CLASSICS

NDON·NEW YORK·TORONTO·MELBOURNE·BOMBAY

The World's Classics

CXXXVI

THE ANALOGY OF RELIGION

BY

JOSEPH BUTLER

OXFORD: HORACE HART
PRINTER TO THE UNIVERSITY

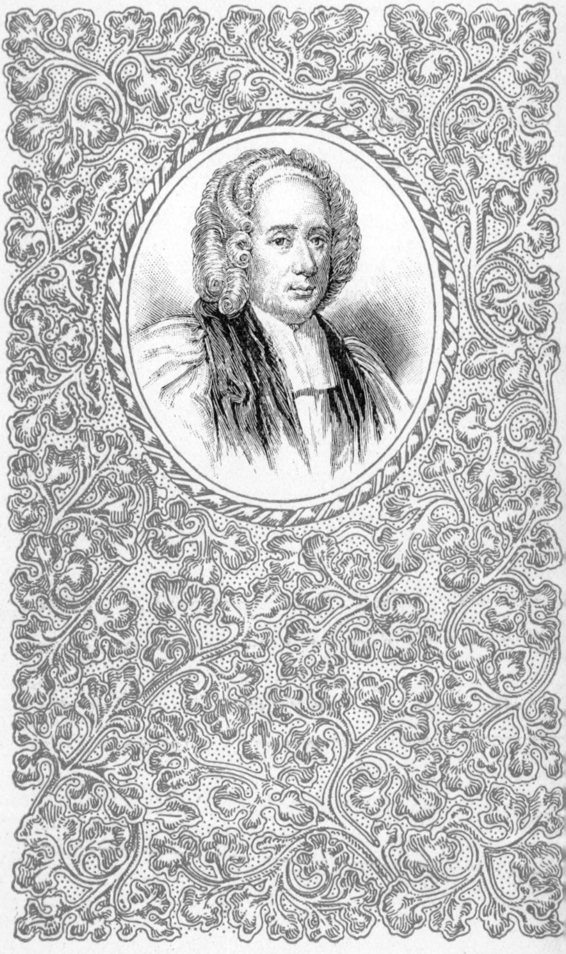

THE ANALOGY OF RELIGION

BY

JOSEPH BUTLER

Butler's Analogy of Religion

Natural and Revealed

to the

Constitution and Course of Nature

EDITED BY

THE RIGHT HON. W. E. GLADSTONE

HENRY FROWDE
OXFORD UNIVERSITY PRESS
LONDON, NEW YORK AND TORONTO

JOSEPH BUTLER

Born, Wantage . . . . May 18, 1692
Died, Bath . . . . . June 16, 1752

'The Analogy of Religion' was first published in 1736. Mr. Gladstone's edition was first published in 1896, and reprinted in 'The World's Classics' in 1907.

EDITOR'S PREFACE

TO HIS EDITION OF BISHOP BUTLER'S WORKS

THE purpose with which this edition of Bishop Butler's Works is published, is to give readier access to the substance and meaning of those works than the student has heretofore enjoyed.

The reasons why such access should be afforded, and that in the largest possible degree, are too wide for statement in a Preface, and will perhaps be sufficiently understood from a collection of Essays which is meant promptly to follow the present publication. But it will be well to set forth the means which have been adopted.

These are in brief as follows:—

1. The *Analogy*, and the other works with slight exceptions, have been broken into sections.

2. Every section has been supplied with a heading, intended to assist the eye, and, as far as may be, the mind of the reader, by an indication of its contents.

3. Indexes to each Volume have been provided: and they are framed upon a separate perusal and following of the Text, as close as the present Editor could make it.

4. He has ventured to add a limited number of Notes, in part explanatory, and in part illustrative.

5. An Appendix has been added to Vol. II. The several pieces which it contains are all of them either by Butler, or associated with his name.

6. The Text of the *Analogy* has been duly con-

sidered under the supervision of the authorities of the University Press, and with the aid furnished by Bishop Fitzgerald's edition of the *Analogy* (Dublin, 1849), in which many corrections of the current edition of 1844 were made, and a collation with the original text of 1736 was embodied.

And now a few words with respect to some of these particulars.

First, the labour of the Editor has in the aggregate been considerable. The smallest and least arduous part of it has also been that where he feels most sanguine as to the results. To provide the students of Butler with this facility for comparison and for reference appeared to him nothing less than a glaring necessity.

The embarrassment heretofore felt has been twofold: it has been experienced alike in perusing Butler, and in testing what has been written upon him.

Dr. Whewell, in 1848, made a step towards it by prefixing to his edition of the *Three Sermons on Human Nature* a brief syllabus in seventy-nine heads. In 1849, publishing an edition of six more of the Fifteen Sermons, as the *Six Sermons on Moral Subjects*, he made a more daring advance, and divided each of them into a continuous series of paragraphs or articles regularly numbered, while he prefixed to them a corresponding list in 160 sentences, each of a very few words. They were such as might have been printed as headings on the margin.

Another editor, Dr. Angus, who has laboured on Butler with care and ability, perceived that something was wanted in order to afford easier access to the *Analogy*, and was struck by the example of Dr. Whewell,

EDITOR'S PREFACE

but concluded that 'this plan seemed a liberty which he was not justified in taking.'[1] And notwithstanding that this very same liberty has now been taken, and that on the largest scale, a tribute of sympathy may still be paid to the temper which made Dr. Angus feel that the mere body and figure of works such as those of Butler were to be handled with scruple and with reverence. It would have been well if the modesty of Butler had allowed him to anticipate that his leading productions would become classics in the philosophical theology of his country, and if he had accordingly furnished them with all facilities for perusal in the mode and form which he was of all men by far the best fitted to determine.

But the dominant consideration with the present Editor has been this, that for want of an easily available power of reference from part to part of works so close in tissue and so profoundly charged with vital matter, the difficulty of mastering Butler has been seriously aggravated, if not multiplied manifold. Most of the editions are without index; but an index is an imperfect help, and the reference to a particular page, good for the particular edition, is valueless for every other. The consequence is that it is often necessary to spend half an hour in looking for a passage. And the further consequence is that, as a high tariff engenders smuggling, so readers, and even critics, of Butler are often compelled or induced to forgo this trouble, and let remote recollection or vague impression shift for itself. It is indeed too easy to show how disastrously censors of Butler in some instances have

[1] Preface to Angus's Butler.

failed to represent him correctly, owing, as I believe, to this cause.

Without sectional divisions, would not our manipulation of the ancient philosophers be hopelessly embarrassed? And yet who is there among them, unless perhaps Aristotle, the tissue of whose thought is closer than that of Butler?

Secondly, with the plan of sectional division has been combined that of sectional headings. And here the Editor must admit that, while the task of framing them is one of a difficulty not to be wholly overcome (as far as his experience enables him to speak) by any amount of labour, the result may probably remain far from satisfactory. Still, on the one hand, these headings may often be useful guides to the eye of a searcher; and, on the other hand, they may supply in a form more direct and easy, if less complete, the same description of help as is aimed at by a more formal analysis.

Thirdly, as to Indexes.

The *Analogy*, to which is subjoined the Clarke correspondence as well as the Two Dissertations, has so close a coherence in itself between every chapter, and indeed every sentence, that, although at numerous points it touches the same subject-matter as the Sermons, there is upon the whole a marked distinction; and it appeared desirable therefore to give a separate Index to each Volume.

While perhaps no writer requires an index so much as Butler, it may be also said that for no writer is it more difficult to frame an index which shall answer its proper purpose. A number of indexes have been framed for the *Analogy*. I do not remember any for the Sermons, which however also require this auxiliary. But what is the proper basis of an index ? Not to present an exhaustive analysis, but rather to supply an aid to the memory of the student. The student ought to find in the several items of an index, under the most natural and (so to speak) salient heads, every point of his author's text to which it is likely that, in default of exact recollection, he may desire to refer. This has been the conception or plan on which these Indexes have been constructed; but the task is difficult, and, though labour has not been spared, the execution may be far from perfect.

Fourthly, this edition is also provided with occasional Notes. Their purpose is limited, and their number not very large.

Dr. Angus indicates in his brief Preface three, indeed four, purposes of his notes, which may here be repeated in substance. First, to give the history of opinions with which the text has dealt. Secondly, to trace the influence of Butler himself on later writers. Thirdly, to question or qualify his arguments, or to explain his expressions. Fourthly, to make good deficiencies in point of evangelical tone.

It appears, however, highly desirable that the student of Butler should not be burdened with unnecessary or distracting notes. In the case of great works like these, as in the case of the *Ethics* of Aristotle, a mass of notes encumbers and obstructs the road to the author's meaning, which may be accessible enough with the aid of close attention and free reference. The student ought not to find extraneous matter too largely interposed between it and his mind. The last of the heads above given is, in the view of the present Editor, illegitimate and causeless. The second, which would open a very wide field, does not seem well suited to fragmentary discussion. The first is useful on account of the amount of tacit reference to prior writers, which Butler, in his anxiety to avoid controversy, has embodied without names in his text; but it should be confined to indicating immediate sources. The third, while requiring circumspection, is proper, and is directly auxiliary to the purposes of the student.

Only in a very few cases of reference to the greatest masters have citations been made for the purpose of corroborative illustration. But, as a general rule, the safest basis of annotation upon Butler probably is to consider not what the text admits, but what it, more or less, requires.

With regard to the Editor's task at large, he is impressed with two convictions in particular. The first of these is, that it was work requisite on broad grounds to be done. The second is, that it might have been—perhaps may yet be—better done by others. Nor does he use the word 'others' vaguely; for he has in view such minds (always of necessity rare) as the mind which produced the masterly Sermon [1] by Dean Church on his illustrious predecessor. The apology for the present effort is comprised in few words: Better thus, than not at all.

W. E. GLADSTONE.

HAWARDEN CASTLE:
  December, 1895.

[1] See the recent Volume, *Blaise Pascal and other Sermons* (Macmillan).

CONTENTS

	PAGE
PREFACE BY THE EDITOR	v
CHRONOLOGY OF BISHOP BUTLER'S LIFE	xiii
EPITAPH ASCRIBED TO DR. FORSTER	xiv
ACCOUNT BY BISHOP HALIFAX OF THE MORAL AND RELIGIOUS SYSTEMS OF BISHOP BUTLER	xv
DEDICATION	xxxvi
ADVERTISEMENT	1
INTRODUCTION	3

PART I
OF NATURAL RELIGION

CHAP.
I. Of a Future Life 19
II. Of the Government of God by Rewards and Punishments; and particularly of the latter 45
III. Of the Moral Government of God . . 60
IV. Of a State of Probation, as implying Trial, Difficulties, and Danger . . . 87
V. Of a State of Probation, as intended for Moral Discipline and Improvement . . 97
VI. Of the Opinion of Necessity, considered as influencing Practice . . . 125
VII. Of the Government of God, considered as a Scheme of Constitution, imperfectly comprehended 144
VIII. Conclusion 158

PART II

OF REVEALED RELIGION

CHAP.   PAGE

I. Of the Importance of Christianity . . 167

II. Of the supposed Presumption against a Revelation, considered as miraculous . . 188

III. Of our Incapacity of judging, what were to be expected in a Revelation; and the Credibility, from Analogy, that it must contain Things appearing liable to Objections . 199

IV. Of Christianity, considered as a Scheme or Constitution, imperfectly comprehended . 218

V. Of the particular System of Christianity; the Appointment of a Mediator, and the Redemption of the World by Him . 226

VI. Of the Want of Universality in Revelation: and of the supposed deficiency in the proof of it 247

VII. Of the particular Evidence for Christianity . 269

VIII. Of the Objections which may be made against arguing from the Analogy of Nature, to Religion 315

IX. Conclusion 330

DISSERTATIONS

I. Of Personal Identity 345
II. Of the Nature of Virtue 355

CORRESPONDENCE BETWEEN DR. BUTLER AND DR. CLARKE 369

INDEX 393

CHRONOLOGY OF BUTLER'S LIFE

Joseph Butler born	May 18, 1692
Entered at Oriel College, Oxford	March 17, 1714
Preacher at the Rolls	1718
B.C.L.	June 10, 1721
Rector of Haughton	1722
Rector of Stanhope	1725
Publication of the *Sermons*	1726
D.C.L.	1733
Clerk of the Closet to Queen Caroline	1736
Publication of the *Analogy*	1736
Bishop of Bristol	Dec. 3, 1738
Dean of St. Paul's	May 23, 1740
Clerk of the Closet to King George II	1746
Bishop of Durham	Oct. 16, 1750
Charge to his Clergy	1751
Death	June 16, 1752

EPITAPH ASCRIBED TO DR. FORSTER

The following Epitaph, said to be written by Dr. Nathanael Forster, is inscribed on a flat marble stone, in the cathedral church of Bristol, placed over the spot where the remains of Bishop Butler are deposited; and which, as it is now almost obliterated, it may be worth while here to preserve.

H. S.
REVERENDUS ADMODUM IN CHRISTO PATER
JOSEPHUS BUTLER, LL.D.
HUJUSCE PRIMO DIOECESEOS
DEINDE DUNELMENSIS EPISCOPUS.
QUALIS QUANTUSQUE VIR ERAT
SUA LIBENTISSIME AGNOVIT AETAS:
ET SI QUID PRAESULI AUT SCRIPTORI AD FAMAM VALENT
MENS ALTISSIMA,
INGENII PERSPICACIS ET SUBACTI VIS,
ANIMUSQUE PIUS, SIMPLEX, CANDIDUS, LIBERALIS,
MORTUI HAUD FACILE EVANESCET MEMORIA.
OBIIT BATHONIAE 16 KALEND. JULII,
A.D. 1752.
ANNOS NATUS 60.

AN ACCOUNT BY BISHOP HALIFAX

OF

THE MORAL AND RELIGIOUS SYSTEMS

OF BISHOP BUTLER [1]

IN what follows I propose to give a short account of the Bishop's *moral and religious systems*, as these are collected from his Works.

I. His way of treating the subject of *morals* is to be gathered from the volume of his Sermons, and particularly from the three first, and from the preface to that volume.

'There is,' as our author with singular sagacity has observed, 'a much more exact correspondence between the natural and moral world, than we are apt to take notice of.'[a] The inward frame of man answers to his outward condition; the several propensities, passions, and affections, implanted in our hearts by the Author of nature, are in a peculiar manner adapted to the circumstances of life in which he hath placed us. This general observation, properly pursued, leads to several important conclusions. The original internal constitution of man, compared with his external condition, enables us to discern what course of action and behaviour that constitution leads to, what is our duty respecting that condition, and furnishes us

[a] Serm. vi.

[1] This portion of the Preface written by Bishop Halifax has been retained as a clear and able summary, which there is no occasion to displace from the ground it has long and usefully occupied.—ED.

besides with the most powerful arguments to the practice of it.

What the inward frame and constitution of man is, is a question of fact; to be determined, as other facts are, from experience, from our internal feelings and external senses, and from the testimony of others. Whether human nature, and the circumstances in which it is placed, might not have been ordered otherwise, is foreign to our inquiry, and none of our concern: our province is, taking both of these as they are, and viewing the connection between them, from that connection to discover, if we can, what course of action is fitted to that nature and those circumstances. From contemplating the bodily senses, and the organs or instruments adapted to them, we learn that the eye was given to see with, the ear to hear with. In like manner, from considering our inward perceptions and the final causes of them, we collect that the feeling of shame, for instance, was given to prevent the doing of things shameful; compassion, to carry us to relieve others in distress; anger, to resist sudden violence offered to ourselves. If, continuing our inquiries in this way, it should at length appear, that the nature, the whole nature, of man leads him to and is fitted for that particular course of behaviour which we usually distinguish by the name of virtue, we are authorized to conclude, that virtue is the law we are born under, that it was so intended by the Author of our being; and we are bound by the most intimate of all obligations, a regard to our own highest interest and happiness, to conform to it in all situations and events.

Human nature is not simple and uniform, but made up of several parts; and we can have no just idea of it as a system or constitution, unless we take into our view the respects and relations which these parts have to each other. As the body is not one member, but many; so our inward structure consists of various instincts, appetites, and propensions. Thus far there is no difference between human creatures and brutes. But besides these common passions and affections, there is another principle, peculiar to mankind, that of conscience, moral sense, reflection, call it what you please, by which they are enabled to review their whole conduct, to approve of some actions in themselves, and to disapprove of others. That this principle will of course have *some* influence on our behaviour, at least at times, will hardly be disputed: but the particular influence which it *ought* to have, the precise degree of power in the regulating of our internal frame that is assigned it by him who placed it there, is a point of the utmost consequence in itself, and on the determination of which the very hinge of our author's moral system turns. If the faculty here spoken of be, indeed, what it is asserted to be, in nature and kind *superior* to every other passion and affection; if it be given, not merely that it may exert its force occasionally, or as our present humour or fancy may dispose us, but that it may at all times exercise an uncontrollable authority and government over all the rest; it will then follow, that, in order to complete the idea of human nature, as a system, we must not only take in each particular bias, propension, instinct, which are seen to belong to it, but we must add besides the principle of conscience, together with the subjection that is due to it from all the other appetites and passions: just as the idea of a civil constitution is formed, not barely from enumerating the several members and ranks of which it is composed, but from these considered as acting in various degrees of subordination to each other, and all under the direction of the same supreme authority, whether that authority be vested in one person or more.

The view here given of the internal constitution of man, and of the supremacy of conscience, agreeable to the conceptions of Bishop Butler, enables us to comprehend the force of that expression, common to him and the ancient moralists, that virtue consists in *following nature*. The meaning cannot be, that it consists in acting agreeably to that propensity of our nature which happens to be the strongest; or which propels us towards certain objects, without any regard to the methods by which they are to be obtained: but the meaning must be, that virtue consists in the due regulation and subjection of all the other appetites and affections to the superior faculty of conscience; from a conformity to which alone our actions are properly *natural*, or correspondent to the nature, to the whole nature of such an agent as man. From hence too it appears, that the Author of our frame is by no means indifferent to virtue and vice, or has left us at liberty to act at random, as humour or appetite may prompt us; but that every man has the rule of right within him; a rule attended in the very notion of it with authority, and such as has the force of a direction and a command from him who made us what we are, what course of behaviour is suited to our nature, and which he expects that we should follow. This moral faculty implies also a presentiment and apprehension, that the judgment which passes on our actions, considered as of good or ill desert, will hereafter be confirmed by the unerring judgment of God; when virtue and happiness, vice and misery, whose ideas are now so closely connected, shall be indissolubly united, and the divine government be found to correspond in the most exact proportion to the nature he has given us. Lastly, this just prerogative or supremacy of conscience it is, which Mr. Pope has described in his Universal Prayer, though perhaps he may have expressed it rather *too* strongly,[1] where he says,

'What conscience dictates to be done,
  Or warns me not to do,
This teach me *more than* hell to shun,
  That *more than* heaven pursue.'

The reader will observe, that this way of treating the subject of morals, by an appeal to *facts*, does not at all interfere with that other way, adopted by Dr. Samuel Clarke and others, which begins with inquiring

[1] Among readers of the present day, most, I hope, will in this matter hold with Pope.—ED.

into the *relations* and *fitness of things,* but rather illustrates and confirms it. That there are essential differences in the qualities of human actions, established by nature, and that this *natural* difference of things prior to and independent of all *will,* creates a natural *fitness* in the agent to act agreeably to it, seems as little to be denied, as that there is the *moral* difference before explained, from which we approve and feel a pleasure in what is right, and conceive a distaste to what is wrong. Still, however, when we are endeavouring to establish either this moral or that natural difference, it ought never to be forgotten, or rather it will require to be distinctly shown, that both of these, when traced up to their source, suppose an intelligent Author of nature and moral Ruler of the world; who originally appointed these differences, and by such an appointment has signified his *will* that we should conform to them, as the only effectual method of securing our *happiness* on the whole under his government. And of this consideration our prelate himself was not unmindful; as may be collected from many expressions in different parts of his writings, and particularly from the following passages in his eleventh Sermon. 'It may be allowed, without any prejudice to the cause of virtue and religion, that our ideas of happiness and misery are of all our ideas the nearest and most important to us; that they will, nay, if you please, that they ought to prevail over those of order, and beauty, and harmony, and proportion, if there should ever be, as it is impossible there ever should be, any inconsistence between them.' And again, 'Though virtue or moral rectitude does indeed consist in affection to and pursuit of what is right and good, as such; yet, when we sit down in a a cool hour, we can neither justify to ourselves this or any other pursuit, till we are convinced that it will be for our happiness, or at least not contrary to it.' [b]

Besides the general system of morality opened above, our author in his volume of Sermons has stated with

[b] Serm. xi.

accuracy the difference between self-love and benevolence—in opposition to those who, on the one hand, make the whole of virtue to consist in benevolence,[c] and to those who, on the other, assert that every particular affection and action is resolvable into self-love. In combating these opinions, he has shown, I think unanswerably, that there are the same kind of indications in human nature, that we were made to promote the happiness of others, as that we were made to promote our own: that it is no just objection to this, that we have dispositions to do *evil* to *others* as well as good; for we have also dispositions to do *evil* as well as good to *ourselves*, to our own most important interests even in this life, for the sake of gratifying a present passion: that the thing to be lamented is, not that men have too great a regard to their own real good, but that they have not enough: that benevolence is not more at variance with or unfriendly to self-love, than any other particular affection is: and that by consulting the happiness of others a man is so far from *lessening* his own, that the very endeavour to do so, though he should fail in the accomplishment, is a source of the highest satisfaction and peace of mind.[d] He has also, in passing, animadverted on the philosopher of Malmesbury, who in his book *Of Human Nature* has advanced, as discoveries in moral science, that benevolence is only the love of power, and compassion the fear of future calamity to ourselves. And this our author has done, not so much with the design of exposing the false reasoning of Mr. Hobbes, but because on so perverse an account of human nature he has raised a system, subversive of all justice and honesty.[e]

II. The religious system of Bishop Butler is chiefly to be collected from the treatise, entitled, *The Analogy*

[c] See the second Dissertation 'Of the Nature of Virtue,' at the end of the *Analogy*.

[d] See Serm. i. and xi. and the Preface to the volume of Sermons.

[e] See the Notes to Serm. i. and v.

of Religion, Natural and Revealed, to the Constitution and Course of Nature.

'All things are double one against another, and God hath made nothing imperfect.'[f] On this single observation of the Son of Sirach, the whole fabric of our prelate's defence of religion, in his *Analogy*, is raised. Instead of indulging to idle speculations, how the world might possibly have been better than it is; or, forgetful of the difference between hypothesis and fact, attempting to explain the divine economy with respect to intelligent creatures, from preconceived notions of his own; he first inquires what the constitution of nature, as made known to us in the way of experiment, actually is; and from this, now seen and acknowledged, he endeavours to form a judgment of that larger constitution, which religion discovers to us. If the dispensation of Providence we are now under, considered as inhabitants of this world, and having a temporal interest to secure in it, be found, on examination, to be analogous to, and of a piece with, that further dispensation, which relates to us as designed for another world, in which we have an eternal interest, depending on our behaviour here; if both may be traced up to the same general laws, and appear to be carried on according to the same plan of administration; the fair presumption is, that both proceed from one and the same Author. And if the principal parts objected to in this latter dispensation be similar to and of the same kind with what we certainly experience under the former; the objections, being clearly inconclusive in one case, because contradicted by plain fact, must, in all reason, be allowed to be inconclusive also in the other.

This way of arguing from what is acknowledged to what is disputed, from things known to other things that resemble them, from that part of the divine establishment which is exposed to our view to that more important one which lies beyond it, is on all hands confessed to be just. By this method Sir Isaac

[f] Ecclus. xlii. 24.

Newton has unfolded the system of nature; by the same method Bishop Butler has explained the system of grace; and thus, to use the words of a writer, whom I quote with pleasure, has 'formed and concluded a happy alliance between faith and philosophy.'ᵍ

And although the argument from analogy be allowed to be imperfect, and by no means sufficient to solve all difficulties respecting the government of God, and the designs of his providence with regard to mankind (a degree of knowledge, which we are not furnished with faculties for attaining, at least in the present state); yet surely it is of importance to learn from it, that the natural and moral world are intimately connected, and parts of one stupendous whole or system; and that the chief objections which are brought against religion may be urged with equal force against the constitution and course of nature, where they are certainly false in fact. And this information we may derive from the work before us; the proper design of which, it may be of use to observe, is not to prove the truth of religion, either natural or revealed, but to confirm that proof, already known, by considerations from analogy.

After this account of the method of reasoning employed by our author, let us now advert to his manner of applying it, first to the subject of natural religion, and secondly to that of revealed.

1. The foundation of all our hopes and fears is a future life; and with this the Treatise begins. Neither the reason of the thing, nor the analogy of nature, according to Bishop Butler, give ground for imagining, that the unknown event, death, will be our destruction. The states in which we have formerly existed, in the womb and in infancy, are not more different from each other than from that of mature age in which we now exist: therefore, that we shall continue to exist hereafter, in a state as different from the present as the present is from those through

ᵍ Mr. Mainwaring's Dissertation, prefixed to his volume of Sermons.

which we have passed already, is a presumption favoured by the analogy of nature. All that we know from reason concerning death, is the effects it has upon animal bodies: and the frequent instances among men of the intellectual powers continuing in high health and vigour, at the very time when a mortal disease is on the point of putting an end to all the powers of sensation, induce us to hope that it may have no effect at all on the human soul, not even so much as to suspend the exercise of its faculties; though, if it have, the suspension of a power by no means implies its extinction, as sleep or a swoon may convince us.[h]

The probability of a future state once granted, an important question arises, How best to secure our interests in that state. We find from what passes daily before us, that the constitution of nature admits of misery as well as happiness; that both of these are the consequences of our own actions; and these consequences we are enabled to foresee. Therefore, that our happiness or misery in a future world may depend on our own actions also, and that rewards and punishments hereafter may follow our good or ill behaviour here, is but an appointment of the same sort with what we experience under the divine government, according to the regular course of nature.[i]

This supposition is confirmed from another circumstance, that the natural government of God, under which we now live, is also moral; in which rewards and punishments are the consequences of actions, considered as virtuous and vicious. Not that every man is rewarded or punished here in exact proportion to his desert; for the essential tendencies of virtue and vice, to produce happiness and the contrary, are often hindered from taking effect from accidental causes. However, there are plainly the rudiments and beginnings of a righteous administration to be discerned in the constitution of nature: from whence we are led to expect, that these accidental hindrances

[h] Part I. chap. i.   [i] Chap. ii.

will one day be removed, and the rule of distributive justice obtain completely in a more perfect state.[k]

The moral government of God, thus established, implies in the notion of it some sort of trial, or a moral possibility of acting wrong as well as right, in those who are the subjects of it. And the doctrine of religion, that the present life is in fact a state of probation for a future one, is rendered credible, from its being analogous throughout to the general conduct of Providence towards us with respect to this world; in which prudence is necessary to secure our temporal interest, just as we are taught that virtue is necessary to secure our eternal interest; and both are trusted to ourselves.[l]

But the present life is not merely a state of probation, implying in it difficulties and danger; it is also a state of discipline and improvement; and that both in our temporal and religious capacity. Thus childhood is a state of discipline for youth; youth for manhood; and that for old age. Strength of body, and maturity of understanding, are acquired by degrees; and neither of them without continual exercise and attention on our part, not only in the beginning of life, but through the whole course of it. So again with respect to our religious concerns, the present world is fitted to be, and to good men is in event, a state of discipline and improvement for a future one. The several passions and propensions implanted in our hearts incline us, in a multitude of instances, to forbidden pleasures: this inward infirmity is increased by various snares and temptations, perpetually occurring from without: hence arises the necessity of recollection and self-government, of withstanding the calls of appetite, and forming our minds to habits of piety and virtue; habits, of which we are capable, and which, to creatures in a state of moral imperfection, and fallen from their original integrity, must be of the greatest use, as an additional security, over and above the principle of conscience, from the dangers to which we are exposed.[m]

[k] Chap. iii.   [l] Chap. iv.   [m] Part I. chap. v.

Nor is the credibility here given, by the analogy of nature, to the general doctrine of religion, destroyed or weakened by any notions concerning necessity. Of itself it is a mere word, the sign of an abstract idea; and as much requires an agent, that is, a necessary agent, in order to effect any thing, as freedom requires a free agent. Admitting it to be speculatively true, if considered as influencing practice, it is the same as false: for it is matter of experience, that, with regard to our present interest, and as inhabitants of this world, we are treated as if we were free; and therefore the analogy of nature leads us to conclude, that, with regard to our future interest, and as designed for another world, we shall be treated as free also. Nor does the opinion of necessity, supposing it possible, at all affect either the general proof of religion, or its external evidence.[n]

Still objections may be made against the wisdom and goodness of the divine government, to which analogy, which can only show the truth or credibility of facts, affords no answer. Yet even here analogy is of use, if it suggest that the divine government is a scheme or system, and not a number of unconnected acts, and that this system is also above our comprehension. Now the government of the natural world appears to be a system of this kind; with parts, related to each other, and together composing a whole: in which system, ends are brought about by the use of means, many of which means, before experience, would have been suspected to have had quite a contrary tendency; which is carried on by general laws, similar causes uniformly producing similar effects: the utility of which general laws, and the inconveniences which would probably arise from the occasional or even secret suspension of them, we are in some sort enabled to discern;[o] but of the whole we are incompetent judges, because of the small part which comes within

[n] Chap. vi.
[o] See a Treatise on Divine Benevolence, by Dr. Thomas Balguy, part ii.

our view. Reasoning then from what we know, it is highly credible, that the government of the moral world is a system also, carried on by general laws, and in which ends are accomplished by the intervention of means; and that both constitutions, the natural and the moral, are so connected, as to form together but one scheme. But of this scheme, as of that of the natural world taken alone, we are not qualified to judge, on account of the mutual respect of the several parts to each other and to the whole, and our own incapacity to survey the whole, or, with accuracy, any single part. All objections therefore to the wisdom and goodness of the divine government may be founded merely on our ignorance; and to such objections our ignorance is the proper, and a satisfactory answer.[p]

2. The chief difficulties concerning natural religion being now removed, our author proceeds, in the next place, to that which is revealed; and as an introduction to an inquiry into the credibility of Christianity begins with the consideration of its importance. The importance of Christianity appeals in two respects. First, in its being a republication of natural religion, in its native simplicity, with authority, and with circumstances of advantage; ascertaining, in many instances of moment, what before was only probable, and particularly confirming the doctrine of a future state of rewards and punishments. Secondly, as revealing a new dispensation of Providence, originating from the pure love and mercy of God, and conducted by the mediation of his son, and the guidance of his Spirit, for the recovery and salvation of mankind, represented in a state of apostasy and ruin. This account of Christianity being admitted to be just, and the distinct offices of these three divine persons being once discovered to us, we are as much obliged in point of duty to acknowledge the relations we stand in to the Son and Holy Ghost, as our Mediator and Sanctifier, as we are obliged in point of duty to acknowledge the relation we stand in to God the Father; although the

[p] Part I. chap. vii.

two former of these relations be learnt from revelation only, and in the last we are instructed by the light of nature ; the obligation in either case arising from the offices themselves, and not at all depending on the manner in which they are made known to us.[q]

The presumptions against revelation in general are, that it is not discoverable by reason, that it is unlike to what is so discovered, and that it was introduced and supported by miracles. But in a scheme so large as that of the universe, unbounded in extent and everlasting in duration, there must of necessity be numberless circumstances which are beyond the reach of our faculties to discern, and which can only be known by divine illumination. And both in the natural and moral government of the world, under which we live, we find many things unlike one to another, and therefore ought not to wonder if the same unlikeness obtain between things visible and invisible ; although it be far from true, that revealed religion is entirely unlike the constitution of nature, as analogy may teach us. Nor is there any thing incredible in revelation, considered as miraculous ; whether miracles be supposed to have been performed at the beginning of the world, or after a course of nature has been established.[1] Not *at the beginning of the world* ; for then there was either no course of nature at all, or a power must have been exerted totally different from what that course is at present : all men and animals cannot have been born, as they are now ; but a pair of each sort must have been produced at first, in a way altogether unlike to that in which they have been since produced ; unless we affirm, that men and animals have existed from eternity in an endless succession : one miracle therefore

[q] Part II. chap. i.

---

[1] The argument in this sentence, purporting to be Butler's, seems to be founded on Part II. ch. ii. §§ 7-9 (II. in the older editions) ; but contains matter which appears to be in the nature of expansion and interpolation into the original text.—ED.

at least there must have been at the beginning of the world, or at the time of man's creation. Not *after the settlement of a course of nature,* on account of miracles being contrary to that course, or, in other words, contrary to experience; for, in order to know whether miracles, worked in attestation of a divine religion, be contrary to experience or not, we ought to be acquainted with other cases, similar or parallel to those, in which miracles are alleged to have been wrought. But where shall we find such similar or parallel cases? The world which we inhabit affords none: we know of no extraordinary revelations from God to man, but those recorded in the Old and New Testament; all of which were established by miracles: it cannot therefore be said, that miracles are incredible, because contrary to experience, when all the experience we have is in favour of miracles, and on the side of religion. Besides, in reasoning concerning miracles, they ought not to be compared with common natural events, but with uncommon appearances, such as comets, magnetism, electricity; which, to one acquainted only with the usual phenomena of nature, and the common powers of matter, must, before proof of their actual existence, be thought incredible.[r]

The presumptions against revelation in general being dispatched, objections against the Christian revelation in particular, against the scheme of it, as distinguished from objections against its evidence, are considered next. Now, supposing a revelation to be really given, it is highly probable beforehand, that it must contain many things appearing to us liable to objections. The acknowledged dispensation of nature is very different from what we should have expected: reasoning then from analogy, the revealed dispensation, it is credible, would be also different. Nor are we in any sort judges at what time, or in what degree, or manner, it is fit or expedient for God to instruct us, in things confessedly of the greatest use, either by natural reason, or by supernatural information. Thus, arguing on speculation

[r] Chap. ii.

only, and without experience, it would seem very unlikely that so important a remedy as that provided by Christianity, for the recovery of mankind from a state of ruin, should have been for so many ages withheld; and, when at last vouchsafed, should be imparted to so few; and, after it has been imparted, should be attended with obscurity and doubt. And just so we might have argued, before experience, concerning the remedies provided in nature for bodily diseases, to which by nature we are exposed: for many of these were unknown to mankind for a number of ages; are known but to few now; some important ones probably not discovered yet; and those which are, neither certain in their application, nor universal in their use: and the same mode of reasoning that would lead us to expect they should have been so, would lead us to expect that the necessity of them should have been superseded, by their being no diseases; as the necessity of the Christian scheme, it may be thought, might also have been superseded, by preventing the fall of man, so that he should not have stood in need of a Redeemer at all.[s]

As to objections against the wisdom and goodness of Christianity, the same answer may be applied to them as was to the like objections against the constitution of nature. For here also, Christianity is a scheme or economy, composed of various parts, forming a whole; in which scheme means are used for the accomplishing of ends; and which is conducted by general laws, of all of which we know as little as we do of the constitution of nature. And the seeming want of wisdom or goodness in this system is to be ascribed to the same cause, as the like appearances of defects in the natural system; our inability to discern the whole scheme, and our ignorance of the relation of those parts which are discernible to others beyond our view.

The objections against Christianity as a matter of fact, and against the wisdom and goodness of it, having

[s] Chap. iii.

from deserved punishment, and restored us to the divine favour. But the fact is otherwise; and real reformation is often found to be of no avail, so as to secure the criminal from poverty, sickness, infamy, and death, the never-failing attendants on vice and extravagance, exceeding a certain degree. By the course of nature then it appears, God does not always pardon a sinner on his repentance. Yet there is provision made, even in nature, that the miseries, which men bring on themselves by unlawful indulgences, may in many cases be mitigated, and in some removed; partly by extraordinary exertions of the offender himself, but more especially and frequently by the intervention of others, who voluntarily, and from motives of compassion, submit to labour and sorrow, such as produce long and lasting inconveniences to themselves, as the means of rescuing another from the wretched effects of former imprudences. Vicarious punishment, therefore, or one person's sufferings contributing to the relief of another, is a providential disposition in the economy of nature: and it ought not to be a matter of surprise, if by a method analogous to this we be redeemed from sin and misery, in the economy of grace. That mankind at present are in a state of degradation, different from that in which they were originally created, is the very ground of the Christian revelation, as contained in the scriptures. Whether we acquiesce in the account, that our being placed in such a state is owing to the crime of our first parents, or choose to ascribe it to any other cause, it makes no difference as to our condition: the vice and unhappiness of the world are still there, notwithstanding all our suppositions; nor is it Christianity that hath put us into this state. We learn also from the same scriptures, what experience and the use of expiatory sacrifices from the most early times might have taught us, that repentance alone is not sufficient to prevent the fatal consequences of past transgressions: but that still there is room for mercy, and that repentance shall be available, though not of itself, yet through the mediation of a divine person, the Messiah; who, from the sublimest principles of compassion, when we were *dead in trespasses and sins*,[u] suffered and died, the innocent for the guilty, *the just for the unjust*,[x] *that we might have redemption through his blood, even the forgiveness of sins*.[y] In what way the death of Christ was of that efficacy it is said to be, in procuring the reconciliation of sinners, the scriptures have not explained: it is enough that the doctrine is revealed; that it is not contrary to any truths which reason and experience teach us; and that it accords in perfect harmony with the usual method of the divine conduct in the government of the world.[z]

Again it hath been said, that if the Christian revelation were true, it must have been universal, and could not have been left upon doubtful evidence. But God, in his natural providence, dispenses his gifts in great variety, not only among creatures of the same species, but to the same individuals also at different times. Had the Christian revelation been universal at first, yet, from the diversity of men's abilities, both of mind and body, their various means of improvement, and other external advantages, some persons must soon have been in a situation, with respect to religious knowledge, much superior to that of others, as much perhaps as they are at present: and all men will be equitably dealt with at last; and to whom little is given, of him little will be required. Then as to the evidence for religion being left doubtful, difficulties of this sort, like difficulties in practice, afford scope and opportunity for a virtuous exercise of the understanding, and dispose the mind to acquiesce and rest satisfied with any evidence that is real. In the daily commerce of life, men are obliged to act upon great uncertainties, with regard to success in their temporal pursuits; and the case with regard to religion is parallel. However, though religion be not intuitively true, the proofs of it which we have are amply sufficient in reason to

---

[u] Ephes. ii. 1. [x] 1 Pet. iii. 18. [y] Coloss. i. 14.
[z] Chap. v.

any one now, after reading the above history, and not knowing whether the whole were not a fiction, be supposed to ask, Whether all that is here related be true? and instead of a direct answer, let him be informed of the several acknowledged facts, which are found to correspond to it in real life; and then let him compare the history and facts together, and observe the astonishing coincidence of both: such a joint review must appear to him of very great weight, and to amount to evidence somewhat more than human. And unless the whole series, and every particular circumstance contained in it, can be thought to have arisen from accident, the truth of Christianity is proved.[b]

The view here given of the moral and religious systems of Bishop Butler, it will immediately be perceived, is chiefly intended for younger students, especially for students in Divinity; to whom it is hoped it may be of use, so as to encourage them to peruse, with proper diligence, the original works of the author himself. For it may be necessary to observe, that neither of the volumes of this excellent prelate are addressed to those who read for amusement, or

---

[b] Chap. vii. To the *Analogy* are subjoined two Dissertations, both originally inserted in the body of the work. One on 'Personal Identity,' in which are contained some strictures on Mr. Locke, who asserts that consciousness makes or constitutes personal identity; whereas, as our author observes, consciousness makes only personality, or is necessary to the idea of a person, i. e. a thinking intelligent being, but presupposes, and therefore cannot constitute, personal identity; just as knowledge presupposes truth, but does not constitute it. Consciousness of past actions does indeed show us the identity of ourselves, or gives us a certain assurance that we are the same persons or living agents now, which we were at the time to which our remembrance can look back: but still we should be the same persons as we were, though this consciousness of what is past were wanting, though all that had been done by us formerly were forgotten; unless it be true, that no person has existed a single moment beyond what he can remember. The other Dissertation is 'Of the Nature of Virtue,' which properly belongs to the moral system of our author, already explained.

induce us to embrace it; and dissatisfaction those proofs may possibly be men's own faults.[a]

Nothing remains but to attend to the posi evidence there is for the truth of Christianity. N besides its direct and fundamental proofs, which miracles and prophecies, there are many collate circumstances, which may be united into one view and all together may be considered as making up on argument. In this way of treating the subject, the revelation, whether real or otherwise, may be supposed to be wholly historical: the general design of which appears to be, to give an account of the condition of religion, and its professors, with a concise narration of the political state of things, as far as religion is affected by it, during a great length of time, near six thousand years of which are already past. More particularly it comprehends an account of God's entering into covenant with one nation, the Jews, that he would be their God, and that they should be his people; of his often interposing in their affairs; giving them the promise, and afterwards the possession, of a flourishing country; assuring them of the greatest national prosperity, in case of their obedience, and threatening the severest national punishment, in case they forsook him, and joined in the idolatry of their pagan neighbours. It contains also a prediction of a particular person to appear in the fulness of time, in whom all the promises of God to the Jews were to be fulfilled: and it relates, that, at the time expected, a person did actually appear, assuming to be the Saviour foretold; that he worked various miracles among them, in confirmation of his divine authority; and, as was foretold also, was rejected and put to death by the very people who had long desired and waited for his coming; but that his religion, in spite of all opposition, was established in the world by his disciples, invested with supernatural powers, for that purpose; of the fate and fortunes of which religion there is a prophetical description, carried down to the end of time. Let

[a] Chap. vi.

curiosity, or to get rid of time. All subjects are not to be comprehended with the same ease; and morality and religion, when treated as sciences, each accompanied with difficulties of its own, can neither of them be understood as they ought, without a very peculiar attention. But morality and religion are not merely to be studied as sciences, or as being speculatively true; they are to be regarded in another and higher light, as a rule of life and manners, as containing authoritative directions by which to regulate our faith and practice. And in this view, the infinite importance of them considered, it can never be an indifferent matter whether they be received or rejected. For both claim to be the voice of God; and whether they be so or not, cannot be known, till their claims be impartially examined. If they indeed come from him, we are bound to conform to them at our peril: nor is it left to our choice, whether we will submit to the obligations they impose upon us or not; for submit to them we must, in such a sense, as to incur the punishments denounced by both against wilful disobedience to their injunctions.

TO THE
RIGHT HONOURABLE

CHARLES LORD TALBOT

BARON OF HENSOL
LORD HIGH CHANCELLOR OF GREAT BRITAIN

THE FOLLOWING TREATISE

IS, WITH ALL RESPECT, INSCRIBED
IN ACKNOWLEDGMENT OF THE HIGHEST OBLIGATIONS
TO
THE LATE LORD BISHOP OF DURHAM
AND TO HIMSELF
BY HIS LORDSHIP'S MOST DUTIFUL
MOST DEVOTED
AND MOST HUMBLE SERVANT

JOSEPH BUTLER

INTRODUCTION

§ 1. *Probable evidence, from lowest to highest, is matter of degree.*

PROBABLE evidence is essentially distinguished from demonstrative by this, that it admits of degrees; and of all variety of them, from the highest moral certainty, to the very lowest presumption. We cannot indeed say a thing is probably true upon one very slight presumption for it; because, as there may be probabilities on both sides of a question, there may be some against it: and though there be not, yet a slight presumption does not beget that degree of conviction, which is implied in saying a thing is probably true.

§ 2. *Presumption is admissible; may be small, or may rise to moral certainty.*

But that the slightest possible presumption is of the nature of a probability, appears from hence; that such low presumption, often repeated, will amount even to moral certainty. Thus a man's having observed the ebb and flow of the tide to-day, affords some sort of presumption, though the lowest imaginable, that it may happen again to-morrow: but the observation of this event for so many days, and months, and ages together, as it has been observed by mankind, gives us a full assurance that it will.

§ 3. *Probability means some likeness to observed truth or fact.*

That which chiefly constitutes probability is expressed in the word likely, i. e. like some truth,[a] or

[a] Verisimile.

true event; like it, in itself, in its evidence, in some more or fewer of its circumstances. For when we determine a thing to be probably true, suppose that an event has or will come to pass, it is from the mind's remarking in it a likeness to some other event, which we have observed has come to pass. And this observation forms, in numberless daily instances, a presumption, opinion, or full conviction, that such event has or will come to pass; according as the observation is, that the like event has sometimes, most commonly, or always so far as our observation reaches, come to pass at like distances of time, or place, or upon like occasions. Hence arises the belief, that a child, if it lives twenty years, will grow up to the stature and strength of a man; that food will contribute to the preservation of its life, and the want of it for such a number of days, be its certain destruction. So likewise the rule and measure of our hopes and fears concerning the success of our pursuits; our expectations that others will act so and so in such circumstances; and our judgment that such actions proceed from such principles; all these rely upon our having observed the like to what we hope, fear, expect, judge; I say upon our having observed the like, either with respect to others or ourselves. And thus, whereas the prince [b] who had always lived in a warm climate, naturally concluded in the way of analogy, that there was no such thing as water's becoming hard, because he had always observed it to be fluid and yielding: we, on the contrary, from analogy conclude, that there is no presumption at all against this: that it is supposable there may be frost in England any given day in January next; probable that there will on some day of the month; and that there is a moral certainty, i. e. ground for an expectation without any doubt of it, in some part or other of the winter.

[b] The story is told by Mr. Locke in the chapter of Probability. [Locke, *On the Understanding*, Bk. iv. c. 15, § 5.]

§ 4. *Is imperfect; and deals with limited beings; yet is for us the guide of life.*

Probable evidence, in its very nature, affords but an imperfect kind of information; and is to be considered as relative only to beings of limited capacities. For nothing which is the possible object of knowledge, whether past, present, or future, can be probable to an infinite Intelligence; since it cannot but be discerned absolutely as it is in itself, certainly true, or certainly false. But to us, probability is the very guide of life.[1]

---

[1] Butler's doctrine of Probability may by some be considered commonplace. But Toland had shortly before taught that in the absence of demonstration we ought to hold our judgments in suspense. See Leslie Stephen, *English Thought in the Eighteenth Century*, c. iii. 14. In his *Place of Christ in Modern Theology*, Dr. Fairbairn observes (p. 11) that Butler's *Analogy* drew more attention than his Sermons on Human Nature, and that ' the fundamental inconsistency' of the supremacy of conscience with the doctrine of probability was never perceived. In proof of the assertion thus hazarded, Dr. Fairbairn has supplied the statement that the reason deals with probabilities which it analyses, whereas the conscience commands; the first being an operation of the mental faculty, while the second is in the domain of religion (pp. 25, 26). Is there any shadow of inconsistency between the two? The conscience, in order that it may legitimately command, requires the state of facts on which it has to judge to be ascertained: and this is ascertained for it by the reason. But Butler's fundamental contention is, that probability involves moral obligation; and the two powers deal with the same process, but at different stages.

This able author falls, I think, into a casual mistake, when he holds that Butler borrowed his doctrine of probability from Locke. But is it not the fact that Locke, in his *Essay on the Understanding*, deals with probability (very rationally) as it stands apart from moral obligation; while Butler, borrowing nothing from him, simply takes up the question at the point where he had laid it down? (Locke, *On the Understanding*, Bk. iv. cc. 15, 16.)

§ 5. *Even on low probabilities, prudence binds to action.*

From these things it follows, that in questions of difficulty, or such as are thought so, where more satisfactory evidence cannot be had, or is not seen; if the result of examination be, that there appears upon the whole, any the lowest presumption on one side, and none on the other, or a greater presumption on one side, though in the lowest degree greater; this determines the question, even in matters of speculation; and in matters of practice, will lay us under an absolute and formal obligation, in point of prudence and of interest,[1] to act upon that presumption or low probability, though it be so low as to leave the mind in very great doubt which is the truth. For surely a man is as really bound in prudence to do what upon the whole appears, according to the best of his judgment, to be for his happiness, as what he certainly knows to be so.

§ 6. *Sometimes, though the chances be less than even,*

Nay further, in questions of great consequence, a reasonable man will think it concerns him to remark lower probabilities and presumptions than these; such as amount to no more than showing one side of a question to be as supposable and credible as the other: nay, such as but amount to much less even than this. For numberless instances might be mentioned respecting the common pursuits of life, where a man would be thought, in a literal sense, distracted, who would not act, and with great application too, not only upon

---

[1] Butler has explained himself elsewhere upon the nature of prudence. See II. viii. 19, and especially Dissertation II. § 8; where, after explaining the nature of prudence, he goes on, 'it should seem that this is virtue, and the contrary behaviour faulty and blamable.'

an even chance, but upon much less,[1] and where the probability or chance was greatly against his succeeding.[c]

§ 7. *Analogy has weight in determining judgment, and practice.*

It is not my design to inquire further into the nature, the foundation, and measure of probability; or whence it proceeds that *likeness* should beget that presumption, opinion, and full conviction, which the human mind is formed to receive from it, and which it does necessarily produce in every one; or to guard against the errors, to which reasoning from analogy is liable. This belongs to the subject of Logic; and is a part of that subject which has not yet been thoroughly considered. Indeed I shall not take upon me to say, how far the extent, compass, and force, of analogical reasoning, can be reduced to general heads and rules; and the whole be formed into a system. But though so little in this way has been attempted by those who have treated of our intellectual powers, and the exercise of them;[2] this does not hinder but that we may be, as we unquestionably are, assured, that analogy is of weight, in various

[c] See Part II. c. vi.

---

[1] It is easy to provide illustrations of what may at first view seem a paradox. Suppose that with a journey in prospect we hear that the ordinary road to the place of our destination is infested by robbers, that a party had been stopped in the preceding week, and that the criminals had not been discovered. But another road, nearly, though not quite, as convenient, was perfectly safe. The odds against our being molested in the first case might be slight, or might be (say) three or five to one; but every prudent person would in such a case take the safe road. Comp. II. vi. 24.

[2] This may seem to glance at Locke's discussion of probability, referred to above, as inadequate.

degrees, towards determining our judgment and our practice.[1] Nor does it in any wise cease to be of weight in those cases, because persons, either given to dispute, or who require things to be stated with greater exactness than our faculties appear to admit of in practical matters, may find other cases in which it is not easy to say, whether it be, or be not, of any weight; or instances of seeming analogies, which are really of none. It is enough to the present purpose to observe, that this general way of arguing is evidently natural, just, and conclusive. For there is no man can make a question, but that the sun will rise tomorrow, and be seen, where it is seen at all, in the figure of a circle, and not in that of a square.

[1] Butler passes from probability to analogy without describing the resemblance between them.

Fitzgerald (Butler's *Analogy*, by William Fitzgerald, Dublin, 1849) says (p. 1), ' Analogy is properly the *resemblance of relations*'; and ' in the common use of modern metaphysical writers, is used to express such arguments from resemblance as fall short of full proof.' And he cites Mill (*Logic*, ii. 97, 98), describing Butler: ' The analogies, with which his argument deals, are, indeed, in general, of that imperfect sort, which do not amount to strict inductions. But, according to his view, they differ from induction not so much in *kind* as in *degree*.' We may perhaps say: to establish a sound analogy, the resemblance of relations need not be entire, but ought to be very substantive and marked.

Analogy then (1) is not demonstrative, but probable; (2) is not to be predicated of mere quantity. It would mislead were we to say there was an analogy between the relation of one foot to two feet, and that of one pound to two pounds. For the relation is absolutely identical. We may perhaps adopt Fitzgerald's definition thus modified: analogy *is the resemblance of qualitative relations*. Fitzgerald refers us to Coplestone's *Four Discourses*, and to Whately's *Rhetoric*, I. iii. 7.

§ 8. *From difficulties in nature, Origen infers a likelihood of similar difficulties in scripture.*

Hence, namely from analogical reasoning, Origen [d] has with singular sagacity observed, that *he who believes the scripture to have proceeded from him who is the Author of nature, may well expect to find the same sort of difficulties in it, as are found in the constitution of nature.*[1] And in a like way of reflection it may be added, that he who denies the scripture to have been from God upon account of these difficulties, may, for

[d] Χρὴ μέν τοι γε τὸν ἄπαξ παραδεξάμενον τοῦ κτίσαντος τὸν κόσμον εἶναι ταύτας τὰς γραφὰς πεπεῖσθαι, ὅτι ὅσα περὶ τῆς κτίσεως ἀπαντᾷ τοῖς ζητοῦσι τὸν περὶ αὐτῆς λόγον, ταῦτα καὶ περὶ τῶν γραφῶν. *Philocal.* p. 23, ed. Cant.

---

[1] Fitzgerald (*Life of Butler*, pp. xxxviii, xlii) quotes the following passage from Berkeley's *Minute Philosopher*, with the observation that it clearly contains the germ of the whole argument of the *Analogy*.

'It will be sufficient, if such analogy appears between the dispensations of grace and nature, as may make it probable (although much should be unaccountable in both) to suppose them derived from the same Author, and the workmanship of one and the same hand.'

But, if Berkeley contains the germ of Butler, the passage from Origen, which Butler himself so prominently alleges, contains the main substance of the striking passage from Berkeley. Origen supplied in all likelihood the minute seed, from which grew the tree of the *Analogy*. But there can be little doubt that though the *Minute Philosopher* (1732) appeared four years before the *Analogy* (1736), the mind of Butler had been occupied, and his subject in hand, for a much longer period; probably from the date (1726), or soon after the date, of the publication of the Sermons.

(Origen's observation.) 'This sagacious remark is strangely misapplied by Origen to the establishment of one of his favourite theories, that there is a mystical meaning in every word and even letter of scripture. As a ground for his analogy, he assumes that the words of scripture are the work of God, in the same sense as nature;

the very same reason, deny the world to have been formed by him. On the other hand, if there be an analogy or likeness between that system of things and dispensation of Providence, which revelation informs us of, and that system of things and dispensation of Providence, which experience together with reason informs us of, i. e. the known course of nature; this is a presumption, that they have both the same author and cause; at least so far as to answer objections against the former's being from God, drawn from any thing which is analogical or similar to what is in the latter, which is acknowledged to be from him; for an Author of nature is here supposed.

§ 9. *Facts, with reasons, give the only just basis for inference from the known to the less known.*

Forming our notions of the constitution and government of the world upon reasoning, without foundation for the principles which we assume, whether from the attributes of God, or any thing else, is building a world upon hypothesis, like Descartes.[1] Forming

or that scripture is, in his own phrase, θεόπνευστος μέχρι τοῦ τυχόντος γράμματος.' Fitzgerald.

St. Irenaeus, after adducing instances of strange and unaccountable things in the economy of the world, proceeds: ' Si ergo et in rebus creaturae quaedam quidem adjacent Deo, quaedam autem et in nostram venerunt scientiam, quid mali est, si et eorum, quae in Scripturis requirantur, universis Scripturis spiritualibus existentibus, quaedam quidem absolvamus secundum gratiam Dei, quaedam autem commendemus Deo, et non solum in hoc seculo, sed et in futuro ' (*Adv. Haer.* ii. 47, p. 203). Fitzgerald.

[1] He, says Mr. L. Stephen, determined the starting-point of much English speculation. It was theological. Questioning all which he thought could be doubted, he assumed the certainty of what he thought could not. Self-attesting innate ideas were discoverable in the mind (*English Thought*, i. 9). The movements of the world and the heavens he considered to be due to *tourbillons* or

our notions upon reasoning from principles which are certain, but applied to cases to which we have no ground to apply them, (like those who explain the structure of the human body, and the nature of diseases and medicines from mere mathematics without sufficient *data*,) is an error much akin to the former: since what is assumed in order to make the reasoning applicable, is hypothesis. But it must be allowed just, to join abstract reasonings with the observation of facts, and argue from such facts as are known, to others that are like them; from that part of the divine government over intelligent creatures which comes under our view, to that larger and more general government over them which is beyond it; and from what is present, to collect what is likely, credible, or not incredible, will be hereafter.

§ 10. *Postulating a natural Governor of the world, he will argue thence for religion.*

This method [1] then of concluding and determining being practical, and what, if we will act at all, we cannot but act upon in the common pursuits of life; being evidently conclusive, in various degrees, proportionable to the degree and exactness of the whole analogy or likeness; and having so great authority [2] for its introduction into the subject of religion, even revealed religion; my design is to apply it to that subject in general, both natural and revealed: taking

vortices, the spring of which were to be found in the earth as the centre of the solar system, and in the fixed stars. This scheme it is which Butler seems to have in view (*Biogr. Universelle*, vi. 150).

[1] Viz. of proceeding in argument from facts known, that is to say, the constitution and course of nature, to those unknown, namely 'the larger and more general government' contemplated by natural and revealed religion.

[2] For example, John iii. 12: 'If I have told you earthly things, and ye believe not, how shall ye believe, if I tell you of heavenly things?'

for proved, that there is an intelligent Author of nature, and natural Governor of the world. For as there is no presumption against this prior to the proof of it: so it has been often proved with accumulated evidence; from this argument of analogy and final causes; from abstract reasonings; from the most ancient tradition and testimony; and from the general consent of mankind. Nor does it appear, so far as I can find, to be denied by the generality of those who profess themselves dissatisfied with the evidence of religion.

§ 11. *Some build up world-systems of imagined optimism.*

As there are some, who, instead of thus attending to what is in fact the constitution of nature, form their notions of God's government upon hypothesis: so there are others, who indulge themselves in vain and idle speculations, how the world might possibly have been framed otherwise than it is; and upon supposition that things might, in imagining that they should, have been disposed and carried on after a better model, than what appears in the present disposition and conduct of them.[1] Suppose now a person of such a turn of mind, to go on with his reveries, till he had at length fixed upon some particular plan of nature, as appearing to him the best.——One shall scarce be thought guilty of detraction against human understanding, if one should say, even beforehand, that the plan which this speculative person would fix upon, though he were the wisest of the sons of men, probably would not be the very best, even according to his own notions of *best*; whether he thought that to be so, which afforded occasions and motives for the exercise of the greatest virtue, or which was productive of the greatest happiness, or that these two were necessarily

[1] 'I suppose that Butler had Bayle particularly in his eye in this passage' (see *Crit. Dict.*, Manichaeus, Origen, Paulicians), Fitzgerald.

connected, and run up into one and the same plan. However, it may not be amiss once for all to see, what would be the amount of these emendations and imaginary improvements upon the system of nature, or how far they would mislead us. And it seems there could be no stopping, till we came to some such conclusions as these: that all creatures should at first be made as perfect and as happy as they were capable of ever being: that nothing, to be sure, of hazard or danger should be put upon them to do; some indolent persons would perhaps think nothing at all: or certainly, that effectual care should be taken, that they should, whether necessarily or not, yet eventually and in fact, always do what was right and most conducive to happiness, which would be thought easy for infinite power to effect; either by not giving them any principles which would endanger their going wrong; or by laying the right motive of action in every instance before their minds continually in so strong a manner, as would never fail of inducing them to act conformably to it: and that the whole method of government by punishments should be rejected as absurd; as an awkward roundabout method of carrying things on; nay, as contrary to a principal purpose, for which it would be supposed creatures were made, namely, happiness.

§ 12. *But, even if agreed as to ends, we are incompetent judges of means.*

Now, without considering what is to be said in particular to the several parts of this train of folly and extravagance; what has been above intimated, is a full direct general answer to it, namely, that we may see beforehand that we have not faculties for this kind of speculation. For though it be admitted, that, from the first principles of our nature, we unavoidably judge or determine some ends to be absolutely in themselves preferable to others, and that the ends now mentioned, or if they run up into one, that this one is absolutely the best; and consequently that we must conclude the ultimate end designed, in the constitution of nature and conduct of Providence, is the most virtue and happiness possible: yet we are far from being able to judge what particular disposition of things would be most friendly and assistant to virtue; or what means might be absolutely necessary to produce the most happiness in a system of such extent as our own world may be, taking in all that is past and to come, though we should suppose it detached from the whole of things.[1] Indeed we are so far from being able to judge of this, that we are not judges what may be the necessary means of raising and conducting one person to the highest perfection and happiness of his nature. Nay, even in the little affairs of the present life, we find men of different educations and ranks are not competent judges of the conduct of each other.

§ 13. *e. g., as an end, that virtue must be happiness, and vice misery, for us all,*

Our whole nature leads us to ascribe all moral perfection to God, and to deny all imperfection of him. And this will for ever be a practical proof of his moral character, to such as will consider what a practical proof is; because it is the voice of God speaking in us. And from hence we conclude, that virtue must be the happiness, and vice the misery, of every creature; and that regularity and order and right cannot but prevail finally in a universe under his government.[2] But we are in no sort judges, what are the necessary means of accomplishing this end.

---

[1] This is possibly a first glimpse given us of an idea rooted in Butler's philosophical speculations, that the operations of this world are of an eventual scope exceeding in an unknown degree the breadth of the stage on which they are visibly carried on. See *inf.* c. iii. 26, 28.

[2] It must not be supposed that this final triumph dispenses with all rendering of account for the period

§ 14. *Will build on the experienced conduct of nature to intelligent creatures.*

Let us then, instead of that idle and not very innocent employment of forming imaginary models of a world, and schemes of governing it, turn our thoughts to what we experience to be the conduct of nature with respect to intelligent creatures; which may be resolved into general laws or rules of administration, in the same way as many of the laws of nature respecting inanimate matter may be collected from experiments. And let us compare the known constitution and course of things with what is said to be the moral system of nature; the acknowledged dispensations of Providence, or that government which we find ourselves under, with what religion teaches us to believe and expect; and see whether they are not analogous and of a piece. And upon such a comparison it will, I think, be found, that they are very much so: that both may be traced up to the same general laws, and resolved into the same principles of divine conduct.

§ 15. *And so vindicate both religion and its evidences.*

The analogy here proposed to be considered is of pretty large extent, and consists of several parts, in some, more, in others, less, exact. In some few instances perhaps it may amount to a real practical proof; in others not so. Yet in these it is a confirmation of what is proved other ways. It will undeniably show, what too many want to have shown them, that the system of religion, both natural and revealed, considered only as a system, and prior to the proof of it, is not a subject of ridicule, unless that of nature

which precedes it. We have here to introduce the reasonable supposition, sustained by our experience, that the inequalities of that period will be subservient to the purposes of discipline in the improvement of characters.

be so too. And it will afford an answer to almost all objections against the system both of natural and revealed religion ; though not perhaps an answer in so great a degree, yet in a very considerable degree an answer to the objections against the evidence of it: for objections against a proof, and objections against what is said to be proved, the reader will observe are different things.

§ 16. *Chapter of summaries : Religion.* (a) *Natural, in five heads ;* (b) *Revealed, in six heads.*[1]

Now the divine government of the world, implied in the notion of religion in general and of Christianity, contains in it; that mankind is appointed to live in a future state ; ᵉ that there every one shall be rewarded or punished ; ᶠ rewarded or punished respectively for

ᵉ Part I. Ch. i.   ᶠ Ch. ii.

---

[1] See note on I. ii. 4. Here we have a summary :—

Natural Religion.

1. A future life, I. i.
2. Of reward and punishment, I. ii.
3. For good and evil conduct, I. iii.
4. This life a probation, I. iv.
5. And discipline, I. v.

[Objection of Necessity, I. vi.
Scheme known only in part, I. vii.]

Revealed Religion.

1. Sin, ruin, and a blinded sense, required a further plan, II. i.
2. Proved by miracles, II. ii.
3. Contents partly strange and unexpected, II. iii.
4. Constituting a scheme or system, II. iv.
5. Worked by the Messiah for our recovery, II. v.
6. Partially revealed and with partial evidence, II. vi, vii.

all that behaviour here, which we comprehend under the words, virtuous or vicious, morally good or evil: [g] that our present life is a probation, a state of trial,[h] and of discipline,[i] for that future one; notwithstanding the objections, which men may fancy they have, from notions of necessity, against there being any such moral plan as this at all; [k] and whatever objections may appear to lie against the wisdom and goodness of it, as it stands so imperfectly made known to us at present: [l] that this world being in a state of apostasy and wickedness, and consequently of ruin, and the sense both of their condition and duty being greatly corrupted amongst men, this gave occasion for an additional dispensation of Providence; of the utmost importance; [m] proved by miracles; [n] but containing in it many things appearing to us strange and not to have been expected; [o] a dispensation of Providence, which is a scheme or system of things; [p] carried on by the mediation of a divine person, the Messiah, in order to the recovery of the world; [q] yet not revealed to all men, nor proved with the strongest possible evidence to all those to whom it is revealed; but only to such a part of mankind, and with such particular evidence as the wisdom of God thought fit.[r]

§ 17. *Will show that both rest on analogies from the constitution and course of nature.*

The design then of the following Treatise will be to show, that the several parts principally objected against in this moral and Christian dispensation, including its scheme, its publication, and the proof which God has afforded us of its truth; that the particular parts principally objected against in this whole dispensation, are analogous to what is experienced in the constitution and course of nature, or Providence; that the chief objections themselves

---

[g] Ch. iii.　　[h] Ch. iv.　　[i] Ch. v.　　[k] Ch. vi.
[l] Ch. vii.　　[m] Part II. Ch. i.　　[n] Ch. ii.　　[o] Ch. iii.
[p] Ch. iv.　　[q] Ch. v.　　[r] Ch. vi, vii.

which are alleged against the former, are no other than what may be alleged with like justness against the latter, where they are found in fact to be inconclusive;[1] and that this argument from analogy is in general unanswerable, and undoubtedly of weight on the side of religion,[s] notwithstanding the objections which may seem to lie against it, and the real ground which there may be for difference of opinion, as to the particular degree of weight which is to be laid upon it. This is a general account of what may be looked for in the following Treatise. And I shall begin it with that which is the foundation of all our hopes and of all our fears; all our hopes and fears, which are of any consideration; I mean a future life.

[s] Part II. Ch. viii.

[1] It is charged by some against Butler, that he leaves 'the course of nature, or Providence,' to meet unprotected the storm of objections carried over to it from Religion, which he has in a manner exonerated by the transfer. But it will be observed that, on the contrary, even in this contracted summary he inserts the express proviso on its behalf, conveyed in the words 'where they are found in fact to be inconclusive.' Comp. I. vii. 3.

THE
ANALOGY OF RELIGION

TO THE

CONSTITUTION AND COURSE OF NATURE

PART I

OF NATURAL RELIGION

CHAPTER I[1]

OF A FUTURE LIFE

§ 1. *Let experience test for us the probable effect of death.*

STRANGE difficulties have been raised by some concerning personal identity, or the sameness of living agents, implied in the notion of our existing now and hereafter, or in any two successive moments;

[1] If we set out from the sentence in which Origen has supplied the basis of the *Analogy*, the natural order of the subject would probably suggest dealing with the phenomena and experience of life before considering those of death. But the author seems to have given precedence to this subject on the special and double grounds:

1. That the doctrine of a future life is the foundation of all our principal hopes and fears, so that without it men will not cross the threshold of this inquiry.

2. That it had been darkened and, so to speak, intercepted, by speculations then fresh in the public mind respecting personal identity, a subject lying at the root of the doctrine. (See Locke, *On the Understanding*, II. xxvii. 10.)

He however hereby exposed himself to these incon-

which whoever thinks it worth while, may see considered in the first Dissertation at the end of this Treatise. But without regard to any of them here, let us consider what the analogy of nature, and the several changes

veniences: (1) That death rather hides than exhibits the course of nature with respect to our condition, by shutting off all the evidence of what follows, so that his argument works at a disadvantage from scantiness of material in a narrowed field. (2) That a chapter purporting to treat ' of a future life ' seemed to promise a full discussion of the subject; whereas here the author is confined to a very partial treatment, and does not, indeed cannot, present at all the great moral argument in favour of our survival, while the general doctrine of the natural immortality of the soul (on which he reserves his opinion) seems to have no natural place in the discussion, as it is not derived from the ' constitution and course of nature.'

Hence there may arise with some a sense of disappointment with the contents of the chapter, which may perhaps be removed or mitigated if we bear steadily in mind that the author was confined by the conditions of his work to a closely limited and partial investigation. He has to leave aside all moral arguments whatever : and the sum of what he can do is to rebut adverse presumptions drawn from the extinction of our sensuous life ; to marshal such favourable presumptions as he can gather from certain observed facts, while not venturing to lay great stress upon them ; and to give as the main considerations in his favour, the incapacity of death to destroy perhaps the corporeal but certainly the mental life, and the argument from continuance. Now that last argument in favour of survival assumes a great strength when we can take our stand upon the moral incompleteness of our present existence. But this is for the present a forbidden topic ; and, in connection with merely physical considerations, the contention seems hardly corroborated enough to bear our laying any very great stress upon it.

On the whole it may seem that the best mode of conceiving Butler's attitude is to treat the two heads of argument as one ; and to put it thus. Considering the disproof which has been given of any power possessed by death to destroy mental (and, it might have been added,

OF A FUTURE LIFE 21

which we have undergone, and those which we know we may undergo without being destroyed, suggest, as to the effect which death may, or may not, have upon us; and whether it be not from thence probable, that we may survive this change, and exist in a future state of life and perception.

§ 2. *In us and in other creatures identity survives great changes.*

[I.] From our being born into the present world in the helpless imperfect state of infancy, and having arrived from thence to mature age, we find it to be a general law of nature in our own species, that the same creatures, the same individuals, should exist in degrees of life and perception, with capacities of action, of enjoyment and suffering, in one period of their being, greatly different from those appointed them in another period of it. And in other creatures the same law holds. For the difference of their capacities and states of life at their birth (to go no higher) and in maturity; the change of worms into flies, and the vast enlargement of their locomotive powers by such change: and birds and insects bursting the shell of their habitation, and by this means entering into a new world, furnished with new accommodations for them, and finding a new sphere of action assigned them; these are instances of this general law of nature. Thus all the various and wonderful transformations of animals are to be taken into consideration here.[1]

still more to destroy moral) qualities, and finding these indestructible qualities now actually embodied in a living subject, it is strictly rational, on grounds quite apart from religion, to suggest the survival of that subject after the change brought about by death, as at least a matter of high probability.

Angus (p. 19), citing Chalmers in aid, observes that while this chapter cannot be taken as supplying an affirmative proof of the future life, it is triumphant in the confutation of objections. Observe Butler's own claim in § 32.

[1] Fitzgerald observes that in his comparison of states

§ 3. *Death may be no greater.*

But the states of life in which we ourselves existed formerly in the womb and in our infancy, are almost as different from our present in mature age, as it is possible to conceive any two states or degrees of life can be. Therefore, that we are to exist hereafter in a state as different (suppose) from our present, as this is from our former, is but according to the analogy of nature; according to a natural order or appointment of the very same kind, with what we have already experienced.

§ 4. *Unless it has a power to destroy, continuance after it is to be presumed.*

[II.] We know we are endued with capacities of action, of happiness and misery: for we are conscious of acting, of enjoying pleasure and suffering pain. Now that we have these powers and capacities before death, is a presumption that we shall retain them through and after death; indeed a probability of it abundantly sufficient to act upon, unless there be some positive reason to think that death is the destruc-

Butler does not allow for the fact that death differs from the others in seeming to deprive us wholly of bodily organisation. On the other hand, in the womb we are entirely deprived of any medium in which to act; and Butler's comparison is one not rigid, but only general. It is conceivable that the death-state may be found to differ from known life-states, only in such a way that the differences between one life-state and another may be 'almost,' if not altogether, as great.

Butler is not here dealing with any objection to a future life which may be grounded on the phenomenon of death, but only dealing with the novelty of that state to which it may be introducing us. Death seems to suggest that, if there be a future state, it must be very foreign to the present state. It seems legitimate to reply by showing that even within the known limits of existence it admits of enormous diversities.

tion of those living powers :[1] because there is in every case a probability, that all things will continue as we experience they are, in all respects, except those in which we have some reason to think they will be altered. This is that *kind* [a] of presumption or probability from analogy, expressed in the very word *continuance*, which seems our only natural reason for believing the course of the world will continue to-morrow, as it has done so far as our experience or knowledge of history can carry us back.[2] Nay, it seems our only reason for believing, that any one

[a] I say *kind* of presumption or probability ; for I do not mean to affirm that there is the same *degree* of conviction, that our living powers will continue after death, as there is, that our substances will.

[1] Dr. Eagar, one of the most recent writers on the *Analogy*, and in general a supporter of its arguments, holds that this chapter is ' out of tune with present knowledge ' : which he explains by saying that no one would now suggest that our reflective powers ' might be independent ' of our physical organs (*Butler's Analogy and Modern Thought*, c. iv. p. 102). The assertion is one which Butler has nowhere made. The word is indeed, on account of its ambiguity, altogether unsuitable. He continually recognises in various forms the near relation between the living powers and the bodily organs. But in § 23 he points out that the living powers do not depend upon the body ' in the manner ' in which perception by our organs of sense does. And Dr. Eagar goes on to show (p. 105) that the physical changes in the brain which accompany the act of perception ' are yet different from it,' and to adopt Butler's own language, ' we see with our eyes as with glasses.' The verbal surrender of Butler's argument appears to be a pure mistake. See further on §§ 10 and 14.

[2] Continuance, however, only raises this presumption in connection with purpose ; and while the purpose for which the substance exists remains not yet accomplished in full, the continuance of its existence until the full accomplishment may be reasonably presumed. See note on § 1.

substance now existing will continue to exist a moment longer; the self-existent substance only excepted. Thus if men were assured that the unknown event, death, was not the destruction of our faculties of perception and of action, there would be no apprehension, that any other power or event unconnected with this of death, would destroy these faculties just at the instant of each creature's death; and therefore no doubt but that they would remain after it: which shows the high probability that our living powers will continue after death, unless there be some ground to think that death is their destruction.[b] For, if it would be in a manner certain that we should survive death, provided it were certain that death would not be our destruction, it must be highly probable we shall survive it, if there be no ground to think death will be our destruction.

§ 5. *Mere apprehension to the contrary is of no weight.*

Now though I think it must be acknowledged, that prior to the natural and moral proofs of a future life commonly insisted upon, there would arise a general confused suspicion, that in the great shock and alteration which we shall undergo by death, we, i. e. our

---

[b] *Destruction of living powers* is a manner of expression unavoidably ambiguous; and may signify
Distinguish destruction absolute from destruction of present conditions. either *the destruction of a living being, so as that the same living being shall be uncapable of ever perceiving or acting again at all:* or *the destruction of those means and instruments by which it is capable of its present life, of its present state of perception and of action.* It is here used in the former sense. When it is used in the latter, the epithet *present* is added. The loss of a man's eye is a destruction of living powers in the latter sense. But we have no reason to think the destruction of living powers, in the former sense, to be possible. We have no more reason to think a being endued with living powers, ever loses them during its whole existence, than to believe that a stone ever acquires them.

living powers, might be wholly destroyed; yet even prior to those proofs, there is really no particular distinct ground or reason for this apprehension at all, so far as I can find. If there be, it must arise either from *the reason of the thing*, or from *the analogy of nature*.

§ 6. (a) *In the reason of the thing; for death does not suggest the destruction of the living agent.*

But we cannot argue from *the reason of the thing*, that death is the destruction of living agents, because we know not at all what death is in itself; but only some of its effects, such as the dissolution of flesh, skin, and bones. And these effects do in no wise appear to imply the destruction of a living agent. And besides, as we are greatly in the dark, upon what the exercise of our living powers depends, so we are wholly ignorant what the powers themselves depend upon; the powers themselves as distinguished, not only from their actual exercise, but also from the present capacity of exercising them; and as opposed to their destruction: for sleep, or however a swoon, shows us, not only that these powers exist when they are not exercised, as the passive power of motion does in inanimate matter; but shows also that they exist, when there is no present capacity of exercising them: or that the capacities of exercising them for the present, as well as the actual exercise of them, may be suspended, and yet the powers themselves remain undestroyed. Since then we know not at all upon what the existence of our living powers depends, this shows further, there can no probability be collected from the reason of the thing, that death will be their destruction: because their existence may depend upon somewhat in no degree affected by death; upon somewhat quite out of the reach of this king of terrors.[1] So that there is nothing

[1] We have also probable evidence that their existence does not depend upon any thing that we know to be affected by death. *Inf.* §§ 14, 16, 29.

more certain, than that *the reason of the thing* shows us no connection between death, and the destruction of living agents.

§ 7. *Or* (b) *in the analogy of nature. It destroys only the sensible proof of living powers.*

Nor can we find any thing throughout the whole *analogy of nature*, to afford us even the slightest presumption, that animals ever lose their living powers; much less, if it were possible, that they lose them by death: for we have no faculties wherewith to trace any beyond or through it, so as to see what becomes of them. This event removes them from our view. It destroys the *sensible* proof, which we had before their death, of their being possessed of living powers, but does not appear to afford the least reason to believe that they are, then, or by that event, deprived of them.

§ 8. *Repeats arguments of §§ 3 and 4.*

And our knowing, that they were possessed of these powers, up to the very period to which we have faculties capable of tracing them, is itself a probability of their retaining them, beyond it. And this is confirmed, and a sensible credibility is given to it, by observing the very great and astonishing changes which we have experienced; so great, that our existence in another state of life, of perception and of action, will be but according to a method of providential conduct, the like to which has been already exercised even with regard to ourselves; according to a course of nature, the like to which we have already gone through.

§ 9. *Warning against trespasses of the imagination.*[1]

However, as one cannot but be greatly sensible, how difficult it is to silence imagination enough to make

[1] Butler appears here to charge upon the imagination all the erratic whims and fancies of the brain. These

the voice of reason even distinctly heard in this case; as we are accustomed, from our youth up, to indulge that forward delusive faculty, ever obtruding beyond its sphere; of some assistance indeed to apprehension, but the author of all error: as we plainly lose ourselves in gross and crude conceptions of things, taking for granted that we are acquainted with, what indeed we are wholly ignorant of: it may be proper to consider the imaginary presumptions, that death will be our destruction, arising from these kinds of early and lasting prejudices; and to show how little they can really amount to, even though we cannot wholly divest ourselves of them. And,

§ 10. *Such apprehension* (c) *is futile, unless the living agent be discerptible: which it seems not to be*

[I.] All presumption of death's being the destruction of living beings, must go upon supposition that they are compounded; and so, discerptible.[1] But since

no doubt are regardless of evidence, and apt, too, to palm themselves upon us as if they were fact. But imagination proper is totally different, and knows itself to be a denizen of a world different from the world of fact, and unsuited to masquerading in any character other than its own. It seems necessary to make these allowances in considering the passage. In imagination proper it would appear that Butler was by no means wanting, if we may judge from the mode in which he treats the subject of beauty, referring it as he does to fixed principles. See Serm. xi. 21.

[1] Dr. Eagar refers us to a modern physiological theory, which appears to go far in supporting the ideas propounded here and in § 14. 'In the highly organised multicellular being, most of these cells are what are called *somatic* cells, i.e. cells that are continually being changed and replaced during life, whose persistence is not necessary to the life of the being. But the cell, that has brought life, is of a different kind. It is never replaced, and never loses its life. The cell of the unicellular animal is of this kind, a *germ-cell*. From the nature of the case it

consciousness is a single and indivisible power, it should seem that the subject in which it resides must be so too. For were the motion of any particle of matter absolutely one and indivisible, so as that it should imply a contradiction to suppose part of this motion to exist, and part not to exist, i. e. part of this matter to move, and part to be at rest; then its power of motion would be indivisible; and so also would the subject in which the power inheres, namely, the particle of matter: for if this could be divided into two, one part might be moved and the other at rest, which is contrary to the supposition. In like manner it has been argued,[c] and, for any thing appearing to the contrary, justly, that since the perception or consciousness, which we have of our own existence, is indivisible, so as that it is a contradiction to suppose one part of it should be here and the other there; the perceptive power, or the power of consciousness, is indivisible too: and consequently the subject in which it resides; i. e. the conscious being.

[c] See Dr. Clarke's Letter to Mr. Dodwell, and the defences of it.

---

can have no *somatic* cells' (Eagar, p. 111). I need hardly add that these words are quoted by way of illustration only.

As regards the text, we must closely observe its terms. This is not an argument to prove the immortality of the soul; but only to show that no presumption of its mortality arises out of the fact of death, unless the soul be discerptible, and therefore material. The passage then does not seek to rule the question of the soul's immortality. May it not be truly said, that of the growth and dissolution of the body we know a little, but of the generation and dissolution of the soul, considered as natural processes, nothing whatever? But Butler is not made responsible by what he has written for Clarke's doctrine. It is indivisibility on which he argues; and so he escapes the association with matter which attaches to the word 'indiscerptible.'

On the Natural Immortality of the Soul, see *inf.* §§ 21, 31.

§ 11. *And, if not, the body is mere foreign matter, without* nisus *towards destroying us.*

Now upon supposition that living agent each man calls himself, is thus a single being, which there is at least no more difficulty in conceiving than in conceiving it to be a compound, and of which there is the proof now mentioned; it follows, that our organized bodies are no more ourselves or part of ourselves, than any other matter around us. And it is as easy to conceive, how matter, which is no part of ourselves, may be appropriated to us in the manner which our present bodies are; as how we can receive impressions from, and have power over any matter. It is as easy to conceive, that we may exist out of bodies, as in them; that we might have animated bodies of any other organs and senses wholly different from these now given us, and that we may hereafter animate these same or new bodies variously modified and organized; as to conceive how we can animate such bodies as our present.[1] And lastly, the dissolution of all these several organized bodies, supposing ourselves to have successively animated them, would have no more conceivable tendency to destroy the living beings ourselves, or deprive us of living faculties, the faculties of perception and of action, than the dissolution of any foreign matter, which we are capable of receiving

---

[1] This appears a hazardous assertion. May it not even be asked whether the human faculties have ever yet fully conceived an existence living and active, and yet wholly discharged from body? It is of course another question whether there may not actually be existence under such conditions.

In Dante the spirits cast no shadow from the sun, yet are, as in all other points, absolutely visible in shapes. Compare the case of the anxiety of demons in the N. T. to be in bodies; and the language of St. Paul (2 Cor. xii. 2): 'whether in the body, or out of the body, I cannot tell.'

impressions from, and making use of for the common occasions of life.[1]

§ 12. *Observation likewise proves the body to be no part of ourselves.*

[II.] The simplicity and absolute oneness of a living agent cannot indeed, from the nature of the thing, be properly proved by experimental observations. But as these *fall in* with the supposition of its unity, so they plainly lead us to *conclude* certainly, that our gross organized bodies, with which we perceive the objects of sense, and with which we act, are no part of ourselves;[2] and therefore show us, that we have no reason to believe their destruction to be ours: even without determining whether our living substances be material or immaterial. For we see by experience, that men may lose their limbs, their organs of sense, and even the greatest part of these bodies, and yet remain the same living agents. And persons can trace up the existence of themselves to a time, when the bulk of their bodies was extremely small, in comparison of what it is in mature age: and we cannot but think, that they might then have lost a considerable part of that small body, and yet have remained the same living agents; as they may now lose great part of their present body, and remain so.

---

[1] The impressions from other foreign matter are upon the exterior organs of the body. But these organs, we now know, transmit tidings to the brain, and there the body has communications with the soul, as to which we know that there is nothing similar in the contact of ordinary matter, though their nature remains wholly inscrutable to us.

[2] In scripture, the body is indeed our 'tabernacle': but it is also the temple of the Holy Ghost (1 Cor. vi. 19), and we are formed of body, soul, and spirit (1 Thess. v. 23). To warrant Butler's assertion we must confine it strictly to that which indeed he is arguing upon, namely, the present and natural body as distinct from the future and spiritual body.

§ 13. *As does the fluxion of its particles.*

And it is certain, that the bodies of all animals are in a constant flux, from that never-ceasing attrition, which there is in every part of them. Now things of this kind unavoidably teach us to distinguish, between these living agents ourselves, and large quantities of matter, in which we are very nearly interested: since these may be alienated, and actually are in a daily course of succession, and changing their owners; whilst we are assured, that each living agent remains one and the same permanent being.[d] And this general observation leads us on to the following ones.

§ 14. *Unless the living agent be bulkier than the atom, no presumption against its survival.*

First, That we have no way of determining by experience, what is the certain bulk of the living being each man calls himself: and yet, till it be determined that it is larger in bulk than the solid elementary particles of matter, which there is no ground to think any natural power can dissolve, there is no sort of reason to think death to be the dissolution of it, of the living being, even though it should not be absolutely indiscerptible.

§ 15. *If our bodies be not the ego, no ground to think any other matter is.*

Secondly, From our being so nearly related to and interested in certain systems of matter, suppose our flesh and bones, and afterwards ceasing to be at all related to them, the living agents ourselves remaining all this while undestroyed notwithstanding such alienation; and consequently these systems of matter not being ourselves: it follows further, that we have no ground to conclude any other, suppose *internal systems* of matter, to be the living agents ourselves;

[d] See Dissertation I.

because we can have no ground to conclude this, but
from our relation to and interest in such other systems
of matter: and therefore we can have no reason to
conclude, what befalls those systems of matter at
death, to be the destruction of the living agents. We
have already several times over lost a great part or
perhaps the whole of our body, according to certain
common established laws of nature; yet we remain the
same living agents: when we shall lose as great a part,
or the whole, by another common established law of
nature, death; why may we not also remain the same?
That the alienation has been gradual in one case, and
in the other will be more at once, does not prove any
thing to the contrary. We have passed undestroyed
through those many and great revolutions of matter,
so peculiarly appropriated to us ourselves; why should
we imagine death will be so fatal to us?

§ 16. *No proof that the original solid body, if any,
is affected by death.*[1]

Nor can it be objected, that what is thus alienated
or lost, is no part of our original solid body, but only
adventitious matter; because we may lose entire
limbs, which must have contained many solid parts
and vessels of the original body: or if this be not
admitted, we have no proof, that any of these solid
parts are dissolved or alienated by death. Though,
by the way, we are very nearly related to that extraneous or adventitious matter, whilst it continues united
to and distending the several parts of our solid body.
But after all; the relation a person bears to those
parts of his body, to which he is the most nearly
related; what does it appear to amount to but this,
that the living agent, and those parts of the body,
mutually affect each other? And the same thing, the
same thing in kind though not in degree, may be said
of *all foreign* matter, which gives us ideas, and which
we have any power over. From these observations

[1] See note on § 10.

the whole ground of the imagination is removed, that the dissolution of any matter, is the destruction of a living agent, from the interest he once had in such matter.

§ 17. *Like other instruments, our senses present objects, but do not perceive.*[1]

Thirdly, If we consider our body somewhat more distinctly, as made up of organs and instruments of perception and of motion, it will bring us to the same conclusion. Thus the common optical experiments show, and even the observation how sight is assisted by glasses shows, that we see with our eyes in the same sense as we see with glasses. Nor is there any reason to believe, that we see with them in any other sense; any other, I mean, which would lead us to think the eye itself a percipient. The like is to be said of hearing: and our feeling distant solid matter by means of somewhat in our hand, seems an instance of the like kind, as to the subject we are considering. All these are instances of foreign matter, or such as is no part of our body, being instrumental in preparing objects for, and conveying them to, the perceiving power, in a manner similar or like to the manner in which our organs of sense prepare and convey them. Both are in a like way instruments of our receiving such ideas from external objects, as the Author of nature appointed those external objects to be the occasions of exciting in us. However, glasses are evidently instances of this; namely of matter which is no part of our body, preparing objects for and conveying them towards the perceiving power, in like manner as our bodily organs do. And if we see with our eyes only in the same manner as we do with glasses, the like may justly be concluded, from analogy, of all our other senses. It

---

[1] Plato, *Alcibiades*, i. 51 : ἕτερον ἄρα σκυτοτόμος καὶ κιθαριστὴς χειρῶν καὶ ὀφθαλμῶν οἷς ἐργάζονται ; . . . . ἕτερον ἄρα ἄνθρωπός ἐστι τοῦ σώματος τοῦ ἑαυτοῦ.

is not intended, by any thing here said, to affirm, that the whole apparatus of vision, or of perception by any other of our senses, can be traced through all its steps, quite up to the living power of seeing, or perceiving: but that so far as it can be traced by experimental observations, so far it appears, that our organs of sense prepare and convey on objects, in order to their being perceived, in like manner as foreign matter does, without affording any shadow of appearance, that they themselves perceive.

§ 18. *We can ($\pi\omega s$) part with them; and act, in dreams, without them.*

And that we have no reason to think our organs of sense percipients, is confirmed by instances of persons losing some of them, the living beings themselves, their former occupiers, remaining unimpaired. It is confirmed also by the experience of dreams; by which we find we are at present possessed of a latent, and, what would otherwise be, an unimagined unknown power of perceiving sensible objects, in as strong and lively a manner without our external organs of sense as with them.

§ 19. *Limbs are instruments, and raise no presumption of one dying with them.*

So also with regard to our power of moving, or directing motion by will and choice: upon the destruction of a limb, this active power remains, as it evidently seems, unlessened; so as that the living being, who has suffered this loss, would be capable of moving as before, if it had another limb to move with. It can walk by the help of an artificial leg; just as it can make use of a pole or a lever, to reach towards itself and to move things, beyond the length and the power of its natural arm: and this last it does in the same manner as it reaches and moves, with its natural arm, things nearer and of less weight. Nor is there so much as any appearance of our limbs being endued with a power of moving or directing themselves; though they are adapted, like the several parts of a machine, to be the instruments of motion to each other; and some parts of the same limb, to be instruments of motion to other parts of it.

Thus a man determines, that he will look at such an object through a microscope; or being lame suppose, that he will walk to such a place with a staff a week hence. His eyes and his feet no more determine in these cases, than the microscope and the staff. Nor is there any ground to think they any more put the determination in practice; or that his eyes are the seers or his feet the movers, in any other sense than as the microscope and the staff are. Upon the whole then, our organs of sense and our limbs are certainly instruments, which the living persons ourselves make use of to perceive and move with: there is not any probability, that they are any more; nor consequently, that we have any other kind of relation to them, than what we may have to any other foreign matter formed into instruments of perception and motion, suppose into a microscope or a staff; (I say any other kind of relation, for I am not speaking of the degree of it;) nor consequently is there any probability, that the alienation or dissolution of these instruments is the destruction of the perceiving and moving agent.

§ 20. *If we can survive such matter, why not all matter?*

And thus our finding, that the dissolution of matter, in which living beings were most nearly interested, is not their dissolution; and that the destruction of several of the organs and instruments of perception and of motion belonging to them, is not their destruction; shows demonstratively, that there is no ground to think that the dissolution of any other matter, or destruction of any other organs and instruments, will be the dissolution or destruction of living agents, from the like kind of relation. And we have no reason to think we stand in any other kind of relation to any thing which we find dissolved by death.

§ 21. Obj. *Then brutes may come to rational and moral nature.* Answ. *May, but need not.*[1]

But it is said these observations are equally applicable to brutes: and it is thought an insuperable difficulty, that they should be immortal, and by consequence capable of everlasting happiness. Now this manner of expression is both invidious and weak: but the thing intended by it, is really no difficulty at all, either in the way of natural or moral consideration. For first, Suppose the invidious thing, designed in such a manner of expression, were really implied, as it is not in the least, in the natural immortality of brutes; namely, that they must arrive at great attainments, and become rational and moral agents; even this would be no difficulty: since we know not what latent powers and capacities they may be endued with. There was once, prior to experience, as great presumption against human creatures, as there is against the brute creatures, arriving at that degree of understanding, which we have in mature age. For we can trace up our own existence to the same original with theirs. And we find it to be a general law of nature, that creatures endued with capacities of virtue and religion should be placed in a condition of being, in which they are altogether without the use of them, for a considerable length of their duration; as in infancy and childhood. And great part of the human species go out of the present world, before they come to the exercise of these capacities in any degree at all. But then, secondly, The natural immortality of brutes does not in the least imply, that they are endued with any

---

[1] Angus quotes from Clarke's Reply to Collins: 'Brutes may for all we know become rational agents, as infants do. If not, the system of the universe may require the future existence of brutes, as it requires the present; and after all there are other and stronger arguments for the future life of man, which do not hold equally in the case of brutes.'

latent capacities of a rational or moral nature.[1] And the economy of the universe might require, that there should be living creatures without any capacities of this kind.

§ 22. *Our ignorance regarding them no bar to the argument as it relates to man.*

And all difficulties as to the manner how they are to be disposed of are so apparently and wholly founded in our ignorance, that it is wonderful they should be insisted upon by any, but such as are weak enough to think they are acquainted with the whole system of things. There is then absolutely nothing at all in this objection, which is so rhetorically urged, against the greatest part of the natural proofs or presumptions of the immortality of human minds: I say the greatest part; for it is less applicable to the following observation, which is more peculiar to mankind:

§ 23. *No presumption anywhere against survival of reason, memory, and affections.*[2]

[III.] That as it is evident our *present* powers and capacities of reason, memory, and affection, do not

---

[1] Disclaiming any positive doctrine of a rational and moral nature for brutes, Butler stops short of disclaiming the argument for their immortality, as implied in a spirit distinct from the body, which arises upon §§ 17-19.

The natural immortality of the human soul mentioned here, is again noticed in § 31, but in neither case is there any explicit acceptance of it.

[2] To the whole argument of Butler for the survival of the reason, memory, and affection, Dr. Eagar appears to make a valuable addition by producing the case of the moral powers distinctly and apart (Eagar, p. 107):

'The moral powers of the man likewise grow, but they have no period of decay, confined within the apparent limits of life. They not only last, but maintain their full vigour, and even strengthen, to the end. The brain, as well as the senses, grows weak; but the man does not weaken in truth, honesty, uprightness, love.'

depend upon our gross body in the manner in which perception by our organs of sense does; so they do not appear to depend upon it at all in any such manner, as to give ground to think, that the dissolution of this body will be the destruction of these our *present* powers of reflection, as it will of our powers of sensation; or to give ground to conclude, even that it will be so much as a suspension of the former.

§ 24. *Our state is dual,* (a) *of sensation,* (b) *of reflection. No sign that death touches* (b).

Human creatures exist at present in two states of life and perception, greatly different from each other; each of which has its own peculiar laws, and its own peculiar enjoyments and sufferings. When any of our senses are affected or appetites gratified with the objects of them, we may be said to exist or live in a state of sensation. When none of our senses are affected or appetites gratified, and yet we perceive, and reason, and act; we may be said to exist or live in a state of reflection. Now it is by no means certain, that any thing which is dissolved by death, is any way necessary to the living being in this its state of reflection, after ideas are gained. For, though, from our present constitution and condition of being, our external organs of sense are necessary for conveying in ideas to our reflecting powers, as carriages, and levers, and scaffolds are in architecture: yet when these ideas are brought in, we are capable of reflecting in the most intense degree, and of enjoying the greatest pleasure, and feeling the greatest pain, by means of that reflection, without any assistance from our senses; and without any at all, which we know of, from that body which will be dissolved by death. It does not appear then, that the relation of this gross body to the reflecting being is, in any degree, necessary to thinking; to our intellectual enjoyments or sufferings: nor, consequently, that the dissolution or alienation of the former by death, will be the destruction of those present powers, which render us capable of this state of reflection.

§ 25. *As some mortal diseases leave the ego unaffected, this may be so with all.*

Further, there are instances of mortal diseases, which do not at all affect our present intellectual powers; and this affords a presumption, that those diseases will not destroy these present powers. Indeed, from the observations made above,[e] it appears, that there is no presumption, from their mutually affecting each other, that the dissolution of the body is the destruction of the living agent. And by the same reasoning, it must appear too, that there is no presumption, from their mutually affecting each other, that the dissolution of the body is the destruction of our present reflecting powers: but instances of their not affecting each other, afford a presumption of the contrary. Instances of mortal diseases not impairing our present reflecting powers, evidently turn our thoughts even from imagining such diseases to be the destruction of them. Several things indeed greatly affect all our living powers, and at length suspend the exercise of them; as for instance drowsiness, increasing till it ends in sound sleep: and from hence we might have imagined it would destroy them, till we found by experience the weakness of this way of judging. But in the diseases now mentioned, there is not so much as this shadow of probability, to lead us to any such conclusion, as to the reflecting powers which we have at present. For in those diseases, persons the moment before death appear to be in the highest vigour of life. They discover apprehension, memory, reason, all entire; with the utmost force of affection; sense of a character, of shame and honour; and the highest mental enjoyments and sufferings, even to the last gasp: and these surely prove even

[e] *Sup.* §§ 15, 16.

greater vigour of life than bodily strength does. Now what pretence is there for thinking, that a progressive disease when arrived to such a degree, I mean that degree which is mortal, will destroy those powers, which were not impaired, which were not affected by it, during its whole progress quite up to that degree? And if death by diseases of this kind is not the destruction of our present reflecting powers, it will scarce be thought that death by any other means is.

§ 26. *Death may not even suspend its activity.*

It is obvious that this general observation may be carried on further: and there appears so little connection between our bodily powers of sensation, and our present powers of reflection, that there is no reason to conclude, that death, which destroys the former, does so much as suspend the exercise of the latter, or interrupt our *continuing* to exist in the like state of reflection which we do now. For suspension of reason, memory, and the affections which they excite, is no part of the idea of death, nor is implied in our notion of it. And our daily experiencing these powers to be exercised, without any assistance, that we know of, from those bodies, which will be dissolved by death; and our finding often, that the exercise of them is so lively to the last; these things afford a sensible apprehension, that death may not perhaps be so much as a discontinuance of the exercise of these powers, nor of the enjoyments and sufferings which it implies.[f] So that our posthumous life, whatever there may be

---

[f] There are three distinct questions, relating to a future life, here considered: Whether death be the destruction *Argument a* of living agents; if not, Whether it be the destruction *fortiori.* of their *present* powers of reflection, as it certainly is the destruction of their present powers of sensation; and if not, Whether it be the suspension, or discontinuance of the exercise, of these present reflecting powers. Now, if there be no reason to believe the last, there will be, if that were possible, less for the next, and less still for the first.

in it additional to our present, yet may not be entirely beginning anew; but going on.

§ 27. *Death may resemble a birth, and forthwith enlarge life.*

Death may, in some sort, and in some respects, answer to our birth; which is not a suspension of the faculties which we had before it, or a total change of the state of life in which we existed when in the womb; but a continuation of both, with such and such great alterations.

Nay, for ought we know of ourselves, of our present life and of death; death may immediately, in the natural course of things, put us into a higher and more enlarged state of life, as our birth does; [g] a state in which our capacities, and sphere of perception and of action, may be much greater than at present. For as our relation to our external organs of sense, renders us capable of existing in our present state of sensation; so it may be the only natural hindrance to our existing, immediately and of course, in a higher state of reflection. The truth is, reason does not at all show us, in what state death naturally leaves us.

§ 28. *Distinguish suspension from destruction.*

But were we sure, that it would suspend all our perceptive and active powers; yet the suspension of a power and the destruction of it, are effects so totally different in kind, as we experience from sleep and a swoon, that we cannot in any wise argue from one to the other; or conclude even to the lowest degree of probability, that the same kind of force which is

---

[g] This, according to Strabo, was the opinion of the Brachmans, νομίζειν μὲν γὰρ δὴ τὸν μὲν ἐνθάδε βίον, ὡς ἂν ἀκμὴν κυομένων εἶναι· τὸν δὲ θάνατον, γένεσιν εἰς τὸν ὄντως βίον, καὶ τὸν εὐδαίμονα τοῖς φιλοσοφήσασι. Lib. xv. p. 1039, ed. Amst. 1707. To which opinion perhaps Antoninus may allude in these words, ὡς νῦν περιμένεις, πότε ἔμβρυον ἐκ τῆς γαστρὸς τῆς γυναικός σου ἐξέλθῃ, οὕτως ἐκδέχεσθαι τὴν ὥραν ἐν ᾗ τὸ ψυχάριόν σου τοῦ ἐλύτρου τούτου ἐκπεσεῖται. Lib. ix. c. 3.

sufficient to suspend our faculties, though it be increased ever so much, will be sufficient to destroy them.

§ 29. *Vegetables, not having living powers, supply no analogy.*

These observations together may be sufficient to show, how little presumption there is, that death is the destruction of human creatures. However, there is the shadow of an analogy, which may lead us to imagine it is; the supposed likeness which is observed between the decay of vegetables, and of living creatures. And this likeness is indeed sufficient to afford the poets [1] very apt allusions to the flowers of the field, in their pictures of the frailty of our present life. But in reason, the analogy is so far from holding, that there appears no ground even for the comparison, as to the present question: because one of the two subjects compared is wholly void of that, which is the principal and chief thing in the other, the power of perception and of action; and which is the only thing we are inquiring about the continuance of. So that the destruction of a vegetable is an event not similar or analogous to the destruction of a living agent.

§ 30. *Basis mainly twofold;* (a) *Doctrine of continuance,* (b) *Incapacity of death to destroy.*

But if, as was above intimated, leaving off the delusive custom of substituting imagination in the room of experience, we would confine ourselves to what we do know and understand; if we would argue only from that, and from that form our expectations; it would appear at first sight, that as no probability of living beings ever ceasing to be so, can be concluded from the reason of the thing; so none can be collected from the analogy of nature; because we cannot trace any living beings beyond death. But as we are con-

---

[1] Il. vi. 146; Moschus, ii. 108.

scious that we are endued with capacities of perception and of action, and are living persons; what we are to go upon is, that we shall continue so, till we foresee some accident or event, which will endanger those capacities, or be likely to destroy us: which death does in no wise appear to be.

§ 31. *What is now supernatural may in the new state be natural.*

And thus, when we go out of this world, we may pass into new scenes, and a new state of life and action, just as naturally as we came into the present. And this new state may naturally be a social one. And the advantages of it, advantages of every kind, may naturally be bestowed, according to some fixed general laws of wisdom, upon every one in proportion to the degrees of his virtue. And though the advantages of that future natural state should not be bestowed, as these of the present in some measure are, by the will of the society; but entirely by his more immediate action, upon whom the whole frame of nature depends: yet this distribution may be just as natural, as their being distributed here by the instrumentality of men. And indeed, though one were to allow any confused undetermined sense, which people please to put upon the word *natural*, it would be a shortness of thought scarce credible, to imagine, that no system or course of things can be so, but only what we see at present: [h] especially whilst the probability of a future life, or the natural immortality of the soul, is admitted upon the evidence of reason; [1] because this is really both

[h] See Part II. chap ii. and Part II. chap. iv.

---

[1] This opinion, not explicitly adopted by Butler, appears to come before us from two points of view:

1. As built upon the evidence of reason;
2. As a part of Natural Religion made known by a primitive Revelation (see *inf.* vi. 18, II. ii. 10).

The question discussed in the first chapter is properly

admitting and denying at once, a state of being different from the present to be natural. But the only distinct meaning of that word is, *stated, fixed,* or *settled*: since what is natural, as much requires and presupposes an intelligent agent to render it so, i. e. to effect it continually, or at stated times; as what is supernatural or miraculous does to effect it for once. And from hence it must follow, that persons' notion of what is natural, will be enlarged in proportion to their greater knowledge of the works of God, and the dispensations of his Providence. Nor is there any absurdity in supposing, that there may be beings in the universe, whose capacities, and knowledge, and views, may be so extensive, as that the whole Christian dispensation may to them appear natural, i. e. analogous or conformable to God's dealings with other parts of his creation; as natural as the visible known course of things appears to us. For there seems scarce any other possible sense to be put upon the word, but that only in which it is here used; similar, stated, or uniform.

that of survival (beyond death) rather than that of immortality, or perpetual survival. This latter question is not argued by Butler, but (in i. 29) included under the name of natural immortality. This did not mean an existence absolutely indefeasible, but a life gifted with power of perpetual continuance unless and until the Creator, who had given it, should take it away. Combined with this, however, is an assumption, for many centuries almost universal, that God had revealed to us His design not to take it away, but to leave it in continuing force without end. Upon this proposition hang grave questions of controversy, now widely spread. They cannot with advantage be touched on here. All that belongs to the present occasion is that Butler's argument in this chapter is really on survival after death and the existence of some future state. So that the subject of perpetual survival does not absolutely fall within its scope.

§ 32. *Negative presumptions have now been quashed; and survival shown to be highly probable.*

This credibility of a future life, which has been here insisted upon, how little soever it may satisfy our curiosity, seems to answer all the purposes of religion, in like manner as a demonstrative proof would. Indeed a proof, even a demonstrative one, of a future life, would not be a proof of religion. For, that we are to live hereafter, is just as reconcilable with the scheme of atheism, and as well to be accounted for by it, as that we are now alive is: and therefore nothing can be more absurd than to argue from that scheme, that there can be no future state. But as religion implies a future state, any presumption against such a state, is a presumption against religion. And the foregoing observations remove all presumptions of that sort, and prove, to a very considerable degree of probability,[1] one fundamental doctrine of religion; which, if believed, would greatly open and dispose the mind seriously to attend to the general evidence of the whole.

CHAPTER II

OF THE GOVERNMENT OF GOD BY REWARDS AND PUNISHMENTS; AND PARTICULARLY OF THE LATTER

§ 1. *Future life: its weight due to our capacity to enjoy and suffer.*

THAT which makes the question concerning a future life to be of so great importance to us, is our capacity of happiness and misery. And that which makes the consideration of it to be of so great importance to us, is the supposition of our happiness and misery Here-

[1] In the brief summary of the argument in ch. vii. 4, this is stated in stronger terms as against the absolutely negative conclusion: it is there pronounced 'palpably absurd to conclude, that we shall cease to be, at death.'

after, depending upon our actions Here. Without this indeed, curiosity could not but sometimes bring a subject, in which we may be so highly interested, to our thoughts; especially upon the mortality of others, or the near prospect of our own. But reasonable men would not take any further thought about Hereafter, than what should happen thus occasionally to rise in their minds, if it were certain that our future interest no way depended upon our present behaviour: whereas on the contrary, if there be ground, either from analogy or any thing else, to think it does; then there is reason also for the most active thought and solicitude, to secure that interest; to behave so as that we may escape that misery, and obtain that happiness in another life, which we not only suppose ourselves capable of, but which we apprehend also is put in our own power. And whether there be ground for this last apprehension, certainly would deserve to be most seriously considered, were there no other proof of a future life and interest, than that presumptive one, which the foregoing observations amount to.

§ 2. *Here, enjoyment, and suffering, are mainly set in our own power.*

Now in the present state, all which we enjoy, and a great part of what we suffer, *is put in our own power*. For pleasure and pain are the consequences of our actions: and we are endued by the Author of our nature with capacities of foreseeing these consequences. We find by experience he does not so much as preserve our lives, exclusively of our own care and attention, to provide ourselves with, and to make use of, that sustenance, by which he has appointed our lives shall be preserved; and without which, he has appointed, they shall not be preserved at all. And in general we foresee, that the external things, which are the objects of our various passions, can neither be obtained nor enjoyed, without exerting ourselves in such and such manners: but by thus exerting ourselves, we obtain and enjoy these objects, in which our natural good consists; or by this means God gives us the possession and enjoyment of them. I know not, that we have any one kind or degree of enjoyment, but by the means of our own actions. And by prudence and care, we may, for the most part, pass our days in tolerable ease and quiet: or, on the contrary, we may, by rashness, ungoverned passion, wilfulness, or even by negligence, make ourselves as miserable as ever we please. And many do please to make themselves extremely miserable, i. e. to do what they know beforehand will render them so. They follow those ways, the fruit of which they know, by instruction, example, experience, will be disgrace, and poverty, and sickness, and untimely death. This every one observes to be the general course of things; though it is to be allowed, we cannot find by experience, that all our sufferings are owing to our own follies.

§ 3. *Possible reasons for this. It operates as a forewarning.*

Why the Author of nature does not give his creatures promiscuously such and such perceptions, without regard to their behaviour; why he does not make them happy without the instrumentality of their own actions, and prevent their bringing any sufferings upon themselves; is another matter. Perhaps there may be some impossibilities in the nature of things, which we are unacquainted with.[a] Or less happiness, it may be, would upon the whole be produced by such a method of conduct, than is by the present. Or perhaps divine goodness, with which, if I mistake not, we make very free in our speculations, may not be a bare single disposition to produce happiness; but a disposition to make the good, the faithful, the honest man happy. Perhaps an infinitely perfect Mind may be pleased, with seeing his creatures behave suitably to the nature which he has given them; to the relations which he

[a] Part I. chap. vii.

has placed them in to each other; and to that, which they stand in to himself: that relation to himself, which, during their existence, is even necessary, and which is the most important one of all: perhaps, I say, an infinitely perfect Mind may be pleased with this moral piety of moral agents, in and for itself; as well as upon account of its being essentially conducive to the happiness of his creation. Or the whole end, for which God made, and thus governs the world, may be utterly beyond the reach of our faculties: there may be somewhat in it as impossible for us to have any conception of, as for a blind man to have a conception of colours. But however this be, it is certain matter of universal experience, that the general method of divine administration is, forewarning us, or giving us capacities to foresee, with more or less clearness, that if we act so and so, we shall have such enjoyments, if so and so, such sufferings; and giving us those enjoyments, and making us feel those sufferings, in consequence of our actions.

§ 4. *Due to nature; that is, to the Author of nature.*[1]

'But all this is to be ascribed to the general course of nature.' True. This is the very thing which I am observing. It is to be ascribed to the general course of nature: i. e. not surely to the words or ideas, *course of nature*; but to him who appointed it, and put things into it: or to a course of operation, from its uniformity or constancy, called natural;[b] and which necessarily

[b] *Sup.* i. 30.

---

[1] We have to observe that there are three stages in Butler's argument, viz.—
1. The constitution and course of nature;
2. Natural Religion;
3. Revealed Religion;

and that we are introduced to the existence and governing activity of God, not as a part of natural religion, but as included in the constitution and course of nature. See

implies an operating agent. For when men find themselves necessitated to confess an Author of nature, or that God is the natural governor of the world; they must not deny this again, because his government is uniform; they must not deny that he does things at all, because he does them constantly; because the effects of his acting are permanent, whether his acting be so or not; though there is no reason to think it is not. In short, every man, in every thing he does, naturally acts upon the forethought and apprehension of avoiding evil or obtaining good:[1] and if the natural course of things be the appointment of God, and our natural faculties of knowledge and experience are given us by him; then the good and bad consequences which follow our actions, are his appointment, and our foresight of those consequences, is a warning given us by him, how we are to act.

§ 5. *These pleasures and pains guide us; but in a general way.*

'Is the pleasure then, naturally accompanying every particular gratification of passion, intended to put us upon gratifying ourselves in every such particular instance, and as a reward to us for so doing?' No, certainly. Nor is it to be said, that our eyes were naturally intended to give us the sight of each particular object, to which they do or can extend; objects which are destructive of them, or which, for any other reason, it may become us to turn our eyes from. Yet there is no doubt, but that our eyes were intended for us to

---

Introd. § 16. This idea of a governing agency anterior to and apart from direct moral government, as a constitution and course of nature, finds perhaps a convenient illustration in the laws of political economy, by following or neglecting which wealth is produced or wasted, without any direct reference to moral considerations.

[1] Comp. Πᾶσα τέχνη καὶ πᾶσα μέθοδος, ὁμοίως δὲ πρᾶξίς τε καὶ προαίρεσις, ἀγαθοῦ τινὸς ἐφίεσθαι δοκεῖ. Aristot. *Eth. Nic.* i. 1.

see with. So neither is there any doubt, but that the foreseen pleasures and pains belonging to the passions, were intended, in general, to induce mankind to act in such and such manners.

§ 6. *So that God already rewards and punishes.*

Now from this general observation, obvious to every one, that God has given us to understand, he has appointed satisfaction and delight to be the consequence of our acting in one manner, and pain and uneasiness of our acting in another, and of our not acting at all; and that we find the consequences, which we were beforehand informed of, uniformly to follow; we may learn, that we are at present actually under his government in the strictest and most proper sense; in such a sense, as that he rewards and punishes us for our actions. An Author of nature being supposed, it is not so much a deduction of reason, as a matter of experience, that we are thus under his government: under his government, in the same sense, as we are under the government of civil magistrates. Because the annexing pleasure to some actions, and pain to others, in our power to do or forbear, and giving notice of this appointment beforehand to those whom it concerns; is the proper formal notion of government.

§ 7. *Whether by propelled or by self-acting laws.*

Whether the pleasure or pain which thus follows upon our behaviour, be owing to the Author of nature's acting upon us every moment which we feel it; or to his having at once contrived and executed his own part in the plan of the world; makes no alteration as to the matter before us. For if civil magistrates could make the sanctions of their laws take place, without interposing at all, after they had passed them; without a trial, and the formalities of an execution: if they were able to make their laws execute themselves, or every offender to execute them upon himself; we should be just in the same sense under their government then, as we are now; but in a much higher degree, and more perfect manner.[1]

§ 8. *And by small pains as well as great.*

Vain is the ridicule with which, one foresees, some persons will divert themselves, upon finding lesser pains considered as instances of divine punishment. There is no possibility of answering or evading the general thing here intended, without denying all final causes. For final causes being admitted, the pleasures and pains now mentioned must be admitted too as instances of them. And if they are; if God annexes delight to some actions, and uneasiness to others, with an apparent design to induce us to act so and so; then he not only dispenses happiness and misery, but also rewards and punishes actions. If, for example, the pain which we feel, upon doing what tends to the destruction of our bodies, suppose upon too near approaches to fire, or upon wounding ourselves, be appointed by the Author of nature to prevent our doing what thus tends to our destruction; this is altogether as much an instance of his punishing our actions, and consequently of our being under his

[1] Fitzgerald observes that Butler here differs from Clarke and agrees with Leibnitz (see the Correspondence between them). For Clarke holds as follows: 'The notion of the world's being a great machine, going on without the interposition of God, as a clock continues to go without the assistance of the clock-maker, is the notion of materialism and fate, and tends . . . to exclude Providence.' To which Leibnitz replies, that on this principle a king so superlatively good that he could arrange all matters on behalf of his subjects in a way so admirable that he should never need to interfere with them would be only a nominal king. So far Fitzgerald. The two combatants, however, agreed that God was the Continuator as well as the Maker.—See Corresp. of Clarke and Leibnitz (London, 1717), pp. 21, 45, 67.

government, as declaring by a voice from heaven, that if we acted so, he would inflict such pain upon us, and inflicting it, whether it be greater or less.

§ 9. *God is* (a) *Governor,* (b) *Moral Governor.*

Thus we find, that the true notion or conception of the Author of nature, is that of a master or governor, prior to the consideration of his moral attributes. The fact of our case, which we find by experience, is, that he actually exercises dominion or government over us at present, by rewarding and punishing us for our actions, in as strict and proper a sense of these words, and even in the same sense, as children, servants, subjects, are rewarded and punished by those who govern them.

And thus the whole analogy of nature, the whole present course of things, most fully shows, that there is nothing incredible in the general doctrine of religion, that God will reward and punish men for their actions hereafter: nothing incredible, I mean, arising out of the notion of rewarding and punishing. For the whole course of nature is a present instance of his exercising that government over us, which implies in it rewarding and punishing.

§ 10. *Punishment will here be chiefly considered, because most cavilled at.*

But as divine punishment is what men chiefly object against, and are most unwilling to allow; it may be proper to mention some circumstances in the natural course of punishments at present, which are analogous to what religion teaches us concerning a future state of punishment; indeed so analogous, that as they add a farther credibility to it, so they cannot but raise a most serious apprehension of it in those who will attend to them.

§ 11. *Of human miseries, a large part are self-inflicted.*

It has been now observed, that such and such miseries naturally follow such and such actions of imprudence and wilfulness, as well as actions more commonly and more distinctly considered as vicious; and that these consequences, when they may be foreseen, are properly natural punishments annexed to such actions. For the general thing here insisted upon, is, not that we see a great deal of misery in the world, but a great deal which men bring upon themselves by their own behaviour, which they might have foreseen and avoided.

§ 12. *Often* (a) *following after pleasure reaped,* (b) *exceeding it,* (c) *long delayed,* (d) *hard to foresee.*

Now the circumstances of these natural punishments, particularly deserving our attention, are such as these; That oftentimes they follow, or are inflicted in consequence of, actions, which procure many present advantages, and are accompanied with much present pleasure: for instance, sickness and untimely death is the consequence of intemperance, though accompanied with the highest mirth and jollity: That these punishments are often much greater, than the advantages or pleasures obtained by the actions, of which they are the punishments or consequences: That though we may imagine a constitution of nature, in which these natural punishments, which are in fact to follow, would follow, immediately upon such actions being done, or very soon after; we find on the contrary in our world, that they are often delayed a great while, sometimes even till long after the actions occasioning them are forgot; so that the constitution of nature is such, that delay of punishment is no sort nor degree of presumption of final impunity: That after such delay, these natural punishments or miseries often come, not by degrees, but suddenly, with violence, and at once;

however, the chief misery often does: That as certainty of such distant misery following such actions, is never afforded persons; so perhaps during the actions, they have seldom a distinct full expectation of its following:[c] and many times the case is only thus, that they see in general, or may see, the credibility, that intemperance, suppose, will bring after it diseases; civil crimes, civil punishments; when yet the real probability often is, that they shall escape; but things notwithstanding take their destined course, and the misery inevitably follows at its appointed time, in very many of these cases.

§ 13. *May be due to habits contracted in youth.*

Thus also though youth may be alleged as an excuse for rashness and folly, as being naturally thoughtless, and not clearly foreseeing all the consequences of being untractable and profligate; this does not hinder, but that these consequences follow, and are grievously felt throughout the whole course of mature life. Habits contracted even in that age, are often utter ruin: and men's success in the world, not only in the common sense of worldly success, but their real happiness and misery, depends, in a great degree, and in various ways, upon the manner in which they pass their youth; which consequences they for the most part neglect to consider, and perhaps seldom can properly be said to believe, beforehand.

§ 14. *Note that lost opportunities rarely recur.*

It requires also to be mentioned, that in numberless cases, the natural course of things affords us opportunities for procuring advantages to ourselves at certain times, which we cannot procure when we will; nor ever recall the opportunities, if we have neglected them. Indeed the general course of nature is an example of this. If, during the opportunity of youth, persons are

[c] See Part II. chap. vi.

indocile and self-willed; they inevitably suffer in their future life, for want of those acquirements, which they neglected the natural season of attaining. If the husbandman lets his seedtime pass without sowing, the whole year is lost to him beyond recovery. In like manner, though after men have been guilty of folly and extravagance *up to a certain degree*, it is often in their power, for instance, to retrieve their affairs, to recover their health and character; at least in good measure: yet real reformation is, in many cases, of no avail at all towards preventing the miseries, poverty, sickness, infamy, naturally annexed to folly and extravagance *exceeding that degree*. There is a certain bound to imprudence and misbehaviour, which being transgressed, there remains no place for repentance in the natural course of things.

§ 15. *Neglect often operates as misbehaviour.*

It is further very much to be remarked, that neglects from inconsiderateness, want of attention,[d] not looking about us to see what we have to do, are often attended with consequences altogether as dreadful, as any active misbehaviour, from the most extravagant passion.

§ 16. *Civil punishments, being natural, often also final.*

And lastly, civil government being natural, the punishments of it are so too: and some of these punishments are capital; as the effects of a dissolute course of pleasure are often mortal. So that many natural punishments are final[e] to him, who incurs

[d] Part II. chap. vi.

[e] The general consideration of a future state of punishment, most evidently belongs to the subject of natural religion. But if any of these reflections should be thought to relate more peculiarly to this doctrine, as taught in scripture; the reader is desired to observe, that Gentile writers, both moralists and poets, speak of the future punishment of the wicked, both as to the duration and degree of it, in a like manner of expression and of description, as *Revelation is distinctive in fixing the time, viz. our next state.*

them, if considered only in his temporal capacity:
and seem inflicted by natural appointment, either to
remove the offender out of the way of being further
mischievous; or as an example, though frequently
a disregarded one, to those who are left behind.

§ 17. *All this is not accidental, but constant, and confirmed by religion.*

These things are not, what we call accidental, or to
be met with only now and then; but they are things
of every day's experience: they proceed from general
laws, very general ones, by which God governs the
world, in the natural course of his providence. And
they are so analogous to what religion teaches us
concerning the future punishment of the wicked, so
much of a piece with it, that both would naturally
be expressed in the very same words, and manner of
description. In the Book of *Proverbs*,[f] for instance,
Wisdom is introduced, as frequenting the most public
places of resort, and as rejected when she offers herself
as the natural appointed guide of human life. *How
long*, speaking to those who are passing through it,
how long, ye simple ones, will ye love folly? and the

the scripture does. So that all which can positively be asserted
to be matter of mere revelation, with regard to this doctrine,
seems to be, that the great distinction between the righteous and
the wicked, shall be made at the end of this world; that each
shall *then* receive according to his deserts. Reason did, as it
well might, conclude that it should, finally and upon the whole,
be well with the righteous, and ill with the wicked: but it could
not be determined upon any principles of reason, whether human
creatures might not have been appointed to pass through other
states of life and being, before that distributive justice should
finally and effectually take place. Revelation teaches us, that
the next state of things after the present is appointed for the
execution of this justice; that it shall be no longer delayed;
but *the mystery of God*, the great mystery of his suffering vice
and confusion to prevail, *shall then be finished;* and he will
take to him his great power and will reign, by rendering to every
one according to his works.

[f] Chap. i.

scorners delight in their scorning, and fools hate knowledge? Turn ye at my reproof: behold, I will pour out my spirit upon you, I will make known my words unto you. But upon being neglected, *Because I have called, and ye refused; I have stretched out my hand, and no man regarded; but ye have set at nought all my counsel, and would none of my reproof: I also will laugh at your calamity; I will mock when your fear cometh; when your fear cometh as desolation, and your destruction cometh as a whirlwind; when distress and anguish cometh upon you. Then shall they call upon me, but I will not answer; they shall seek me early, but they shall not find me.* This passage, every one sees, is poetical, and some parts of it are highly figurative; but their meaning is obvious. And the thing intended is expressed more literally in the following words; *For that they hated knowledge, and did not choose the fear of the Lord:——therefore shall they eat of the fruit of their own way, and be filled with their own devices. For the security of the simple shall slay them, and the prosperity of fools shall destroy them.* And the whole passage is so equally applicable, to what we experience in the present world, concerning the consequences of men's actions, and to what religion teaches us is to be expected in another, that it may be questioned which of the two was principally intended.

§ 18. *The force of the topics ought to bring the subject home.*

Indeed when one has been recollecting the proper proofs of a future state of rewards and punishments, nothing methinks can give one so sensible an apprehension of the latter, or representation of it to the mind; as observing, that after the many disregarded checks, admonitions and warnings, which people meet with in the ways of vice and folly and extravagance; warnings from their very nature; from the examples of others; from the lesser inconveniences which they bring upon themselves; from the instructions of wise and virtuous men: after these have been long despised, scorned, ridiculed: after the chief bad consequences, temporal consequences, of their follies, have been delayed for a great while; at length they break in irresistibly, like an armed force: repentance is too late to relieve, and can serve only to aggravate, their distress: the case is become desperate: and poverty and sickness, remorse and anguish, infamy and death, the effects of their own doings, overwhelm them, beyond possibility of remedy or escape. This is an account of what is in fact the general constitution of nature.

§ 19. *Operation of the scheme not uniform, but sufficient to establish a warning likelihood,*

It is not in any sort meant, that according to what appears at present of the natural course of things, men are always uniformly punished in proportion to their misbehaviour: but that there are very many instances of misbehaviour punished in the several ways now mentioned, and very dreadful instances too; sufficient to show what the laws of the universe may admit; and, if thoroughly considered, sufficient fully to answer all objections against the credibility of a future state of punishments, from any imaginations, that the frailty of our nature and external temptations, almost annihilate the guilt of human vices: as well as objections of another sort; from necessity; from suppositions, that the will of an infinite Being cannot be contradicted; or that he must be incapable of offence and provocation.[g]

§ 20. *And rebuke the audacity of this age.*

Reflections of this kind are not without their terrors to serious persons, the most free from enthusiasm, and of the greatest strength of mind; but it is fit things be stated and considered as they really are. And

[g] See chaps. iv. and vi.

there is, in the present age, a certain fearlessness, with regard to what may be hereafter under the government of God, which nothing but an universally acknowledged demonstration on the side of atheism can justify; and which makes it quite necessary, that men be reminded, and if possible made to feel, that there is no sort of ground for being thus presumptuous, even upon the most sceptical principles.

§ 21. *There may be persons born only to serve as warning examples.*

For, may it not be said of any person upon his being born into the world, he may behave so, as to be of no service to it, but by being made an example of the woful effects of vice and folly? That he may, as any one may, if he will, incur an infamous execution, from the hands of civil justice; or in some other course of extravagance shorten his days; or bring upon himself infamy and diseases worse than death? So that it had been better for him, even with regard to the present world, that he had never been born. And is there any pretence of reason, for people to think themselves secure, and talk as if they had certain proof, that, let them act as licentiously as they will, there can be nothing analogous to this, with regard to a future and more general interest, under the providence and government of the same God?

CHAPTER III

OF THE MORAL GOVERNMENT OF GOD

§ 1. *Government, like Creation, may be proved referable to design.*

As the manifold appearances of design and of final causes, in the constitution of the world, prove it to be the work of an intelligent Mind; so the particular final causes of pleasure and pain distributed amongst his creatures, prove that they are under his government; what may be called his natural government of creatures endued with sense and reason. This, however, implies somewhat more than seems usually attended to, when we speak of God's natural government of the world. It implies government of the very same kind with that, which a master exercises over his servants, or a civil magistrate over his subjects. These latter instances of final causes, as really prove an intelligent *Governor* of the world, in the sense now mentioned, and before [a] distinctly treated of; as any other instances of final causes prove an intelligent *Maker* of it.

§ 2. *Where reward and punishment are just, the government is moral.*

But this alone does not appear at first sight to determine any thing certainly, concerning the moral character of the Author of nature, considered in this relation of governor; does not ascertain his government to be moral, or prove that he is the righteous judge of the world. Moral government consists, not barely in rewarding and punishing men for their actions, which the most tyrannical person may do: but in rewarding the righteous, and punishing the wicked;

[a] Chap. ii.

in rendering to men according to their actions, considered as good or evil. And the perfection of moral government consists in doing this, with regard to all intelligent creatures, in an exact proportion to their personal merits or demerits.

§ 3. *Just; that is, not simply benevolent, but righteous.*[1]

Some men seem to think the only character of the Author of nature to be that of simple absolute benevolence. This, considered as a principle of action and infinite in degree, is a disposition to produce the greatest possible happiness, without regard to persons' behaviour, otherwise than as such regard would produce higher degrees of it. And supposing this to be the only character of God, veracity and justice in him would be nothing but benevolence conducted by wisdom. Now surely this ought not to be asserted, unless it can be proved; for we should speak with cautious reverence upon such a subject. And whether it can be proved or no, is not the thing here to be inquired into; but whether in the constitution and conduct of the world, a righteous government be not discernibly planned out: which necessarily implies a righteous governor. There may possibly be in the creation beings, to whom the Author of nature manifests himself under this most amiable of all characters, this of infinite absolute benevolence; for it is the most amiable, supposing it not, as perhaps it is not, incompatible with justice: but he manifests himself to us under the character of a righteous governor. He may, consistently with this, be simply and absolutely benevolent, in the sense now explained: but he is, for he has given us a proof in the constitution and conduct of the world that he is, a governor over servants, as he rewards and punishes us for our actions. And in the constitution and conduct of it, he may also have given, besides the reason of the thing, and the natural presages of conscience, clear and distinct

[1] See Dissertation on Virtue, §§ 12-16.

intimations, that his government is righteous or moral: clear to such as think the nature of it deserving their attention; and yet not to every careless person, who casts a transient reflection upon the subject.[b]

§ 4. *This government is moral, not absolutely, but in degree.*

But it is particularly to be observed, that the divine government, which we experience ourselves under in the present state, taken alone, is allowed not to be the perfection of moral government. And yet this by no means hinders, but that there may be somewhat, be it more or less, truly moral in it. A righteous government may plainly appear to be carried on to some degree: enough to give us the apprehension that it shall be completed, or carried on to that degree of perfection which religion teaches us it shall; but which cannot appear, till much more of the divine administration be seen, than can in the present life. And the design of this chapter is to inquire, how far this is the case: how far, over and above the moral nature [c] which God has given us, and our natural notion of him as righteous governor of those his creatures, to whom he has given this nature; [d] I say how far besides this, the principles and beginnings of a moral government over the world may be discerned, notwithstanding and amidst all the confusion and disorder of it.

[b] The objections against religion, from the evidence of it not being universal, nor so strong as might possibly have been, may be urged against natural religion, as well as against revealed. And therefore the consideration of them belongs to the first part of this Treatise, as well as the second. But as these objections are chiefly urged against revealed religion, I chose to consider them in the second part. And the answer to them there, chap. vi, as urged against Christianity, being almost equally applicable to them as urged against the religion of nature; to avoid repetition, the reader is referred to that chapter.

Insufficiency of proof. Lies against Religion in both forms.

[c] Dissertation II.   [d] Chap. vi.

§ 5. *The balance in favour of virtue not invariable; nor always clear.*

Now one might mention here, what has been often urged with great force, that in general, less uneasiness and more satisfaction, are the natural consequences [e] of a virtuous than of a vicious course of life, in the present state, as an instance of a moral government established in nature; an instance of it, collected from experience and present matter of fact. But it must be owned a thing of difficulty to weigh and balance pleasures and uneasiness, each amongst themselves, and also against each other, so as to make an estimate with any exactness, of the overplus of happiness on the side of virtue. And it is not impossible, that, amidst the infinite disorders of the world, there may be exceptions to the happiness of virtue; even with regard to those persons, whose course of life from their youth up has been blameless;

§ 6. *Especially in cases of reformed life.*

And more with regard to those, who have gone on for some time in the ways of vice, and have afterwards reformed. For suppose an instance of the latter case; a person with his passions inflamed, his natural faculty of self-government impaired by habits of indulgence, and with all his vices about him, like so many harpies, craving for their accustomed gratification: who can say how long it might be, before such a person would find more satisfaction in the reasonableness and present good consequences of virtue, than difficulties and self-denial in the restraints of it? Experience also shows, that men can, to a great degree, get over their sense of shame, so as that by professing themselves to be without principle, and avowing even direct villainy, they can support themselves against the infamy of it. But as the ill actions of any one will probably be more

[e] See Lord Shaftesbury's *Inquiry concerning Virtue*, Part II.

talked of, and oftener thrown in his way, upon his reformation; so the infamy of them will be much more felt, after the natural sense of virtue and of honour is recovered. Uneasinesses of this kind ought indeed to be put to the account of former vices: yet it will be said, they are in part the consequences of reformation.

§ 7. *But clear as a whole, and as initial.*

Still I am far from allowing it doubtful, whether virtue, upon the whole, be happier than vice in the present world. But if it were, yet the beginnings of a righteous administration may beyond all question be found in nature, if we will attentively inquire after them. And,

§ 8. *God, then, being Governor, may be also moral Governor.*

[I.] In whatever manner the notion of God's moral government over the world might be treated, if it did not appear, whether he were in a proper sense our governor at all: yet when it is certain matter of experience, that he does manifest himself to us under the character of a governor, in the sense explained; [f] it must deserve to be considered, whether there be not reason to apprehend, that he may be a righteous or moral governor. Since it appears to be fact, that God does govern mankind by the method of rewards and punishments, according to some settled rules of distribution; it is surely a question to be asked, What presumption is there against his finally rewarding and punishing them according to this particular rule, namely, as they act reasonably, or unreasonably, virtuously or viciously?

[f] Chap. ii.

§ 9. *The moral rule of award is more natural than any other.*

Since rendering men happy or miserable by this rule, certainly falls in, much more falls in, with our natural apprehensions and sense of things, than doing so by any other rule whatever: since rewarding and punishing actions by any other rule, would appear much harder to be accounted for, by minds formed as he has formed ours. Be the evidence of religion then more or less clear, the expectation which it raises in us, that the righteous shall, upon the whole, be happy, and the wicked miserable, cannot however possibly be considered as absurd or chimerical; because it is no more than an expectation, that a method of government already begun, shall be carried on, the method of rewarding and punishing actions; and shall be carried on by a particular rule, which unavoidably appears to us at first sight more natural than any other, the rule which we call distributive justice. Nor,

§ 10. *Mental states attaching to good and evil conduct, and the forecast allowed by fixed laws, all go to affirm it.*

[II.] Ought it to be entirely passed over, that tranquillity, satisfaction, and external advantages, being the natural consequences of prudent management of ourselves, and our affairs; and rashness, profligate negligence, and wilful folly, bringing after them many inconveniences and sufferings; these afford instances of a right constitution of nature: as the correction of children, for their own sakes, and by way of example, when they run into danger or hurt themselves, is a part of right education. And thus, that God governs the world by general fixed laws, that he has endued us with capacities of reflecting upon this constitution of things, and foreseeing the good and bad consequences of our behaviour; plainly implies some sort of moral government: since from such a constitution of things it cannot but follow, that prudence and imprudence, which are of the nature of virtue and vice,[g] must be, as they are, respectively rewarded and punished.

§ 11. *As do civil punishments, and the fear of them.*

[III.] From the natural course of things, vicious actions are, to a great degree, actually punished as mischievous to society; and besides punishment actually inflicted upon this account, there is also the fear and apprehension of it in those persons, whose crimes have rendered them obnoxious to it, in case of a discovery; this state of fear being itself often a very considerable punishment. The natural fear and apprehension of it too, which restrains from such crimes, is a declaration of nature against them. It is necessary to the very being of society, that vices destructive of it, should be punished *as being so*; the vices of falsehood, injustice, cruelty: which punishment therefore is as natural as society; and so is an instance of a kind of moral government, naturally established and actually taking place. And, since the certain natural course of things is the conduct of Providence or the government of God, though carried on by the instrumentality of men; the observation here made amounts to this, that mankind find themselves placed by him in such circumstances, as that they are unavoidably accountable for their behaviour, and are often punished, and sometimes rewarded under his government, in the view of their being mischievous, or eminently beneficial to society.

§ 12. *Good acts are sometimes punished; but never as being good.*

If it be objected that good actions, and such as are beneficial to society, are often punished, as in the case of persecution and in other cases; and that ill and mischievous actions are often rewarded: it may be

[g] See Dissertation II. (§ 8).

answered distinctly; first, that this is in no sort necessary, and consequently not natural, in the sense in which it is necessary, and therefore natural, that ill or mischievous actions should be punished: and in the next place, that good actions are never punished, considered as beneficial to society, nor ill actions rewarded, under the view of their being hurtful to it. So that it stands good, without any thing on the side of vice to be set over against it, that the Author of nature has as truly directed, that vicious actions, considered as mischievous to society, should be punished, and put mankind under a necessity of thus punishing them; as he has directed and necessitated us to preserve our lives by food.

§ 13. *Regard is had not to acts only, but to their quality as virtuous or vicious.*

[IV.] In the natural course of things, virtue *as such* is actually rewarded, and vice *as such* punished: which seems to afford an instance or example, not only of government, but of moral government, begun and established; moral in the strictest sense; though not in that perfection of degree, which religion teaches us to expect. In order to see this more clearly, we must distinguish between actions themselves, and that quality ascribed to them, which we call virtuous or vicious. The gratification itself of every natural passion must be attended with delight: and acquisitions of fortune, however made, are acquisitions of the means or materials of enjoyment. An action then, by which any natural passion is gratified or fortune acquired, procures delight or advantage; abstracted from all consideration of the morality of such action. Consequently, the pleasure or advantage in this case, is gained by the action itself, not by the morality, the virtuousness or viciousness of it; though it be, perhaps, virtuous or vicious. Thus, to say such an action or course of behaviour, procured such pleasure or advantage, or brought on such inconvenience and pain, is quite a different thing from saying, that such good or bad effect was owing to the virtue or vice of such action or behaviour. In one case, an action abstracted from all moral consideration, produced its effect: in the other case, for it will appear that there are such cases, the morality of the action, the action under a moral consideration, i. e. the virtuousness or viciousness of it, produced the effect. Now I say virtue as such, naturally procures considerable advantages to the virtuous, and vice as such, naturally occasions great inconvenience and even misery to the vicious, in very many instances. The immediate effects of virtue and vice upon the mind and temper, are to be mentioned as instances of it. Vice as such is naturally attended with some sort of uneasiness, and, not uncommonly, with great disturbance and apprehension. That inward feeling, which, respecting lesser matters, and in familiar speech, we call being vexed with oneself, and in matters of importance and in more serious language, remorse; is an uneasiness naturally arising from an action of a man's own, reflected upon by himself as wrong, unreasonable, faulty, i. e. vicious in greater or less degrees: and this manifestly is a different feeling from that uneasiness, which arises from a sense of mere loss or harm. What is more common, than to hear a man lamenting an accident or event, and adding——but however he has the satisfaction that he cannot blame himself for it; or on the contrary, that he has the uneasiness of being sensible it was his own doing ? Thus also the disturbance and fear, which often follow upon a man's having done an injury, arise from a sense of his being blameworthy; otherwise there would, in many cases, be no ground of disturbance, nor any reason to fear resentment or shame. On the other hand, inward security and peace, and a mind open to the several gratifications of life, are the natural attendants of innocence and virtue. To which must be added the complacency, satisfaction, and even joy of heart, which accompany the exercise, the real exercise, of gratitude, friendship, benevolence.

§ 14. *Reckon in, too, the fears and hopes of a future life;*

And here, I think, ought to be mentioned, the fears of future punishment, and peaceful hopes of a better life, in those who fully believe, or have any serious apprehension of religion: because these hopes and fears are present uneasiness and satisfaction to the mind, and cannot be got rid of by great part of the world, even by men who have thought most thoroughly upon that subject of religion. And no one can say, how considerable this uneasiness and satisfaction may be, or what upon the whole it may amount to.

§ 15. *And the favour and disfavour especially of the good;*

In the next place comes in the consideration, that all honest and good men are disposed to befriend honest good men as such, and to discountenance the vicious as such, and do so in some degree; indeed in a considerable degree: from which favour and discouragement cannot but arise considerable advantage and inconvenience. And though the generality of the world have little regard to the morality of their own actions, and may be supposed to have less to that of others, when they themselves are not concerned; yet let any one be known to be a man of virtue, somehow or other he will be favoured, and good offices will be done him, from regard to his character without remote views, occasionally, and in some low degree, I think, by the generality of the world, as it happens to come in their way. Public honours too and advantages are the natural consequences, are sometimes at least the consequences in fact, of virtuous actions; of eminent justice, fidelity, charity, love to our country, considered in the view of being virtuous. And sometimes even death itself, often infamy and external inconveniences, are the public consequences of vice as vice. For instance, the sense which mankind have of tyranny, injustice, oppression, additional to the mere feeling or fear of misery, has doubtless been instrumental in bringing about revolutions, which make a figure even in the history of the world. For it is plain, men resent injuries as implying faultiness, and retaliate, not merely under the notion of having received harm, but of having received wrong; and they have this resentment in behalf of others, as well as of themselves. So likewise even the generality are, in some degree, grateful and disposed to return good offices, not merely because such an one has been the occasion of good to them, but under the view, that such good offices implied kind intention and good desert in the doer.

§ 16. *And the moral quality seen in* (a) *civil government,* (b) *care of children,* (c) *in virtues* per se, *never in vices,* (d) *in pardons given in absence of guilt.*

To all this may be added two or three particular things, which many persons will think frivolous; but to me nothing appears so, which at all comes in towards determining a question of such importance, as, whether there be, or be not, a moral institution of government, in the strictest sense moral, *visibly* established and begun in nature. The particular things are these: That in domestic government, which is doubtless natural, children and others also are very generally punished for falsehood and injustice and ill-behaviour, as such, and rewarded for the contrary; which are instances where veracity, and justice, and right behaviour as such, are naturally enforced by rewards and punishments, whether more or less considerable in degree: That, though civil government be supposed to take cognizance of actions in no other view than as prejudicial to society, without respect to the immorality of them; yet as such actions are immoral, so the sense which men have of the immorality of them, very greatly contributes, in different ways, to bring offenders to justice: and that entire absence of all crime and guilt in the moral sense, when plainly appearing, will almost of course procure, and circumstances of aggravated guilt prevent, a remission of the penalties annexed to civil crimes, in many cases, though by no means in all.

§ 17. *Sum of results on behalf of well-doing as such,* διχῶς.

Upon the whole then, besides the good and bad effects of virtue and vice upon men's own minds, the course of the world does, in some measure, turn upon the approbation and disapprobation of them as such, in others. The sense of well and ill-doing, the presages of conscience, the love of good characters and dislike of bad ones, honour, shame, resentment, gratitude; all these, considered in themselves, and in their effects, do afford manifest real instances of virtue as such naturally favoured, and of vice as such discountenanced, more or less, in the daily course of human life; in every age, in every relation, in every general circumstance of it. That God has given us a moral nature,[h] may most justly be urged as a proof of our being under his moral government: but that he has placed us in a condition, which gives this nature, as one may speak, scope to operate, and in which it does unavoidably operate; i.e. influence mankind to act, so as thus to favour and reward virtue, and discountenance and punish vice; this is not the same, but a further, additional proof of his moral government: for it is an instance of it. The first is a proof, that he will finally favour and support virtue effectually: the second is an example of his favouring and supporting it at present, in some degree.

§ 18. *This regard to the* quale *is due to* (a) *our moral nature,* (b) *its effect upon related destinies.*

If a more distinct inquiry be made, whence it arises, that virtue as such is often rewarded, and vice as such

[h] See Dissertation II. (§§ 1-3).

is punished, and this rule never inverted: it will be found to proceed, in part, immediately from the moral nature itself, which God has given us; and also in part, from his having given us, together with this nature, so great a power over each other's happiness and misery. For *first*, it is certain, that peace and delight, in some degree and upon some occasions, is the necessary and present effect of virtuous practice; an effect arising immediately from that constitution of our nature. We are so made, that well-doing as such gives us satisfaction, at least, in some instances; ill-doing as such, in none. And *secondly*, from our moral nature, joined with God's having put our happiness and misery in many respects in each other's power, it cannot but be, that vice as such, some kinds and instances of it at least, will be infamous, and men will be disposed to punish it as in itself detestable; and the villain will by no means be able always to avoid feeling that infamy, any more than he will be able to escape this further punishment, which mankind will be disposed to inflict upon him, under the notion of his deserving it.

§ 19. *Any like regard to vice a dream or a monster.*

But there can be nothing on the side of vice, to answer this; because there is nothing in the human mind contradictory, as the logicians speak, to virtue. For virtue consists in a regard to what is right and reasonable, as being so; in a regard to veracity, justice, charity, in themselves: and there is surely no such thing, as a like natural regard to falsehood, injustice, cruelty. If it be thought, that there are instances of an approbation of vice, as such, in itself, and for its own sake, (though it does not appear to me, that there is any such thing at all; but supposing there be,) it is evidently monstrous: as much so, as the most acknowledged perversion of any passion whatever. Such instances of perversion then being left out as merely imaginary, or, however, unnatural; it must follow, from the frame of our nature, and from our condition, in the respects now described, that *vice cannot at all be, and virtue cannot but be, favoured as such by others, upon some occasions*; and happy in itself, in some degree. For what is here insisted upon, is not the degree in which virtue and vice are thus distinguished, but only the thing itself, that they are so in some degree; though the whole good and bad effect of virtue and vice as such, is not inconsiderable in degree. But that they must be thus distinguished in some degree, is in a manner necessary: it is matter of fact of daily experience, even in the greatest confusion of human affairs.

§ 20. *Perverse rules intrude, but not so as to drown the voice of nature in Providence.*

It is not pretended but that in the natural course of things, happiness and misery appear to be distributed by other rules, than only the personal merit and demerit of characters. They may sometimes be distributed by way of mere discipline. There may be the wisest and best reasons, why the world should be governed by general laws, from whence such promiscuous distribution perhaps must follow; and also why our happiness and misery should be put in each other's power, in the degree which they are. And these things, as in general they contribute to the rewarding virtue and punishing vice, as such: so they often contribute also, not to the inversion of this, which is impossible; but to the rendering persons prosperous, though wicked; afflicted, though righteous; and, which is worse, to the *rewarding some actions*, though vicious, and *punishing other actions*, though virtuous. But all this cannot drown the voice of nature in the conduct of Providence, plainly declaring itself for virtue, by way of distinction from vice, and preference to it. For our being so constituted as that virtue and vice are thus naturally favoured and discountenanced, rewarded and punished respectively as such, is an intuitive proof of the intent of nature, that it should be so: otherwise the constitution of our mind, from which it thus immediately and directly proceeds, would be absurd. But it cannot be said, because virtuous actions are sometimes punished, and vicious actions rewarded, that nature intended it. For, though this great disorder is brought about, as all actions are done, by means of some natural passion; yet *this may be*, as it undoubtedly is, brought about by the perversion of such passion, implanted in us for other, and those very good purposes. And indeed these other and good purposes, even of every passion, may be clearly seen.

§ 21. *God takes the side of the* vir bonus.

We have then a declaration, in some degree of present effect, from him who is supreme in nature, which side he is of, or what part he takes: a declaration for virtue, and against vice. So far therefore as a man is true to virtue, to veracity and justice, to equity and charity, and the right of the case, in whatever he is concerned; so far he is on the side of the divine administration, and cooperates with it: and from hence, to such a man, arises naturally a secret satisfaction and sense of security, and implicit hope of somewhat further. And,

§ 22. *The tendencies of virtue and vice run ahead of the present facts.*

[V.] This hope is confirmed by the necessary tendencies of virtue, which, though not of present effect, yet are at present discernible in nature; and so afford an instance of somewhat moral in the essential constitution of it. There is, in the nature of things, a tendency in virtue and vice to produce the good and bad effects now mentioned, in a greater degree than they do in fact produce them. For instance; good and bad men would be much more rewarded and punished as such, were it not, that justice is often artificially eluded, that characters are not known, and many, who would thus favour virtue and discourage vice, are hindered from doing so by accidental causes. These tendencies of virtue and vice are obvious with regard to *individuals*. But it may require more particularly to be considered, that power in a *society*, by being under the direction of virtue, naturally increases, and has a necessary tendency to prevail over opposite power, not under the direction of it; in like manner as power, by being under the direction of reason, increases, and has a tendency to prevail over brute force. There are several brute creatures of equal, and several of superior strength, to that of men; and possibly the sum of the whole strength of brutes may be greater than that of mankind: but reason gives us the advantage and superiority over them; and thus man is the acknowledged governing animal upon the earth. Nor is this superiority considered by any as accidental; but as what reason has a tendency, in the nature of the thing, to obtain. And yet perhaps difficulties may be raised about the meaning, as well as the truth, of the assertion, that virtue has the like tendency.

§ 23. *Compare the tendency of reason to overcome brute force by union, or with time; this too not uniform.*

To obviate these difficulties, let us see more distinctly, how the case stands with regard to reason; which is so readily acknowledged to have this advantageous tendency. Suppose then two or three men, of the best and most improved understanding, in a desolate open plain, attacked by ten times the number of beasts of prey: would their reason secure them the victory in this unequal combat? Power then, though joined with reason, and under its direction, cannot be expected to prevail over opposite power, though merely brutal, unless the one bears some proportion to the other. Again: put the imaginary case, that rational and irrational creatures were of like external shape and manner: it is certain, before there were opportunities for the first to distinguish each other, to separate from their adversaries, and to form an union among themselves, they might be upon a level, or in several respects upon great disadvantage; though united they might be vastly superior: since union is of such efficacy, that ten men united, might be able to accomplish, what ten thousand of the same natural strength and understanding wholly ununited, could not. In this case then, brute force might more than maintain its ground against reason, for want of union among the rational creatures. Or suppose a number of men to land upon an island inhabited only by wild beasts; a number of men who, by the regulations of civil government, the inventions of art, and the experience of some years, could they be preserved so long, would be really sufficient to subdue the wild beasts, and to preserve themselves in security from them: yet a conjuncture of accidents might give such advantage to the irrational animals, as that they might at once overpower, and even extirpate, the whole species of rational ones. Length of time then, proper scope and opportunities, for reason to exert itself, may be absolutely necessary to its prevailing over brute force. Further still: there are many instances of brutes succeeding in attempts, which they could not have undertaken, had not their irrational nature rendered them incapable of foreseeing the danger of such attempts, or the fury of passion hindered their attending to it; and there are instances of reason and real prudence preventing men's undertaking what, it hath appeared afterwards, they might have succeeded in by a lucky rashness. And in certain conjunctures, ignorance and folly, weakness and discord, may have their advantages. So that rational animals have not necessarily the superiority over irrational ones: but, how improbable soever it may be, it is evidently possible, that, in some globes, the latter may be superior. And were the former wholly at variance and disunited, by false self-interest and envy, by treachery and injustice, and consequent rage and malice against each other, whilst the latter were firmly united among themselves by instinct; this might greatly contribute to the introducing such an inverted order of things. For every one would consider it as inverted: since reason has, in the nature of it, a tendency to prevail over brute force; notwithstanding the possibility it may not prevail, and the necessity, which there is, of many concurring circumstances to render it prevalent.

§ 24. *So virtue tends to the acquisition of power;*

Now I say, virtue in a society has a like tendency to procure superiority and additional power: whether this power be considered as the means of security from opposite power, or of obtaining other advantages. And it has this tendency, by rendering public good, an object and end, to every member of the society; by putting every one upon consideration and diligence, recollection and self-government, both in order to see what is the most effectual method, and also in order to perform their proper part, for obtaining and preserving it; by uniting a society within itself, and so increasing its strength; and, which is particularly to be mentioned, uniting it by means of veracity and justice. For as these last are principal bonds of union, so benevolence or public spirit, undirected, unrestrained by them, is, nobody knows what.

§ 25. *And is likely to prevail, if with a fair field.*

And suppose the invisible world, and the invisible dispensations of Providence, to be, in any sort, analogous to what appears: or that both together make up one uniform scheme, the two parts of which, the part which we see, and that which is beyond our observation, are analogous to each other: then, there must be a like natural tendency in the derived power, throughout the universe, under the direction of virtue, to prevail in general over that, which is not under its direction; as there is in reason, derived reason in the universe, to prevail over brute force. But then, in order to the prevalence of virtue, or that it may actually produce, what it has a tendency to produce; the like concurrences are necessary, as are, to the prevalence of reason. There must be some proportion, between the natural power or force which is, and that which is not, under the direction of virtue: there must be sufficient length of time; for the complete success of virtue, as of reason, cannot, from the nature of the thing, be otherwise than gradual: there must be, as one may speak, a fair field of trial, a stage large and extensive enough, proper occasions and opportunities, for the virtuous to join together, to exert themselves against lawless force, and to reap the fruit of their united labours. Now indeed it is to be hoped, that the disproportion between the good and bad, even here on earth, is not so great, but that the former have natural power sufficient to their prevailing to a considerable degree, if circumstances would permit this power to be united. For, much less, very much less, power under the direction of virtue, would prevail over much greater not under the direction of it.

§ 26. *Virtue, hindered and militant here, may have full scope hereafter;*

However, good men over the face of the earth cannot unite; as for other reasons, so because they cannot be sufficiently ascertained of each other's characters. And the known course of human things, the scene we are now passing through, particularly the shortness of life, denies to virtue its full scope in several other respects. The natural tendency which we have been considering, though real, is *hindered from being* carried into effect in the present state: but these hindrances may be removed in a future one. Virtue, to borrow the Christian allusion, is militant here; and various untoward accidents contribute to its being often overborne: but it may combat with greater advantage hereafter, and prevail completely, and enjoy its consequent rewards, in some future states. Neglected as it is, perhaps unknown, perhaps despised and oppressed here; there may be scenes in eternity, lasting enough, and in every other way adapted, to afford it a sufficient sphere of action; and a sufficient sphere for the natural consequences of it to follow in fact. If the soul be naturally immortal,[1] and this state be a progress towards a future one, as childhood is towards mature age; good men may naturally unite, not only amongst themselves, but also with other orders of virtuous creatures, in that future state.

§ 27. *Is, per se, a bond of union;*

For virtue, from the very nature of it, is a principle and bond of union, in some degree, amongst all who are endued with it, and known to each other; so as that by it, a good man cannot but recommend himself to the favour and protection of all virtuous beings, throughout the whole universe, who can be acquainted with his character, and can any way interpose in his behalf in any part of his duration.

§ 28. *And may far hence win over spirits capable of improvement.*

And one might add, that suppose all this advantageous tendency of virtue to become effect, amongst one or more orders of creatures, in any distant scenes and periods, and to be seen by any orders of vicious creatures, throughout the universal kingdom of God; this happy effect of virtue would have a tendency, by way of example, and possibly in other ways, to amend those of them, who are capable of amendment, and being recovered to a just sense of virtue. If our notions

---

[1] Natural immortality of the soul is put hypothetically here, as *sup.* i. 21, 31.

of the plan of Providence were enlarged in any sort proportionable to what late discoveries have enlarged our views with respect to the material world; representations of this kind would not appear absurd or extravagant. However, they are not to be taken as intended for a literal delineation of what is in fact the particular scheme of the universe, which cannot be known without revelation: for suppositions are not to be looked on as true, because not incredible: but they are mentioned to show, that our finding virtue to be hindered from procuring to itself such superiority and advantages, is no objection against its having, in the essential nature of the thing, a tendency to procure them. And the suppositions now mentioned do plainly show this: for they show, that these hindrances are so far from being necessary, that we ourselves can easily conceive, how they may be removed in future states, and full scope be granted to virtue. And all these advantageous tendencies of it are to be considered as declarations of God in its favour. This however is taking a pretty large compass: though it is certain, that, as the material world appears to be, in a manner boundless and immense; there must be *some* scheme of Providence vast in proportion to it.

§ 29. *Suppose an ideal state.*

But let us return to the earth our habitation; and we shall see this happy tendency of virtue, by imagining an instance not so vast and remote: by supposing a kingdom or society of men upon it, perfectly virtuous, for a succession of many ages; to which, if you please, may be given a situation advantageous for universal monarchy. In such a state, there would be no such thing as faction: but men of the greatest capacity would of course, all along, have the chief direction of affairs willingly yielded to them; and they would share it among themselves without envy. Each of these would have the part assigned him, to which his genius was peculiarly adapted: and others, who had not any distinguished genius, would be safe, and think themselves very happy, by being under the protection and guidance of those who had. Public determinations would really be the result of the united wisdom of the community: and they would faithfully be executed, by the united strength of it. Some would in a higher way contribute, but all would in some way contribute, to the public prosperity: and in it, each would enjoy the fruits of his own virtue. And as injustice whether by fraud or force, would be unknown among themselves; so they would be sufficiently secured from it in their neighbours. For cunning and false self-interest, confederacies in injustice, ever slight, and accompanied with faction and intestine treachery; these on one hand would be found mere childish folly and weakness, when set in opposition against wisdom, public spirit, union inviolable, and fidelity on the other: allowing both a sufficient length of years to try their force.

§ 30. *Such a state would acquire immense power.*

Add the general influence, which such a kingdom would have over the face of the earth, by way of example particularly, and the reverence which would be paid it. It would plainly be superior to all others, and the world must gradually come under its empire: not by means of lawless violence; but partly by what must be allowed to be just conquest; and partly by other kingdoms submitting themselves voluntarily to it, throughout a course of ages, and claiming its protection, one after another, in successive exigencies. The head of it would be an universal monarch, in another sense than any mortal has yet been; and the eastern style would be literally applicable to him, that *all people, nations, and languages should serve him.* And though indeed our knowledge of human nature, and the whole history of mankind, show the impossibility, without some miraculous interposition, that a number of men, here on earth, should unite in one society or government, in the fear of God and universal practice of virtue; and that such a government should continue so united for a succession of ages: yet admitting or supposing this, the effect would be as now drawn out. And thus, for instance, the wonderful power and prosperity promised to the Jewish nation in the scripture, would be, in a great measure, the consequence of what is predicted of them; that the *people should be all righteous, and inherit the land for ever*;[1] were we to understand the latter phrase of a long continuance only, sufficient to give things time to work. The predictions of this kind, for there are many of them, cannot come to pass, in the present known course of nature; but suppose them come to pass, and then, the dominion and preeminence promised must naturally follow, to a very considerable degree.

§ 31. *If these anticipations seem trifles for virtue, what, if they were for vice?*

Consider now the general system of religion: that the government of the world is uniform, and one, and moral; that virtue and right shall finally have the advantage, and prevail over fraud and lawless force, over the deceits, as well as the violence of wickedness, under the conduct of one supreme governor: and from the observations above made, it will appear, that God has, by our reason, given us to see a peculiar connection in the several parts of this scheme, and a tendency towards the completion of it arising out of the very nature of virtue: which tendency is to be considered as somewhat moral in the essential constitution of things. If any one should think all this to be of little importance; I desire him to consider, what he would think, if vice had, essentially, and in its nature, these advantageous tendencies; or if virtue had essentially the direct contrary ones.

[1] Isa. lx. 21.

§ 32. *His aim is to show whither the facts of nature point.*

But it may be objected, that, notwithstanding all these natural effects and these natural tendencies of virtue; yet things may be now going on throughout the universe, and may go on hereafter, in the same mixed way as here at present upon earth: virtue sometimes prosperous, sometimes depressed; vice sometimes punished, sometimes successful. The answer to which is, that it is not the purpose of this chapter, nor of this Treatise, properly to prove God's perfect moral government over the world, or the truth of Religion; but to observe what there is in the constitution and course of nature, to confirm the proper proof of it, supposed to be known: and that the weight of the foregoing observations to this purpose may be thus distinctly proved.

§ 33. *But this mixed state, if continued, would not conclude in favour of vice.*

Pleasure and pain are indeed to a certain degree, say to a very high degree, distributed amongst us without any apparent regard to the merit or demerit of characters. And were there nothing else concerning this matter discernible in the constitution and course of nature; there would be no ground from the constitution and course of nature to hope or to fear, that men would be rewarded or punished hereafter according to their deserts: which, however, it is to be remarked, implies, that even then there would be no ground from appearances to think, that vice upon the whole would have the advantage, rather than that virtue would. And thus the proof of a future state of retribution would rest upon the usual known arguments for it: which are I think plainly unanswerable; and would be so, though there were no additional confirmation of them from the things above insisted on. But these things are a very strong confirmation of them. For,

§ 34. *For God is shown to have taken sides already in the contest.*

First, They show, that the Author of nature is not indifferent to virtue and vice. They amount to a declaration from him, determinate and not to be evaded, in favour of one, and against the other: such a declaration, as there is nothing to be set over against or answer, on the part of vice. So that were a man, laying aside the proper proof of religion, to determine from the course of nature only, whether it were most probable, that the righteous or the wicked would have the advantage in a future life; there can be no doubt, but that he would determine the probability to be, that the former would. The course of nature then, in the view of it now given, furnishes us with a real practical proof of the obligations of religion.

§ 35. *The change we hope is in degree only, not in kind.*

Secondly, When, conformably to what religion teaches us, God shall reward and punish virtue and vice as such, so as that every one shall, upon the whole, have his deserts; this distributive justice will not be a thing different in *kind*, but only in *degree*, from what we experience in his present government. It will be that in *effect*, toward which we now see a *tendency*. It will be no more than the *completion* of that moral government, the *principles and beginning* of which have been shown, beyond all dispute, discernible in the present constitution and course of nature. And from hence it follows,

§ 36. *The lower degree warrants hope of the higher.*

Thirdly, That, as under the natural government of God, our experience of those kinds and degrees of happiness and misery, which we do experience at present, gives just ground to hope for and to fear, higher degrees and other kinds of both in a future state, supposing a future state admitted : so under his moral government, our experience, that virtue and vice are, in the manners above mentioned, actually rewarded and punished at present, in a certain degree, gives just ground to hope and to fear, that they *may be* rewarded and punished in an higher degree hereafter. It is acknowledged indeed that this alone is not sufficient ground to think, that they *actually will be* rewarded and punished in an higher degree, rather than in a lower: but then,

§ 37. *Essential tendency supplies a firmer basis than accidental hindrance.*

Lastly, There is sufficient ground to think so, from the good and bad tendencies of virtue and vice. For these tendencies are essential, and founded in the nature of things: whereas the hindrances to their becoming effect are, in numberless cases, not necessary, but artificial only. Now it may be much more strongly argued, that these tendencies, as well as the actual rewards and punishments, of virtue and vice, which arise directly out of the nature of things, will remain hereafter, than that the accidental hindrances of them will. And if these hindrances do not remain ; those rewards and punishments cannot but be carried on much further towards the perfection of moral government: i. e. the tendencies of virtue and vice will become effect: but when, or where, or in what particular way, cannot be known at all, but by revelation.

§ 38. *Sum of the foregoing arguments.*

Upon the whole: There is a kind of moral government implied in God's natural government: [k] virtue and vice are naturally rewarded and punished as beneficial and mischievous to society ; [l] and rewarded and punished directly as virtue and vice.[m] The notion

[k] *Sup.* §§ 8–11. [l] *Ibid.* [m] *Sup.* §§ 12, 13

then of a moral scheme of government is not fictitious, but natural; for it is suggested to our thoughts by the constitution and course of nature: and the execution of this scheme is actually begun, in the instances here mentioned. And these things are to be considered as a declaration of the Author of nature, for virtue, and against vice: they give a credibility to the supposition of their being rewarded and punished hereafter; and also ground to hope and to fear, that they may be rewarded and punished in higher degrees than they are here. And as all this is confirmed, so the argument for religion, from the constitution and course of nature, is carried on further, by observing, that there are natural tendencies, and, in innumerable cases, only artificial hindrances, to this moral scheme's being carried on much further towards perfection, than it is at present.[n] The notion then of a moral scheme of government, much more perfect than what is seen, is not a fictitious, but a natural notion; for it is suggested to our thoughts, by the essential tendencies of virtue and vice. And these tendencies are to be considered as intimations, as implicit promises and threatenings, from the Author of nature, of much greater rewards and punishments to follow virtue and vice, than do at present. And indeed, every *natural* tendency, which is to continue, but which is hindered from becoming effect by only *accidental* causes, affords a presumption, that such tendency will, some time or other, become effect: a presumption in degree proportionable to the length of the duration, through which such tendency will continue. And from these things together, arises a real presumption, that the moral scheme of government established in nature, shall be carried on much further towards perfection hereafter; and, I think, a presumption that it will be absolutely completed. But from these things, joined with the moral nature which God has given us, considered as given us by him, arises a practical proof [o]

---

[n] *Sup.* §§ 22–26.

[o] See this proof drawn out briefly, chap. vi.

that it will be completed: a proof from fact; and therefore a distinct one from that, which is deduced from the eternal and unalterable relations, the fitness and unfitness of actions.

CHAPTER IV

OF A STATE OF PROBATION, AS IMPLYING TRIAL, DIFFICULTIES, AND DANGER

§ 1. *This probationary life involves trial, difficulty, danger, and future account.*

THE general doctrine of religion, that our present life is a state of probation for a future one, comprehends under it several particular things, distinct from each other. But the first, and most common meaning of it seems to be, that our future interest is now depending, and depending upon ourselves; that we have scope and opportunities here, for that good and bad behaviour, which God will reward and punish hereafter; together with temptations to one, as well as inducements of reason to the other. And this is, in great measure, the same with saying, that we are under the moral government of God, and to give an account of our actions to him. For the notion of a future account and general righteous judgment, implies some sort of temptations to what is wrong: otherwise there would be no moral possibility of doing wrong, nor ground for judgment, or discrimination. But there is this difference, that the word *probation* is more distinctly and particularly expressive of allurements to wrong, or difficulties in adhering uniformly to what is right, and of the danger of miscarrying by such temptations, than the words *moral government*. A state of probation then, as thus particularly implying in its trial, difficulties, and danger, may require to be considered distinctly by itself.

§ 2. *Does the like for this world by natural government,*

And as the moral government of God, which religion teaches us, implies, that we are in a state of trial with regard to a future world: so also his natural government over us implies, that we are in a state of trial, in the like sense, with regard to the present world. Natural government by rewards and punishments, as much implies natural trial, as moral government does moral trial. The natural government of God here meant [a] consists in his annexing pleasure to some actions, and pain to others, which are in our power to do or forbear, and in giving us notice of such appointment beforehand. This necessarily implies, that he has made our happiness and misery, or our interest, to depend in part upon ourselves. And so far as men have temptations to any course of action which will probably occasion them greater temporal inconvenience and uneasiness, than satisfaction; so far their temporal interest is in danger from themselves, or they are in a state of trial with respect to it. Now people often blame others, and even themselves, for their misconduct in their temporal concerns. And we find many are greatly wanting to themselves, and miss of that natural happiness, which they might have obtained in the present life: perhaps every one does in some degree. But many run themselves into great inconvenience, and into extreme distress and misery: not through incapacity of knowing better, and doing better for themselves, which would be nothing to the present purpose; but through their own fault. And these things necessarily imply temptation, and danger of miscarrying, in a greater or less degree, with respect to our worldly interest or happiness. Every one too, without having religion in his thoughts, speaks of the hazards which young people run, upon their setting out in the world: hazards from other causes, than merely their ignorance, and unavoidable accidents.

[a] Chap. ii.

And some courses of vice, at least, being contrary to men's worldly interest or good; temptations to these must at the same time be temptations to forego our present and our future interest. Thus in our natural or temporal capacity, we are in a state of trial, i.e. of difficulty and danger, analogous, or like to our moral and religious trial.

§ 3. *This probation, in both spheres, is twofold:* (a) *by temptation* ab extra ;

This will more distinctly appear to any one, who thinks it worth while, more distinctly, to consider, what it is which constitutes our trial in both capacities, and to observe, how mankind behave under it.

And that which constitutes this our trial, in both these capacities, must be somewhat either in our external circumstances, or in our nature. For, on the one hand, persons may be betrayed into wrong behaviour upon surprise, or overcome upon any other very singular and extraordinary external occasions; who would, otherwise, have preserved their character of prudence and of virtue : in which cases, every one, in speaking of the wrong behaviour of these persons, would impute it to such particular external circumstances.

§ 4. *And* (b) *by ill habits contracted, and passions.*

And on the other hand, men who have contracted habits of vice and folly of any kind, or have some particular passions in excess, will seek opportunities, and, as it were, go out of their way, to gratify themselves in these respects, at the expense of their wisdom and their virtue; led to it, as every one would say, not by external temptations, but by such habits and passions. And the account of this last case is, that particular passions are no more coincident [1] with

---

[1] In the Sermons Butler has set forth that self-love is entirely distinct from particular passions and affections. Serm. i. 6, xi. 8; also Serm. ii. 15.

prudence, or that reasonable self-love,[1] the end of which is our worldly interest, than they are with the principle of virtue and religion; but often draw contrary ways to one, as well as to the other: and so such particular passions are as much temptations, to act imprudently with regard to our worldly interest, as to act viciously.[b] However, as when we say, men are misled by external circumstances of temptation; it cannot but be understood, that there is somewhat within themselves, to render those circumstances temptations, or to render them susceptible of impressions from them: so when we say, they are misled by passions; it is always supposed, that there are occasions, circumstances, and objects, exciting these passions, and affording means for gratifying them. And therefore, temptations from within, and from without, coincide, and mutually imply each other. Now the several external objects of the appetites, passions, and affections, being present to the senses, or offering themselves to the mind, and so exciting emotions suitable to their nature; not only in cases

---

[b] See Sermons preached at the Rolls, 1726, 2nd ed. p. 205, &c. Pref. p. 25, &c. Serm. p. 21, &c. [I have no means of tracing this reference exactly, but I think it contemplates Preface § 30, and perhaps Serm. III. §§ 3, 4.—ED.]

---

[1] I understand Butler here to mean no more than his words actually convey, namely, that there is a form or attitude of self-love which addresses itself to our worldly interest, and that it is reasonable: but not that this interest is the only one contemplated by self-love. There is a parallel passage in Serm. iii. 12: 'Self-love then, though confined to the interest of the present world, does in general perfectly coincide with virtue:' 'though' being equivalent to 'even if,' 'even when.' It may be admitted that the grammatical form is awkward: but the alternative interpretation seems to be nothing less than absurd. For Butler associates reasonable self-love with conscience as the 'chief or superior principles' in our nature. Serm. iii. 13 *sub fin*.

where they can be gratified consistently with innocence and prudence, but also in cases where they cannot, and yet can be gratified imprudently and viciously: this as really puts them in danger of voluntarily foregoing their present interest or good, as their future; and as really renders self-denial necessary to secure one, as the other: i. e. we are in a like state of trial with respect to both, by the very same passions, excited by the very same means.

§ 5. *The trial is identic: but is, in the temporal sphere, of our prudence;*

Thus mankind having a temporal interest depending upon themselves, and a prudent course of behaviour being necessary to secure it; passions inordinately excited, whether by means of example, or by any other external circumstance, towards such objects, at such times, or in such degrees, as that they cannot be gratified consistently with worldly prudence; are temptations, dangerous, and too often successful temptations, to forego a greater temporal good for a less; i. e. to forego what is, upon the whole, our temporal interest, for the sake of a present gratification.

§ 6. *In the religious, of our virtue.*[1]

This is a description of our state of trial in our temporal capacity. Substitute now the word *future* for *temporal*, and *virtue* for *prudence*; and it will be

---

[1] Inasmuch as prudence is here so clearly distinguished from virtue, he appears, when he says elsewhere that it has the nature of virtue (see Diss. II. 8), to mean that it has a share of that nature. In its reckoning with the future it draws to itself and assimilates virtuous elements, while it likewise has regard to other inducements not in themselves virtuous, though allied with virtue, and consequent upon it.

just as proper a description of our state of trial in our religious capacity; so analogous are they to each other.

§ 7. *Some are deceived into wrong; others face it with deliberate intent, and for both spheres.*

If, from consideration of this our like state of trial in both capacities, we go on to observe further, how mankind behave under it; we shall find there are some, who have so little sense of it, that they scarce look beyond the passing day: they are so taken up with present gratifications, as to have, in a manner, no feeling of consequences, no regard to their future ease or fortune in this life; any more than to their happiness in another. Some appear to be blinded and deceived by inordinate passion, in their worldly concerns, as much as in religion. Others are, not deceived, but, as it were, forcibly carried away by the like passions, against their better judgment, and feeble resolutions too of acting better. And there are men, and truly they are not a few, who shamelessly avow, not their interest, but their mere will and pleasure, to be their law of life: and who, in open defiance of every thing that is reasonable, will go on in a course of vicious extravagance, foreseeing, with no remorse and little fear, that it will be their temporal ruin; and some of them, under the apprehension of the consequences of wickedness in another state. And to speak in the most moderate way, human creatures are not only continually liable to go wrong voluntarily, but we see likewise that they often actually do so, with respect to their temporal interests, as well as with respect to religion.

§ 8. *Our state in each is analogous to the other.*

Thus our difficulties and dangers, or our trials, in our temporal and our religious capacity, as they proceed from the same causes, and have the same effect upon men's behaviour, are evidently analogous, and of the same kind

§ 9. *Our dangers aggravated by* (a) *acts of others,* (b) *ill training,* (c) *corruptions in religion,* (d) *our own prior acts.*

It may be added, that as the difficulties and dangers of miscarrying in our religious state of trial, are greatly increased, and one is ready to think, in a manner wholly *made*, by the ill behaviour of others; by a wrong education, wrong in a moral sense, sometimes positively vicious; by general bad example; by the dishonest artifices which are got into business of all kinds; and, in very many parts of the world, by religion's being corrupted into superstitions,[1] which indulge men in their vices: so in like manner, the difficulties of conducting ourselves prudently in respect to our present interest, and our danger of being led aside from pursuing it, are greatly increased, by a foolish education; and, after we come to mature age, by the extravagance and carelessness of others, whom we have intercourse with; and by mistaken notions, very generally prevalent, and taken up from common opinion, concerning temporal happiness, and wherein it consists. And persons, by their own negligence and folly in their temporal affairs, no less than by a course of vice, bring themselves into new difficulties; and, by habits of indulgence, become less qualified to go through them: and one irregularity after another, embarrasses things to such a degree, that they know not whereabout they are; and often makes the path of conduct so intricate and perplexed, that it is difficult to trace it out; difficult even to determine what is the prudent or the moral part. Thus, for instance, wrong behaviour [2] in one stage of life, youth; wrong,

[1] Here Butler evidently looks beyond the Christian pale. In other passages he specially regards it. See II. i. 13, vi. 5. In Six Sermons, i. 4, he points out the provision of the Divine word, whereby, with the corruption, the confutation is transmitted.

[2] Butler is not here repeating himself from § 4. Our

I mean, considering ourselves only in our temporal capacity, without taking in religion; this, in several ways, increases the difficulties of right behaviour in mature age; i.e. puts us into a more disadvantageous state of trial in our temporal capacity.

§ 10. *In neither sphere are the demands on us extravagant.*

We are an inferior part of the creation of God. There are natural appearances of our being in a state of degradation.[c] And we certainly are in a condition, which *does not seem*, by any means, the most advantageous we could imagine or desire, either in our natural or moral capacity, for securing either our present or future interest. However, this condition, low and careful and uncertain as it is, does not afford any just ground of complaint. For, as men may manage their temporal affairs with prudence, and so pass their days here on earth in tolerable ease and satisfaction, by a moderate degree of care: so likewise with regard to religion, there is no more required than what they are well able to do, and what they must be greatly wanting to themselves, if they neglect. And for persons to have that put upon them, which they are well able to go through, and no more, we naturally consider as an equitable thing; supposing it done by proper authority. Nor have we any more reason to complain of it, with regard to the Author of nature, than of his not having given us other advantages, belonging to other orders of creatures.

[c] Part II. chap. v.

ill conduct impairs our subsequent position διχᾶς—
1. By the habits formed, biassing us *ab intra* (§ 4).
2. By marring our environment *ab extra*, e. g. by ill repute.

The second is what he here deals with exclusively.

§ 11. *The religious part is accredited by the natural part.*

But the thing here insisted upon is, that the state of trial which Religion teaches us we are in, is rendered credible, by its being throughout uniform and of a piece with the general conduct of Providence towards us, in all other respects within the compass of our knowledge. Indeed if mankind, considered in their natural capacity, as inhabitants of this world only, found themselves, from their birth to their death, in a settled state of security and happiness, without any solicitude or thought of their own : or if they were in no danger of being brought into inconveniences and distress, by carelessness, or the folly of passion, through bad example, the treachery of others, or the deceitful appearances of things : were this our natural condition, then it might seem strange, and be some presumption against the truth of religion, that it represents our future and more general interest, as not secure of course, but as depending upon our behaviour, and requiring recollection and self-government to obtain it. For it might be alleged, ' What you say is our condition in one respect, is not in any wise of a sort with what we find, by experience, our condition is in another. Our whole present interest is secured to our hands, without any solicitude of ours; and why should not our future interest, if we have any such, be so too ? ' But since, on the contrary, thought and consideration, the voluntary denying ourselves many things which we desire, and a course of behaviour, far from being always agreeable to us; are absolutely necessary to our acting even a common decent, and common prudent part, so as to pass with any satisfaction through the present world, and be received upon any tolerable good terms in it : since this is the case, all presumption against self-denial and attention being necessary to secure our higher interest, is removed. Had we not experience, it might, perhaps speciously, be urged, that it is improbable any thing of hazard and danger should be put upon us by an infinite Being ; when every thing which is hazard and danger in our manner of conception, and will end in error, confusion, and misery, is now already certain in his foreknowledge.

§ 12. *Though why we are put in hazard we cannot say.*

And indeed, why any thing of hazard and danger should be put upon such frail creatures as we are, may well be thought a difficulty in speculation;[1] and cannot but be so, till we know the whole, or, however, much more of the case. But still the constitution of nature is as it is. Our happiness and misery are trusted to our conduct, and made to depend upon it. Somewhat, and, in many circumstances, a great deal too, is put upon us, either to do, or to suffer, as we choose. And all the various miseries of life, which people bring upon themselves by negligence and folly, and might have avoided by proper care, are instances of this: which miseries are beforehand just as contingent and undetermined as their conduct, and left to be determined by it.

§ 13. *In religion, as in nature, we do not accept, but acquire*

These observations are an answer to the objections against the credibility of a state of trial, as implying temptations, and real danger of miscarrying with regard to our general interest, under the moral government of God : and they show, that, if we are at all to be considered in such a capacity, and as having such an interest ; the general analogy of Providence must lead us to apprehend ourselves in danger of mis-

---

[1] This mystery, however, like most others, seems to run up into the one grand mystery, the permitted introduction of evil into the universe, through the creation of free wills.

carrying, in different degrees, as to this interest, by our neglecting to act the proper part belonging to us in that capacity. For we have a present interest, under the government of God which we experience here upon earth. And this interest, as it is not forced upon us, so neither is it offered to our acceptance, but to our acquisition; in such sort, as that we are in danger of missing it, by means of temptations to neglect, or act contrary to it; and without attention and self-denial, must and do miss of it. It is then perfectly credible, that this may be our case, with respect to that chief and final good, which religion proposes to us.

CHAPTER V

OF A STATE OF PROBATION, AS INTENDED FOR MORAL DISCIPLINE AND IMPROVEMENT

§ 1. *We cannot supply fully the why of our condition.*

From the consideration of our being in a probation-state, of so much difficulty and hazard, naturally arises the question, how we came to be placed in it. But such a general inquiry as this would be found involved in insuperable difficulties. For, though some of these difficulties would be lessened by observing, that all wickedness is voluntary, as is implied in its very notion; and that many of the miseries of life have apparent good effects: yet, when we consider other circumstances belonging to both, and what must be the consequence of the former in a life to come; it cannot but be acknowledged plain folly and presumption, to pretend to give an account of the whole reasons of this matter: the whole reasons of our being allotted a condition, out of which so much wickedness and misery, so circumstanced, would in fact arise. Whether it be not beyond our faculties, not only to find out, but even to understand, the whole account of this; or, though we should be supposed capable of understanding it, yet, whether it would be of service or prejudice to us to be informed of it, is impossible to say.

§ 2. *No proof lies against this why: and religion shows its aim to be our improvement.*

But as our present condition can in no wise be shown inconsistent with the perfect moral government of God: so religion teaches us we were placed in it, that we might qualify ourselves, by the practice of virtue, for another state which is to follow it. And this, though but a partial answer, a very partial one indeed, to the inquiry now mentioned; yet, is a more satisfactory answer to another, which is of real, and of the utmost importance to us to have answered: the inquiry, What is our business here? The known end then, why we are placed in a state of so much affliction, hazard, and difficulty, is, our improvement in virtue and piety, as the requisite qualification for a future state of security and happiness.

§ 3. *That this life is to a future one as youth to manhood, is credible.*

Now the beginning of life, considered as an education for mature age in the present world, appears plainly, at first sight, analogous to this our trial for a future one: the former being in our temporal capacity, what the latter is in our religious capacity. But some observations common to both of them, and a more distinct consideration of each, will more distinctly show the extent and force of the analogy between them; and the credibility, which arises from hence, as well as from the nature of the thing, that the present life was intended to be a state of discipline for a future one.

§§ 2–5] DISCIPLINE AND IMPROVEMENT

§ 4. *Our environment corresponds with our selves.*

[I.] Every species of creatures is, we see, designed for a particular way of life; to which, the nature, the capacities, temper, and qualifications of each species, are as necessary, as their external circumstances. Both come into the notion of such state, or particular way of life, and are constituent parts of it. Change a man's capacities or character to the degree, in which it is conceivable they may be changed; and he would be altogether incapable of a human course of life, and human happiness: as incapable, as if, his nature continuing unchanged, he were placed in a world, where he had no sphere of action, nor any objects to answer his appetites, passions, and affections of any sort. One thing is set over against another, as an ancient writer expresses it. Our nature corresponds to our external condition. Without this correspondence, there would be no possibility of any such thing as human life and human happiness: which life and happiness are, therefore, a *result* from our nature and condition jointly: meaning by human life, not living in the literal sense, but the whole complex notion commonly understood by those words. So that, without determining what will be the employment and happiness, the particular life of good men hereafter; there must be some determinate capacities, some necessary character and qualifications, without which persons cannot but be utterly incapable of it: in like manner, as there must be some, without which men would be incapable of their present state of life. Now,

§ 5. *Our powers of storage, self-adaptation, attaining fitness and facility by use.*

[II.] The constitution of human creatures, and indeed of all creatures which come under our notice, is such, as that they are capable of naturally becoming qualified for states of life, for which they were once wholly unqualified. In imagination we may indeed conceive of creatures, as incapable of having any of their faculties naturally enlarged, or as being unable naturally to acquire any new qualifications: but the faculties of every species known to us are made for enlargement; for acquirements of experience and habits. We find ourselves in particular endued with capacities, not only of perceiving ideas, and of knowledge or perceiving truth, but also of storing up our ideas and knowledge by memory. We are capable, not only of acting, and of having different momentary impressions made upon us; but of getting a new facility in any kind of action, and of settled alterations in our temper or character. The power of the two last is the power of habits. But neither the perception of ideas, nor knowledge of any sort, are habits; though absolutely necessary to the forming of them. However, apprehension, reason, memory, which are the capacities of acquiring knowledge, are greatly improved by exercise. Whether the word *habit* is applicable to all these improvements, and in particular how far the powers of memory and of habits may be powers of the same nature, I shall not inquire. But that perceptions come into our minds readily and of course, by means of their having been there before, seems a thing of the same sort, as readiness in any particular kind of action, proceeding from being accustomed to it.

§ 6. *Habits, bodily and mental, are both passive and active.*

And aptness to recollect practical observations of service in our conduct, is plainly habit in many cases. There are habits of perception, and habits of action. An instance of the former, is our constant and even involuntary readiness, in correcting the impressions of our sight concerning magnitudes and distances, so as to substitute judgment in the room of sensation imperceptibly to ourselves. And it seems as if all other associations of ideas not naturally connected might be called *passive habits*; as properly as our readiness in understanding languages upon sight, or hearing of words. And our readiness in speaking and writing them is an instance of the latter, of active habits. For distinctness, we may consider habits, as belonging to the body, or the mind: and the latter will be explained by the former. Under the former are comprehended all bodily activities or motions, whether graceful or unbecoming, which are owing to use: under the latter, general habits of life and conduct; such as those of obedience and submission to authority, or to any particular person; those of veracity, justice, and charity; those of attention, industry, self-government, envy, revenge. And habits of this latter kind seem produced by repeated acts,[1] as well as the former.

§ 7. *These last begot by inward principles carried into act.*

And in like manner as habits belonging to the body are produced by external acts: so habits of the mind are produced by the exertion of inward practical principles, i.e. by carrying them into act, or acting upon them; the principles of obedience, of veracity, justice, and charity. Nor can those habits be formed by any external course of action, otherwise than as it proceeds from these principles: because it is only these inward principles exerted, which are strictly acts of obedience, of veracity, of justice, and of charity. So likewise habits of attention, industry, self-government, are in the same manner acquired by exercise; and habits of envy and revenge by indulgence, whether in outward act, or in thought and intention, i.e. inward act: for such intention is an act. Resolutions also to do well are properly acts. And endeavouring to

[1] Comp. Aristotle, *Eth. Nic.* II. i. 7, 8: καὶ ἑνὶ δὴ λόγῳ ἐκ τῶν ὁμοίων ἐνεργειῶν αἱ ἕξεις γίνονται. διὸ δεῖ τὰς ἐνεργείας ποιὰς ἀποδιδόναι.

enforce upon our own minds a practical sense of virtue, or to beget in others that practical sense of it, which a man really has himself, is a virtuous act. All these, therefore, may and will contribute towards forming good habits.

§ 8. *Passive habit loses in power by repetition, active gains.*

But going over the theory of virtue in one's thoughts, talking well, and drawing fine pictures, of it; this is so far from necessarily or certainly conducing to form an habit of it, in him who thus employs himself, that it may harden the mind in a contrary course, and render it gradually more insensible, i. e. form an habit of insensibility, to all moral considerations. For, from our very faculty of habits, passive impressions, by being repeated, grow weaker. Thoughts, by often passing through the mind, are felt less sensibly: being accustomed to danger, begets intrepidity, i. e. lessens fear; to distress, lessens the passions of pity; to instances of others' mortality, lessens the sensible apprehension of our own. And from these two observations together; that practical habits are formed and strengthened by repeated acts, and that passive impressions grow weaker by being repeated upon us; it must follow, that active habits may be gradually forming and strengthening, by a course of acting upon such and such motives and excitements, whilst these motives and excitements themselves are, by proportionable degrees, growing less sensible, i. e. are continually less and less sensibly felt, even as the active habits strengthen. And experience confirms this: for active principles, at the very time that they are less lively in perception than they were, are found to be, somehow, wrought more thoroughly into the temper and character, and become more effectual in influencing our practice. The three things just mentioned may afford instances of it.

§ 9. *Though perhaps with diminished emotion.*

Perception of danger is a natural excitement of passive fear, and active caution: and by being inured to danger, habits of the latter are gradually wrought, at the same time that the former gradually lessens. Perception of distress in others is a natural excitement, passively to pity, and actively to relieve it: but let a man set himself to attend to, inquire out, and relieve distressed persons, and he cannot but grow less and less sensibly affected with the various miseries of life, with which he must become acquainted; when yet, at the same time, benevolence, considered not as a passion, but as a practical principle of action, will strengthen: and whilst he passively compassionates the distressed less, he will acquire a greater aptitude actively to assist and befriend them. So also at the same time that the daily instances of men's dying around us give us daily a less sensible passive feeling or apprehension of our own mortality, such instances greatly contribute to the strengthening a practical regard to it in serious men; i.e. to forming an habit of acting with a constant view to it.

§ 10. *The passive may give aid in forming the active.*

And this seems again further to show, that passive impressions made upon our minds by admonition, experience, example, though they may have a remote efficacy, and a very great one, towards forming active habits, yet, can have this efficacy no otherwise than by inducing us to such a course of action: and that it is not being affected so and so, but acting, which forms those habits: only it must be always remembered, that real endeavours to enforce good impressions upon ourselves are a species of virtuous action. Nor do we know how far it is possible, in the nature of things, that effects should be wrought in us at once, equivalent to habits, i.e. what is wrought by use and exercise. However, the thing insisted upon is, not what may be possible, but what is in fact the appointment of nature: which is, that active habits are to be formed by exercise.

§11. *The formation hard to trace, but proved by experience.*

Their progress may be so gradual, as to be imperceptible of its steps: it may be hard to explain the faculty, by which we are capable of habits, throughout its several parts; and to trace it up to its original, so as to distinguish it from all others in our mind: and it seems as if contrary effects were to be ascribed to it. But the thing in general, that our nature is formed to yield, in some such manner as this, to use and exercise, is matter of certain experience.

§12. *Habit gives readiness, ease, pleasure.*

Thus, by accustoming ourselves to any course of action, we get an aptness to go on, a facility, readiness, and often pleasure, in it. The inclinations which rendered us averse to it grow weaker: the difficulties in it, not only the imaginary but the real ones, lessen: the reasons for it offer themselves of course to our thoughts upon all occasions: and the least glimpse of them is sufficient to make us go on, in a course of action, to which we have been accustomed. And practical principles appear to grow stronger, absolutely in themselves, by exercise; as well as relatively, with regard to contrary principles; which, by being accustomed to submit, do so habitually, and of course. And thus a new character, in several respects, may be formed; and many habitudes of life, not given by nature, but which nature directs us to acquire.

§13. *Without habit, nothing in us would mature.*

[III.] Indeed we may be assured, that we should never have had these capacities of improving by experience, acquired knowledge, and habits, had they not been necessary, and intended to be made use of. And accordingly we find them so necessary, and so much intended, that without them we should be utterly incapable of that, which was the end for which we were made, considered in our temporal capacity only: the employments and satisfactions of our mature state of life.

§ 14. *Mature powers given at birth would embarrass and disable.*

Nature does in no wise qualify us wholly, much less at once, for this mature state of life. Even maturity of understanding and bodily strength, are not only arrived to gradually, but are also very much owing to the continued exercise of our powers of body and mind from infancy. But if we suppose a person brought into the world with both these in maturity, as far as this is conceivable; he would plainly at first be as unqualified for the human life of mature age, as an idiot.[1] He would be in a manner distracted, with astonishment, and apprehension, and curiosity, and suspense: nor can one guess, how long it would be, before he would be familiarized to himself and the objects about him enough, even to set himself to any thing. It may be questioned too, whether the natural information of his sight and hearing would be of any manner of use at all to him in acting, before experience. And it seems, that men would be strangely headstrong and self-willed, and disposed to exert themselves with an impetuosity, which would render society insupportable, and the living in it impracticable; were it not for some acquired moderation and self-government, some aptitude and readiness in restraining themselves, and concealing their sense of things. Want of every

---

[1] This argument (perhaps somewhat succinctly expressed) admirably illustrates what he has argued above (§ 4) as to the correspondence between self and the environment.

thing of this kind which is learnt would render a man as uncapable of society, as want of language would; or as his natural ignorance of any of the particular employments of life would render him uncapable of providing himself with the common conveniences, or supplying the necessary wants of it.

§ 15. *Nature leaves us unfurnished,*

In these respects, and probably in many more, of which we have no particular notion, mankind is left, by nature, an unformed, unfinished creature; utterly deficient and unqualified, before the acquirement of knowledge, experience, and habits, for that mature state of life, which was the end of his creation, considering him as related only to this world.

§ 16. *But with a capacity for furnishing,*

But then, as nature has endued us with a power of supplying those deficiencies, by acquired knowledge, experience, and habits: so likewise we are placed in a condition, in infancy, childhood, and youth, fitted for it; fitted for our acquiring those qualifications of all sorts, which we stand in need of in mature age. Hence children, from their very birth, are daily growing acquainted with the objects about them, with the scene in which they are placed, and to have a future part; and learning somewhat or other, necessary to the performance of it. The subordinations, to which they are accustomed in domestic life, teach them self-government in common behaviour abroad, and prepare them for subjection and obedience to civil authority.

§ 17. *By effort, and progress of life.*

What passes before their eyes, and daily happens to them, gives them experience, caution against treachery and deceit, together with numberless little rules of action and conduct, which we could not live without; and which are learnt so insensibly and so perfectly, as to be mistaken perhaps for instinct: though they are the effect of long experience and exercise; as much so as language, or knowledge in particular business, or the qualifications and behaviour belonging to the several ranks and professions. Thus the beginning of our days is adapted to be, and is, a state of education in the theory and practice of mature life. We are much assisted in it by example, instruction, and the care of others; but a great deal is left to ourselves to do. And of this, as part is done easily and of course; so part requires diligence and care, the voluntary foregoing many things which we desire, and setting ourselves to what we should have no inclination to, but for the necessity or expedience of it. For, that labour and industry, which the station of so many absolutely requires, they would be greatly unqualified for, in maturity; as those in other stations would be, for any other sorts of application; if both were not accustomed to them in their youth. And according as persons behave themselves, in the general education which all go through, and in the particular ones adapted to particular employments; their character is formed, and made appear; they recommend themselves more or less; and are capable of, and placed in, different stations in the society of mankind.

§ 18. *Analogy between preparation for maturity, and for survival.*

The former part of life then is to be considered as an important opportunity, which nature puts into our hands; and which, when lost, is not to be recovered. And our being placed in a state of discipline throughout this life, for another world, is a providential disposition of things, exactly of the same kind, as our being placed in a state of discipline during childhood, for mature age. Our condition in both respects is uniform and of a piece, and comprehended under one and the same general law of nature.

§ 19. *Which might hold even were the* how *of this preparation undiscoverable.*

And if we were not able at all to discern, how or in what way the present life could be our preparation for another; this would be no objection against the credibility of its being so. For we do not discern, how food and sleep contribute to the growth of the body: nor could have any thought that they would, before we had experience. Nor do children at all think, on the one hand, that the sports and exercises, to which they are so much addicted, contribute to their health and growth; nor, on the other, of the necessity which there is for their being restrained in them: nor are they capable of understanding the use of many parts of discipline, which nevertheless they must be made to go through, in order to qualify them for the business of mature age. Were we not able then to discover, in what respects the present life could form us for a future one: yet nothing would be more supposable than that it might, in some respects or other, from the general analogy of Providence.

§ 20. *Is corroborated, if we take God's moral government into view.*

And this, for ought I see, might reasonably be said, even though we should not take in the consideration of God's moral government over the world. But,

[IV.] Take in this consideration, and consequently, that the character of virtue and piety is a necessary qualification for the future state; and then we may distinctly see, how, and in what respects, the present life may be a preparation for it: since we *want, and are capable of, improvement in that character, by moral and religious habits;* and *the present life is fit to be a state of discipline for such improvement:* in like manner as we have already observed, how, and in what respects, infancy, childhood, and youth, are a necessary preparation, and a natural state of discipline, for mature age.

§ 21. *The future life is probably active; common; and more sensibly under divine government.*

Nothing which we at present see would lead us to the thought of a solitary unactive state hereafter : but, if we judge at all from the analogy of nature, we must suppose, according to the scripture account of it, that it will be a community. And there is no shadow of any thing unreasonable in conceiving, though there be no analogy for it, that this community will be, as the scripture represents it, under the more immediate, or, if such an expression may be used, the more sensible government of God. Nor is our ignorance, what will be the employments of this happy community, nor our consequent ignorance, what particular scope or occasion there will be for the exercise of veracity, justice, and charity, amongst the members of it with regard to each other ; any proof, that there will be no sphere of exercise for those virtues. Much less, if that were possible, is our ignorance any proof, that there will be no occasion for that frame of mind, or character, which is formed by the daily practice of those particular virtues here, and which is a result from it. This at least must be owned in general, that, as the government established in the universe is moral, the character of virtue and piety must, in some way or other, be the condition of our happiness, or the qualification for it.

§ 22. *Habits are the fitting antidote for our liability to lapse,*

Now from what is above observed, concerning our natural power of habits, it is easy to see, that we are *capable* of moral improvement by discipline. And how greatly we *want* it, need not be proved to any one who is acquainted with the great wickedness of mankind ; or even with those imperfections, which the best are conscious of. But it is not perhaps distinctly attended to by every one, that the occasion which human creatures have for discipline, to improve in them this character of virtue and piety, is to be traced up higher than to excess in the passions, by indulgence and habits of vice. Mankind, and perhaps all finite creatures, from the very constitution of their nature, before habits of virtue, are deficient, and in danger of deviating from what is right: and therefore stand in need of virtuous habits, for a security against this danger.[1]

§ 23. *Which arises because we have propensions not subjected to virtue.*

For, together with the general principle of moral understanding, we have in our inward frame various affections towards particular external objects. These affections are naturally, and of right, subject to the government of the moral principle, as to the occasions upon which they may be gratified ; as to the times, degrees, and manner, in which the objects of them may be pursued : but then the principle of virtue can neither excite them, nor prevent their being excited. On the contrary, they are naturally felt, when the objects of them are present to the mind, not only before all consideration, whether they can be obtained by lawful means, but after it is found they cannot. For the natural objects of affection continue so ; the necessaries, conveniences, and pleasures of life, remain naturally desirable ; though they cannot be obtained innocently : nay, though they cannot possibly be obtained at all. And when the objects of any affection whatever cannot be obtained without unlawful means ; but may be obtained by them : such affection, though its being excited, and its continuing some time in the mind, be as innocent as it is natural and necessary ; yet cannot but be conceived to have a tendency to incline persons to venture upon such unlawful means : and therefore must be conceived as putting them in some danger of it.

[1] *Inf.* § 29.

§ 24. *Habit gives us a security* ab intra.

Now what is the general security against this danger, against their actually deviating from right? As the danger is, so also must the security be, from within: from the practical principle of virtue.[a] And the strengthening or improving this principle, considered as practical, or as a principle of action, will lessen the danger, or increase the security against it. And this moral principle is capable of improvement, by proper discipline and exercise: by recollecting the practical impressions which example and experience have made upon us: and, instead of following humour and mere inclination, by continually attending to the equity and right of the case, in whatever we are engaged, be it in greater or less matters; and accustoming ourselves always to act upon it; as being itself the just and natural motive of action: and as this moral course of behaviour must necessarily, under divine government be our final interest. *Thus the principle of virtue, improved into an habit, of which improvement we are*

---

[a] It may be thought, that a sense of interest would as effectually restrain creatures from doing wrong. But if by a *sense of interest* is meant a speculative conviction or belief, that such and such indulgence would occasion them greater uneasiness, upon the whole, than satisfaction; it is contrary to present experience to say, that this sense of interest is sufficient to restrain them from thus indulging themselves. *Sense of interest, as mere pleasure, insufficient, as comprehensive regard to happiness, is part of virtue.* And if by a *sense of interest* is meant a practical regard to what is upon the whole our happiness: this is not only coincident with the principle of virtue or moral rectitude, but is a part of the idea itself. And it is evident this reasonable self-love wants to be improved, as really as any principle in our nature. For we daily see it overmatched, not only by the more boisterous passions, but by curiosity, shame, love of imitation, by any thing, even indolence; especially if the interest, the temporal interest, suppose, which is the end of such self-love, be at a distance. So greatly are profligate men mistaken, when they affirm they are wholly governed by interestedness and self-love. And so little cause is there for moralists to disclaim this principle. See pp. 80–83.

thus capable, will plainly be, in proportion to the strength of it, a security against the danger which finite creatures are in, from the very nature of propension, or particular affections.

§ 25. *May have place in a future life; is anyhow an advance in virtue.*

This way of putting the matter, supposes particular affections to remain in a future state; which it is scarce possible to avoid supposing. And if they do; we clearly see, that acquired habits of virtue and self-government may be necessary for the regulation of them. However, though we were not distinctly to take in this supposition, but to speak only in general; the thing really comes to the same. For habits of virtue, thus acquired by discipline, are improvement in virtue: and improvement in virtue must be advancement in happiness, if the government of the universe be moral.

§ 26. *Liberty renders falling possible, but does not account for it.*

From these things we may observe, and it will further show this our natural and original need of being improved by discipline, how it comes to pass, that creatures made upright fall; and that those who preserve their uprightness, by so doing, raise themselves to a more secure state of virtue. To say that the former is accounted for by the nature of liberty, is to say no more, than that an event's actually happening is accounted for by a mere possibility of its happening.

§ 27. *It seems explained by the nature of particular propensions.*

But it seems distinctly conceivable from the very nature of particular affections or propensions. For, suppose creatures intended for such a particular state of life, for which such propensions were necessary:

suppose them endued with such propensions, together with moral understanding, as well including a practical sense of virtue, as a speculative perception of it; and that all these several principles, both natural and moral, forming an inward constitution of mind, were in the most exact proportion possible; i. e. in a proportion the most exactly adapted to their intended state of life: such creatures would be made upright, or finitely perfect. Now particular propensions, from their very nature, must be felt, the objects of them being present; though they cannot be gratified at all, or not with the allowance of the moral principle. But if they can be gratified without its allowance, or by contradicting it; then they must be conceived to have some tendency, in how low a degree soever, yet some tendency, to induce persons to such forbidden gratification. This tendency, in some one particular propension, may be increased, by the greater frequency of occasion naturally exciting it, than of occasions exciting others. The least voluntary indulgence in forbidden circumstances, though but in thought, will increase this wrong tendency; and may increase it further, till, peculiar conjunctures perhaps conspiring, it becomes effect; and danger of deviating from right, ends in actual deviation from it; a danger necessarily arising from the very nature of propension; and which therefore could not have been prevented, though it might have been escaped, or got innocently through. The case would be, as if we were to suppose a strait path marked out for a person, in which such a degree of attention would keep him steady: but if he would not attend in this degree, any one of a thousand objects, catching his eye, might lead him out of it.

§ 28. *Disobedience, single, produces disorder, of undefined amount; if repeated, habit.*

Now it is impossible to say, how much even the first full overt act of irregularity might disorder the inward constitution; unsettle the adjustments, and alter the proportions, which formed it, and in which the uprightness of its make consisted : but repetition of irregularities would produce habits. And thus the constitution would be spoiled ; and creatures made upright, become corrupt and depraved in their settled character, proportionately to their repeated irregularities in occasional acts.

§ 29. *Is the counterpart to that capacity of betterment, which might raise us up to safety.*

But on the contrary, these creatures might have improved and raised themselves, to an higher and more secure state of virtue, by the contrary behaviour: by steadily following the moral principle, supposed to be one part of their nature ; and thus withstanding that unavoidable danger of defection, which necessarily arose from propension, the other part of it. For, by thus preserving their integrity for some time, their danger would lessen ; since propensions, by being inured to submit, would do it more easily and of course : and their security against this lessening danger would increase ; since the moral principle would gain additional strength by exercise : both which things are implied in the notion of virtuous habits. Thus then vicious indulgence is not only criminal in itself, but also depraves the inward constitution and character. And virtuous self-government is not only right in itself, but also improves the inward constitution or character : and may improve it to such a degree, that though we should suppose it impossible, for particular affections to be absolutely coincident with the moral principle ; and consequently should allow, that such creatures as have been above supposed, would for ever remain defectible ; yet their danger of actually deviating from right may be almost infinitely lessened, and they fully fortified against what remains of it : if that may be called danger, against which there is an adequate effectual security. But still, this their higher perfection may continue to consist in habits of virtue formed in a state of discipline, and this their more complete security remain to proceed from them. And thus it is plainly conceivable, that creatures without blemish, as they came out of the hands of God, may be in danger of going wrong ; and so may stand in need of the security of virtuous habits, additional to the moral principle wrought into their natures by him. That which is the ground of their danger, or their want of security, may be considered as a deficiency in them, to which virtuous habits are the natural supply.[1] And as they are naturally capable of being raised and improved by discipline, it may be a thing fit and requisite that they should be placed in circumstances with an eye to it : in circumstances peculiarly fitted to be, to them, a state of discipline for their improvement in virtue.

§ 30. *Need of training enhanced for us who have 'corrupted our natures.'*

But how much more strongly must this hold with respect to those, who have corrupted their natures, are fallen from their original rectitude, and whose passions are become excessive by repeated violations of their inward constitution? Upright creatures may want to be improved: depraved creatures want to be renewed. Education and discipline, which may be in all degrees and sorts of gentleness and of severity, is expedient for those : but must be absolutely necessary for these. For these, discipline of the severer sort too, and in the higher degrees of it, must be necessary, in order to wear out vicious habits; to recover their primitive strength of self-government, which indulgence must have weakened ; to repair, as well as raise into an habit, the moral principle, in order to their arriving at a secure state of virtuous happiness.

[1] *Sup.* § 22.

§ 31. *The varied lessons of the present state peculiarly fit it for discipline.*

Now whoever will consider the thing, may clearly see, that the present world is *peculiarly fit* to be a state of discipline for this purpose, to such as will set themselves to mend and improve. For, the various temptations with which we are surrounded; our experience of the deceits of wickedness; having been in many instances led wrong ourselves; the great viciousness of the world; the infinite disorders consequent upon it; our being made acquainted with pain and sorrow, either from our own feeling of it, or from the sight of it in others; these things, though some of them may indeed produce wrong effects upon our minds, yet when duly reflected upon, have, all of them, a direct tendency to bring us to a settled moderation and reasonableness of temper: the contrary both to thoughtless levity, and also to that unrestrained self-will, and violent bent to follow present inclination, which may be observed in undisciplined minds. Such experience, as the present state affords, of the frailty of our nature; of the boundless extravagance of ungoverned passion; of the power which an infinite Being has over us, by the various capacities of misery which he has given us; in short, that kind and degree of experience, which the present state affords us, that the constitution of nature is such as to admit the possibility, the danger, and the actual event, of creatures losing their innocence and happiness, and becoming vicious and wretched; hath a tendency to give us a practical sense of things, very different from a mere speculative knowledge that we are liable to vice, and capable of misery. And who knows, whether the security of creatures in the highest and most settled state of perfection, may not in part arise, from their having had such a sense of things as this, formed, and habitually fixed within them, in some state of probation? And passing through the present world with that moral attention, which is necessary to the acting a right part in it, may leave everlasting impressions of this sort upon our minds. But to be a little more distinct : allurements to what is wrong ; difficulties in the discharge of our duty ; our not being able to act an uniform right part without some thought and care; and the opportunities which we have, or imagine we have, of avoiding what we dislike, or obtaining what we desire, by unlawful means, when we either cannot do it at all, or at least not so easily, by lawful ones ; these things, i.e. the snares and temptations of vice, are what render the present world peculiarly fit to be a state of discipline, to those who will preserve their integrity: because they render being upon our guard, resolution, and the denial of our passions, necessary in order to that end.

§ 32. *Wherein habit is confirmed by persistent effort, and by wariness against temptations.*

And the exercise of such particular recollection, intention of mind, and self-government, in the practice of virtue, has, from the make of our nature, a peculiar tendency to form habits of virtue ; as implying, not only a real, but also a more continued, and a more intense exercise of the virtuous principle; or a more constant and a stronger effort of virtue exerted into act. Thus suppose a person to know himself to be in particular danger, for some time, of doing any thing wrong, which yet he fully resolves not to do : continued recollection, and keeping upon his guard, in order to make good his resolution, is a *continued* exerting of that act of virtue in a *high degree*, which need have been, and perhaps would have been, only *instantaneous* and *weak*, had the temptation been so. It is indeed ridiculous to assert, that self-denial is essential to virtue and piety : but it would have been nearer the truth, though not strictly the truth itself, to have said, that it is essential to discipline and improvement.[1]

---

[1] Because if the state of virtue be perfect, all the inclinations are right, and there is nothing to deny or mortify. Comp. also Aristotle, *Eth. Nic.* II. iii. 1.

For though actions materially virtuous, which have no sort of difficulty, but are perfectly agreeable to our particular inclinations, may possibly be done only from these particular inclinations, and so may not be any exercise of the principle of virtue, i. e. not be virtuous actions at all; yet, on the contrary, they may be an exercise of that principle: and when they are, they have a tendency to form and fix the habit of virtue. But when the exercise of the virtuous principle is more continued, oftener repeated, and more intense; as it must be in circumstances of danger, temptation, and difficulty, of any kind and in any degree; this tendency is increased proportionably, and a more confirmed habit is the consequence.

§ 33. *This law, even if limited by the law of a mean in moral character, is not subverted.*

This undoubtedly holds to a certain length: but how far it may hold, I know not. Neither our intellectual powers, nor our bodily strength, can be improved beyond such a degree: and both may be over-wrought. Possibly there may be somewhat analogous to this, with respect to the moral character; which is scarce worth considering. And I mention it only, lest it should come into some persons' thoughts, not as an exception to the foregoing observations, which perhaps it is; but as a confutation of them, which it is not. And there may be several other exceptions. Observations of this kind cannot be supposed to hold minutely, and in every case. It is enough that they hold in general. And these plainly hold so far, as that from them may be seen distinctly, which is all that is intended by them, that *the present world is peculiarly fit to be a state of discipline, for our improvement in virtue and piety:* in the same sense as some sciences, by requiring and engaging the attention, not to be sure of such persons as will not, but of such as will, set themselves to them; are fit to form the mind to habits of attention.

§ 34. *Life as a discipline of vice to the majority is thereby enhanced as a discipline of virtue to the good.*

Indeed the present state is so far from proving, in event, a discipline of virtue to the generality of men, that, on the contrary, they seem to make it a discipline of vice. And the viciousness of the world is, in different ways, the great temptation, which renders it a state of virtuous discipline, in the degree it is, to good men. The whole end, and the whole occasion, of mankind's being placed in such a state as the present, is not pretended to be accounted for. That which appears amidst the general corruption, is, that there are some persons, who, having within them the principle of amendment and recovery, attend to and follow the notices of virtue and religion, be they more clear or more obscure, which are afforded them ; and that the present world is, not only an exercise of virtue in these persons, but an exercise of it in ways and degrees, peculiarly apt to improve it : apt to improve it, in some respects, even beyond what would be, by the exercise of it, required in a perfectly virtuous society, or in a society of equally imperfect virtue with themselves. But that the present world does not actually become a state of moral discipline to many, even to the generality, i. e. that they do not improve or grow better in it, cannot be urged as a proof, that it was not intended for moral discipline, by any who at all deserve the analogy of nature.

§ 35. *The enormous waste in creation, though unaccountable, does not disprove design.*

For, of the numerous seeds of vegetables and bodies of animals, which are adapted and put in the way, to improve to such a point or state of natural maturity and perfection, we do not see perhaps that one in a million actually does. Far the greatest part of them decay before they are improved to it ; and appear to be absolutely destroyed. Yet no one, who does not deny all final causes, will deny, that those seeds and bodies, which do attain to that point of maturity and perfection, answer the end for which they were really designed by nature; and therefore that nature designed them for such perfection.[1] And I cannot forbear adding, though it is not to the present purpose, that the *appearance* of such an amazing *waste* in nature, with respect to these seeds and bodies, by foreign causes, is to us as unaccountable, as, what is much more terrible, the present and future ruin of so many moral agents by themselves, i. e. by vice.

§ 36. *Obedience from hope or fear forms habits, and grows into morality.*[2]

Against this whole notion of moral discipline, it may be objected, in another way; that so far as a course of behaviour, materially virtuous, proceeds from hope and fear, so far it is only a discipline and strengthening of self-love. But doing what God commands, because he commands it, is obedience, though it proceeds from hope or fear. And a course of such obedience will form habits of it. And a constant regard to veracity, justice and charity, may form distinct habits of these particular virtues; and will certainly form habits of self-government, and of denying our inclinations, whenever veracity, justice or charity requires it. Nor is there any foundation for this great nicety, with which some affect to distinguish in this case, in order to depreciate all religion proceeding from hope or fear. For, veracity, justice and charity, regard to God's authority, and to our own chief interest, are not only all three coincident; but each of them is, in itself, a just and natural motive or principle of action. And he who begins a good life from any one of them, and

---

[1] The waste impairs design as a whole: but not as to all the parts. So the argument, if reduced, is not destroyed.

[2] See Shaftesbury, *Inquiry concerning Virtue*, Part III. iii. 3.

perseveres in it, as he is already in some degree, so he cannot fail of becoming more and more, of that character, which is correspondent to the constitution of nature as moral; and to the relation, which God stands in to us as moral Governor of it: nor consequently can he fail of obtaining that happiness which this constitution and relation necessarily suppose connected with that character.

§ 37. *Passive virtue, or resignation, is also good. Training in patience may be needful.*

These several observations, concerning the active principle of virtue and obedience to God's commands, are applicable to passive submission or resignation to his will:[1] which is another essential part of a right character, connected with the former, and very much in our power to form ourselves to. It may be imagined, that nothing but afflictions can give occasion for, or require this virtue; that it can have no respect to, nor be any way necessary to qualify for, a state of perfect happiness: but it is not experience which can make us think thus. Prosperity itself, whilst any thing supposed desirable is not ours, begets extravagant and unbounded thoughts. Imagination is altogether as much a source of discontent, as any thing in our external condition. It is indeed true, that there can be no scope for patience, when sorrow shall be no more: but there may be need of a temper of mind, which shall have been formed by patience.

§ 38. *Self-love, not always conforming to God's will, may require aid from the habit of resignation.*[2]

For, though self-love, considered merely as an active principle leading us to pursue our chief interest, cannot

[1] In Serm. xiv. §§ 5, 6, on the love of God, a much larger scope is given to resignation: perhaps one beyond what the word itself in strictness admits.

[2] In the Second Sermon on Human Nature, § 15, self-love is described as a principle superior in kind to passion;

but be uniformly coincident with the principle of obedience to God's commands, our interest being rightly understood; because this obedience, and the pursuit of our own chief interest, must be in every case one and the same thing: yet it may be questioned, whether self-love, considered merely as the desire of our own interest or happiness, can, from its nature, be thus absolutely and uniformly coincident with the will of God; any more than particular affections can:[b] coincident in such sort, as not to be liable to be excited upon occasions and in degrees, impossible to be gratified consistently with the constitution of things, or the divine appointments. So that *habits* of resignation may, upon this account, be requisite for all creatures: habits, I say; which signify what is formed by use. However, in general it is obvious that both self-love and particular affections in human creatures, considered only as passive feelings, distort and rend the mind; and therefore stand in need of discipline.[1] Now denial of those particular affections, in a course of active virtue and obedience to God's will, has a tendency to moderate them; and seems also to have a tendency to habituate the mind, to be easy and satisfied with that degree of happiness which is allotted us, i. e. to moderate self-love.

§ 39. *Passive obedience is suited to affliction, and integrates the active.*

But the proper discipline for resignation is affliction. For a right behaviour under that trial; recollecting ourselves so as to consider it in the view, in which religion teaches us to consider it, as from the hand of

[b] *Sup.* § 23.

---

but then it is self-love under watch and ward, so to speak: 'reasonable' and 'cool' self-love.

[1] Comp. Serm. xi. 7.

God; receiving it as what he appoints, or thinks proper to permit, in his world and under his government; this will habituate the mind to a dutiful submission. And such submission, together with the active principle of obedience, make up the temper and character in us, which answers to his sovereignty; and which absolutely belongs to the condition of our being, as dependent creatures. Nor can it be said, that this is only breaking the mind to a submission to mere power; for mere power may be accidental, and precarious, and usurped: but it is forming within ourselves the temper of resignation to his rightful authority, who is, by nature, supreme over all.

§ 40. *Character proper for this life and another depends upon action.*

Upon the whole: Such a character, and such qualifications, are necessary for a mature state of life in the present world, as nature alone does in no wise bestow; but has put it upon us, in great part, to acquire, in our progress from one stage of life to another, from childhood to mature age: put it upon us to acquire them, by giving us capacities of doing it, and by placing us, in the beginning of life, in a condition fit for it. And this is a general analogy to our condition in the present world, as in a state of moral discipline for another. It is in vain then to object against the credibility of the present life's being intended for this purpose, that all the trouble and the danger, unavoidably accompanying such discipline, might have been saved us, by our being made at once the creatures and the characters, *which we were to be.* For we experience, that *what we were to be,* was to be the effect of *what we would do:* and that the general conduct of nature is, not to save us trouble or danger, but to make us capable of going through them, and to put it upon us to do so.

§ 41. *Attainment of right qualifications parallel to the supply of legitimate wants.*

Acquirements of our own, experience and habits, are the *natural* supply to our deficiencies, and security against our dangers: since it is as plainly natural to set ourselves to acquire the qualifications, as the external things, which we stand in need of. In particular, it is as plainly a general law of nature, that we should, with regard to our temporal interest, form and cultivate practical principles within us, by attention, use, and discipline, as any thing whatever is a natural law; chiefly in the beginning of life, but also throughout the whole course of it. And the alternative is left to our choice: either to improve ourselves, and better our condition; or, in default of such improvement, to remain deficient and wretched. It is therefore perfectly credible, from the analogy of nature, that the same may be our case, with respect to the happiness of a future state, and the qualifications necessary for it.

§ 42. *Manifestation of character may be πολλαχῶς a further purpose of our probation.*

There is a third thing, which may seem implied in the present world's being a state of probation; that it is a theatre of action, for the manifestation of persons' characters, with respect to a future one: not to be sure to an all-knowing Being, but to his creation or part of it. This may, perhaps, be only a consequence of our being in a state of probation in the other senses. However, it is not impossible, that men's showing and making manifest what is in their heart, what their real character is, may have respect to a future life, in ways and manners which we are not acquainted with: particularly it may be a means, for the Author of nature does not appear to do any thing without means, of their being disposed of suitably to their characters; and of its being known to the creation, by way of example, that they are thus disposed of. But not to enter upon any conjectural account of this; one may just mention, that the manifestation of persons' characters contributes very much, in various ways, to the carrying on a great part of that general course of nature, respecting mankind, which comes under our observation at present. I shall only add, that probation, in both these senses, as well as in that treated of in the foregoing chapter, is implied in moral government: since by persons' behaviour under it, their characters cannot but be manifested, and, if they behave well, improved.

CHAPTER VI[1]

OF THE OPINION OF NECESSITY, CONSIDERED AS INFLUENCING PRACTICE

§ 1. *If this opinion comports with nature, why not also with religion?*

THROUGHOUT the foregoing Treatise it appears, that the condition of mankind, considered as inhabitants of this world only, and under the government of God which we experience, is greatly analogous to our condition, as designed for another world, or under that further government, which religion teaches us. If there-

---

[1] This chapter may be said not to fall strictly within the lines of the proper argument of the work. It removes, however, out of Butler's way a superficial objection, which he shows to be inapplicable to the treatment of practical questions. He may have done this because the idea was too prominent among the philosophical notions of the day to be simply passed by with safety. For he tells us (§ 14) that the opinion of necessity was the fashionable plea for unbelief. It is to be borne in mind that the notions of the fatalists received a powerful support from the Calvinistic school, most powerfully represented by Jonathan Edwards, whose work, however, did not appear until 1754.

fore any assert, as a fatalist must, that the opinion of universal necessity is reconcilable with the former;[1] there immediately arises a question in the way of analogy, whether he must not also own it to be reconcilable with the latter, i. e. with the system of religion itself, and the proof of it. The reader then will observe, that the question now before us is not absolute, Whether the opinion of fate be reconcilable with religion; but hypothetical, Whether, upon supposition of its being reconcilable with the constitution of nature, it be not reconcilable with religion also: or, what pretence a fatalist, not other persons, but a fatalist, has to conclude from his opinion, that there can be no such thing as religion. And as the puzzle and obscurity, which must unavoidably arise from arguing upon so absurd[2] a supposition as that of universal necessity, will, I fear, easily be seen; it will, I hope, as easily be excused.

But since it has been all along taken for granted, as a thing proved, that there is an intelligent Author of nature, or natural Governor of the world; and since an objection may be made against the proof of this, from the opinion of universal necessity, as it may be supposed, that such necessity will itself account for the origin and preservation of all things: it is requisite, that this objection be distinctly answered; or that it be shown, that a fatality, supposed consistent with what we certainly experience, does not destroy the proof of an intelligent Author and Governor of nature; before we proceed to consider, whether it destroys the proof of a moral Governor of it, or of our being in a state of religion.

---

[1] A fatalist holds as such 'the opinion of universal necessity.' Mr. Stephen (*English Thought*, c. v. § 18) distinguishes fatalism, as an occasional necessity, from universal necessity, charges Butler with confounding them, and hence infers Butler's weakness as a metaphysician. But we see from this passage that fatalism is in Butler's view a synonym for universal necessity.

[2] Comp. § 8.

§ 2. *Fate or no fate, agency by choice is matter of experience.*

Now, when it is said by a fatalist, that the whole constitution of nature, and the actions of men, that every thing, and every mode and circumstance of every thing, is necessary, and could not possibly have been otherwise; it is to be observed, that this necessity does not exclude deliberation, choice, preference, and acting from certain principles, and to certain ends: because all this is matter of undoubted experience, acknowledged by all, and what every man may, every moment, be conscious of.

§ 3. *Only alleges an incident of being, no way explains the* how.

And from hence it follows, that necessity, alone and of itself, is in no sort an account of the constitution of nature, and how things came *to be* and *to continue* as they are; but only an account of this *circumstance* relating to their origin and continuance, that they could not have been otherwise than they are and have been. The assertion, that every thing is by necessity of nature, is not an answer to the question; Whether the world came into being as it is, by an intelligent agent forming it thus, or not: but to quite another question; Whether it came into being as it is, in that way and manner which we call *necessarily*, or in that way and manner which we call *freely*. For suppose further, that one who was a fatalist, and one who kept to his natural sense of things, and believed himself a free agent, were disputing together, and vindicating their respective opinions; and they should happen to instance in a house: they would agree that it was built by an architect. Their difference concerning necessity and freedom would occasion no difference of judgment concerning this; but only concerning another matter; whether the architect built it necessarily or freely. Suppose then they should proceed to inquire concerning the constitution of nature: in a lax way of speaking, one of them might say, it was by necessity; and the other, by freedom: but if they had any meaning to their words, as the latter must mean a free agent, so the former must at length be reduced to mean an agent, whether he would say one or more, acting by necessity: for abstract notions can do nothing.

§ 4. *God exists by a necessity antecedent to design: this is but a manner of speech.*

Indeed we ascribe to God a necessary existence, uncaused by any agent. For we find within ourselves the idea of infinity, i. e. immensity and eternity, impossible, even in imagination, to be removed out of being. We seem to discern intuitively, that there must, and cannot but be somewhat, external to ourselves, answering this idea, or the archetype of it. And from hence (for *this abstract*, as much as any other, implies a *concrete*) we conclude, that there is and cannot but be, an infinite, an immense eternal Being existing, prior to all design contributing to his existence, and exclusive of it. And from the scantiness of language, a manner of speaking has been introduced; that necessity is the foundation, the reason, the account of the existence of God. But it is not alleged, nor can it be at all intended, that *every thing* exists as it does, by this kind of necessity; a necessity antecedent in nature to design: it cannot, I say, be meant that every thing exists as it does, by this kind of necessity, upon several accounts; and particularly because it is admitted, that design, in the actions of men, contributes to many alterations in nature. For if any deny this, I shall not pretend to reason with them.

§ 5. *Fatalism postulates an agent, as much as freedom.*

From these things it follows; first, That when a fatalist asserts, that every thing is *by necessity*, he must mean, *by an agent acting necessarily;* he must, I say, mean this, for I am very sensible he would not choose to mean it : and secondly, That the necessity, by which such an agent is supposed to act, does not exclude intelligence and design. So that, were the system of fatality admitted, it would just as much account for the formation of the world, as for the structure of an house, and no more. Necessity as much requires and supposes a necessary agent, as freedom requires and supposes a free agent, to be the former of the world. And the appearances of *design* and of *final causes* in the constitution of nature as really prove this acting agent to be an *intelligent designer*, or to act from choice ; upon the scheme of necessity, supposed possible, as upon that of freedom.

§ 6. *Destroys no proof of religion.*

It appearing thus, that the notion of necessity does not destroy the proof, that there is an intelligent Author of nature and natural Governor of the world ; the present question, which the analogy before mentioned [a] suggests, and which, I think, it will answer, is this : Whether the opinion of necessity, supposed consistent with possibility, with the constitution of the world, and the natural government which we experience exercised over it, destroys all reasonable ground of belief, that we are in a state of religion : or whether that opinion be reconcilable with religion ; with the system, and the proof of it.

§ 7. *A child, trained as not accountable, would be insupportable, and would find his own life so.*

Suppose then a fatalist to educate any one, from his youth up, in his own principles ; that the child should reason upon them, and conclude, that since he cannot possibly behave otherwise than he does, he is not a subject of blame or commendation, nor can deserve

[a] *Sup.* § 1.

to be rewarded or punished: imagine him to eradicate the very perceptions of blame and commendation out of his mind, by means of this system; to form his temper, and character, and behaviour to it; and from it to judge of the treatment he was to expect, say, from reasonable men, upon his coming abroad into the world: as the fatalist judges from this system, what he is to expect from the Author of nature, and with regard to a future state. I cannot forbear stopping here to ask, whether any one of common sense would think fit, that a child should be put upon these speculations, and be left to apply them to practice. And a man has little pretence to reason, who is not sensible, that we are all children in speculations of this kind. However, the child would doubtless be highly delighted to find himself freed from the restraints of fear and shame, with which his playfellows were fettered and embarrassed; and highly conceited in his superior knowledge, so far beyond his years. But conceit and vanity would be the least bad part of the influence, which these principles must have, when thus reasoned and acted upon, during the course of his education. He must either be allowed to go on and be the plague of all about him, and himself too, even to his own destruction: or else correction must be continually made use of, to supply the want of those natural perceptions of blame and commendation, which we have supposed to be removed; and to give him a practical impression, of what he had reasoned himself out of the belief of, that he was in fact an accountable child, and to be punished for doing what he was forbid. It is therefore in reality impossible, but that the correction which he must meet with, in the course of his education, must convince him, that if the scheme he was instructed in were not false; yet that he reasoned inconclusively upon it, and somehow or other misapplied it to practice and common life: as what the fatalist experiences of the conduct of Providence at present, ought in all reason to convince him, that this scheme is misapplied when applied to the subject of religion.[b] But supposing the child's temper could remain still formed to the system, and his expectation of the treatment he was to have in the world be regulated by it; so as to expect that no reasonable man would blame or punish him, for any thing which he should do, because he could not help doing it: upon this supposition it is manifest he would, upon his coming abroad into the world, be insupportable to society, and the treatment which he would receive from it would render it so to him; and he could not fail of doing somewhat, very soon, for which he would be delivered over into the hands of civil justice. And thus, in the end, he would be convinced of the obligations he was under to his wise instructor.

§ 8. *The scheme, however tested, lands in absurdity.*

Or suppose this scheme of fatality, in any other way, applied to practice, such practical application of it will be found equally absurd;[1] equally fallacious in a practical sense: for instance, that if a man be destined to live such a time, he shall live to it, though he take no care of his own preservation; or if he be destined to die before that time, no care can prevent it: therefore all care about preserving one's life is to be neglected: which is the fallacy instanced in by the ancients.

§ 9. *Our entire state is as if we were free.*

But now on the contrary, none of these practical absurdities can be drawn, from reasoning upon the supposition, that we are free; but all such reasoning with regard to the common affairs of life is justified by experience. And therefore, though it were admitted that this opinion of necessity were speculatively true; yet, with regard to practice, it is as if it were false, so far as our experience reaches; that is, to the whole

[b] *Sup.* § 21.

[1] Comp. § 1.

of our present life. For, the constitution of the present world, and the condition in which we are actually placed, is, as if we were free. And it may perhaps justly be concluded, that since the whole process of action, through every step of it, suspense, deliberation, inclining one way, determining, and at last doing as we determine, is as if we were free, therefore we are so. But the thing here insisted upon is, that under the present natural government of things, we find we are treated and dealt with, as if we were free, prior to all consideration whether we are or not.

§ 10. *It misleads then if true: so may it not again mislead, and* in maximis?

Were this opinion therefore of necessity admitted to be ever so true; yet such is in fact our condition and the natural course of things, that whenever we apply it to life and practice, this application of it always misleads us, and cannot but mislead us, in a most dreadful manner, with regard to our present interest. And how can people think themselves so very secure then, that the same application of the same opinion may not mislead them also, in some analogous manner, with respect to a future, a more general and more important interest? For, religion being a practical subject; and the analogy of nature showing us, that we have not faculties to apply this opinion, were it a true one, to practical subjects; whenever we do apply it to the subject of religion, and thence conclude, that we are free from its obligations, it is plain this conclusion cannot be depended upon. There will still remain just reason to think, whatever appearances are, that we deceive ourselves; in somewhat of a like manner, as when people fancy they can draw contradictory conclusions from the idea of infinity.

§ 11. *It being as if false, to entertain it is against reason.*

From these things together, the attentive reader will see it follows, that if upon supposition of freedom the evidence of religion be conclusive, it remains so, upon supposition of necessity; because the notion of necessity is not applicable to practical subjects: i. e. with respect to them, is as if it were not true. Nor does this contain any reflection upon reason: but only upon what is unreasonable. For to pretend to act upon reason, in opposition to practical principles, which the Author of our nature gave us to act upon; and to pretend to apply our reason to subjects, with regard to which, our own short views, and even our experience, will show us, it cannot be depended upon; and such, at best, the subject of necessity must be; this is vanity, conceit, and unreasonableness.

§ 12. *As it allows of will and character in us, so it may in our Author.*

But this is not all. For we find within ourselves a will, and are conscious of a character. Now if this, in us, be reconcilable with fate, it is reconcilable with it, in the Author of nature. And besides, natural government and final causes imply a character and a will in the Governor and Designer;[c] a will concerning the creatures whom he governs. The Author

[c] By *will* and *character* is meant [1] that, which, in speaking of men, we should express, not only by these words, but also by the words *temper, taste, dispositions, practical principles, that whole frame of mind, from whence we act in one manner rather than another*.

---

[1] Not that each of the δυνάμεις he proceeds to mention is a synonym for character or for will; but that, as powers contributing to determine action, they are included in the phrase 'will and character' from which action immediately springs.

of nature then being certainly of some character or other, notwithstanding necessity; it is evident this necessity is as reconcilable with the particular character of benevolence, veracity, and justice in him, which attributes are the foundation of religion, as with any other character: since we find this necessity no more hinders *men* from being benevolent, than cruel; true, than faithless; just, than unjust; or if the fatalist pleases, what we call unjust. For it is said indeed, that what, upon supposition of freedom, would be just punishment; upon supposition of necessity, becomes manifestly unjust: because it is punishment inflicted for doing that which persons could not avoid doing. As if the necessity, which is supposed to destroy the injustice of murder, for instance, would not also destroy the injustice of punishing it. However, as little to the purpose as this objection is in itself, it is very much to the purpose to observe from it, how the notions of justice and injustice remain, even whilst we endeavour to suppose them removed; how they force themselves upon the mind, even whilst we are making suppositions destructive of them: for there is not, perhaps, a man in the world, but would be ready to make this objection at first thought.

§ 13. *It leaves intact the relation of God to veracity and justice,*

But though it is most evident, that universal necessity, if it be reconcilable with any thing, is reconcilable with that character in the Author of nature, which is the foundation of religion; 'Yet, does it not plainly destroy the proof, that he is of that character, and consequently the proof of religion?' By no means. For we find, that happiness and misery are not our fate, in any such sense as not to be the consequences of our behaviour; but that they are the consequences of it.[d] We find God exercises the same kind of govern-

[d] Chap. ii.

ment over us, with that, which a father exercises over his children, and a civil magistrate over his subjects. Now, whatever becomes of abstract questions concerning liberty and necessity, it evidently appears to us, that veracity and justice must be the natural rule and measure of exercising this authority or government, to a Being who can have no competitions or interfering of interests, with his creatures and his subjects.

§ 14. *And all that shows his government to correspond with our nature.*

But as the doctrine of liberty, though we experience its truth, may be perplexed with difficulties, which run up into the most abstruse of all speculations; and as the opinion of necessity seems to be the very basis, upon which infidelity grounds itself; it may be of some use to offer a more particular proof of the obligations of religion, which may distinctly be shown not to be destroyed by this opinion.

The proof from final causes of an intelligent Author of nature is not affected by the opinion of necessity; supposing necessity a thing possible in itself, and reconcilable with the constitution of things.[e] And it is a matter of fact, independent on this or any other speculation, that he governs the world by the method of rewards and punishments:[f] and also that he hath given us a moral faculty, by which we distinguish between actions, and approve some as virtuous and of good desert, and disapprove others as vicious and of ill desert.[g] Now this moral discernment implies, in the notion of it, a rule of action, and a rule of a very peculiar kind: for it carries in it authority and a right of direction; authority in such a sense, as that we cannot depart from it without being self-condemned.[h] And that the dictates of this moral faculty, which are by nature a rule to us, are moreover the laws of God,

[e] *Sup.* §§ 1, 2.   [f] Chap. ii.   [g] Dissert. II.
[h] Serm. ii. at the Rolls.

laws in a sense including sanctions; may be thus proved. Consciousness of a rule or guide of action, in creatures who are capable of considering it as given them by their Maker, not only raises immediately a sense of duty, but also a sense of security in following it, and of danger in deviating from it. A direction of the Author of nature, given to creatures capable of looking upon it as such, is plainly a command from him: and a command from him necessarily includes in it, at least, an implicit promise in case of obedience, or threatening in case of disobedience. But then the sense or perception of good and ill desert,[1] which is contained in the moral discernment, renders the sanction explicit, and makes it appear, as one may say, expressed. For since his method of government is to reward and punish actions, his having annexed to some actions an inseparable sense of good desert, and to others of ill, this surely amounts to declaring, upon whom his punishments shall be inflicted, and his rewards be bestowed. For he must have given us this discernment and sense of things, as a presentiment of what is to be hereafter: that is, by way of information beforehand, what we are finally to expect in his world.

§ 15. *As then God governs, we infer the duty of worship to him.*

There is then most evident ground to think, that the government of God, upon the whole, will be found to correspond to the nature which he has given us: and that in the upshot and issue of things, happiness and misery shall, in fact and event, be made to follow virtue and vice respectively; as he has already, in so peculiar a manner, associated the ideas of them in our minds. And from hence might easily be deduced the obligations of religious worship, were it only to be considered as a means of preserving upon our minds a sense of this moral government of God, and securing

[1] Dissert. II.

our obedience to it: which yet is an extremely imperfect view of that most important duty.

§ 16. *Against this general proof, necessity has nothing to say.*

Now I say, no objection from necessity can lie against this general proof of religion. None against the proposition reasoned upon, that we have such a moral faculty and discernment; because this is a mere matter of fact, a thing of experience, that human kind is thus constituted: none against the conclusion; because it is immediate and wholly from this fact. For the conclusion, that God will finally reward the righteous and punish the wicked, is not here drawn, from its appearing to us fit [k] that *he should;* but from its appearing, that he has told us, *he will.* And this he hath certainly told us, in the promise and threatening, which it hath been observed the notion of a command implies, and the sense of good and ill desert which he has given us, more distinctly expresses. And this reasoning from fact is confirmed, and in some degree even verified, by other facts; by the natural tenden-

---

[k] However, I am far from intending to deny, that the will of God is determined, by what is fit, by the right and reason of the case; though one chooses to decline matters of such abstract speculation, and to speak with caution when one does speak of them. But if it be intelligible to say, that *it is fit and reasonable for every one to consult his own happiness*, then *fitness of action, or the right and reason of the case*, is an intelligible manner of speaking. And it seems as inconceivable, to suppose God to approve one course of action, or one end, preferably to another, which yet his acting at all from design implies that he does, without supposing somewhat prior in that end, to be the ground of the preference; as to suppose him to discern an abstract proposition to be true, without supposing somewhat prior in it, to be the ground of the discernment. It doth not therefore appear, that moral right is any more relative to perception, than abstract truth is: or that it is any more improper, to speak of the fitness and rightness of actions and ends, as founded in the nature of things, than to speak of abstract truth, as thus founded.

The will of God is determined by what is fit.

cies of virtue and of vice;[1] and by this, that God, in the natural course of his providence, punishes vicious actions as mischievous to society; and also vicious actions as such in the strictest sense.[m] So that the general proof of religion is unanswerably real, even upon the wild supposition which we are arguing upon.

§ 17. *Nor against the evidence* ab extra *afforded by long duration.*

It must likewise be observed further, that natural religion hath, besides this, an external evidence; which the doctrine of necessity, if it could be true, would not affect. For suppose a person, by the observations and reasoning above, or by any other, convinced of the truth of religion; that there is a God, who made the world, who is the moral Governor and Judge of mankind, and will upon the whole deal with every one according to his works: I say, suppose a person convinced of this by reason; but to know nothing at all of antiquity, or the present state of mankind. It would be natural for such an one to be inquisitive, what was the history of this system of doctrine; at what time, and in what manner, it came first into the world; and whether it were believed by any considerable part of it. And were he upon inquiry to find, that a particular person, in a late age, first of all proposed it, as a deduction of reason, and that mankind were before wholly ignorant of it: then, though its evidence from reason would remain, there would be no additional probability of its truth, from the account of its discovery. But instead of this being the fact of the case, on the contrary, he would find, what could not but afford him a very strong confirmation of its truth: First, That somewhat of this system, with more or fewer additions and alterations, hath been professed in all ages and countries, of which we have any certain information relating to this matter. Secondly, That it is certain historical fact, so far as

[1] *Sup.* chap. iii. §§ 22–24. [m] *Sup.* chap. iii. §§ 11–13.

we can trace things up, that this whole system of belief, that there is one God, the Creator and moral Governor of the world, and that mankind is in a state of religion, was received in the first ages.

§ 18. *Which began with a primitive revelation.*[1]

And Thirdly, That as there is no hint or intimation in history, that this system was first reasoned out; so there is no express historical or traditional evidence, as ancient as history, that it was taught first by revelation. Now these things must be allowed to be of great weight. The first of them, general consent, shows this system to be conformable to the common sense of mankind. The second, namely, that religion was believed in the first ages of the world, especially as it does not appear that there were then any superstitious or false additions to it, cannot but be a further confirmation of its truth. For it is a proof of this alternative: either that it came into the world by revelation; or that it is natural, obvious, and forces itself upon the mind. The former of these is the conclusion of learned men. And whoever will consider, how unapt for speculation rude and uncultivated minds are, will, perhaps from hence alone, be strongly inclined to believe it the truth. And as it is shown in the second part [n] of this Treatise, that there is nothing of such peculiar presumption against a revelation in the beginning of the world, as there is supposed to be against subsequent ones: a sceptic could not, I think, give any account, which would appear more probable even to himself, of the early pretences to revelation; than by supposing some real original one, from whence they were copied.[2] And the third thing above mentioned,

---

[n] Part II. chap. ii.

[1] On the origin of natural religion comp. II. ii. 10.

[2] Unless the sceptic (supposed to be a theist) held it to be impossible for the Creator to find any means beyond what external nature supplies for conveying his will to

that there is express historical or traditional evidence as ancient as history, of the system of religion being taught mankind by revelation; this must be admitted as some degree of real proof, that it was so taught. For why should not the most ancient tradition be admitted, as some additional proof of a fact, against which there is no presumption? And this proof is mentioned here, because it has its weight to show, that religion came into the world by revelation, prior to all consideration of the proper authority of any book supposed to contain it; and even prior to all consideration, whether the revelation itself be uncorruptly handed down and related, or mixed and darkened with fables. Thus the historical account, which we have, of the origin of religion, taking in all circumstances, is a real confirmation of its truth, no way affected by the opinion of necessity. And the *external* evidence,[1] even of natural religion, is by no means inconsiderable.

§ 19. *Our perceptions, though faulty, are still our guides, and are not to be superseded by fashion.*

But it is carefully to be observed, and ought to be recollected after all proofs of virtue and religion, which are only general; that as speculative reason may be neglected, prejudiced, and deceived, so also may our moral understanding be impaired and perverted, and the dictates of it not impartially attended to. This indeed proves nothing against the reality of our speculative or practical faculties of perception; against their being intended by nature, to inform us in the theory of things, and instruct us how we are to behave, and what we are to expect in consequence of our

the minds of his creatures: or else held, as is now pretended by some, that all approaches to religion were made by innumerable slow and gradual steps, reaching, after this illimitable series, the idea of God: which is against all testimony concerning the earliest history of our race.

[1] *Videlicet*, that of history, monuments, and traditions; to which some reference has already been made.

§§ 19, 20] AS INFLUENCING PRACTICE

behaviour. Yet our liableness, in the degree we are liable, to prejudice and perversion, is a most serious admonition to us to be upon our guard, with respect to what is of such consequence, as our determinations concerning virtue and religion: and particularly not to take custom, and fashion, and slight notions of honour, or imaginations of present ease, use, and convenience to mankind, for the only moral rule.º

§ 20. *Suppose the fatalist to argue against religion that punishment of necessary action is incredible,*

The foregoing observations, drawn from the nature of the thing, and the history of religion, amount, when taken together, to a real practical proof of it, not to be confuted: such a proof as, considering the infinite importance of the thing, I apprehend, would be admitted fully sufficient, in reason, to influence the actions of men, who act upon thought and reflection; if it were admitted that there is no proof of the contrary. But it may be said: 'There are many probabilities, which cannot indeed be confuted, i.e. shown to be no probabilities, and yet may be overbalanced by greater probabilities on the other side; much more by demonstration. And there is no occasion to object against particular arguments alleged for an opinion, when the opinion itself may be clearly shown to be false, without meddling with such arguments at all, but leaving them just as they are.ᵖ Now the method of government by rewards and punishments, and especially rewarding and punishing good and ill desert as such respectively, must go upon supposition, that we are free and not necessary agents.[1] And it is incredible, that the Author

º Dissert. II.
ᵖ Pages 1, 10 [corresponding with Introd. §§ 1, 2, 14–16, in the present edition. I fail, however, to trace the reference intended by the author.—Ed.].

---

[1] Fitzgerald thinks it important to distinguish between the 'religious necessitarian,' who in regard to a particular

of nature should govern us upon a supposition as true, which he knows to be false; and therefore absurd to think, he will reward or punish us for our actions hereafter; especially that he will do it under the notion, that they are of good or ill desert.'

§ 21. *Necessary action is not punishable: but we have the experimental fact of moral government;*

Here then the matter is brought to a point. And the answer to all this is full, and not to be evaded: that the whole constitution and course of things, the whole analogy of Providence, shows beyond possibility of doubt, that the conclusion from this reasoning is false; wherever the fallacy lies. The doctrine of freedom indeed clearly shows where: in supposing ourselves necessary, when in truth we are free agents. But upon the supposition of necessity, the fallacy lies in taking for granted, that it is incredible necessary agents should be rewarded and punished. But that, somehow or other, the conclusion now mentioned is false, is most certain. For it is fact, that God does govern even brute creatures by the method of rewards and punishments, in the natural course of things. And men are rewarded and punished for their actions, punished for actions mischievous to society as being so, punished for vicious actions as such; by the natural instrumentality of each other, under the present conduct of Providence. Nay even the affection of gratitude, and the passion of resentment, and the rewards and punishments following from them, which in general are to be considered as natural, i.e. from the Author of nature; these rewards and punishments, being naturally q annexed to actions considered as implying

q Serm. viii. at the Rolls.

action denies that he could have willed otherwise, and the irreligious, who allows that there is a persuasion of our being free, though a false persuasion. But Butler's argument strikes alike both of these unfounded and mischievous opinions.

good intention and good desert, ill intention and ill desert; these natural rewards and punishments, I say, are as much a contradiction to the conclusion above, and show its falsehood, as a more exact and complete rewarding and punishing of good and ill desert as such.

§ 22. *Which consequently shows our actions not to be necessary.*

So that if it be incredible, that necessary agents should be thus rewarded and punished; then, men are not necessary but free; since it is matter of fact, that they are thus rewarded and punished. But if, on the contrary, which is the supposition we have been arguing upon, it be insisted, that men are necessary agents; then, there is nothing incredible in the further supposition of necessary agents being thus rewarded and punished: since we ourselves are thus dealt with.

§ 23. *So, as an opinion referable to practice, it is false.*

From the whole therefore it must follow, that a necessity supposed possible, and reconcilable with the constitution of things, does in no sort prove that the Author of Nature will not, nor destroy the proof that he will, finally and upon the whole, in his eternal government, render his creatures happy or miserable, by some means or other, as they behave well or ill. Or, to express this conclusion in words conformable to the title of the chapter, the analogy of nature shows us, that the opinion of necessity, considered as practical, is false. And if necessity, upon the supposition above mentioned, doth not destroy the proof of natural religion, it evidently makes no alteration in the proof of revealed.

§ 24. *But, if at peace with fact, it would be at peace with religion.*

From these things likewise we may learn, in what sense to understand that general assertion, that the opinion of necessity is essentially destructive of all religion. First, in a practical sense; that by this notion, atheistical men pretend to satisfy and encourage themselves in vice, and justify to others their disregard to all religion. And secondly, in the strictest sense; that it is a contradiction to the whole constitution of nature, and to what we may every moment experience in ourselves, and so overturns every thing.[1] But by no means is this assertion to be understood, as if necessity, supposing it could possibly be reconciled with the constitution of things and with what we experience, were not also reconcilable with religion: for upon this supposition, it demonstrably is so.

CHAPTER VII

OF THE GOVERNMENT OF GOD, CONSIDERED AS A SCHEME OR CONSTITUTION, IMPERFECTLY COMPREHENDED

§ 1. *Analogy proves the fact rather than the right of the divine government.*

THOUGH it be, as it cannot but be, acknowledged, that the analogy of nature gives a strong credibility to the general doctrine of religion, and to the several particular things contained in it, considered as so many matters of fact; and likewise that it shows this credibility not to be destroyed by any notions of necessity: yet still, objections may be insisted upon, against the wisdom, equity, and goodness of the divine government implied in the notion of religion, and against the method by which this government is conducted; to which objections analogy can be no direct answer.

[1] Some commentators on Butler hold that 'necessity' is admissible and just, in the sense of foreknowledge. So Angus and Chalmers. But he nowhere acknowledges such a sense: and surely as vision is a thing totally separate from causation, so is prevision: and it is a confusion of ideas to mix certainty with necessity.

For the credibility, or the certain truth, of a matter of fact, does not immediately prove any thing concerning the wisdom or goodness of it: and analogy can do no more, immediately or directly, than show such and such things to be true or credible, considered only as matters of fact.

§ 2. *Effects something, if showing it to be* (a) *a scheme,* (b) *imperfectly comprehended.*

But still, if, upon supposition of a moral constitution of nature and a moral government over it, analogy suggests and makes it credible that this government must be a scheme, system, or constitution of government, as distinguished from a number of single unconnected acts of distributive justice and goodness; and likewise, that it must be a scheme, so imperfectly comprehended, and of such a sort in other respects, as to afford a direct general answer to all objections against the justice and goodness of it: then analogy is, remotely, of great service in answering those objections; both by suggesting the answer, and showing it to be a credible one.

§ 3. *So much it effects.*

Now this, upon inquiry, will be found to be the case. For, First, Upon supposition that God exercises a moral government over the world, the analogy of his natural government suggests and makes it credible, that his moral government must be a scheme, quite beyond our comprehension: and this affords a general answer to all objections against the justice and goodness of it. And, Secondly, A more distinct observation of some particular things contained in God's scheme of natural government, the like things being supposed, by analogy, to be contained in his moral government, will further show, how little weight [1] is to be laid upon these objections.

[1] Compare Introd. § 17.

§ 4. *In both points the moral government is analogous to the natural.*

[I.] Upon supposition that God exercises a moral government over the world, the analogy of his natural government suggests and makes it credible, that his moral government must be a scheme, quite beyond our comprehension: and this affords a general answer to all objections against the justice and goodness of it. It is most obvious, analogy renders it highly credible, that, upon supposition of a moral government, it must be a scheme; for the world, and the whole natural government of it, appears to be so: to be a scheme, system, or constitution, whose parts correspond to each other, and to a whole; as really as any work of art, or as any particular model of a civil constitution and government. In this great scheme of the natural world, individuals have various peculiar relations to other individuals of their own species. And whole species are, we find, variously related to other species, upon this earth.

§ 5. *Earthly relations may extend beyond earth.*

Nor do we know, how much further these kinds of relations may extend.[1] And, as there is not any action or natural event, which we are acquainted with, so single and unconnected, as not to have a respect to some other actions and events: so possibly each of them, when it has not an immediate, may yet have a remote, natural relation to other actions and events, much beyond the compass of this present world. There seems indeed nothing, from whence we can so much

---

[1] *Inf.* viii. 1. It seems as if Butler's disposition to refer to portions of the universe outside this earth as possibly concerned in an earthly dispensation, may have been due to his considering the vastness and weight of the Divine Incarnation in relation to the smallness of this world, and possibly of its inhabitants, as compared with the immense range of creation at large.

as make a conjecture, whether all creatures, actions, and events, throughout the whole of nature, have relations to each other. But, as it is obvious, that all events have future unknown consequences; so if we trace any, as far as we can go, into what is connected with it, we shall find, that if such event were not connected with somewhat further in nature unknown to us, somewhat both past and present, such event could not possibly have been at all.

§ 6. *We cannot give an entire account of any one thing.*[1]

Nor can we give the whole account of any one thing whatever: of all its causes, ends, and necessary adjuncts; those adjuncts, I mean, without which it could not have been. By this most astonishing connection, these reciprocal correspondencies and mutual relations, every thing which we see in the course of nature is actually brought about. And things seemingly the most insignificant imaginable are perpetually observed to be necessary conditions to other things of the greatest importance: so that any one thing whatever may, for ought we know to the contrary, be a necessary condition to any other. The natural world then, and natural government of it, being such an incomprehensible scheme; so incomprehensible, that a man must, really in the literal sense, know nothing at all, who is not sensible of his ignorance in it: this immediately suggests, and strongly shows the credibility, that the moral world and government of it may be so too.

§ 7. *Natural government may be subservient to moral, and blent with it.*

Indeed the natural and moral constitution and government of the world are so connected, as to make

---

[1] Butler's views of human ignorance are set forth in Serm. xv, which deals professedly with the subject: much of it in the manner of the *Analogy*. See particularly Serm. xv. §§ 3–9, and 12 with its note.

up together but one scheme: and it is highly probable, that the first is formed and carried on merely in subserviency to the latter; as the vegetable world is for the animal, and organized bodies for minds. But the thing intended here is, without inquiring how far the administration of the natural world is subordinate to that of the moral, only to observe the credibility, that one should be analogous or similar to the other:

§ 8. *Each part of moral government may be subservient to other parts, or to the whole.*

That therefore every act of divine justice and goodness may be supposed to look much beyond itself, and its immediate object;[1] may have some reference to other parts of God's moral administration, and to a general moral plan: and that every circumstance of this his moral government may be adjusted beforehand with a view to the whole of it. Thus for example: the determined length of time, and the degrees and ways, in which virtue is to remain in a state of warfare and discipline, and in which wickedness is permitted to have its progress; the times appointed for the execution of justice; the appointed instruments of it; the kinds of rewards and punishments, and the manners of their distribution; all particular instances of divine justice and goodness, and every circumstance of them, may have such respects to each other, as to make up altogether a whole, connected and related in all its parts: a scheme or system, which is as properly one as the natural world is, and of the like kind.

§ 9. *Our ignorance of the whole precludes judgments upon the parts;*

And supposing this to be the case; it is most evident, that we are not competent judges of this scheme, from

[1] This is in fact proved by the proof of a *scheme*, since each part of a scheme necessarily has reference to the other parts.

the small parts of it which come within our view in the present life : and therefore no objections against any of these parts can be insisted upon by reasonable men.

§ 10. *And answers objections against Providence,*

This our ignorance, and the consequence here drawn from it, are universally acknowledged upon other occasions ; and though scarce denied, yet are universally forgot, when persons come to argue against religion. And it is not perhaps easy, even for the most reasonable men, always to bear in mind the degree of our ignorance, and make due allowances for it. Upon these accounts, it may not be useless to go on a little further, in order to show more distinctly, how just an answer our ignorance is, to objections against the scheme of Providence.

§ 11. *And would hold in the main even were there no scheme, or the scheme a defect.*

Suppose then a person boldly to assert, that the things complained of, the origin and continuance of evil, might easily have been prevented by repeated interpositions ; [a] interpositions so guarded and circumstanced, as would preclude all mischief arising from them ; or, if this were impracticable, that a scheme of government is itself an imperfection ; since more good might have been produced, without any scheme, system, or constitution at all, by continued single unrelated acts of distributive justice and goodness ; because these would have occasioned no irregularities. And further than this, it is presumed, the objections will not be carried. Yet the answer is obvious : that were these assertions true, still the observations above, concerning our ignorance in the scheme of divine government, and the consequence drawn from it, would hold, in great measure ; enough to vindicate religion, against all objections from the disorders of the present

[a] *Inf.* §§ 17–19.

state. Were these assertions true, yet the government of the world might be just and good notwithstanding; for, at the most, they would infer nothing more than that it might have been better.

§ 12. *Which are indeed but arbitrary untested assertions.*

But indeed they are mere arbitrary assertions: no man being sufficiently acquainted with the possibilities of things, to bring any proof of them, to the lowest degree of probability. For however possible what is asserted may seem; yet many instances may be alleged, in things much less out of our reach, of suppositions absolutely impossible, and reducible to the most palpable self-contradictions, which, not every one by any means would perceive to be such, nor perhaps any one at first sight suspect.

§ 13. *The answer may lie in some unknown relation, or impossibility.*

From these things, it is easy to see distinctly, how our ignorance, as it is the common, is really a satisfactory answer to all objections against the justice and goodness of Providence. If a man, contemplating any one providential dispensation, which had no relation to any others, should object, that he discerned in it a disregard to justice, or a deficiency of goodness; nothing would be less an answer to such objection, than our ignorance in other parts of Providence, or in the possibilities of things, no way related to what he was contemplating. But when we know not but the parts objected against may be relative to other parts unknown to us; and when we are unacquainted with what is, in the nature of the thing, practicable in the case before us; then our ignorance is a satisfactory answer: because, some unknown relation, or some unknown impossibility, may render what is objected against, just and good; nay good in the highest practicable degree.

§ 14. *Experience shows us ends are subserved by means we should think unlikely;*

[II.] And how little weight is to be laid upon such objections, will further appear, by a more distinct observation of some particular things contained in the natural government of God, the like to which may be supposed, from analogy, to be contained in his moral government.

First, As in the scheme of the natural world, no ends appear to be accomplished without means: so we find that means very undesirable, often conduce to bring about ends in such a measure desirable, as greatly to overbalance the disagreeableness of the means. And in cases where such means are conducive to such ends, it is not reason, but experience, which shows us, that they are thus conducive. Experience also shows many means to be conducive and necessary to accomplish ends, which means, before experience, we should have thought, would have had even a contrary tendency.

§ 15. *And such provisions of the moral scheme may be good, even indispensable.*

Now from these observations relating to the natural scheme of the world, the moral being supposed analogous to it, arises a great credibility, that the putting our misery in each other's power to the degree it is, and making men liable to vice to the degree we are; and in general, that those things which are objected against the moral scheme of Providence, may be, upon the whole, friendly and assistant to virtue, and productive of an overbalance of happiness: i.e. the things objected against may be means, by which an overbalance of good will, in the end, be found produced. And from the same observations, it appears to be no presumption against this, that we do not, if indeed we do not, see those means to have any such tendency; or that they seem to us to have a contrary one. Thus those things, which we call irregularities, may not be so at all: because they may be means of accomplishing wise and good ends more considerable. And it may be added, as above,[b] that they may also be the only means, by which these wise and good ends are capable of being accomplished.

§ 16. *Evils may work for good, though we might have been better without them.*[1]

After these observations it may be proper to add, in order to obviate an absurd and wicked conclusion from any of them, that though the constitution of our nature, from whence we are capable of vice and misery, may, as it undoubtedly does, contribute to the perfection and happiness of the world; and though the actual permission of evil may be beneficial to it: (i. e. it would have been more mischievous, not that a wicked person had himself abstained from his own wickedness, but that any one had forcibly prevented it, than that it was permitted:) yet notwithstanding, it might have been much better for the world, if this very evil had never been done. Nay, it is most clearly conceivable, that the very commission of wickedness may be benefi-

---

[b] *Sup.* § 13.

---

[1] Not that vice contributes, but that freedom of choice between good and evil contributes, to elevate our condition. Fitzgerald shows how Jonathan Edwards, overleaping all barriers, carries us into peril, teaching as follows:

(*a*) That no sensible man will declare it, for certain, to be impossible that it is best for the world that there should be such a thing as moral evil in it.

(*b*) That if so, God must choose it, and with a wise and holy choice.

(*c*) That men will sin *as sin*, which God does not.

But is it not rather true that men do not will sin as sin, but for the sake of obtaining enjoyment by it? The whole speculation, however, is on forbidden ground, useless as to results; and we see a pious man on the borders, at the least, of sheer impiety.

§§ 16-18] IMPERFECTLY COMPREHENDED 153

cial to the world, and yet, that it would be infinitely more beneficial for men to refrain from it.

§ 17. *Like those disorders which bring their own cure.*

For thus, in the wise and good constitution of the natural world, there are disorders which bring their own cures; diseases, which are themselves remedies. Many a man would have died, had it not been for the gout or a fever; yet it would be thought madness to assert, that sickness is a better or more perfect state than health; though the like, with regard to the moral world, has been asserted. But,

§ 18. *Natural government, worked under general laws, thus allows action with forethought.*

Secondly, The natural government of the world is carried on by general laws.[1] For this there may be wise and good reasons: the wisest and best, for ought we know to the contrary. And that there are such reasons, is suggested to our thoughts by the analogy of nature: by our being made to experience good ends to be accomplished, as indeed all the good which we enjoy is accomplished, by this means, that the laws, by which the world is governed, are general. For we have scarce any kind of enjoyments, but what we are, in some way or other, instrumental in procuring ourselves, by acting in a manner which we foresee likely to procure them: now this foresight could not be at all, were not the government of the world carried on by general laws. And though, for ought we know to the contrary, every single case may be, at length, found to have been provided for even by these: yet to prevent all irregularities, or remedy them as they arise, by the wisest and best general laws, may be impossible in the nature of things; as we see it is absolutely impossible in civil government.

[1] Comp. Berkeley, *Principles of Human Knowledge*, pp. 30, 31.

§ 19. *Irregular interpositions might do more harm than good.*

But then we are ready to think, that, the constitution of nature remaining as it is, and the course of things being permitted to go on, in other respects, as it does, there might be interpositions to prevent irregularities; though they could not have been prevented or remedied by any general laws. And there would indeed be reason to wish, which, by the way, is very different from a right to claim, that all irregularities were prevented or remedied by present interpositions, if these interpositions would have no other effect than this. But it is plain they would have some visible and immediate bad effects: for instance, they would encourage idleness and negligence; and they would render doubtful the natural rule of life, which is ascertained by this very thing, that the course of the world is carried on by general laws. And further, it is certain they would have distant effects, and very great ones too; by means of the wonderful connections before mentioned.[c] So that we cannot so much as guess, what would be the whole result of the interpositions desired. It may be said, any bad result might be prevented by further interpositions, whenever there was occasion for them: but this again is talking quite at random, and in the dark.[d] Upon the whole then, we see wise reasons, why the course of the world should be carried on by general laws, and good ends accomplished by this means: and, for ought we know, there may be the wisest reasons for it, and the best ends accomplished by it. We have no ground to believe, that all irregularities could be remedied as they arise, or could have been precluded, by general laws. We find that interpositions would produce evil, and prevent good: and, for ought we know, they would produce greater evil than they would prevent; and prevent greater good than they would produce. And if this be the case, then the not

[c] *Sup.* §§ 5–9.   [d] *Sup.* §§ 12, 13.

interposing is so far from being a ground of complaint, that it is an instance of goodness. This is intelligible and sufficient: and going further, seems beyond the utmost reach of our faculties.

§ 20. *Our ignorance, not being total, need not blind us to the positive proofs of religion.*[1]

But it may be said, that 'after all, these supposed impossibilities and relations are what we are unacquainted with; and we must judge of religion, as of other things, by what we do know, and look upon the rest as nothing: or however, that the answers here given to what is objected against Religion, may equally be made use of to invalidate the proof of it; since their stress lies so very much upon our ignorance.' But,

First, Though total ignorance in any matter does indeed equally destroy, or rather preclude, all proof concerning it, and objections against it; yet partial ignorance does not. For we may in any degree be convinced, that a person is of such a character, and consequently will pursue such ends; though we are greatly ignorant, what is the proper way of acting, in order the most effectually to obtain those ends: and in this case, objections against his manner of acting, as seemingly not conducive to obtain them, might be answered by our ignorance; though the proof that such ends were intended, might not at all be invalidated by it. Thus, the proof of religion is a proof of the moral character of God, and consequently that his government is moral, and that every one upon the whole shall receive according to his deserts; a proof that this is the designed end of his government. But we are not competent judges, what is the proper way of acting, in order the most effectually to accomplish this end.[e] Therefore our ignorance is an answer to objec-

* Introd. § 12.

---

[1] Our ignorance, being in the nature of a limitation, does not presumptively blind us within the range still permitted to us.

tions against the conduct of Providence, in permitting irregularities, as seeming contradictory to this end. Now, since it is so obvious, that our ignorance may be a satisfactory answer to objections against a thing, and yet not affect the proof of it; till it can be shown, it is frivolous to assert, that our ignorance invalidates the proof of religion, as it does the objections against it.

§ 21. *Were religion unknown, moral duties would remain*, (a) *as right*, (b) *as perhaps rewardable.*

Secondly, Suppose unknown impossibilities, and unknown relations, might justly be urged to invalidate the proof of religion, as well as to answer objections against it: and that in consequence of this, the proof of it were doubtful. Yet still, let the assertion be despised, or let it be ridiculed, it is undeniably true, that moral obligations would remain certain, though it were not certain what would, upon the whole, be the consequences of observing or violating them. For, these obligations arise immediately and necessarily from the judgment of our own mind, unless perverted, which we cannot violate without being self-condemned. And they would be certain too, from considerations of interest. For though it were doubtful, what will be the future consequences of virtue and vice; yet it is, however, credible, that they may have those consequences, which Religion teaches us they will: and this credibility is a certain [f] obligation in point of prudence, to abstain from all wickedness, and to live in the conscientious practice of all that is good. But,

§ 22. *Shows how ignorance, while answering objections, need not injure proofs.*[1]

Thirdly, The answers above given to the objections against Religion cannot equally be made use of to

[f] Introd. § 5; and Part II. ch. vi.

---

[1] That ignorance may be a plea valid to exclude objection

§§ 21-23] IMPERFECTLY COMPREHENDED   157

invalidate the proof of it. For, upon supposition that God exercises a moral government over the world, analogy does most strongly lead us to conclude, that this moral government must be a scheme, or constitution, beyond our comprehension. And a thousand particular analogies show us, that parts of such a scheme, from their relation to other parts, may conduce to accomplish ends, which we should have thought they had no tendency at all to accomplish: nay ends, which, before experience, we should have thought such parts were contradictory to, and had a tendency to prevent. And therefore all these analogies show, that the way of arguing made use of in objecting against religion is delusive: because they show it is not at all incredible, that, could we comprehend the whole, we should find the permission of the disorders objected against to, be consistent with justice and goodness; and even to be instances of them. Now this is not applicable to the proof of Religion, as it is to the objections against it; [g] and therefore cannot invalidate that proof, as it does these objections.[1]

§ 23. *The ignorance is such ignorance, as experience shows to disable in like cases.*

Lastly, From the observation now made, it is easy to see, that the answers above given to the objections

[g] Serm. at the Rolls, p. 312, 2nd ed.

without marring proof is almost self-evident: but in this section Butler further shows that the very things, which in ignorance we might condemn, may prove to be themselves actual goods, which would bring them to be not merely neutralised, but actual witnesses in favour.

[1] The objections are inadmissible because it is plain that the things objected to may not be bad, but even good; and the objection may be subverted, even reversed. But no similar observation applies to the matters which have been alleged in proof of religion.

The proofs may be fully known: whereas the disability of objection comes from this, that we know only in part, and that a very small part.

against Providence, though, in a general way of speaking, they may be said to be taken from our ignorance; yet are by no means taken merely from that, but from somewhat which analogy shows us concerning it. For analogy shows us positively, that our ignorance in the possibilities of things, and the various relations in nature, renders us incompetent judges, and leads us to false conclusions, in cases similar to this, in which we pretend to judge and to object. So that the things above insisted upon are not mere suppositions of unknown impossibilities and relations: but they are suggested to our thoughts, and even forced upon the observation of serious men, and rendered credible too, by the analogy of nature. And therefore, to take these things into the account, is to judge by experience and what we do know: and it is not judging so, to take no notice of them.

CHAPTER VIII

CONCLUSION

§ 1. *This scene of human life is* (a) *related to something beyond it,* (b) *progressive,* (c) *not fully comprehensible.*

THE observations of the last chapter lead us to consider this little scene of human life, in which we are so busily engaged, as having a reference, of some sort or other, to a much larger plan of things. Whether we are, any way, related to the more distant parts of the boundless universe, into which we are brought, is altogether uncertain. But it is evident, that the course of things, which comes within our view, is connected with somewhat past, present, and future, beyond it.[a] So that we are placed, as one may speak, in the middle of a scheme, not a fixed but a progressive one, every way incomprehensible: incomprehensible, in a

[a] *Sup.* ch. vii. §§ 5, 6.

manner equally, with respect to what has been, what now is, and what shall be hereafter. And this scheme cannot but contain in it somewhat as wonderful, and as much beyond our thought and conception,[b] as any thing in that of religion.

§ 2. *No escape found by denying an intelligent Author;*

For, will any man in his senses say, that it is less difficult to conceive, how the world came to be and to continue as it is, without, than with, an intelligent Author and Governor of it? Or, admitting an intelligent Governor of it, that there is some other rule of government more natural, and of easier conception, than that which we call moral? Indeed, without an intelligent Author and Governor of nature, no account at all can be given, how this universe, or the part of it particularly in which we are concerned, came to be, and the course of it to be carried on, as it is: nor any, of its general end and design, without a moral Governor of it. That there is an intelligent Author of nature, and natural Governor of the world, is a principle gone upon in the foregoing Treatise; as proved, and generally known and confessed to be proved.

§ 3. *Whose character and goodness give us an interest in his scheme.*

And the very notion of an intelligent Author of nature, proved by particular final causes, implies a will and a character.[c] Now, as our whole nature, the nature which he has given us, leads us to conclude his will and character to be moral, just, and good: so we can scarce in imagination conceive, what it can be otherwise. However, in consequence of this his will and character, whatever it be, he formed the universe as it is, and carries on the course of it as he does, rather than in any other manner; and has assigned to us, and to all living creatures, a part and a lot in it. Irra-

[b] See Part II. ch. ii.   [c] *Sup.* ch. vi. § 12.

tional creatures act this their part, and enjoy and undergo the pleasures and the pains allotted them, without any reflection. But one would think it impossible, that creatures endued with reason could avoid reflecting sometimes upon all this: reflecting, if not from whence we came, yet, at least, whither we are going; and what the mysterious scheme, in the midst of which we find ourselves, will, at length, come out and produce: a scheme in which it is certain we are highly interested, and in which we may be interested even beyond conception.

§ 4. *To presume extinction at death is* πολλαχῶς *irrational.*

For many things prove it palpably absurd to conclude, that we shall cease to be, at death. Particular analogies do most sensibly show us, that there is nothing to be thought strange, in our being to exist in another state of life. And that we are now living beings, affords a strong probability that we shall *continue* so; unless there be some positive ground, and there is none from reason or analogy, to think death will destroy us.[1] Were a persuasion of this kind ever so well grounded, there would, surely, be little reason to take pleasure in it. But indeed it can have no other ground, than some such imagination, as that of our gross bodies being ourselves;[2] which is contrary to experience. Experience too most clearly shows us the folly of concluding, from the body and the living agent affecting each other mutually, that the dissolution of the former is the destruction of the latter. And there are remarkable instances of their

---

[1] See I. i. 4.

[2] I.e. our whole selves: or ourselves so far as to determine the fate of the whole. Still the body of the Christian is a temple of the Holy Ghost (1 Cor. iii. 16; vi. 19). Butler would probably have distinguished between the body here mentioned, and the sensuous or 'gross' bodies which he denies to be 'ourselves.'

not affecting each other, which lead us to a contrary conclusion. The supposition then, which in all reason we are to go upon, is, that our living nature will *continue* after death.

§ 5. *Hence a scope for hope and fear in the future; which, like as in the present, may bear upon conduct.*

And it is infinitely unreasonable to form an institution of life, or to act, upon any other supposition. Now all expectation of immortality, whether more or less certain, opens an unbounded prospect to our hopes and our fears: since we see the constitution of nature is such, as to admit of misery as well as to be productive of happiness, and experience ourselves to partake of both in some degree; and since we cannot but know, what higher degrees of both we are capable of. And there is no presumption against believing further, that our future interest depends upon our present behaviour: for we see our present interest doth; and that the happiness and misery, which are naturally annexed to our actions, very frequently do not follow, till long after the actions are done, to which they are respectively annexed. So that were speculation to leave us uncertain, whether it were likely, that the Author of nature, in giving happiness and misery to his creatures, hath regard to their actions or not: yet, since we find by experience that he hath such regard, the whole sense of things which he has given us, plainly leads us, at once and without any elaborate inquiries, to think, that it may, indeed must, be to good actions chiefly that he hath annexed happiness, and to bad actions misery; or that he will, upon the whole, reward those who do well, and punish those who do evil.

§ 6. *Natural government has a moral element, leaning to virtue, operative in part,*

To confirm this from the constitution of the world, it has been observed, that some sort of moral government is necessarily implied in that natural government of God, which we experience ourselves under: that good and bad actions, at present, are naturally rewarded and punished, not only as beneficial and mischievous to society, but also as virtuous and vicious: and that there is, in the very nature of the thing, a tendency to their being rewarded and punished in a much higher degree than they are at present. And though this higher degree of distributive justice, which nature thus points out and leads towards, is prevented for a time from taking place: it is by obstacles, which the state of this world unhappily throws in its way, and which therefore are in their nature temporary. Now, as these things in the natural conduct of Providence are observable on the side of virtue; so there is nothing to be set against them on the side of vice. A moral scheme [1] of government then is visibly established, and, in some degree, carried into execution:

§ 7. *And, subject to risk and labour, promises an enlarged action in a future state.*

And this, together with the essential tendencies of virtue and vice duly considered, naturally raise in us an apprehension, that it will be carried on further towards perfection in a future state, and that every one shall there receive according to his deserts. And if this be so, then our future and general interest, under the moral government of God, is appointed to depend upon our behaviour; notwithstanding the difficulty, which this may occasion, of securing it, and the danger of losing it: just in the same manner as our temporal interest, under his natural government, is appointed to depend upon our behaviour; notwithstanding the like difficulty and danger. For, from our original constitution, and that of the world which we inhabit, we are naturally trusted with ourselves; with our own conduct and our own interest. And from the same constitution of nature, especially joined with that

[1] See *sup.* iii. 4, 5.

course of things which is owing to men, we have temptations to be unfaithful in this trust; to forfeit this interest, to neglect it, and run ourselves into misery and ruin. From these temptations arise the difficulties of behaving so as to secure our temporal interest, and the hazard of behaving so as to miscarry in it. There is therefore nothing incredible in supposing there may be the like difficulty and hazard with regard to that chief and final good, which religion lays before us.

§ 8. *We can partly give the why of our position; but not fully.*

Indeed the whole account, how it came to pass that we were placed in such a condition as this, must be beyond our comprehension. But it is in part accounted for by what religion teaches us, that the character of virtue and piety must be a necessary qualification for a future state of security and happiness, under the moral government of God; in like manner, as some certain qualifications or other are necessary for every particular condition of life, under his natural government: and that the present state was intended to be a school of discipline, for improving in ourselves that character.

§ 9. *We observe an intention for our improvement.*

Now this intention of nature is rendered highly credible by observing; that we are plainly made for improvement of all kinds: that it is a general appointment of Providence, that we cultivate practical principles, and form within ourselves habits of action, in order to become fit for what we were wholly unfit for before: that in particular, childhood and youth is naturally appointed to be a state of discipline for mature age: and that the present world is peculiarly fitted for a state of moral discipline.

§ 10. *Fatalism is disabled from objecting.*

And, whereas objections are urged against the whole notion of moral government and a probation-state, from the opinion of necessity; it has been shown, that God has given us the evidence, as it were, of experience, that all objections against religion, on this head, are vain and delusive.

§ 11. *Natural government is a buttress to moral.*

He has also, in his natural government, suggested an answer to all our short-sighted objections, against the equity and goodness of his moral government: and in general he has exemplified to us the latter by the former.

§ 12. *Hence we are bound to self-discipline and piety.*

These things, which, it is to be remembered, are matters of fact, ought, in all common sense, to awaken mankind; to induce them to consider in earnest their condition, and what they have to do. It is absurd, absurd to the degree of being ridiculous, if the subject were not of so serious a kind, for men to think themselves secure in a vicious life; or even in that immoral thoughtlessness, which far the greatest part of them are fallen into. And the credibility of religion, arising from experience and facts here considered, is fully sufficient, in reason, to engage them to live in the general practice of all virtue and piety; under the serious apprehension, though it should be mixed with some doubt,[d] of a righteous administration established in nature, and a future judgment in consequence of it: especially when we consider, how very questionable it is, whether any thing at all can be gained by vice;[e] how unquestionably little, as well as precarious, the pleasures and profits of it are at the best; and how soon they must be parted with at the longest.[1] For,

[d] Part II. ch. vi.   [e] *Sup.* ch. iii. §§ 5–7.

---

[1] Argued more at length in Serm. iii. on Human Nature, §§ 9–11.

in the deliberations of reason, concerning what we are to pursue and what to avoid, as temptations to any thing from mere passion are supposed out of the case: so inducements to vice, from cool expectations of pleasure and interest so small and uncertain and short, are really so insignificant, as, in the view of reason, to be almost nothing in themselves; and in comparison with the importance of religion, they quite disappear and are lost.

§ 13. *Temporal regards, adverse to vice ; coincide with virtue.*

Mere passion indeed may be alleged, though not as a reason, yet as an excuse, for a vicious course of life. And how sorry an excuse it is, will be manifest by observing, that we are placed in a condition, in which we are unavoidably inured to govern our passions, by being necessitated to govern them; and to lay ourselves under the same kind of restraints, and as great ones too, from temporal regards, as virtue and piety, in the ordinary course of things, require. The plea of ungovernable passion then, on the side of vice, is the poorest of all things: for it is no reason, and but a poor excuse.

§ 14. *Religious proofs are religious motives.*

But the proper motives to religion are the proper proofs of it, from our moral nature, from the presages of conscience, and our natural apprehension of God under the character of a righteous Governor and Judge; a nature and conscience and apprehension given us by him: and from the confirmation of the dictates of reason, by *life and immortality brought to light by the Gospel ; and the wrath of God revealed from heaven against all ungodliness and unrighteousness of men.*

THE END OF THE FIRST PART.

THE ANALOGY OF RELIGION

TO THE
CONSTITUTION AND COURSE OF NATURE

PART II
OF REVEALED RELIGION

CHAPTER I

OF THE IMPORTANCE OF CHRISTIANITY

§ 1. *A Revelation was* (a) *required,* (b) *serviceable.*

SOME persons, upon pretence of the sufficiency of the light of nature, avowedly reject all revelation, as, in its very notion, incredible, and what must be fictitious. And indeed it is certain, no revelation would have been given, had the light of nature been sufficient in such a sense, as to render one not wanting and useless. But no man, in seriousness and simplicity of mind, can possibly think it so, who considers the state of religion in the heathen world before revelation, and its present state in those places which have borrowed no light from it: particularly the doubtfulness of some of the greatest men, concerning things of the utmost importance, as well as the natural inattention and ignorance of mankind in general. It is impossible to say, who would have been able to have reasoned out that whole system, which we call natural religion, in its genuine simplicity, clear of superstition: but there is certainly no ground to affirm that the generality could.[1] If they

---

[1] For the origin of natural religion see *sup.* I. vi. 18, and *inf.* ii. 10.

could, there is no sort of probability that they would. Admitting there were, they would highly want a standing admonition to remind them of it, and inculcate it upon them.[1] And further still, were they as much disposed to attend to religion, as the better sort of men are: yet even upon this supposition, there would be various occasions for supernatural instruction and assistance, and the greatest advantages might be afforded by them. So that to say revelation is a thing superfluous, what there was no need of, and what can be of no service, is, I think, to talk quite wildly and at random. Nor would it be more extravagant to affirm, that mankind is so entirely at ease in the present state, and life so completely happy, that it is a contradiction to suppose our condition capable of being, in any respect, better.

§ 2. *Weigh well Christianity as to* (a) *its importance,* (b) *its credibility, as added to natural religion.*

There are other persons, not to be ranked with these, who seem to be getting into a way of neglecting, and, as it were, overlooking revelation, as of small importance, provided natural religion be kept to. With little regard either to the evidence of the former, or to the objections against it, and even upon supposition of its truth: 'the only design of it,' say they, 'must be, to establish a belief of the moral system of nature, and to enforce the practice of natural piety and virtue. The belief and practice of these things were, perhaps,

---

[1] Fitzgerald refers, for the development of this argument, to Leland's *Advantage and Necessity of Christian Revelation; shown from the state of Religion in the ancient heathen world*. 2nd ed., Dublin, 1765. The ground of this necessity would lie partly in the sins and shortcomings of the individuals, partly in the degradation of the current religions of the heathen world, which had sunk far below the level of natural religion. Butler's propositions do not stand in need of particular illustrations, but such illustrations, infinite in detail, are of the deepest interest.

much promoted by the first publication of Christianity: but whether they are believed and practised, upon the evidence and motives of nature or of revelation, is no great matter.'[a] This way of considering revelation, though it is not the same with the former,[1] yet borders nearly upon it, and very much, at length, runs up into it: and requires to be particularly considered, with regard to the persons who seem to be getting into this way. The consideration of it will likewise further show the extravagance of the former opinion, and the truth of the observations in answer to it, just mentioned. And an inquiry into the importance of Christianity, cannot be an improper introduction to a Treatise concerning the credibility of it.

§ 3. *If its commands be divine, it is certain.*

Now if God has given a revelation to mankind, and commanded those things which are commanded in Christianity; it is evident, at first sight, that it cannot in any wise be an indifferent matter, whether we obey or disobey those commands: unless we are certainly assured, that we know all the reasons for them, and that all those reasons are now ceased, with regard to mankind in general, or to ourselves in particular. And it is absolutely impossible we can be assured of this. For our ignorance of these reasons proves nothing in the case: since the whole analogy of nature shows, what is indeed in itself evident, that there may be infinite reasons for things, with which we are not acquainted.

---

[a] Invenis multos——propterea nolle fieri Christianos, quia quasi sufficiunt sibi de bona vita sua. Bene vivere opus est, ait. Quid mihi praecepturus Christus? Ut bene vivam? Jam bene vivo. Quid mihi necessarius est Christus? Nullum homicidium, nullum furtum, nullam rapinam facio res alienas non concupisco, nullo adulterio contaminor. Nam inveniatur in vita mea aliquid quod reprehendatur, et qui reprehenderit faciat Christianum. *Aug. in Psal.* xxxi.

---

[1] Viz. (§ 1) 'to say revelation is a thing superfluous.'

§ 4. *It purports to teach religion, as* (a) *natural,* (b) *revealed.*

But the importance of Christianity will more distinctly appear, by considering it more distinctly: first, as a republication, and external institution, of natural or essential religion, adapted to the present circumstances of mankind, and intended to promote natural piety and virtue: and secondly, as containing an account of a dispensation of things not discoverable by reason, in consequence of which, several distinct precepts are enjoined us. For though natural religion is the foundation and principal part of Christianity, it is not in any sense the whole of it.

§ 5. *Viz. as a republication.*[1]

[I.] Christianity is a republication of natural religion. It instructs mankind in the moral system of the world: that it is the work of an infinitely perfect Being, and under his government; that virtue is his law; and that he will finally judge mankind in righteousness, and render to all according to their works, in a future state. And, which is very material, it teaches natural religion in its genuine simplicity; free from those superstitions, with which it was totally corrupted, and under which it was in a manner lost.

§ 6. *With fresh authority.*

Revelation is further, an authoritative publication of natural religion, and so affords the evidence of testimony for the truth of it. Indeed the miracles and prophecies recorded in scripture, were intended to prove a particular dispensation of Providence, the redemption of the world by the Messiah: but this does not hinder, but that they may also prove God's general providence over the world, as our moral Governor and Judge. And they evidently do prove it;

---

[1] See, on this republication, the first of the Six Sermons, § 3.

because this character of the Author of nature, is necessarily connected with and implied in that particular revealed dispensation of things: it is likewise continually taught expressly, and insisted upon, by those persons who wrought the miracles and delivered the prophecies. So that indeed natural religion seems as much proved by the scripture revelation, as it would have been, had the design of revelation been nothing else than to prove it.

§ 7. *For miracle (including prophecy) adds to credibility.*

But it may possibly be disputed, how far miracles can prove natural religion; and notable objections may be urged against this proof of it, considered as a matter of speculation: but considered as a practical thing, there can be none. For suppose a person to teach natural religion to a nation, who had lived in total ignorance or forgetfulness of it; and to declare he was commissioned by God so to do: suppose him in proof of his commission, to foretell things future, which no human foresight could have guessed at; to divide the sea with a word; feed great multitudes with bread from heaven; cure all manner of diseases; and raise the dead, even himself, to life: would not this give additional credibility to his teaching, a credibility beyond what that of a common man would have; and be an authoritative publication of the law of nature, i.e. a new proof of it? It would be a practical one, of the strongest kind, perhaps, which human creatures are capable of having given them. The law of Moses then, and the gospel of Christ, are authoritative publications of the religion of nature; they afford a proof of God's general providence, as moral Governor of the world, as well as of his particular dispensations of providence towards sinful creatures, revealed in the law and the gospel. As they are the only evidence of the latter, so they are an additional evidence of the former.

§ 8. *Has force in confirming a wavering mind.*

To show this further, let us suppose a man of the greatest and most improved capacity, who had never heard of revelation, convinced upon the whole, notwithstanding the disorders of the world, that it was under the direction and moral government of an infinitely perfect Being; but ready to question, whether he were not got beyond the reach of his faculties: suppose him brought, by this suspicion, into great danger of being carried away by the universal bad example of almost every one around him, who appeared to have no sense, no practical sense at least, of these things: and this, perhaps, would be as advantageous a situation with regard to religion, as nature alone ever placed any man in. What a confirmation now must it be to such a person, all at once, to find, that this moral system of things was revealed to mankind, in the name of that infinite Being, whom he had from principles of reason believed in; and that the publishers of the revelation proved their commission from him, by making it appear, that he had entrusted them with a power of suspending and changing the general laws of nature.

§ 9. *Eminently brings life and immortality to light.*

Nor must it by any means be omitted, for it is a thing of the utmost importance, that life and immortality are eminently brought to light by the gospel.[1] The great doctrines of a future state, the danger of a course of wickedness, and the efficacy of repentance, are not only confirmed in the gospel, but are taught,

---

[1] But if immortality were known already and independent of the gospel, it is only in a feeble and secondary sense that we can say of it (as e.g. of right and wrong) that it was brought to light by the gospel. See I. i. 31. Evidently Butler's position would be far stronger if, with many Christian writers of the earliest centuries, he had been liberated from the belief that the soul was indefeasibly immortal.

especially the last is, with a degree of light, to which that of nature is but darkness.

§ 10. *Miracle, taken up and recorded by the church, has advanced natural religion.*

Further: As Christianity served these ends and purposes, when it was first published, by the miraculous publication itself; so it was intended to serve the same purposes in future ages, by means of the settlement of a visible church: [1] of a society, distinguished from common ones, and from the rest of the world, by peculiar religious institutions; by an instituted method of instruction, and an instituted form of external religion. Miraculous powers were given to the first preachers of Christianity, in order to their introducing it into the world: a visible church was established, in order to continue it, and carry it on successively throughout all ages. Had Moses and the Prophets, Christ and his Apostles, only taught, and by miracles proved, religion to their contemporaries; the benefits of their instructions would have reached but to a small part of mankind.[2] Christianity must have been, in a great degree, sunk and forgot in a very few ages. To prevent this, appears to have been one reason why a visible church was instituted: to be, like a city upon an hill, a standing memorial to the world of the

---

[1] For the development of this idea see Sermon before the S.P.G., § 4.

[2] At first sight a doubt may be suggested as to the validity of this argument from the prolonged existence in modern times of sects who can hardly be said to have collectively a visible church, such as Congregationalists and Quakers. But the answer is, I think, conclusive. All the positive teaching of these bodies, upon which their vitality depends, is in truth included within the creeds of the universal church (with some small allowance perhaps for partial exaggerations). So that they are, so to speak, *in tow* of the visible church, carried onwards with and by it. At least, it supplies for them that portion of Christian evidence, in which they seem to be defective.

duty which we owe our Maker: to call men continually, both by example and instruction, to attend to it, and, by the form of religion, ever before their eyes, remind them of the reality: to be the repository of the oracles of God: to hold up the light of revelation in aid to that of nature, and propagate it throughout all generations to the end of the world—the light of revelation, considered here in no other view, than as designed to enforce natural religion. And in proportion as Christianity is professed and taught in the world, religion, natural or essential religion, is thus distinctly and advantageously laid before mankind, and brought again and again to their thoughts, as a matter of infinite importance.

§ 11. *Especially as a church implies positive teaching institutions.*

A visible church has also a further tendency to promote natural religion, as being an instituted method of education, originally intended to be of more peculiar advantage to those who would conform to it. For one end of the institution was, that by admonition and reproof, as well as instruction; by a general regular discipline, and public exercises of religion; *the body of Christ*, as the scripture speaks, should be *edified;* i. e. trained up in piety and virtue for a higher and better state. This settlement then appearing thus beneficial; tending in the nature of the thing to answer, and in some degree actually answering, those ends; it is to be remembered, that the very notion of it implies positive institutions; for the visibility of the church consists in them. Take away every thing of this kind, and you lose the very notion itself. So that if the things now mentioned are advantages, the reason and importance of positive institutions in general is most obvious; since without them these advantages could not be secured to the world. And it is mere idle wantonness, to insist upon knowing the reasons, why such particular ones were fixed upon rather than others.

§ 12. *Thus natural religion has had supernatural aid.*

The benefit arising from this supernatural assistance, which Christianity affords to natural religion, is what some persons are very slow in apprehending. And yet it is a thing distinct in itself, and a very plain obvious one. For will any in good earnest really say, that the bulk of mankind in the heathen world were in as advantageous a situation with regard to natural religion, as they are now amongst us: that it was laid before them, and enforced upon them, in a manner as distinct, and as much tending to influence their practice?

§ 13. *Despite perversions of Christianity,*

The objections against all this, from the perversion of Christianity, and from the supposition of its having had but little good influence, however innocently they may be proposed, yet cannot be insisted upon as conclusive, upon any principles, but such as lead to downright atheism: because the manifestation of the law of nature by reason, which, upon all principles of theism, must have been from God, has been perverted and rendered ineffectual in the same manner. It may indeed, I think, truly be said, that the good effects of Christianity have not been small; nor its supposed ill effects, any effects at all of it, properly speaking. Perhaps too the things themselves done have been aggravated; and if not, Christianity hath been often only a pretence; and the same evils in the main would have been done upon some other pretence. However, great and shocking as the corruptions and abuses of it have really been, they cannot be insisted upon as arguments against it, upon principles of theism.

§ 14. *Divine government leaves its provisions open to abuse.*

For one cannot proceed one step in reasoning upon natural religion, any more than upon Christianity, without laying it down as a first principle, that the dispensations of Providence are not to be judged of by their perversions, but by their genuine tendencies: not by what they do actually seem to effect, but by what they would effect if mankind did their part; that part which is justly put and left upon them. It is altogether as much the language of one as of the other; *He that is unjust, let him be unjust still: and he that is holy, let him be holy still.*[b] The light of reason does not, any more than that of revelation, force men to submit to its authority; both admonish them of what they ought to do and avoid, together with the consequences of each; and after this, leave them at full liberty to act just as they please, till the appointed time of judgment. Every moment's experience shows, that this is God's general rule of government.

§ 15. *As such a republication, Christianity has a title to be examined.*

To return then: Christianity being a promulgation of the law of nature; being moreover an authoritative promulgation of it; with new light, and other circumstances of peculiar advantage, adapted to the wants of mankind; these things fully show its importance. And it is to be observed further, that as the nature of the case requires, so all Christians are commanded to contribute, by their profession of Christianity, to preserve it in the world, and render it such a promulgation and enforcement of religion. For it is the very scheme of the gospel, that each Christian should, in his degree, contribute towards continuing and carrying it on: all by uniting in the public profession and external practice of Christianity; some by instructing, by having the oversight and taking care of this religious community, the church of God. Now this further shows the importance of Christianity; and, which is what I chiefly intend, its importance in a practical sense: or the high obligations we are under,

[b] Rev. xxii. 11.

to take it into our most serious consideration; and the danger there must necessarily be, not only in treating it despitefully, which I am not now speaking of, but in disregarding and neglecting it. For this is neglecting to do what is expressly enjoined us, for continuing those benefits to the world, and transmitting them down to future times. And all this holds, even though the only thing to be considered in Christianity, were its subserviency to natural religion. But,

§ 16. *Is also a new plan of recovery for a world in ruins.*

[II.] Christianity is to be considered in a further view: as containing an account of a dispensation of things, not at all discoverable by reason, in consequence of which several distinct precepts are enjoined us. Christianity is not only an external institution of natural religion, and a new promulgation of God's general providence, as righteous Governor and Judge of the world; but it contains also a revelation of a particular dispensation of Providence, carrying on by his Son and Spirit, for the recovery and salvation of mankind, who are represented, in scripture, to be in a state of ruin.

§ 17. *Revelation is especially of the Son and Spirit.*

And in consequence of this revelation being made, we are commanded *to be baptized,* not only *in the name of the Father,* but also, *of the Son, and of the Holy Ghost:* and other obligations of duty, unknown before, to the Son and the Holy Ghost, are revealed. Now the importance of these duties may be judged of, by observing that they arise, not from positive command merely, but also from the offices, which appear, from scripture, to belong to those divine persons in the gospel dispensation; or from the relations, which, we are there informed, they stand in to us. By reason is revealed the relation, which God the Father stands in to us. Hence arises the obligation of duty which we are under to him. In scripture are revealed the relations, which the Son and Holy Spirit stand in to us. Hence arise the obligations of duty, which we are under to them.

§ 18. *Hence baptism is triune.*

The truth of the case, as one may speak, in each of these three respects being admitted: that God is the Governor of the world, upon the evidence of reason; that Christ is the Mediator between God and man, and the Holy Ghost our Guide and Sanctifier, upon the evidence of revelation: the truth of the case, I say, in each of these respects being admitted; it is no more a question, why it should be commanded, that we be baptized in the name of the Son and of the Holy Ghost, than that we be baptized in the name of the Father. This matter seems to require to be more fully stated.[c]

§ 19. *Christianity has two parts, both essential:* (a) *inward,* (b) *outward.*

Let it be remembered then, that religion comes under the twofold consideration of internal and external: for the latter is as real a part of religion, of true religion as the former. Now when religion is considered under the first notion, as an inward principle, to be exerted in such and such inward acts of the mind and heart; the essence of natural religion may be said to consist in religious regards to *God the Father Almighty:* and the essence of revealed religion, as distinguished from natural, to consist in religious regards to *the Son,* and to *the Holy Ghost.* And the obligation we are under, of paying these religious regards to each of these divine persons respectively, arises from the respective relations which they each stand in to us. How these relations

---

[c] See *The Nature, Obligation, and Efficacy of the Christian Sacraments,* &c. [by Archdeacon Waterland, 1734), and Colliber, *Of revealed Religion,* as there quoted.

are made known, whether by reason or revelation, makes no alteration in the case: because the duties arise out of the relations themselves, not out of the manner in which we are informed of them.

§ 20. *Dictates religious regards to Son and Spirit.*

The Son and Spirit have each his proper office in that great dispensation of Providence, the redemption of the world; the one our Mediator, the other our Sanctifier. Does not then the duty of religious regards to both these divine persons, as immediately arise, to the view of reason, out of the very nature of these offices and relations; as the inward good-will and kind intention, which we owe to our fellow-creatures, arises out of the common relations between us and them? But it will be asked, 'What are the inward religious regards, appearing thus obviously due to the Son and Holy Spirit; as arising, not merely from command in scripture, but from the very nature of the revealed relations, which they stand in to us?' I answer, the religious regards of reverence, honour, love, trust, gratitude, fear, hope.

§ 21. *Form of the outward is governed by command.*

In what external manner this inward worship is to be expressed, is a matter of pure revealed command: as perhaps the external manner, in which God the Father is to be worshipped, may be more so, than we are ready to think: but the worship, the internal worship itself, to the Son and Holy Ghost, is no further matter of pure revealed command, than as the relations they stand in to us are matter of pure revelation: for the relations being known, the obligations to such internal worship are obligations of reason, arising out of those relations themselves. In short, the history of the gospel as immediately shows us the reason of these obligations, as it shows us the meaning of the words, Son and Holy Ghost.

§ 22. *Our relation to Christ is strictly moral, and under moral sanctions.*

If this account of the Christian religion be just; those persons who can speak lightly of it, as of little consequence, provided natural religion be kept to, plainly forget, that Christianity, even what is peculiarly so called, as distinguished from natural religion, has yet somewhat very important, even of a moral nature. For the office of our Lord being made known, and the relation he stands in to us, the obligation of religious regards to him is plainly moral, as much as charity to mankind is; since this obligation arises, before external command, immediately out of that his office and relation itself. Those persons appear to forget, that revelation is to be considered, as informing us of somewhat new, in the state of mankind, and in the government of the world: as acquainting us with some relations we stand in, which could not otherwise have been known. And these relations being real, (though before revelation we could be under no obligations from them, yet upon their being revealed,) there is no reason to think, but that neglect of behaving suitably to them will be attended with the same kind of consequences under God's government, as neglecting to behave suitably to any other relations made known to us by reason. And ignorance, whether unavoidable or voluntary, so far as we can possibly see, will just as much, and just as little, excuse in one case as in the other: the ignorance being supposed equally unavoidable, or equally voluntary, in both cases.

§ 23. *Disregard whereof may entail penalty in a natural way.*

If therefore Christ be indeed the Mediator between God and man, i. e. if Christianity be true; if he be indeed our Lord, our Saviour, and our God; no one can say, what may follow, not only the obstinate, but the careless disregard to him, in those high relations.

Nay no one can say, what may follow such disregard, even in the way of natural consequence.[d] For, as the natural consequences of vice in this life are doubtless to be considered as judicial punishments inflicted by God; so likewise, for ought we know, the judicial punishments of the future life may be, in a like way or a like sense, the natural consequence of vice:[e] of men's violating or disregarding the relations which God has placed them in here, and made known to them.

§ 24. *Same is true as to use of enjoined means of grace.*

Again: If mankind are corrupted and depraved in their moral character, and so are unfit for that state, which Christ is gone to prepare for his disciples; and if the assistance of God's Spirit be necessary to renew their nature, in the degree requisite to their being qualified for that state; all which is implied in the express, though figurative declaration, *Except a man be born of the Spirit, he cannot enter into the kingdom of God:*[f] supposing this, is it possible any serious person can think it a slight matter, whether or no he makes use of the means, expressly commanded by God, for obtaining this divine assistance? Especially since the whole analogy of nature shows, that we are not to expect any benefits without making use of the appointed means for obtaining or enjoying them. Now reason shows us nothing, of the particular immediate means of obtaining either temporal or spiritual benefits. This therefore we must learn, either from experience or revelation. And experience, the present case does not admit of.

§ 25. *Conclusion: that to treat Christianity with levity is wildly rash.*

The conclusion from all this evidently is, that, Christianity being supposed either true or credible, it

---

[d] *Sup.* I. i. 31.   [e] Chap. v.   [f] John iii. 5.

is unspeakable irreverence, and really the most presumptuous rashness, to treat it as a light matter. It can never justly be esteemed of little consequence, till it be positively supposed false. Nor do I know a higher and more important obligation which we are under, than that of examining most seriously into the evidence of it, supposing its credibility; and of embracing it, upon supposition of its truth.

§ 26. *Commands distinguished as* (a) *positive,* (b) *moral.*

The two following deductions may be proper to be added, in order to illustrate the foregoing observations, and to prevent their being mistaken.

First, Hence we may clearly see, where lies the distinction between what is positive and what is moral in religion. Moral *precepts* are precepts, the reasons of which we see: positive *precepts* are precepts, the reasons of which we do not see.[g] Moral *duties* arise out of the nature of the case itself, prior to external command. Positive *duties* do not arise out of the nature of the case, but from external command; nor would they be duties at all, were it not for such command, received from him whose creatures and subjects we are.

§ 27. *But the positive have a moral force; and may rest either on natural or revealed religion*

But the manner in which the nature of the case, or the fact of the relation, is made known, this doth not

[g] This is the distinction between moral and positive precepts considered respectively as such. But yet, *How the two* since the latter have somewhat of a moral nature, *agree, and* we may see the reason of them, considered in *differ.* this view. Moral and positive precepts are in some respects alike, in other respects different. So far as they are alike, we discern the reasons of both; so far as they are different, we discern the reasons of the former, but not of the latter. See *sup.* § 10 *sqq.* [But I do not see the relevancy of the reference.—ED.], and *inf.* § 27.

denominate any duty either positive or moral. That we be baptized in the name of the Father, is as much a positive duty, as that we be baptized in the name of the Son; because both arise equally from revealed command: though the relation which we stand in to God the Father is made known to us by reason; the relation we stand in to Christ, by revelation only. On the other hand, the dispensation of the gospel admitted, gratitude as immediately becomes due to Christ, from his being the voluntary minister of this dispensation, as it is due to God the Father, from his being the fountain of all good; though the first is made known to us by revelation only, the second by reason. Hence also we may see, and, for distinctness sake, it may be worth mentioning, that positive institutions come under a twofold consideration. They are either institutions founded on natural religion, as baptism in the name of the Father; though this has also a particular reference to the gospel dispensation, for it is in the name of God, as the Father of our Lord Jesus Christ: or they are external institutions founded on revealed religion; as baptism in the name of the Son, and of the Holy Ghost.

§ 28. *In principle they have a moral basis: but take the second place.*

Secondly, From the distinction between what is moral and what is positive in religion, appears the ground of that peculiar preference, which the scripture teaches us to be due to the former.

The reason of positive institutions in general is very obvious; though we should not see the reason, why such particular ones are pitched upon rather than others. Whoever therefore, instead of cavilling at words, will attend to the thing itself, may clearly see, that positive institutions in general, as distinguished from this or that particular one, have the nature of moral commands; since the reasons of them appear. Thus, for instance, the *external* worship of God is a moral duty, though no particular mode of it be so. Care then is to be taken, when a comparison is made between positive and moral duties, that they be compared no further than as they are different; no further than as the former are positive, or arise out of mere external command, the reasons of which we are not acquainted with; and as the latter are moral, or arise out of the apparent reason of the case, without such external command. Unless this caution be observed, we shall run into endless confusion.

§ 29. *In case of conflict, the moral precept prevails.*

Now this being premised, suppose two standing precepts enjoined by the same authority; that, in certain conjunctures, it is impossible to obey both; that the former is moral, i.e. a precept of which we see the reasons, and that they hold in the particular case before us; but that the latter is positive, i. e. a precept of which we do not see the reasons: it is indisputable that our obligations are to obey the former; because there is an apparent reason for this preference, and none against it. Further, positive institutions, I suppose all those which Christianity enjoins, are means to a moral end: and the end must be acknowledged more excellent than the means. Nor is observance of these institutions any religious obedience at all, or of any value, otherwise than as it proceeds from a moral principle. This seems to be the strict logical way of stating and determining this matter; but will, perhaps, be found less applicable to practice, than may be thought at first sight.

§ 30. *Has double title, from (a) scripture, (b) natural law.*

And therefore, in a more practical, though more lax way of consideration, and taking the words, *moral law* and *positive institutions*, in the popular sense; I add, that the whole moral law is as much matter of revealed command, as positive institutions are : for the scripture enjoins every moral virtue. In this respect then they are both upon a level. But the moral law is, moreover, written upon our hearts; interwoven into our very nature. And this is a plain intimation of the Author of it, which is to be preferred, when they interfere.

§ 31. *Men strive to substitute rite for virtue; but in vain.*

But there is not altogether so much necessity for the determination of this question, as some persons seem to think. Nor are we left to reason alone to determine it. For, first, Though mankind have, in all ages, been greatly prone to place their religion in peculiar positive rites, by way of equivalent for obedience to moral precepts; yet, without making any comparison at all between them, and consequently without determining which is to have the preference, the nature of the thing abundantly shows all notions of that kind to be utterly subversive of true religion : as they are, moreover, contrary to the whole general tenor of scripture; and likewise to the most express particular declarations of it, that nothing can render us accepted of God, without moral virtue. Secondly, Upon the occasion of mentioning together positive and moral duties, the scripture always puts the stress of religion upon the latter, and never upon the former : which, though no sort of allowance to neglect the former, when they do not interfere with the latter, yet is a plain intimation, that when they do, the latter are to be preferred.

§ 32. *Our Lord has settled the matter, by his teaching on the Sabbath.*

And further, as mankind are for placing the stress of their religion any where, rather than upon virtue; lest both the reason of the thing, and the general spirit of Christianity, appearing in the intimation now mentioned, should be ineffectual against this prevalent folly: our Lord himself, from whose command alone the obligation of positive institutions arises, has taken occasion to make the comparison between them and moral precepts; when the Pharisees censured him, for *eating with publicans and sinners;* and also when they censured his disciples, for *plucking the ears of corn on the Sabbath-day.* Upon this comparison, he has determined expressly, and in form, which shall have the preference when they interfere. And by delivering his authoritative determination in a proverbial manner of expression, he has made it general: *I will have mercy,*[1] *and not sacrifice.*[h] The propriety of the word *proverbial* is not the thing insisted upon: though I think the manner of speaking is to be called so. But that the manner of speaking very remarkably renders the determination general, is surely indisputable. For, had it, in the latter case, been said only, that God preferred mercy to the rigid observance of the Sabbath; even then, by parity of reason, most justly might we have argued, that he preferred mercy likewise, to the observance of other ritual institutions; and in general, moral duties, to positive ones. And thus the determination would have been general; though its being so were inferred and not expressed. But as the passage really stands in the gospel, it is much stronger. For the sense and the very literal words of our Lord's answer are as applicable to any other instance of a comparison, between positive and moral duties, as to this upon which they were spoken. And if, in case of competition, mercy is to be preferred to positive institutions, it will scarce be thought, that justice is to give place to them.

[h] Matt. ix. 13 and xii. 7.

---

[1] 'Obedience to positive command, it will be noticed, is often a more decisive test of religious character, than the practice of moral duties. The latter may spring from a principle of natural morality; the former, if not the result of hypocrisy or of mechanical habit, is an evidence of reverence for the divine will.' Angus.

§ 33. *Superiority of virtue to observance taught by the Old Testament.*

It is remarkable too, that, as the words are a quotation from the Old Testament, they are introduced, on both the forementioned occasions, with a declaration, that the Pharisees did not understand the meaning of them. This, I say, is very remarkable. For, since it is scarce possible, for the most ignorant person, not to understand the literal sense of the passage, in the prophet;[i] and since understanding the literal sense would not have prevented their *condemning the guiltless*;[k] it can hardly be doubted, that the thing which our Lord really intended in that declaration was, that the Pharisees had not learnt from it, as they might, wherein the *general* spirit of religion consists: that it consists in moral piety and virtue, as distinguished from forms, and ritual observances. However, it is certain we may learn this from his divine application of the passage, in the gospel.

§ 34. *The obligation to obey positive precepts is moral.*

But, as it is one of the peculiar weaknesses of human nature, when, upon a comparison of two things, one is found to be of greater importance than the other, to consider this other as of scarce any importance at all: it is highly necessary that we remind ourselves, how great presumption it is, to make light of any institutions of divine appointment; that our obligations to obey all God's commands whatever are absolute and indispensable; and that commands merely positive, admitted to be from him, lay us under a moral obligation to obey them: an obligation moral in the strictest and most proper sense.

---

[i] Hos. vi.   [k] See Matt. xii. 7.

§ 35. *We are to accept the sense of scripture, not import it.*

To these things I cannot forbear adding, that the account now given of Christianity most strongly shows and enforces upon us the obligation of searching the scriptures, in order to see, what the scheme of revelation really is; instead of determining beforehand, from reason, what the scheme of it must be.[1] Indeed if in revelation there be found any passages, the seeming meaning of which is contrary to natural religion; we may most certainly conclude, such seeming meaning not to be the real one. But it is not any degree of a presumption against an interpretation of scripture, that such interpretation contains a doctrine, which the light of nature cannot discover;[m] or a precept, which the law of nature does not oblige to.

CHAPTER II

OF THE SUPPOSED PRESUMPTION AGAINST A REVELATION, CONSIDERED AS MIRACULOUS

§ 1. *Will deal* (a) *with presumption,* (b) *with positive evidence.*

HAVING shown the importance of the Christian revelation, and the obligations which we are under seriously to attend to it, upon supposition of its truth, or its credibility: the next thing in order, is to consider the supposed presumptions against revelation in general; which shall be the subject of this chapter: and the objections against the Christian in particular; which shall be the subject of some following ones.[a] For it seems the most natural method, to remove these prejudices against Christianity, before we proceed to

[1] See chap. iii.   [m] *Inf.* ii. 3,4.   [a] Chaps. iii, iv, v, vi.

the consideration of the positive evidence for it, and the objections against that evidence.[b]

§ 2. *He discusses under protest a plea he deems frivolous.*

It is, I think, commonly supposed, that there is some peculiar presumption, from the analogy of nature, against the Christian scheme of things; at least against miracles: so as that stronger evidence is necessary to prove the truth and reality of them, than would be sufficient to convince us of other events, or matters of fact. Indeed the consideration of this supposed presumption cannot but be thought very insignificant, by many persons. Yet, as it belongs to the subject of this Treatise; so it may tend to open the mind, and remove some prejudices: however needless the consideration of it be, upon its own account.

§ 3. *Nature sustains no presumption against the gospel idea,*

[I.] I find no appearance of a presumption, from the analogy of nature, against the general scheme of Christianity, that God created and invisibly governs the world by Jesus Christ; and by him also will hereafter judge it in righteousness, i.e. render to every one according to his works: and that good men are under the secret influence of his Spirit. Whether these things are, or are not, to be called miraculous, is, perhaps, only a question about words; or however, is of no moment in the case. If the analogy of nature raises any presumption against this general scheme of Christianity, it must be, either because it is not discoverable by reason or experience; or else, because it is unlike that course of nature, which is. But analogy raises no presumption against the truth of this scheme, upon either of these accounts.

[b] Chap. vii.

§ 4. (a) *Because it is undiscoverable ; like so much else ;*

First, There is no presumption, from analogy, against the truth of it, upon account of its not being discoverable by reason or experience. For suppose one who never heard of revelation, of the most improved understanding, and acquainted with our whole system of natural philosophy and natural religion : such an one could not but be sensible, that it was but a very small part of the natural and moral system of the universe, which he was acquainted with. He could not but be sensible, that there must be innumerable things, in the dispensations of Providence past, in the invisible government over the world at present carrying on, and in what is to come ; of which he was wholly ignorant,[c] and which could not be discovered without revelation. Whether the scheme of nature be, in the strictest sense, infinite or not ; it is evidently vast, even beyond all possible imagination. And doubtless that part of it, which is opened to our view, is but as a point, in comparison of the whole plan of Providence, reaching throughout eternity past and future ; in comparison of what is even now going on in the remote parts of the boundless universe ; nay in comparison of the whole scheme of this world. And therefore, that things lie beyond the natural reach of our faculties, is no sort of presumption against the truth and reality of them : because it is certain, there are innumerable things, in the constitution and government of the universe, which are thus beyond the natural reach of our faculties.

§ 5. *Or (b) because not always like nature : which is not uniform ; nor is moral government.*

Secondly, Analogy raises no presumption against any of the things contained in this general doctrine of scripture now mentioned, upon account of their being unlike the known course of nature. For there is no pre-

---

[c] *Sup.* I. vii. 2–4.

sumption at all from analogy, that the *whole* course of things, or divine government, naturally unknown to us, and *every* thing in it, is like to any thing in that which is known; and therefore no peculiar presumption against any thing [1] in the former, upon account of its being unlike to any thing in the latter. And in the constitution and natural government of the world, as well as in the moral government of it, we see things, in a great degree, unlike one another: and therefore ought not to wonder at such unlikeness between things visible and invisible. However, the scheme of Christianity is by no means entirely unlike the scheme of nature; as will appear in the following part of this Treatise.

§ 6. *So that analogy supplies no adverse presumption.* [2]

The notion of a miracle, considered as a proof of a divine mission, has been stated with great exactness by divines; and is, I think, sufficiently understood by every one. There are also invisible miracles, the Incarnation of Christ, for instance, which, being secret, cannot be alleged as a proof of such a mission; but

[1] That is, against any particular thing. For, were there an universal or general unlikeness, it would contradict the purpose of this work as declared in the title.

[2] Butler's argument is not concerned with proving the Christian miracles, but only with showing that the fact of their having been used to prove Christianity raises no presumption against its truth.

The definition of a miracle had not been perhaps as closely examined in mediaeval, or even in Butler's days, as in our own. *Aliquid dicitur esse miraculum, quod fit praeter ordinem totius naturae creatae.* So Aquinas, *Summa*, I. Qu. cx. Art. 4. What seems the essence is perhaps this, that the act should reasonably convey to the human mind the belief that it could only be done by an exertion of the divine power above and beyond the settled order of things. It is conceivable that a miracle of one age might, owing to the advance of natural knowledge and resource, cease to be a miracle for another.

require themselves to be proved by visible [1] miracles. Revelation itself too is miraculous; and miracles are the proof of it: and the supposed presumption against these shall presently be considered. All which I have been observing here is, that, whether we choose to call every thing in the dispensations of Providence, not discoverable without revelation, nor like the known course of things, miraculous; and whether the general Christian dispensation now mentioned is to be called so, or not; the foregoing observations seem certainly to show, that there is no presumption against it from the analogy of nature.

§ 7. *Was there a primaeval revelation? is a question of common fact,*

[II.] There is no presumption, from analogy, against some operations, which we should now call miraculous; particularly none against a revelation at the beginning of the world: nothing of such presumption against it, as is supposed to be implied or expressed in the word *miraculous*. For a miracle, in its very notion, is relative to a course of nature; and implies somewhat different from it, considered as being so. Now, either there was no course of nature at the time which we are speaking of: or if there were, we are not acquainted what the course of nature is, upon the first peopling of worlds. And therefore the question, whether mankind had a revelation made to them at that time, is to be considered, not as a question concerning a miracle but as a common question of fact. And we have the like reason, be it more or less, to admit the report of tradition, concerning this question, and concerning common matters of fact of the same antiquity; for instance, what part of the earth was first peopled.

---

[1] Evidently meaning sensible: cf. the miracle of the 'rushing mighty wind,' and the speech in tongues previously unknown to the speaker (Acts ii. 4) on the day of Pentecost, and thereafter.

§ 8. *Certainly foreign to the present course of nature.*

Or thus: When mankind was first placed in this state, there was a power exerted, totally different from the present course of nature. Now, whether this power, thus wholly different from the present course of nature, for we cannot properly apply to it the word *miraculous*;[1] whether this power stopped immediately after it had made man, or went on, and exerted itself further in giving him a revelation, is a question of the same kind, as whether an ordinary power exerted itself in such a particular degree and manner, or not.

§ 9. *Our Lord's miracles not a question of degree.*

Or suppose the power exerted in the formation of the world be considered as miraculous, or rather, be called by that name; the case will not be different: since it must be acknowledged, that such a power was exerted. For supposing it acknowledged, that our Saviour spent some years in a course of working miracles: there is no more presumption, worth mentioning, against his having exerted this miraculous power, in a certain degree greater, than in a certain degree less; in one or two more instances, than in one or two fewer; in this, than in another manner.

It is evident then, that there can be no peculiar presumption, from the analogy of nature, against supposing a revelation, when man was first placed upon the earth.

§ 10. *Upon the evidences, religion first came by revelation. Inferred doubly.*[2]

Add, that there does not appear the least intimation in history or tradition, that religion was first reasoned

---

[1] The following up of creation by revelation can hardly be called miraculous: for there was not at the time, so far as known to us, and perhaps hardly could be, any 'course of nature' from which it could be (see § 7) 'somewhat different.'

[2] On the origin of natural religion, comp. I. vi. 18.

out: but the whole of history and tradition makes for the other side, that it came into the world by revelation. Indeed the state of religion in the first ages, of which we have any account, seems to suppose and imply, that this was the original of it amongst mankind. And these reflections together, without taking in the peculiar authority of scripture, amount to real and a very material degree of evidence, that there was a revelation at the beginning of the world. Now this, as it is a confirmation of natural religion, and therefore mentioned in the former part of this Treatise:[d] so likewise it has a tendency to remove any prejudices against a subsequent revelation.

§ 11. *Strong presumptions lie against many known facts.*

[III.] But still it may be objected, that there is some peculiar presumption, from analogy, against miracles; particularly against revelation, after the settlement and during the continuance of a course of nature.

Now with regard to this supposed presumption, it is to be observed in general, that before we can have ground for raising what can, with any propriety, be called an *argument* from analogy, for or against revelation considered as somewhat miraculous, we must be acquainted with a similar or parallel case. But the history of some other world, seemingly in like circumstances with our own, is no more than a parallel case: and therefore nothing short of this can be so. Yet, could we come at a presumptive proof, for or against a revelation, from being informed, whether such world had one, or not; such a proof, being drawn from one single instance only, must be infinitely precarious. More particularly: First of all; There is a very strong presumption against common speculative truths, and against the most ordinary facts, before the proof of them; which yet is overcome by almost any proof.[1]

---

[d] *Sup.* I. vi. 18.

[1] It is difficult to comprehend Butler's mode of arrival

§ 11] A REVELATION WITH MIRACLE 195

There is a presumption of millions to one, against the story of Caesar, or of any other man. For suppose

at this proposition, and the proposition itself seems hard to defend. Butler founds probability upon likeness (Introd. § 3). Improbability therefore requires an unlikeness of the same kind. But there is no such unlikeness in these most ordinary facts, which are here declared improbable. True, the improbability spoken of is one before proof. But surely it is a startling assertion that very high improbability can be overcome by almost any thing in the nature of proof; which I take to be the meaning of Butler's words. Suppose it autumn: I am looking at a great tree with an hundred thousand leaves, and the fall of the leaf has commenced at what may be called an uniform rate. A leaf falls: the chances (appreciable by me) that that particular leaf would fall at that particular moment was one to ten thousand. Still these chances, as I should say, constituted something in its nature different from an improbability. But could I have seen into the physical condition of the ligaments which connected each leaf with the tree, according as they still lived or came near to death, I might then have said the early fall of this leaf is probable, of that one improbable. But the improbability to be real must be somewhat in the thing itself and in its relation to other things. There is improbability, antecedent to proof, in the life of Alexander the Great or of Mahomet, but it is because those lives are so unlike the lives of common men, or the ordinary course of nature. Accordingly Bishop Fitzgerald quotes with a just approval the contention of Mill (*Logic*, ii. 192, 194) that these observations of Butler afford no answer to the argument of Hume against miracles, because that argument proceeds upon 'contrariety to the uniform course of experience.' Chance, on which Butler here rests, can only be predicated where there is no substantial unlikeness, as in the case of the tickets in a lottery. The case of Caesar (standing alone) imports an element of improbability, founded on unlikeness: but an improbability removable by proof (see Fitzgerald's *Analogy*, p. 184 *n*.).

The word presumption, then, appears, as well as improbability, to be inapplicable to the case now before us.

a number of common facts so and so circumstanced, of which one had no kind of proof, should happen to come into one's thoughts; every one would, without any possible doubt, conclude them to be false. And the like may be said of a single common fact.

§ 12. (a) *The real question: Is there a presumption against miracles, such as to make them incredible?*

And from hence it appears, that the question of importance, as to the matter before us, is, concerning the degree of the peculiar presumption supposed against miracles; not whether there be any peculiar presumption at all against them. For, if there be the presumption of millions to one, against the most common facts; what can a small presumption, additional to this, amount to, though it be peculiar? It cannot be estimated, and is as nothing. The only material question is, whether there be any such presumption against miracles, as to render them in any sort incredible.

§ 13. (b) *Antecedent to proof, the presumption against miracles in general less than against particular facts.*

Secondly, If we leave out the consideration of religion, we are in such total darkness, upon what causes, occa-

Mill takes his distinction in a convenient form between improbability before the fact, and improbability after the fact.

All this is quite independent of the validity of Hume's argument. If we set up contrariety to the uniform law of nature it may surely be observed, (1) that nature is extremely various; (2) that we are not entitled to assert that we know the limit of these variations; (3) that as by our will we can set in motion forces antagonistic to other known natural forces, so it is possible that, by willpower other and greater than ours, other natural forces may be contravened; (4) that this action of will is as much a part of the law and course of nature as any other portion of the operations established by experience.

This subject is discussed in Mr. Leslie Stephen's *History of English Thought in the Eighteenth Century*, ch. viii. § 28.

sions, reasons, or circumstances, the present course of nature depends; that there does not appear any improbability for or against supposing, that five or six thousand years may have given scope for causes, occasions, reasons, or circumstances, from whence miraculous interpositions may have arisen. And from this, joined with the foregoing observation, it will follow, that there must be a presumption, beyond all comparison, greater, against the *particular* common facts just now instanced in, than against miracles *in general;* before any evidence of either.[1]

§ 14. (c) *But religion supplies particular reasons for them.*

But, thirdly, Take in the consideration of religion, or the moral system of the world, and then we see distinct particular reasons for miracles: to afford mankind instruction additional to that of nature, and to attest the truth of it. And this gives a real credibility to the supposition, that it might be part of the original plan of things, that there should be miraculous interpositions.

§ 15. (d) *They are to be compared with the extraordinaries of nature.*

Then, lastly, Miracles must not be compared to common natural events; or to events which, though uncommon, are similar to what we daily experience: but to the extraordinary phenomena of nature. And then the comparison will be between the presumption against miracles, and the presumption against such uncommon appearances, suppose, as comets, and against there being any such powers in nature as magnetism and electricity, so contrary to the properties of other bodies not endued with these powers.[2] And

---

[1] This argument appears to be entangled in the fallacious idea propounded in § 11.

[2] These powers differ from the case of miracles in that

before any one can determine, whether there be any peculiar presumption against miracles, more than against other extraordinary things; he must consider, what, upon first hearing, would be the presumption against the last-mentioned appearances and powers, to a person acquainted only with the daily, monthly, and annual course of nature respecting this earth, and with those common powers of matter which we every day see.

§ 16. *Thus they appear rather to have a degree of positive title to belief.*

Upon all this I conclude; That there certainly is no such presumption against miracles, as to render them in any wise incredible: that on the contrary, our being able to discern reasons for them, gives a positive credibility to the history of them, in cases where those reasons hold: and that it is by no means certain, that there is any peculiar presumption at all, from analogy, even in the lowest degree, against miracles, as distinguished from other extraordinary phenomena: though it is not worth while to perplex the reader with inquiries into the abstract nature of evidence, in order to determine a question, which, without such inquiries, we see [e] is of no importance.

[e] P. 169 [in edition of 1844. But the reference appears to be to p. 210, § 2.]

---

they are capable of systematic verification; but are available for Butler's purpose in that, as we learn new effects and characteristics of these laws, we find the bounds of nature wider than we had supposed; and the broad differences between them and other laws, which were not always known, prepare us to anticipate other differences of great breadth and strangeness. Fitzgerald observes, that miracles may be regarded as physical events having moral antecedents: which fall under Butler's reference to 'reasons.'

CHAPTER III

OF OUR INCAPACITY OF JUDGING, WHAT WERE TO BE EXPECTED IN A REVELATION; AND THE CREDIBILITY, FROM ANALOGY, THAT IT MUST CONTAIN THINGS APPEARING LIABLE TO OBJECTIONS.

§ 1. *Enumerates divers objections taken to the Christian scheme.*

BESIDES the objections against the evidence for Christianity, many are alleged against the scheme of it; against the whole manner in which it is put and left with the world; as well as against several particular relations in scripture: objections drawn from the deficiencies of revelation; from things in it appearing to men *foolishness*; [a] from its containing matters of offence, which have led, and it must have been foreseen would lead, into strange enthusiasm and superstition, and be made to serve the purposes of tyranny and wickedness; from its not being universal; and, which is a thing of the same kind, from its evidence not being so convincing and satisfactory as it might have been: for this last is sometimes turned into a positive argument against its truth [b]. It would be tedious, indeed impossible, to enumerate the several particulars comprehended under the objections here referred to; they being so various, according to the different fancies of men. There are persons, who think it a strong objection against the authority of scripture, that it is not composed by rules of art, agreed upon by critics, for polite and correct writing. And the scorn is inexpressible, with which some of the prophetic parts of scripture are treated: partly through the rashness of interpreters; but very much also, on account of the hieroglyphical and figurative language,

[a] 1 Cor. i. 23.   [b] See chap. vi.

in which they are left us. Some of the principal things of this sort shall be particularly considered in following chapters.

§ 2. *Mostly frivolous; except those against the evidence.*

But my design at present is to observe in general, with respect to this whole way of arguing, that, upon supposition of a revelation, it is highly credible beforehand, we should be incompetent judges of it to a great degree: and that it would contain many things appearing to us liable to great objections; in case we judge of it otherwise, than by the analogy of nature. And therefore, though objections against the evidence of Christianity are most seriously to be considered; yet objections against Christianity itself are, in a great measure, frivolous: almost all objections against it, excepting those which are alleged against the particular proofs of its coming from God.

§ 3. *Cautious not to vilify reason, whereby we judge even of revelation.*

I express myself with caution, lest I should be mistaken to vilify reason;[1] which is indeed the only faculty we have wherewith to judge concerning any thing, even revelation itself: or be misunderstood to assert, that a supposed revelation cannot be proved false, from internal characters. For, it may contain clear immoralities or contradictions; and either of these would prove it false. Nor will I take upon me to affirm, that nothing else can possibly render any supposed revelation incredible. Yet still the observation above is, I think, true beyond doubt; that objections against Christianity, as distinguished from objections against its evidence, are frivolous. To make out this, is the general design of the present chapter.

[1] See *inf.* ix. 7.

§ 4. *Dislike of consequences no relevant plea.*

And with regard to the whole of it, I cannot but particularly wish, that the proofs might be attended to; rather than the assertions cavilled at, upon account of any unacceptable consequences, whether real or supposed, which may be drawn from them. For, after all, that which is true, must be admitted, though it should show us the shortness of our faculties; and that we are in no wise judges of many things, of which we are apt to think ourselves very competent ones. Nor will this be any objection with reasonable men, at least upon second thought it will not be any objection with such, against the justness of the following observations.

§ 5. *Taking objection to nature, we are likely to object to revelation.*

As God governs the world, and instructs his creatures, according to certain laws or rules, in the known course of nature, known by reason together with experience: so the scripture informs us of a scheme of divine Providence, additional to this. It relates, that God has, by revelation, instructed men in things concerning his government, which they could not otherwise have known; and reminded them of things, which they might otherwise know: and attested the truth of the whole by miracles. Now if the natural and the revealed dispensation of things are both from God, if they coincide with each other, and together make up one scheme of Providence; our being incompetent judges of one, must render it credible, that we may be incompetent judges also of the other. Since, upon experience, the acknowledged constitution and course of nature is found to be greatly different from what, before experience, would have been expected; and such as, men fancy, there lie great objections against: this renders it beforehand highly credible, that they may find the revealed dispensation likewise, if they judge of it as they do of the constitution of nature, very different from expectations formed beforehand; and liable, in appearance, to great objections: objections against the scheme itself, and against the degrees and manners of the miraculous interpositions, by which it was attested and carried on.

§ 6. *As a bad judge of ordinary temporal government would be the like of extraordinary.*

Thus suppose a prince to govern his dominions in the wisest manner possible, by common known laws; and that upon some exigencies he should suspend these laws; and govern, in several instances, in a different manner: if one of his subjects were not a competent judge beforehand, by what common rules the government should or would be carried on; it could not be expected, that the same person would be a competent judge, in what exigencies, or in what manner, or to what degree, those laws commonly observed would be suspended or deviated from. If he were not a judge of the wisdom of the ordinary administration, there is no reason to think he would be a judge of the wisdom of the extraordinary. If he thought he had objections against the former; doubtless, it is highly supposable, he might think also, that he had objections against the latter. And thus, as we fall into infinite follies and mistakes, whenever we pretend, otherwise than from experience and analogy, to judge of the constitution and course of nature; it is evidently supposable beforehand, that we should fall into as great, in pretending to judge, in like manner, concerning revelation. Nor is there any more ground to expect that this latter should appear to us clear of objections, than that the former should.

§ 7. *What inspiration, or revelation, would or should be, we are bad judges.*

These observations, relating to the whole of Christianity, are applicable to inspiration in particular. As we are in no sort judges beforehand, by what laws or rules, in what degree, or by what means, it were to have been expected, that God would naturally instruct us: so upon supposition of his affording us light and instruction by revelation, additional to what he has afforded us by reason and experience, we are in no sort judges, by what methods, and in what proportion, it were to be expected, that this supernatural light and instruction would be afforded us. We know not beforehand, what degree or kind of natural information, it were to be expected God would afford men, each by his own reason and experience: nor how far he would enable and effectually dispose them to communicate it, whatever it should be, to each other: nor whether the evidence of it would be certain, highly probable, or doubtful: nor whether it would be given with equal clearness and conviction to all. Nor could we guess, upon any good ground I mean, whether natural knowledge, or even the faculty itself, by which we are capable of attaining it, reason, would be given us at once, or gradually. In like manner, we are wholly ignorant, what degree of new knowledge, it were to be expected, God would give mankind by revelation, upon supposition of his affording one: or how far, or in what way, he would interpose miraculously, to qualify them, to whom he should originally make the revelation, for communicating the knowledge given by it; and to secure their doing it to the age in which they should live; and to secure its being transmitted to posterity. We are equally ignorant, whether the evidence of it would be certain, or highly probable, or doubtful:[c] or whether all who should have any degree of instruction from it, and any degree of evidence of its truth, would have the same: or whether the scheme would be revealed at once, or unfolded gradually. Nay we are not in any sort able to judge, whether it were to have been expected, that the revelation should have been committed to writing; or left to be handed down, and consequently corrupted, by verbal tradition, and

[c] See chap. vi.

at length sunk under it, if mankind so pleased, and during such time as they are permitted, in the degree they evidently are, to act as they will.

§ 8. *E. g. as between written and oral forms.*

But it may be said, 'that a revelation in some of the above mentioned circumstances, one, for instance, which was not committed to writing, and thus secured against danger of corruption, would not have answered its purpose.' I ask, what purpose? It would not have answered all the purposes, which it has now answered, and in the same degree: but it would have answered others, or the same in different degrees. And which of these were the purposes of God, and best fell in with his general government, we could not at all have determined beforehand.

§ 9. *Thus ignorant* a parte ante, *we are incompetent* a parte post.

Now since it has been shown, that we have no principles of reason, upon which to judge beforehand, how it were to be expected revelation should have been left, or what was most suitable to the divine plan of government, in any of the forementioned respects; it must be quite frivolous to object afterwards as to any of them, against its being left in one way, rather than another: for this would be to object against things, upon account of their being different from expectations, which have been shown to be without reason. And thus we see, that the only question concerning the truth of Christianity is, whether it be a real revelation: not whether it be attended with every circumstance which we should have looked for: and concerning the authority of scripture, whether it be what it claims to be; not whether it be a book of such sort, and so promulged, as weak men are apt to fancy a book containing a divine revelation should. And therefore, neither obscurity, nor seeming inaccuracy of style, nor various readings, nor early disputes about the authors of particular parts; nor any other things of the like kind, though they had been much more considerable in degree than they are, could overthrow the authority of the scripture: unless the prophets, apostles, or our Lord, had promised, that the book containing the divine revelation should be secure from those things.

§ 10. *Attack feasible only on* (a) *proofs of miracle,* (b) *prophecy.*

Nor indeed can any objections overthrow such a kind of revelation as the Christian claims to be, since there are no objections against the morality of it,[d] but such as can show, that there is no proof of miracles wrought originally in attestation of it; no appearance of any thing miraculous in its obtaining in the world; nor any of prophecy, that is, of events foretold, which human sagacity could not foresee.

§ 11. *If but partially proven, their authority will abide.*

If it can be shown, that the proof alleged for all these is absolutely none at all, then is revelation overturned.[1] But were it allowed, that the proof of any one or all of them is lower than is allowed; yet, whilst any proof of them remains, revelation will stand upon much the same foot it does at present, as to all the purposes of life and practice, and ought to have the like influence upon our behaviour.

[d] *Inf.* § 26.

---

[1] I suppose we may fill up the argument thus. The disproof in this or that case would not affect the credit generally due. If the general proof of all were weakened but not destroyed, we should not, under the rules of probability and good sense, be discharged from all duty in regard to them.

§ 12. *Arguments good for ordinary books will not always hold in the case of scripture.*

From the foregoing observations too, it will follow, and those who will thoroughly examine into revelation will find it worth remarking; that there are several ways of arguing, which, though just with regard to other writings, are not applicable to scripture: at least not to the prophetic parts of it. We cannot argue, for instance, that this cannot be the sense or intent of such a passage of scripture; for, if it had, it would have been expressed more plainly, or have been represented under a more apt figure or hieroglyphic: yet we may justly argue thus, with respect to common books. And the reason of this difference is very evident; that in scripture we are not competent judges, as we are in common books, how plainly it were to have been expected, what is the true sense should have been expressed, or under how apt an image figured. The only question is, what appearance there is, that this is the sense; and scarce at all, how much more determinately or accurately it might have been expressed or figured.

§ 13. *Internal improbabilities* (a) *hard to establish,* (b) *may be set aside by evidence.*

'But is it not self-evident, that internal improbabilities of all kinds weaken external probable proof?' Doubtless. But to what practical purpose can this be alleged here, when it has been proved before,[e][1] that

[e] *Sup.* ii. 11, 12.

---

[1] Again we appear to be entangled in the argument of §§ 11 and 12, ch. ii. Still, the statement there does not go beyond propounding that an adverse presumption of millions to one may be overcome by almost any proof. That such a presumption, as Butler there has in view, does not 'rise to moral certainty' is plain at once from the fact that the things referred to are ('the most common

real internal improbabilities which rise even to moral certainty, are overcome by the most ordinary testimony; and when it now has been made appear, that we scarce know what are improbabilities, as to the matter we are here considering: as it will further appear from what follows.

§ 14. *Why preconceived notions are sure to mislead.*

For though from the observations above made it is manifest, that we are not in any sort competent judges, what supernatural instruction were to have been expected; and though it is self-evident, that the objections of an incompetent judgment must be frivolous: yet it may be proper to go one step further, and observe; that if men will be regardless of these things, and pretend to judge of the scripture by preconceived expectations; the analogy of nature shows beforehand not only that it is highly credible they may, but also probable that they will, imagine they have strong objections against it, however really unexceptionable: for so, prior to experience, they would think they had, against the circumstances and degrees and the whole manner of that instruction, which is afforded by the ordinary course of nature. Were the instruction which God affords to brute creatures by instincts and mere propensions, and to mankind by these together with reason, matter of probable proof, and not of certain observation; it would be rejected as incredible, in many instances of it, only upon account of the means by which this instruction is given, the seeming dis-

facts') such as do actually happen. These are not 'real internal improbabilities,' for they do not grow out of any thing in the things themselves, but are a mere conjecture as to the number of possibilities, any one of which might have become fact, instead of that which did become so. This discussion must turn not upon mere adverse chances, but on improbabilities which are intrinsic. The closing lines of the section stand clear of this difficulty. See *sup.* § 11 of ch. ii.

proportions, the limitations, necessary conditions, and circumstances of it.

§ 15. *E.g. as to* (a) *comparative access to different kinds of knowledge,* (b) *invention,* (c) *language.*

For instance: Would it not have been thought highly improbable, that men should have been so much more capable of discovering, even to certainty, the general laws of matter, and the magnitudes, paths and revolutions of the heavenly bodies; than the occasions and cures of distempers, and many other things, in which human life seems so much more nearly concerned, than in astronomy? How capricious and irregular a way of information, would it be said, is that of *invention,* by means of which nature instructs us in matters of science, and in many things, upon which the affairs of the world greatly depend: that a man should, by this faculty, be made acquainted with a thing in an instant, when perhaps he is thinking of somewhat else, which he has in vain been searching after, it may be, for years. So likewise the imperfections attending the only method, by which nature enables and directs us to communicate our thoughts to each other, are innumerable. Language is, in its very nature, inadequate, ambiguous, liable to infinite abuse, even from negligence; and so liable to it from design, that every man can deceive and betray by it.

§ 16. *Greater certainty of brutes in their mental operations.*

And, to mention but one instance more; that brutes, without reason, should act, in many respects, with a sagacity and foresight vastly greater than what men have in those respects, would be thought impossible. Yet it is certain they do act with such superior foresight: whether it be their own indeed, is another question.

§ 17. *Case would probably be similar in any (supposed) further revelation.*

From these things, it is highly credible beforehand, that upon supposition God should afford men some additional instruction by revelation, it would be with circumstances, in manners, degrees, and respects, which we should be apt to fancy we had great objections against the credibility of. Nor are the objections against the scripture, nor against Christianity in general, at all more or greater, than the analogy of nature would beforehand—not perhaps give ground to expect; for this analogy may not be sufficient, in some cases, to ground an expectation upon; but no more nor greater, than analogy would show it, beforehand, to be supposable and credible, that there might seem to lie against revelation.

§ 18. *Objection from the disorderly use of miraculous gifts futile.*

By applying these general observations to a particular objection, it will be more distinctly seen, how they are applicable to others of the like kind: and indeed to almost all objections against Christianity, as distinguished from objections against its evidence. It appears from scripture, that, as it was not unusual in the apostolic age, for persons, upon their conversion to Christianity, to be endued with miraculous gifts; so, some of those persons exercised these gifts in a strangely irregular and disorderly manner; and this is made an objection against their being really miraculous. Now the foregoing observations quite remove this objection, how considerable soever it may appear at first sight. For, consider a person endued with any of these gifts; for instance, that of tongues: it is to be supposed, that he had the same power over this miraculous gift, as he would have had over it, had it been the effect of habit, of study and use, as it ordinarily is; or the same power over it, as he had over any other natural endowment.[1] Consequently, he would use it in the same manner he did any other; either regularly, and upon proper occasions only, or irregularly, and upon improper ones: according to his sense of decency, and his character of prudence. Where then is the objection? Why, if this miraculous power was indeed given to the world to propagate Christianity, and attest the truth of it, we might, it seems, have expected, that other sort of persons should have been chosen to be invested with it; or that these should, at the same time, have been endued with prudence; or that they should have been continually restrained and directed in the exercise of it: i. e. that God should have miraculously interposed, if at all, in a different manner, or higher degree. But, from the observations made above, it is undeniably evident, that we are not judges in what degrees and manners it were to have been expected he should miraculously interpose; upon supposition of his doing it in some degree and manner.

§ 19. *Similar risk in other gifts.*

Nor, in the natural course of Providence, are superior gifts of memory, eloquence, knowledge, and other talents of great influence, conferred only on persons of prudence and decency, or such as are disposed to make the properest use of them. Nor is the instruction and admonition naturally afforded us for the conduct of life, particularly in our education, commonly given in a manner the most suited to recommend it; but often with circumstances apt to prejudice us against such instruction.

§ 20. *Analogy of nature and revelation in the relations of lower to higher knowledge.*

One might go on to add, that there is a great resemblance between the light of nature and of revelation,

---

[1] This seems to be expressly declared in 1 Cor. xiv. 32, 'and the spirits of the prophets are subject to the prophets.'

in several other respects. Practical Christianity, or that faith and behaviour which renders a man a Christian, is a plain and obvious thing: like the common rules of conduct, with respect to our ordinary temporal affairs. The more distinct and particular knowledge of those things, the study of which the apostle calls *going on unto perfection*,[f] and of the prophetic parts of revelation, like many parts of natural and even civil knowledge, may require very exact thought, and careful consideration. The hindrances too, of natural, and of supernatural light and knowledge, have been of the same kind.

§ 21. *So it is as to the further opening of scripture.*

And as it is owned the whole scheme of scripture is not yet understood; so, if it ever comes to be understood, before the *restitution of all things*,[g] and without miraculous interpositions; it must be in the same way as natural knowledge is come at: by the continuance and progress of learning and of liberty; and by particular persons attending to, comparing and pursuing, intimations scattered up and down it, which are overlooked and disregarded by the generality of the world. For this is the way, in which all improvements are made; by thoughtful men's tracing on obscure hints, as it were, dropped us by nature accidentally, or which seem to come into our minds by chance. Nor is it at all incredible, that a book, which has been so long in the possession of mankind, should contain many truths as yet undiscovered. For, all the same phenomena, and the same faculties of investigation, from which such great discoveries in natural knowledge have been made in the present and last age, were equally in the possession of mankind, several thousand years before. And possibly it might be intended, that events, as they come to pass, should open and ascertain the meaning of several parts of scripture.

[f] Heb. vi. 1.   [g] Acts iii. 21.

§ 22. *Natural knowledge sometimes of high stamp: is given not as we expect, but differently.*[1]

It may be objected, that this analogy fails in a material respect: for that natural knowledge is of little or no consequence. But I have been speaking of the general instruction which nature does or does not afford us. And besides, some parts of natural knowledge, in the more common restrained sense of the words, are of the greatest consequence to the ease and convenience of life. But suppose the analogy did, as it does not, fail in this respect; yet it might be abundantly supplied, from the whole constitution and course of nature: which shows, that God does not dispense his gifts according to our notions of the advantage and consequence they would be of to us. And this in general, with his method of dispensing knowledge in particular, would together make out an analogy full to the point before us.

§ 23. *That the supply of light is only partial.*

But it may be objected still further and more generally; 'The scripture represents the world as in a state of ruin, and Christianity as an expedient to recover it, to help in these respects where nature fails: in particular, to supply the deficiencies of natural light. Is it credible then, that so many ages should have been let pass, before a matter of such a sort, of so great and

---

[1] Dr. Angus in his analysis of the chapter brings out the numerous points of this short section:

(*a*) Objection is taken to natural knowledge as unimportant.

(*b*) That is, irrelevant.

(*c*) Also untrue.

(*d*) The argument is that God gives not as we expect, but differently.

(*e*) Herein a full analogy between nature and revelation is exhibited.

See *Butler's Analogy*, edited by Dr. Angus, p. 180.

so general importance, was made known to mankind; and then that it should be made known to so small a part of them? Is it conceivable, that this supply should be so very deficient, should have the like obscurity and doubtfulness, be liable to the like perversions, in short, lie open to all the like objections, as the light of nature itself?'[h]

§ 24. *In both schemes, remedies are incomplete.*

Without determining how far this in fact is so, I answer; it is by no means incredible, that it might be so, if the light of nature and of revelation be from the same hand. Men are naturally liable to diseases: for which God, in his good providence, has provided natural remedies.[i] But remedies existing in nature have been unknown to mankind for many ages: are known but to few now: probably many valuable ones are not known yet. Great has been and is the obscurity and difficulty, in the nature and application of them. Circumstances seem often to make them very improper, where they are absolutely necessary. It is after long labour and study, and many unsuccessful endeavours, that they are brought to be as useful as they are; after high contempt and absolute rejection of the most useful we have; and after disputes and doubts, which have seemed to be endless. The best remedies too, when unskilfully, much more if dishonestly applied, may produce new diseases: and with the rightest application the success of them is often doubtful. In many cases they are not at all effectual: where they are, it is often very slowly: and the application of them, and the necessary regimen accompanying it, is, not uncommonly, so disagreeable, that some will not submit to them; and satisfy themselves with the excuse, that, if they would, it is not certain whether it would be successful. And many persons, who labour under diseases, for which there are known natural remedies, are not so happy as to be always, if ever,

[h] Chap. vi.   [i] See chap. v.

in the way of them. In a word, the remedies which nature has provided for diseases are neither certain, perfect, nor universal.

§ 25. *If we ask perfect remedies, why not ask banishment of disease?*

And indeed the same principles of arguing, which would lead us to conclude, that they must be so, would lead us likewise to conclude, that there could be no occasion for them; i.e. that there could be no diseases at all. And therefore our experience that there are diseases shows, that it is credible beforehand, upon supposition nature has provided remedies for them, that these remedies may be, as by experience we find they are, not certain, nor perfect, nor universal; because it shows, that the principles upon which we should expect the contrary are fallacious.

§ 26. *In revelation, reason is to judge* (a) *the meaning,* (b) *the morality,* (c) *the evidence.*

And now, what is the just consequence from all these things? Not that reason is no judge of what is offered to us as being of divine revelation. For this would be to infer, that we are unable to judge of any thing, because we are unable to judge of all things. Reason can, and it ought to judge, not only of the meaning, but also of the morality and the evidence, of revelation. First, It is the province of reason to judge of the morality of the scripture; i.e. not whether it contains things different from what we should have expected from a wise, just, and good Being; for objections from hence have been now obviated: but whether it contains things plainly contradictory to wisdom, justice, or goodness; to what the light of nature teaches us of God. And I know nothing of this sort objected against scripture, excepting such objections as are formed upon suppositions, which would equally conclude, that the constitution of nature is contradictory to wisdom, justice, or goodness; which most certainly it is not.

§ 27. *Some precepts, not contrary to immutable morality, are made moral only by command.*

Indeed there are some particular precepts in scripture, given to particular persons, requiring actions, which would be immoral and vicious, were it not for such precepts. But it is easy to see, that all these are of such a kind, as that the precept changes the whole nature of the case and of the action; and both constitutes and shows that not to be unjust or immoral, which, prior to the precept, must have appeared and really have been so: which may well be, since none of these precepts are contrary to immutable morality. If it were commanded, to cultivate the principles and act from the spirit of treachery, ingratitude, cruelty; the command would not alter the nature of the case or of the action, in any of these instances. But it is quite otherwise in precepts, which require only the doing an external action: for instance, taking away the property or life of any. For men have no right to either life or property, but what arises solely from the grant of God: when this grant is revoked, they cease to have any right at all in either: and when this revocation is made known, as surely it is possible it may be, it must cease to be unjust to deprive them of either. And though a course of external acts, which without command would be immoral, must make an immoral habit; yet a few detached commands have no such natural tendency.[1]

---

[1] I suppose that violence offered by order of law may help to illustrate Butler's meaning: especially as in the case of an executioner. I deal more fully with this subject in my reply to Miss Hennell in a separate essay On the Censors of Butler. See Coleridge's account of Executioners in Germany: *Letters* (1895), vol. i. p. 294.

§ 28. *Objection urged against these lies against nature at large, and trial of all kinds.*

I thought proper to say thus much of the few scripture precepts, which require, not vicious actions, but actions which would have been vicious had it not been for such precepts; because they are sometimes weakly urged as immoral, and great weight is laid upon objections drawn from them. But to me there seems no difficulty at all in these precepts, but what arises from their being offences: i. e. from their being liable to be perverted,[1] as indeed they are, by wicked designing men, to serve the most horrid purposes; and, perhaps, to mislead the weak and enthusiastic. And objections from this head are not objections against revelation; but against the whole notion of religion, as a trial; and against the general constitution of nature. Secondly,[2] Reason is able to judge, and must, of the evidence of revelation, and of the objections urged against that evidence: which shall be the subject of a following chapter.[k]

§ 29. *Other objections being frivolous, let us try those against the proofs.*

But the consequence of the foregoing observations is, that the question upon which the truth of Christianity depends is scarce at all, what objections there are against its scheme, since there are none against the morality of it; but *what objections there are against its*

[k] Chap. vii.

---

[1] Perverted, that is, seemingly, by unwarranted imitation. We need not examine the precise propriety of the word offences, since Butler has given his own definition of it *pro hâc vice*, as acts liable to be perverted. The application given a few centuries ago to some of the Old Testament commands may perhaps serve here as an illustration.

[2] On this head see *inf.*, ch. vii.

evidence: or, what proof there remains of it, after due allowances made for the objections against that proof: because it has been shown, that the *objections against Christianity, as distinguished from objections against its evidence, are frivolous.* For surely very little weight, if any at all, is to be laid upon a way of arguing and objecting, which, when applied to the general constitution of nature, experience shows not to be conclusive: and such, I think, is the whole way of objecting treated of throughout this chapter. It is resolvable into principles, and goes upon suppositions, which mislead us to think, that the Author of nature would not act, as we experience he does; or would act, in such and such cases, as we experience he does not in like cases. But the unreasonableness of this way of objecting will appear yet more evidently from hence, that the chief things thus objected against are justified, as shall be further shown,[1] by distinct, particular, and full analogies, in the constitution and course of nature.

§ 30. *We can judge whether a revelation* (a) *tends to virtue and* (b) *is due to mere human motive.*

But it is to be remembered, that, as frivolous as objections of the foregoing sort against revelation are, yet, when a supposed revelation is more consistent with itself, and has a more general and uniform tendency to promote virtue, than, all circumstances considered, could have been expected from enthusiasm and political views; this is a presumptive proof of its not proceeding from them, and so of its truth : because we are competent judges, what might have been expected from enthusiasm and political views.

[1] Chap. iv. latter part, and chaps. v, vi.

CHAPTER IV

OF CHRISTIANITY, CONSIDERED AS A SCHEME OR CONSTITUTION, IMPERFECTLY COMPREHENDED

§ 1. *Objections against nature have been answered: same answer may serve for Christianity.*[1]

It hath been now shown,[a] that the analogy of nature renders it highly credible beforehand, that supposing a revelation to be made, it must contain many things very different from what we should have expected, and such as appear open to great objections: and that this observation, in good measure, takes off the force of those objections, or rather precludes them. But it may be alleged, that this is a very partial answer to such objections, or a very unsatisfactory way of obviating them: because it doth not show at all, that the things objected against can be wise, just, and good; much less, that it is credible they are so. It will therefore be proper to show this distinctly; by applying to these objections against the wisdom, justice, and goodness of Christianity, the answer above [b] given to the like objections against the constitution of nature: before we consider the particular analogies

---

[a] In the foregoing chapter.
[b] Part I. ch. vii. to which this all along refers.

---

[1] To show this distinctly, Butler, as if foreseeing the objection of those who now hold that he has only shifted the burden to the shoulders of Nature, expressly declines in this section to expose that line of defence to the attack: and holds it his duty, on the merits of the case, to show by a threefold argument that he is entitled to bar the objections as they are in themselves, and not only by showing that they apply elsewhere.

He has already done the same for Nature, not only in I. vii., but in his Introduction, § 17.

§§ 1, 2] IMPERFECTLY COMPREHENDED

in the latter, to the particular things objected against in the former. Now that which affords a sufficient answer to objections against the wisdom, justice, and goodness of the constitution of nature, is its being a constitution, a system, or scheme, imperfectly comprehended; a scheme in which means are made use of to accomplish ends; and which is carried on by general laws. For from these things it has been proved, not only to be possible, but also to be credible, that those things which are objected against may be consistent with wisdom, justice, and goodness; nay, may be instances of them: and even that the constitution and government of nature may be perfect in the highest possible degree. If Christianity then be a scheme, and of the like kind; it is evident, the like objections against it must admit of the like answer. And,

§ 2. *It is imperfectly comprehended; and our ignorance bars our objections.*

[I.] Christianity is a scheme, quite beyond our comprehension. The moral government of God is exercised, by gradually conducting things so in the course of his providence, that every one, at length and upon the whole, shall receive according to his deserts; and neither fraud nor violence, but truth and right, shall finally prevail. Christianity is a particular scheme under this general plan of Providence, and a part of it, conducive to its completion, with regard to mankind: consisting itself also of various parts, and a mysterious economy, which has been carrying on from the time the world came into its present wretched state, and is still carrying on, for its recovery, by a divine person, the Messiah; who is to *gather together in one the children of God that are scattered abroad,*[c] and establish *an everlasting kingdom, wherein dwelleth righteousness.*[d] And in order to it; after various manifestations of things, relating to this great and general scheme of Providence, through a succession of many ages: (for

[c] John xi. 52.   [d] 2 Pet. iii. 13.

the Spirit of Christ which was in the prophets, testified beforehand his sufferings, and the glory that should follow: unto whom it was revealed, that not unto themselves, but unto us they did minister the things which are now reported unto us by them that have preached the gospel; which things the angels desire to look into: [e]—after various dispensations, looking forward, and preparatory, to this final salvation: *in the fulness of time,* when infinite wisdom thought fit; he, *being in the form of God,——made himself of no reputation, and took upon him the form of a servant, and was made in the likeness of men: and being found in fashion as a man, he humbled himself, and became obedient to death, even the death of the cross: wherefore God also hath highly exalted him, and given him a name, which is above every name: that at the name of Jesus every knee should bow, of things in heaven, and things in the earth, and things under the earth; and that every tongue should confess that Jesus Christ is Lord, to the glory of God the Father.*[f] Parts likewise of this economy are the miraculous mission of the Holy Ghost, and his ordinary assistances given to good men: the invisible government, which Christ at present exercises over his church that which he himself refers to in these words; *In my Father's house are many mansions——I go to prepare a place for you:*[g] and his future return to *judge the world in righteousness,* and completely re-establish the kingdom of God. *For the Father judgeth no man, but hath committed all judgment unto the Son: that all men should honour the Son, even as they honour the Father.*[h] *All power is given unto him in heaven and in earth.*[i] *And he must reign, till he hath put all enemies under his feet. Then cometh the end, when he shall have delivered up the kingdom to God, even the Father; when he shall have put down all rule and all authority and power. And when all things shall be subdued unto him, then shall the Son also himself be subject unto him that put all things under him, that God may be all in all.*[k]

[e] 1 Pet. i. 11, 12.   [f] Phil. ii. 6–11.   [g] John xiv. 2.
[h] John v. 22, 23.   [i] Matt. xxviii. 18.   [k] 1 Cor. xv. 24–28.

Now little, surely, need be said to show, that this system, or scheme of things, is but imperfectly comprehended by us. The scripture expressly asserts it to be so. And indeed one cannot read a passage relating to this *great mystery of godliness*,[1] but what immediately runs up into something which shows us our ignorance in it; as every thing in nature shows us our ignorance in the constitution of nature. And whoever will seriously consider that part of the Christian scheme, which is revealed in scripture, will find so much more unrevealed, as will convince him, that, to all the purposes of judging and objecting, we know as little of it, as of the constitution of nature. Our ignorance, therefore, is as much an answer to our objections against the perfection of one, as against the perfection of the other.[m]

§ 3. *Here, as in nature, means to attain ends are used; which may both be the very best.*

[II.] It is obvious too, that in the Christian dispensation, as much as in the natural scheme of things, means are made use of to accomplish ends. And the observation of this furnishes us with the same answer, to objections against the perfection of Christianity, as to objections of the like kind, against the constitution of nature. It shows the credibility, that the things objected against, how *foolish*[n] soever they appear to men, may be the very best means of accomplishing the very best ends. And their appearing *foolishness* is no presumption against this, in a scheme so greatly beyond our comprehension.[o]

§ 4. *Nature operates by general laws, hard to trace out.*

[III.] The credibility, that the Christian dispensation may have been, all along, carried on by general laws,[p] no less than the course of nature, may require

---

[1] 1 Tim. iii. 16.   [m] *Sup.* I. vii. 13 *sqq.*   [n] 1 Cor. i.
[o] *Sup.* I. vii. 13 *sqq.*   [p] *Sup.* I. vii. 18.

to be more distinctly made out. Consider then, upon what ground it is we say, that the whole common course of nature is carried on according to general foreordained laws. We know indeed several of the general laws of matter: and a great part of the natural behaviour of living agents is reducible to general laws. But we know in a manner nothing, by what laws, storms and tempests, earthquakes, famine, pestilence, become the instruments of destruction to mankind. And the laws, by which persons born into the world at such a time and place are of such capacities, geniuses, tempers; the laws, by which thoughts come into our mind, in a multitude of cases; and by which innumerable things happen, of the greatest influence upon the affairs and state of the world; these laws are so wholly unknown to us, that we call the events which come to pass by them, accidental: though all reasonable men know certainly, that there cannot, in reality, be any such thing as chance; and conclude, that the things which have this appearance are the result of general laws, and may be reduced into them. It is then but an exceeding little way, and in but a very few respects, that we can trace up the natural course of things before us, to general laws. And it is only from analogy, that we conclude the whole of it to be capable of being reduced into them: only from our seeing, that part is so. It is from our finding, that the course of nature, in some respects and so far, goes on by general laws, that we conclude this of the rest.

§ 5. *The same may hold as to revelation.*

And if that be a just ground for such a conclusion, it is a just ground also, if not to conclude, yet to apprehend, to render it supposable and credible, which is sufficient for answering objections, that God's miraculous interpositions may have been, all along in like manner, by *general* laws of wisdom. Thus, that miraculous powers should be exerted, at such times, upon such occasions, in such degrees and manners, and with regard to such persons, rather than others; that the affairs of the world, being permitted to go on in their natural course so far, should, just at such a point, have a new direction given them by miraculous interpositions; that these interpositions should be exactly in such degrees and respects only; all this may have been by general laws. These laws are unknown indeed to us: but no more unknown, than the laws from whence it is, that some die as soon as they are born, and others live to extreme old age; that one man is so superior to another in understanding; with innumerable more things, which, as was before observed, we cannot reduce to any laws or rules at all, though it is taken for granted, they are as much reducible to general ones, as gravitation. Now, if the revealed dispensations of Providence, and miraculous interpositions, be by general laws, as well as God's ordinary government in the course of nature, made known by reason and experience; there is no more reason to expect, that every exigence, as it arises, should be provided for by these general laws of miraculous interpositions, than that every exigence in nature should, by the general laws of nature: yet there might be wise and good reasons, that miraculous interpositions should be by general laws: and that these laws should not be broken in upon, or deviated from, by other miracles.

§ 6. *As to apparent gaps and anomalies, the two are parallel.*

Upon the whole then: The appearance of deficiencies and irregularities in nature is owing to its being a scheme but in part made known, and of such a certain particular kind in other respects. Now we see no more reason why the frame and course of nature should be such a scheme, than why Christianity should. And that the former is such a scheme, renders it credible, that the latter, upon supposition of its truth, may be so too. And as it is manifest, that Christianity is a scheme revealed but in part, and a scheme in which means are made use of to accomplish ends, like to that of nature: so the credibility, that it may have been all along carried on by general laws, no less than the course of nature, has been distinctly proved. And from all this it is beforehand credible that there might, I think probable that there would, be the like appearance of deficiencies and irregularities in Christianity, as in nature: i.e. that Christianity would be liable to the like objections, as the frame of nature. And these objections are answered by these observations concerning Christianity; as the like objections against the frame of nature are answered by the like observations concerning the frame of nature.

§ 7. Obj. *Christianity uses means that are cumbrous and roundabout.* Ans. *We are not fit judges; and why.*

THE objections against Christianity, considered as a matter of fact,[q] having, in general, been obviated in the preceding chapter; and the same, considered as made against the wisdom and goodness of it, having been obviated in this: the next thing, according to the method proposed, is to show, that the principal objections, in particular, against Christianity, may be answered, by particular and full analogies in nature. And as one of them is made against the whole scheme of it together, as just now described, I choose to consider it here, rather than in a distinct chapter by itself. The thing objected against this scheme of the gospel is, ' that it seems to suppose God was reduced to the necessity of a long series of intricate means, in order to accomplish his ends, the recovery and salvation of the world: in like sort as men, for want of understanding or power, not being able to come at their ends directly,

[q] [This sign of reference is left by me as I found it, except that, as elsewhere, I substitute for the variable paging the actual place in the Treatise as fixed in this Edition, viz. I. vii. 1 *sqq*. But the sign ought, I think, to be attached to the last words of the sentence, ' analogies in nature.'—ED.]

are forced to go roundabout ways, and make use of many perplexed contrivances to arrive at them.' Now every thing which we see shows the folly of this, considered as an objection against the truth of Christianity. For, according to our manner of conception, God makes use of variety of means, what we often think tedious ones, in the natural course of providence, for the accomplishment of all his ends. Indeed it is certain there is somewhat in this matter quite beyond our comprehension: but the mystery is as great in nature as in Christianity. We know what we ourselves aim at, as final ends: and what courses we take, merely as means conducing to those ends. But we are greatly ignorant how far things are considered by the Author of nature, under the single notion of means and ends; so as that it may be said, this is merely an end, and that merely means, in his regard. And whether there be not some peculiar absurdity in our very manner of conception, concerning this matter, somewhat contradictory arising from our extremely imperfect views of things, it is impossible to say.

§ 8. *Herein it plainly corresponds with nature.*

However, thus much is manifest, that the whole natural world and government of it is a scheme or system; not a fixed, but a progressive one: a scheme, in which the operation of various means takes up a great length of time, before the ends they tend to can be attained. The change of seasons, the ripening of the fruits of the earth, the very history of a flower, is an instance of this: and so is human life. Thus vegetable bodies, and those of animals, though possibly formed at once, yet grow up by degrees to a mature state. And thus rational agents, who animate these latter bodies, are naturally directed to form each his own manners and character, by the gradual gaining of knowledge and experience, and by a long course of action. Our existence is not only successive, as it must be of necessity; but one state of our life and being is appointed by God, to be a preparation for another; and that, to be the means of attaining to another succeeding one: infancy to childhood; childhood to youth; youth to mature age. Men are impatient, and for precipitating things: but the Author of nature appears deliberate throughout his operations; accomplishing his natural ends by slow successive steps. And there is a plan of things beforehand laid out, which, from the nature of it, requires various systems of means, as well as length of time, in order to the carrying on its several parts into execution. Thus, in the daily course of natural providence, God operates in the very same manner, as in the dispensation of Christianity: making one thing subservient to another: this, to somewhat further; and so on, through a progressive series of means, which extend, both backward and forward, beyond our utmost view. Of this manner of operation, every thing we see in the course of nature is as much an instance, as any part of the Christian dispensation.

CHAPTER V

OF THE PARTICULAR SYSTEM OF CHRISTIANITY; THE APPOINTMENT OF A MEDIATOR, AND THE REDEMPTION OF THE WORLD BY HIM

§ 1. *Mediation, or the instrumentality of others, met everywhere in nature.*

THERE is not, I think, any thing relating to Christianity, which has been more objected against, than the mediation of Christ, in some or other of its parts. Yet, upon thorough consideration, there seems nothing less justly liable to it. For,

[I.] The whole analogy of nature removes all imagined presumption against the general notion of *a mediator between God and man.*[a] For we find all living

[a] 1 Tim. ii. 5.

creatures are brought into the world, and their life in infancy is preserved, by the instrumentality of others: and every satisfaction of it, some way or other, is bestowed by the like means. So that the visible government, which God exercises over the world, is by the instrumentality and mediation of others. And how far his invisible government be or be not so, it is impossible to determine at all by reason. And the supposition, that part of it is so, appears, to say the least, altogether as credible as the contrary. There is then no sort of objection, from the light of nature, against the general notion of a mediator between God and man, considered as a doctrine of Christianity, or as an appointment in this dispensation : since we find by experience, that God does appoint mediators, to be the instruments of good and evil to us ; the instruments of his justice and his mercy. And the objection here referred to is urged, not against mediation in that high, eminent, and peculiar sense, in which Christ is our Mediator ; but absolutely against the whole notion itself of a mediator at all.

§ 2. *Punishment may come of course, i.e. in the way of natural consequence.*

[II.] As we must suppose, that the world is under the proper moral government of God, or in a state of religion, before we can enter into consideration of the revealed doctrine, concerning the redemption of it by Christ ; so that supposition is here to be distinctly taken notice of. Now the divine moral government which religion teaches us, implies, that the consequence of vice shall be misery, in some future state, by the righteous judgment of God. That such consequent punishment shall take effect by his appointment, is necessarily implied. But, as it is not in any sort to be supposed, that we are made acquainted with all the ends or reasons, for which it is fit future punishments should be inflicted, or why God has appointed such and such consequent misery should follow vice ; and as we are altogether in the dark, how or in what manner it shall follow, by what immediate occasions, or by the instrumentality of what means; there is no absurdity in supposing it may follow in a way analogous to that, in which many miseries follow such and such courses of action at present; poverty, sickness, infamy, untimely death by diseases, death from the hands of civil justice. There is no absurdity in supposing future punishment may follow wickedness of course, as we speak, or in the way of natural consequence from God's original constitution of the world; from the nature he has given us, and from the condition in which he places us: or in a like manner, as a person rashly trifling upon a precipice, in the way of natural consequence, falls down; in the way of natural consequence, breaks his limbs, suppose; in the way of natural consequence of this, without help perishes.

§ 3. *And natural consequence is the act of God.*

Some good men may perhaps be offended with hearing it spoken of as a supposable thing, that the future punishments of wickedness may be in the way of natural consequence: as if this were taking the execution of justice out of the hands of God, and giving it to nature. But they should remember, that when things come to pass according to the course of nature, this does not hinder them from being his doing, who is the God of nature: and that the scripture ascribes those punishments to divine justice which are known to be natural; and which must be called so, when distinguished from such as are miraculous. But after all, this supposition, or rather this way of speaking, is here made use of only by way of illustration of the subject before us. For since it must be admitted, that the future punishment of wickedness is not a matter of arbitrary appointment, but of reason, equity, and justice; it comes, for ought I see, to the same thing, whether it is supposed to be inflicted in a way analogous to that, in which the temporal punishments of vice and folly are inflicted, or in any other way. And though there were a difference, it is allowable, in the present case, to make this supposition, plainly not an incredible one; that future punishment may follow wickedness in the way of natural consequence, or according to some general laws of government already established in the universe.

§ 4. *Partial impunity or relief is familiar to us in nature.*

[III.] Upon this supposition, or even without it, we may observe somewhat, much to the present purpose, in the constitution of nature or appointments of Providence: the provision which is made, that all the bad natural consequences of men's actions should not always actually follow; or that such bad consequences, as, according to the settled course of things, would inevitably have followed, if not prevented, should, in certain degrees, be prevented. We are apt presumptuously to imagine, that the world might have been so constituted, as that there would not have been any such thing as misery or evil. On the contrary we find the Author of nature permits it: but then he has provided reliefs, and in many cases perfect remedies for it, after some pains and difficulties: reliefs and remedies even for that evil, which is the fruit of our own misconduct; and which, in the course of nature, would have continued, and ended in our destruction, but for such remedies. And this is an instance both of severity and of indulgence, in the constitution of nature. Thus all the bad consequences, now mentioned, of a man's trifling upon a precipice, might be prevented. And though all were not, yet some of them might, by proper interposition, if not rejected: by another's coming to the rash man's relief, with his own laying hold on that relief, in such sort as the case required. Persons may do a great deal themselves towards preventing the bad consequences of their follies: and more may be done by themselves, together with the assistance of others their fellow-creatures; which assistance nature requires and prompts us to. This is the general constitution of the world. Now suppose it had been so constituted, that after such actions were done, as were foreseen naturally to draw after them misery to the doer, it should have been no more in human power to have prevented that naturally consequent misery, in any instance, than it is, in all; no one can say, whether such a more severe constitution of things might not yet have been really good. But, that, on the contrary, provision is made by nature, that we may and do, to so great degree, prevent the bad natural effects of our follies; this may be called mercy or compassion in the original constitution of the world: compassion, as distinguished from goodness in general. And, the whole known constitution and course of things affording us instances of such compassion, it would be according to the analogy of nature, to hope, that, however ruinous the natural consequences of vice might be, from the general laws of God's government over the universe; yet provision might be made, possibly might have been originally made, for preventing those ruinous consequences from inevitably following: at least from following universally, and in all cases.

§ 5. *Total impunity is often reckoned on.*

Many, I am sensible, will wonder at finding this made a question, or spoken of as in any degree doubtful. The generality of mankind are so far from having that awful sense of things, which the present state of vice and misery and darkness seems to make but reasonable, that they have scarce any apprehension or thought at all about this matter, any way: and some serious persons may have spoken unadvisedly concerning it.[1]

[1] Butler seems to have had here in view those unhappy devices of what is called Universalism, that are now so much more widely promulgated.

§ 6. *Yet neglect has grave consequences ; sin, probably, awful ones.*

But let us observe, what we experience to be, and what, from the very constitution of nature, cannot but be, the consequences of irregular and disorderly behaviour ; even of such rashness, wilfulness, neglects, as we scarce call vicious. Now it is natural to apprehend, that the bad consequences of irregularity will be greater, in proportion as the irregularity is so. And there is no comparison between these irregularities, and the greater instances of vice, or a dissolute profligate disregard to all religion ; if there be any thing at all in religion. For consider what it is for creatures, moral agents, presumptuously to introduce that confusion and misery into the kingdom of God, which mankind have in fact introduced ; to blaspheme the Sovereign Lord of all ; to contemn his authority ; to be injurious, to the degree they are, to their fellow-creatures, the creatures of God. Add that the effects of vice in the present world are often extreme misery, irretrievable ruin, and even death. And upon putting all this together, it will appear, that as no one can say, in what degree fatal the unprevented consequences of vice may be, according to the general rule of divine government ; so it is by no means intuitively certain, how far these consequences could possibly, in the nature of the thing, be prevented, consistently with the eternal rule of right, or with what is, in fact, the moral constitution of nature. However, there would be large ground to hope, that the universal government was not so severely strict, but that there was room for pardon, or for having those penal consequences prevented. Yet,

§ 7. *Nor does subsequent good behaviour cancel the past in nature ;*

[IV.] There seems no probability, that any thing we could do would alone and of itself prevent them : prevent their following, or being inflicted. But one would think, at least, it were impossible that the contrary should be thought certain. For we are not acquainted with the whole of the case. We are not informed of all the reasons, which render it fit that future punishments should be inflicted: and therefore cannot know, whether any thing we could do would make such an alteration, as to render it fit that they should be remitted. We do not know what the whole natural or appointed consequences of vice are; nor in what way they would follow, if not prevented: and therefore can in no sort say, whether we could do any thing which would be sufficient to prevent them. Our ignorance being thus manifest, let us recollect the analogy of nature or providence. For, though this may be but a slight ground to raise a positive opinion upon, in this matter; yet it is sufficient to answer a mere arbitrary assertion, without any kind of evidence, urged by way of objection against a doctrine, the proof of which is not reason, but revelation. Consider then: people ruin their fortunes by extravagance; they bring diseases upon themselves by excess; they incur the penalties of civil laws; and surely civil government is natural; will sorrow for these follies past, and behaving well for the future, alone and of itself prevent the natural consequences of them? On the contrary, men's natural abilities of helping themselves are often impaired: or if not, yet they are forced to be beholden to the assistance of others, upon several accounts, and in different ways: assistance which they would have had no occasion for, had it not been for their misconduct; but which, in the disadvantageous condition they have reduced themselves to, is absolutely necessary to their recovery, and retrieving their affairs.

§ 8. *And probably not under revelation.*

Now since this is our case, considering ourselves merely as inhabitants of this world, and as having a temporal interest here, under the natural government of God, which however has a great deal moral in it: why is it not supposable that this may be our case also, in our more important capacity, as under his perfect moral government, and having a more general and future interest depending? If we have misbehaved in this higher capacity, and rendered ourselves obnoxious to the future punishment, which God has annexed to vice: it is plainly credible, that behaving well for the time to come may be—not useless, God forbid—but wholly insufficient, alone and of itself, to prevent that punishment; or to put us in the condition, which we should have been in, had we preserved our innocence.

§ 9. *The wide early prevalence of sacrifices shows how repentance was held insufficient.*

And though we ought to reason with all reverence, whenever we reason concerning the divine conduct: yet it may be added, that it is clearly contrary to all our notions of government, as well as to what is, in fact, the general constitution of nature, to suppose that doing well for the future should, in all cases, prevent all the judicial bad consequences of having done evil, or all the punishment annexed to disobedience. And we have manifestly nothing from whence to determine, in what degree, and in what cases, reformation would prevent this punishment, even supposing that it would in some. And though the efficacy of repentance itself alone, to prevent what mankind had rendered themselves obnoxious to, and recover what they had forfeited, is now insisted upon, in opposition to Christianity: yet, by the general prevalence of propitiatory sacrifices over the heathen world, this notion, of repentance alone being sufficient to expiate guilt, appears to be contrary to the general sense of mankind.

I 3

§ 10. *Punishment, then, was to be expected.*

Upon the whole, then: Had the laws, the general laws of God's government, been permitted to operate, without any interposition in our behalf, the future punishment, for ought we know to the contrary, or have any reason to think, must inevitably have followed, notwithstanding any thing we could have done to prevent it. Now,

§ 11. *Mediation, then, was* (a) *appropriate,* (b) *requisite,* (c) *effectual.*

[V.] In this darkness, or this light of nature, call it which you please, revelation comes in; confirms every doubting fear, which could enter into the heart of man, concerning the future unprevented consequence of wickedness; supposes the world to be in a state of ruin; (a supposition which seems the very ground of the Christian dispensation, and which, if not provable by reason, yet is in no wise contrary to it;) teaches us too, that the rules of divine government are such, as not to admit of pardon immediately and directly upon repentance, or by the sole efficacy of it: but then teaches at the same time, what nature might justly have hoped, that the moral government of the universe was not so rigid, but that there was room for an interposition, to avert the fatal consequences of vice; which therefore, by this means, does admit of pardon. Revelation teaches us, that the unknown laws of God's more general government, no less than the particular laws by which we experience he governs us at present, are compassionate,[b] as well as good in the more general notion of goodness: and that he hath mercifully provided, that there should be an interposition to prevent the destruction of human kind; whatever that destruction unprevented would have been. *God so loved the world, that he gave his only begotten Son, that whosoever believeth,* not, to

[b] *Sup.* § 4.

be sure, in a speculative, but in a practical sense, *that whosoever believeth in him should not perish :* ᶜ gave his Son in the same way of goodness to the world, as he affords particular persons the friendly assistance of their fellow-creatures; when, without it, their temporal ruin would be the certain consequence of their follies: in the same way of goodness, I say; though in a transcendent and infinitely higher degree. And the Son of God *loved us and gave himself for us,* with a love, which he himself compares to that of human friendship: though, in this case, all comparisons must fall infinitely short of the thing intended to be illustrated by them. He interposed in such a manner as was necessary and effectual to prevent that execution of justice upon sinners, which God had appointed should otherwise have been executed upon them: or in such a manner, as to prevent that punishment from actually following, which, according to the general laws of divine government, must have followed the sins of the world, had it not been for such interposition.ᵈ

ᶜ John iii. 16.

ᵈ It cannot, I suppose, be imagined, even by the most cursory reader, that it is, in any sort, affirmed or implied in any thing said in this chapter, that none can have the benefit of the general redemption, but such as have the advantage of being made acquainted with it in the present life. But it may be needful to mention, that several questions, which have been brought into the subject before us, and determined, and not in the least entered into here: questions which have be, I fear, rashly determined, and perhaps with equal rashness contrary ways. For instance, whether God could have saved the world by other means than the death of Christ, consistently with the general laws of his government. And had not Christ come into the world, what would have been the future condition of the better sort of men; those just persons over the face of the earth, for whom, Manasses in his prayer asserts, repentance was not appointed. The meaning of the first of these questions is greatly ambiguous: and neither of them can properly be answered, without going upon that infinitely absurd supposition, that we know the whole of the case. And perhaps the very inquiry, *What would have followed if God had not done as he has?* may have in it some very *Of large questions left aside.*

§ 12. *Our sad plight has the sin in Paradise for its occasion.*

If any thing here said should appear, upon first thought, inconsistent with divine goodness; a second, I am persuaded, will entirely remove that appearance. For were we to suppose the constitution of things to be such, as that the whole creation must have perished, had it not been for somewhat, which God had appointed should be, in order to prevent that ruin: even this supposition would not be inconsistent, in any degree, with the most absolutely perfect goodness. But still it may be thought, that this whole manner of treating the subject before us supposes mankind to be naturally in a very strange state. And truly so it does. But it is not Christianity, which has put us into this state. Whoever will consider the manifold miseries, and the extreme wickedness of the world: that the best have great wrongnesses within themselves, which they complain of, and endeavour to amend; but that the generality grow more profligate and corrupt with age: that heathen moralists thought the present state to be a state of punishment: and, what might be added, that the earth our habitation has the appearances of being a ruin: whoever, I say, will consider all these, and some other obvious things, will think he has little reason to object against the scripture account, that mankind is in a state of degradation; against this being the fact: how difficult soever he may think it to account for, or even to form a distinct conception of the occasions and circumstances of it. But that the crime of our first parents was the occasion of our being placed in a more disadvantageous condition, is a thing throughout and particularly analogous to what we see in the daily course of natural Providence; as the recovery of the world by the interposition of Christ has been shown to be so in general.

great impropriety; and ought not to be carried on any further, than is necessary to help our partial and inadequate conceptions of things.

§ 13. *The mediation is by a foreshadowed Priest-victim;*

[VI.] The particular manner in which Christ interposed in the redemption of the world, or his office as *Mediator*, in the largest sense, *between God and man*, is thus represented to us in the scripture. *He is the light of the world;* [e] the revealer of the will of God in the most eminent sense. He is a propitiatory sacrifice; [f] *the Lamb of God:* [g] and, as he voluntarily offered himself up, he is styled our High-Priest. [h] And, which seems of peculiar weight, he is described beforehand in the Old Testament, under the same characters of a priest, and an expiatory victim. [i] And whereas it is objected, that all this is merely by way of allusion to the sacrifices of the Mosaic law, the apostle on the contrary affirms, that the *law was a shadow of good things to come, and not the very image of the things:* [k] and that *the priests that offer gifts according to the law— serve unto the example and shadow of heavenly things, as Moses was admonished of God when he was about to make the tabernacle: for See, saith he, that thou make all things according to the pattern showed to thee in the mount:* [l] i.e. the Levitical priesthood was a shadow of the priesthood of Christ; in like manner as the tabernacle made by Moses was according to that showed him in the mount. The priesthood of Christ, and the tabernacle in the mount, were the originals: of the former of which the Levitical priesthood was a type; and of the latter the tabernacle made by Moses was a copy. The doctrine of this Epistle then plainly is, that the legal sacrifices were allusions to the great and final atonement to be made by the blood of Christ; and not that this was an allusion to those. Nor can any thing be more express and determinate,

[e] John i. and viii. 12.
[f] Rom. iii. 25 and v. 11 ; 1 Cor. v. 7 ; Eph. v. 2 ; 1 John ii. 2 ; Matt. xxvi. 28.
[g] John i. 29, 36 ; and throughout the Book of Revelation.
[h] Throughout the Epistle to the Hebrews.
[i] Isa. liii ; Dan. ix. 24 ; Ps. cx. 4.   [k] Heb. x. 1.
[l] Heb. viii. 4, 5.

than the following passage. *It is not possible that the blood of bulls and of goats should take away sin. Wherefore when he cometh into the world, he saith, Sacrifice and offering,* i.e. of bulls and of goats, *thou wouldest not, but a body hast thou prepared me——Lo, I come to do thy will, O God——By which will we are sanctified, through the offering of the body of Jesus Christ once for all.*[m] And to add one passage more of the like kind: *Christ was once offered to bear the sins of many; and unto them that look for him shall he appear the second time, without sin;* i.e. without bearing sin, as he did at his first coming, by being an offering for it; without having our *iniquities* again *laid upon him,* without being any more a sin offering: *unto them that look for him shall he appear the second time, without sin, unto salvation.*[n]

§ 14. *With an efficacy transcending that of example, instruction, or government.*

Nor do the inspired writers at all confine themselves to this manner of speaking concerning the satisfaction of Christ; but declare an efficacy in what he did and suffered for us, additional to and beyond mere instruction, example, and government, in great variety of expression: *That Jesus should die for that nation,* the Jews: *and not for that nation only, but that also,* plainly by the efficacy of his death, *he should gather together in one the children of God that were scattered abroad:* [o] that *he suffered for sins, the just for the unjust:* [p] that *he gave his life, himself, a ransom:* [q] that *we are bought, bought with a price:* [r] that *he redeemed us with his blood; redeemed us from the curse of the law, being made a curse for us:* [s] that he is our *advocate,* inter-

---

[m] Heb. x. 4, 5, 7, 9, 10. [n] Heb. ix. 28.
[o] John xi. 51, 52. [p] 1 Pet iii. 18.
[q] Matt. xx. 28; Mark x. 45; 1 Tim. ii. 6.
[r] 2 Pet. ii. 1; Rev. xiv. 4; 1 Cor. vi. 20.
[s] 1 Pet. i. 19; Rev. v. 9; Gal. iii. 13.

cessor, and *propitiation :* [t] that *he was made perfect, or consummate, through sufferings : and being thus made perfect, he became the author of salvation :* [u] that *God was in Christ reconciling the world to himself ; by the death of his Son, by the cross ; not imputing their trespasses unto them :* [x] and lastly, that *through death he destroyed him that had the power of death.*[y] Christ then having thus *humbled himself, and become obedient to death, even the death of the cross ; God also hath highly exalted him, and given him a name, which is above every name : hath given all things into his hand : hath committed all judgment unto him ; that all men should honour the Son, even as they honour the Father.*[z] For, *Worthy is the Lamb that was slain, to receive power, and riches, and wisdom, and strength, and honour, and glory, and blessing. And every creature which is in heaven, and on the earth, heard I, saying, Blessing, and honour, and glory, and power, be unto him that sitteth upon the throne, and unto the Lamb for ever and ever.*[a]

§ 15. *It was also* (a) *by a Prophet,*

These passages of scripture seem to comprehend and express the chief parts of Christ's office, as Mediator between God and man, so far, I mean, as the nature of this his office is revealed ; and it is usually treated of by divines under three heads.

First, He was, by way of eminence, the Prophet: *that Prophet that should come into the world,*[b] to declare the divine will. He published anew the law of nature, which men had corrupted ; and the very knowledge of which, to some degree, was lost among them. He taught mankind, taught us authoritatively, to *live soberly, righteously, and godly in this present world,* in expectation of the future judgment of God. He confirmed

---
[t] Heb. vii. 25 ; 1 John ii. 1, 2.   [u] Heb. ii. 10 and v. 9.
[x] 2 Cor. v. 19 ; Rom. v. 10 ; Eph. ii. 16.
[y] Heb. ii. 14. See also a remarkable passage in the Book of Job, xxxiii. 24.
[z] Phil. ii. 8, 9 ; John iii. 35 and v. 22, 23.
[a] Rev. v. 12, 13.   [b] John vi. 14

the truth of this moral system of nature, and gave us additional evidence of it; the evidence of testimony [c] He distinctly revealed the manner in which God would be worshipped, the efficacy of repentance, and the rewards and punishments of a future life. Thus he was a prophet in a sense in which no other ever was. To which is to be added, that he set us a perfect *example, that we should follow his steps.*

§ 16. (b) *Who had a Church or kingdom.*

Secondly, He has a *kingdom which is not of this world.* He founded a church, to be to mankind a standing memorial of religion, and invitation to it; which he promised to be with always even to the end. He exercises an invisible government over it, himself, and by his Spirit: over that part of it, which is militant here on earth, a government of discipline, *for the perfecting of the saints, for the edifying his body: till we all come in the unity of the faith, and of the knowledge of the Son of God, unto a perfect man, unto the measure of the stature of the fulness of Christ.*[d] Of this church, all persons scattered over the world, who live in obedience to his laws, are members. For these he is *gone to prepare a place,* and *will come again to receive them unto himself, that where he is, there they may be also; and reign with him for ever and ever :* [e] and likewise *to take vengeance on them that know not God, and obey not his gospel.*[f]

Against these parts of Christ's office I find no objections, but what are fully obviated in the beginning of this chapter.

§ 17. (c) *By an expiation;*

Lastly, Christ offered himself a propitiatory sacrifice, and made atonement for the sins of the world; which is mentioned last, in regard to what is objected against it. Sacrifices of expiation were commanded the Jews,

[c] *Sup.* II. i. 4 *sqq.*   [d] Eph. iv. 12, 13.
[e] John xiv. 2, 3; Rev. iii. 21 and xi. 15.   [f] 2 Thess. i. 8.

and obtained amongst most other nations, from tradition, whose original probably was revelation. And they were continually repeated, both occasionally, and at the returns of stated times; and made up great part of the external religion of mankind. *But now once in the end of the world Christ appeared to put away sin by the sacrifice of himself.*[g] And this sacrifice was, in the highest degree and with the most extensive influence, of that efficacy for obtaining pardon of sin, which the heathens may be supposed to have thought their sacrifices to have been, and which the Jewish sacrifices really were in some degree, and with regard to some persons.

§ 18. *Whereof the mode is not revealed to us.*

How and in what particular way it had this efficacy, there are not wanting persons who have endeavoured to explain: but I do not find that the scripture has explained it. We seem to be very much in the dark concerning the manner in which the ancients understood atonement to be made, i.e. pardon to be obtained by sacrifices. And if the scripture has, as surely it has, left this matter of the satisfaction of Christ, mysterious, left somewhat in it unrevealed, all conjectures about it must be, if not evidently absurd, yet at least uncertain. Nor has any one reason to complain for want of further information, unless he can show his claim to it.

§ 19. *Some have exaggerated expiation, others reduce it to example.*

Some have endeavoured to explain the efficacy of what Christ has done and suffered for us, beyond what the scripture has authorized: others, probably because they could not explain it, have been for taking it away, and confining his office as Redeemer of the world to his instruction, example, and government of the church. Whereas the doctrine of the gospel appears to be, not

[g] Heb. ix. 26.

only that he taught the efficacy of repentance, but rendered it of the efficacy which it is, by what he did and suffered for us: that he obtained for us the benefit of having our repentance accepted unto eternal life: not only that he revealed to sinners, that they were in a capacity of salvation, and how they might obtain it; but moreover that he put them into this capacity of salvation, by what he did and suffered for them; put us into a capacity of escaping future punishment, and obtaining future happiness. And it is our wisdom thankfully to accept the benefit, by performing the conditions, upon which it is offered, on our part, without disputing how it was procured on his. For,

§ 20. *Whether* (a) *means other than mediation could have been used, we cannot judge.*

[VII.] Since we neither know by what means punishment in a future state would have followed wickedness in this; nor in what manner it would have been inflicted, had it not been prevented; nor all the reasons why its infliction would have been needful; nor the particular nature of that state of happiness, which Christ is gone to prepare for his disciples: and since we are ignorant how far any thing which we could do, would, alone and of itself, have been effectual to prevent that punishment, to which we were obnoxious, and recover that happiness, which we had forfeited; it is most evident we are not judges, antecedently to revelation, whether a mediator was or was not necessary, to obtain those ends: to prevent that future punishment, and bring mankind to the final happiness of their nature.

§ 21. *Nor* (b) *of the particulars of the mediatorial work.*

And for the very same reasons, upon supposition of the necessity of a mediator, we are no more judges, antecedently to revelation, of the whole nature of his office, or the several parts of which it consists; of what

satisfaction of Christ is, either that they do not consider God's settled and uniform appointments as his appointments at all : or else they forget that vicarious punishment is a providential appointment of every day's experience : and then, from their being unacquainted with the more general laws of nature or divine government over the world, and not seeing how the sufferings of Christ could contribute to the redemption of it, unless by arbitrary and tyrannical will ; they conclude his sufferings could not contribute to it any other way.

§ 23. *Notice its tendency to vindicate the laws of God.*

And yet, what has been often alleged in justification of this doctrine, even from the apparent natural tendency of this method of our redemption ; its tendency to vindicate the authority of God's laws, and deter his creatures from sin ; this has never yet been answered, and is, I think, plainly unanswerable : though I am far from thinking it an account of the whole of the case. But without taking this into consideration, it abundantly appears, from the observations above made, that this objection is, not an objection against Christianity, but against the whole general constitution of nature. And if it were to be considered as an objection against Christianity, or considering it as it is, an objection against the constitution of nature ; it amounts to no more in conclusion than this, that a divine appointment cannot be necessary or expedient, because the objector does not discern it to be so : though he must own that the nature of the case is such, as renders him incapable of judging, whether it be so or not ; or of seeing it to be necessary, though it were so.

§ 24. *This cavil, 'We see not why, ergo it cannot be,' almost more foolish than guilty.*

It is indeed a matter of great patience to reasonable men, to find people arguing in this manner : objecting against the credibility of such particular things revealed in scripture, that they do not see the necessity or expediency of them. For though it is highly right, and the most pious exercise of our understanding, to inquire with due reverence into the ends and reasons of God's dispensations: yet when those reasons are concealed, to argue from our ignorance, that such dispensations cannot be from God, is infinitely absurd. The presumption of this kind of objections seems almost lost in the folly of them. And the folly of them is yet greater, when they are urged, as usually they are, against things in Christianity analogous or like to those natural dispensations of Providence, which are matter of experience. Let reason be kept to: and if any part of the scripture account of the redemption of the world by Christ can be shown to be really contrary to it, let the scripture, in the name of God, be given up: but let not such poor creatures as we go on objecting against an infinite scheme, that we do not see the necessity or usefulness of all its parts, and call this reasoning; and, which still further heightens the absurdity in the present case, parts which we are not actively concerned in. For it may be worth mentioning.

§ 25. *We cannot expect information on the divine conduct, as large as on our own duty.*

Lastly, That not only the reason of the thing, but the whole analogy of nature, should teach us, not to expect to have the like information concerning the divine conduct, as concerning our own duty. God instructs us by experience, (for it is not reason, but experience which instructs us,) what good or bad consequences will follow from our acting in such and such manners: and by this he directs us, how we are to behave ourselves. But, though we are sufficiently instructed for the common purposes of life: yet it is but an almost infinitely small part of natural providence, which we are at all let into. The case is the same with regard to revelation. The doctrine of a mediator between God and man, against which it is objected, that the expediency of some things in it is not understood, relates only to what was done on God's part in the appointment, and on the mediator's in the execution of it. For what is required of us, in consequence of this gracious dispensation, is another subject, in which none can complain for want of information. The constitution of the world, and God's natural government over it, is all mystery, as much as the Christian dispensation. Yet under the first he has given men all things pertaining to life; and under the other, all things pertaining unto godliness. And it may be added, that there is nothing hard to be accounted for in any of the common precepts of Christianity: though if there were, surely a divine command is abundantly sufficient to lay us under the strongest obligations to obedience. But the fact is, that the reasons of all the Christian precepts are evident. Positive institutions are manifestly necessary to keep up and propagate religion amongst mankind. And our duty to Christ, the internal and external worship of him; this part of the religion of the gospel, manifestly arises out of what he has done and suffered, his authority and dominion, and the relation which he is revealed to stand in to us.[h]

CHAPTER VI

OF THE WANT OF UNIVERSALITY IN REVELATION: AND OF THE SUPPOSED DEFICIENCY IN THE PROOF OF IT

§ 1. *These two objections do not justify rejection,*

It has been thought by some persons, that if the evidence of revelation appears doubtful, this itself turns into a positive argument against it: because it cannot be supposed, that, if it were true, it would be left to subsist upon doubtful evidence. And the objection against revelation from its not being universal is often insisted upon as of great weight.

[h] *Sup.* II. i. 16–18.

Now the weakness of these opinions may be shown, by observing the suppositions on which they are founded: which are really such as these; that it cannot be thought God would have bestowed any favour at all upon us, unless in the degree, which, we think, he might, and which, we imagine, would be most to our particular advantage; and also that it cannot be thought he would bestow a favour upon any, unless he bestowed the same upon all: suppositions which we find contradicted, not by a few instances in God's natural government of the world, but by the general analogy of nature together.

§ 2. *In temporal matters; nor, therefore, in spiritual; as regards* (a) *imperfect communication,*

Persons who speak of the evidence of religion as doubtful, and of this supposed doubtfulness as a positive argument against it, should be put upon considering, what that evidence indeed is, which they act upon with regard to their temporal interests. For, it is not only extremely difficult, but in many cases absolutely impossible, to balance pleasure and pain, satisfaction and uneasiness, so as to be able to say on which side the overplus is. There are the like difficulties and impossibilities in making the due allowances for a change of temper and taste, for satiety, disgusts, ill health: any of which render men incapable of enjoying, after they have obtained what they most eagerly desired. Numberless too are the accidents, besides that one of untimely death, which may even probably disappoint the best concerted schemes: and strong objections are often seen to lie against them, not to be removed or answered, but which seem overbalanced by reasons on the other side; so as that the certain difficulties and dangers of the pursuit are, by every one, thought justly disregarded, upon account of the appearing greater advantages in case of success, though there be but little probability of it. Lastly, every one observes our liableness, if we be not upon our guard, to be deceived by the falsehood of men, and the false appearances of things: and this danger must be greatly increased, if there be a strong bias within, suppose from indulged passion, to favour the deceit. Hence arises that great uncertainty and doubtfulness of proof, wherein our temporal interest really consists; what are the most probable means of attaining it; and whether those means will eventually be successful. And numberless instances there are, in the daily course of life, in which all men think it reasonable to engage in pursuits, though the probability is greatly against succeeding; and to make such provision for themselves, as it is supposable they may have occasion for, though the plain acknowledged probability is, that they never shall.

§ 3. *Or* (b) *want of universality in the gift.*

Then those who think the objection against revelation, from its light not being universal, to be of weight, should observe, that the Author of nature, in numberless instances, bestows that upon some, which he does not upon others, who seem equally to stand in need of it. Indeed he appears to bestow all his gifts with the most promiscuous variety among creatures of the same species: health and strength, capacities of prudence and of knowledge, means of improvement, riches, and all external advantages. And as there are not any two men found, of exactly like shape and features: so it is probable there are not any two, of an exactly like constitution, temper and situation, with regard to the goods and evils of life. Yet, notwithstanding these uncertainties and varieties, God does exercise a natural government over the world: and there is such a thing as a prudent and imprudent institution of life, with regard to our health and our affairs, under that his natural government.

§ 4. *Diverse degrees of evidence have here been combined with diversity of time;*

As neither the Jewish nor Christian revelation have been universal; and as they have been afforded to a greater or less part of the world, at different times: so likewise, at different times, both revelations have had different degrees of evidence. The Jews who lived during the succession of prophets, that is, from Moses till after the Captivity, had higher evidence of the truth of their religion, than those had, who lived in the interval between the last-mentioned period, and the coming of Christ. And the first Christians had higher evidence of the miracles wrought in attestation of Christianity, than what we have now. They had also a strong presumptive proof of the truth of it, perhaps of much greater force, in way of argument, than many think, of which we have very little remaining; I mean the presumptive proof of its truth, from the influence which it had upon the lives of the generality of its professors. And we, or future ages, may possibly have a proof of it, which they could not have, from the conformity between the prophetic history, and the state of the world and of Christianity.

§ 5. *Also of persons, places, circumstances.*

And further: If we were to suppose the evidence, which some have of religion, to amount to little more than seeing that it may be true; but that they remain in great doubts and uncertainties about both its evidence and its nature, and great perplexities concerning the rule of life: others to have a full conviction of the truth of religion, with a distinct knowledge of their duty: and others severally to have all the intermediate degrees of religious light and evidence, which lie between these two——If we put the case, that for the present, it was intended, revelation should be no more than a small light, in the midst of a world greatly overspread, notwithstanding it, with ignorance and darkness: that certain glimmerings of this light should extend, and be directed, to remote distances, in such a manner as that those who really partook of it should not discern from whence it originally came: that some in a nearer situation to it should have its light obscured, and, in different ways and degrees, intercepted: and that others should be placed within its clearer influence, and be much more enlivened, cheered, and directed by it; but yet that even to these it should be no more than *a light shining in a dark place:* all this would be perfectly uniform, and of a piece with the conduct of Providence, in the distribution of its other blessings. If the fact of the case really were, that some have received no light at all from the scripture; as many ages and countries in the heathen world: that others, though they have, by means of it, had essential or natural religion enforced upon their consciences, yet have never had the genuine scripture-revelation, with its real evidence, proposed to their consideration; and the ancient Persians [1] and modern Mahometans [2] may possibly be instances of people in a situation somewhat like to this: that others, though they have had the scripture laid before them as of divine revelation, yet have had it with the system and evidence of Christianity so interpolated,[3] the system so corrupted, the evidence so blended with false miracles, as to leave the mind in the utmost doubtfulness and uncertainty about the whole; which may be the state of some

---

[1] The author probably had in his mind the comparative purity of Zoroastrian doctrine.

[2] There are three things here to be borne in mind:

(*a*) That Mahometanism, among undeveloped races, still manifests a considerable force of aggressive energy.

(*b*) That its proclamation of the divine unity is a fact of gigantic moment.

(*c*) That the worst of all its developments, in the terrible wickedness of the government of Turkey, has only been exhibited in full to the world during the latter portion of the nineteenth century.

[3] See *sup.* II. i. 13.

thoughtful men, in most of those nations who call themselves Christian: and lastly, that others have had Christianity offered to them in its genuine simplicity, and with its proper evidence, as persons in countries and churches of civil and of Christian liberty; but however that even these persons are left in great ignorance in many respects, and have by no means light afforded them enough to satisfy their curiosity, but only to regulate their life, to teach them their duty, and encourage them in the careful discharge of it:

§ 6. *All these cases have parallels in nature.*

I say, if we were to suppose this somewhat of a general true account of the degrees of moral and religious light and evidence, which were intended to be afforded mankind, and of what has actually been and is their situation, in their moral and religious capacity; there would be nothing in all this ignorance, doubtfulness, and uncertainty, in all these varieties, and supposed disadvantages of some in comparison of others, respecting religion, but may be paralleled by manifest analogies in the natural dispensations of Providence at present, and considering ourselves merely in our temporal capacity.

§ 7. *But God's plan is one of allowances, and so of universal equity.*

Nor is there any thing shocking in all this, or which would seem to bear hard upon the moral administration in nature, if we would really keep in mind, that every one shall be dealt equitably with: instead of forgetting this, or explaining it away, after it is acknowledged in words. All shadow of injustice, and indeed all harsh appearances, in this various economy of Providence, would be lost; if we would keep in mind, that every merciful allowance shall be made, and no more be required of any one, than what might have been equitably expected of him, from the circumstances in which he was placed; and not what might have been expected, had he been placed in other circumstances: i.e. in scripture language, that every man shall be *accepted according to what he had, not according to what he had not.*[a] This however doth not by any means imply, that all persons' condition here is equally advantageous with respect to futurity. And Providence's designing to place some in greater darkness with respect to religious knowledge, is no more a reason why they should not endeavour to get out of that darkness, and others to bring them out of it; than why ignorant and slow people in matters of other knowledge should not endeavour to learn, or should not be instructed.

§ 8. *Unlikeness of creatures makes probable unlikeness of situations for like creatures.*

It is not unreasonable to suppose, that the same wise and good principle, whatever it was, which disposed the Author of nature to make different kinds and orders of creatures, disposed him also to place creatures of like kinds in different situations:[1] and that the same principle which disposed him to make creatures of different moral capacities, disposed him also to place creatures of like moral capacities in different religious situations; and even the same creatures, in different periods of their being. And the account or reason of this is also most probably the account why the constitution of things is such, as that

[a] 2 Cor. viii. 12.

---

[1] 'Of like kinds' may mean, I presume, likeness of kind, class, property, or quality, short of likeness in every particular of each property or quality. It is observable that when St. Paul pleads the dominion of the potter over his clay, to confront an objector, he does not proceed to any assertion that the potter, in selecting clay for different vessels, has no regard to the suitableness of the material for each respectively. Rom. ix. 21-23.

creatures of moral natures or capacities, for a considerable part of that duration in which they are living agents, are not at all subjects of morality and religion ; but grow up to be so, and grow up to be so more and more, gradually from childhood to mature age.

§ 9. *The complexity of nature infers* per se *great varieties.*

What, in particular, is the account or reason of these things, we must be greatly in the dark, were it only that we know so very little even of our own case. Our present state may possibly be the consequence of somewhat past, which we are wholly ignorant of: as it has a reference to somewhat to come, of which we know scarce any more than is necessary for practice. A system or constitution, in its notion, implies variety ; and so complicated an one as this world, very great variety. So that were revelation universal, yet from men's different capacities of understanding, from the different lengths of their lives, their different educations and other external circumstances, and from their difference of temper and bodily constitution ; their religious situations would be widely different, and the disadvantage of some in comparison of others, perhaps, altogether as much as at present. And the true account, whatever it be, why mankind, or such a part of mankind, are placed in this condition of ignorance, must be supposed also the true account of our further ignorance, in not knowing the reasons why, or whence it is, that they are placed in this condition. But the following practical reflections may deserve the serious consideration of those persons, who think the circumstances of mankind or their own, in the forementioned respects, a ground of complaint.

§ 10. (a) *Doubtfulness of evidence may constitute a part of moral probation.*

First, The evidence of religion not appearing obvious, may constitute one particular part of some men's trial in the religious sense: as it gives scope for a virtuous exercise, or vicious neglect of their understanding, in examining or not examining into that evidence. There seems no possible reason to be given, why we may not be in a state of moral probation, with regard to the exercise of our understanding upon the subject of religion, as we are with regard to our behaviour in common affairs. The former is as much a thing within our power and choice as the latter. And I suppose it is to be laid down for certain, that the same character, the same inward principle, which, after a man is convinced of the truth of religion, renders him obedient to the precepts of it, would, were he not thus convinced, set him about an examination of it, upon its system and evidence being offered to his thoughts: and that in the latter state his examination would be with an impartiality, seriousness, and solicitude, proportionable to what his obedience is in the former.

§ 11. (b) *Neglect of evidence is a form of depravity.*

And as inattention, negligence, want of all serious concern, about a matter of such a nature and such importance, when offered to men's consideration, is, before a distinct conviction of its truth, as real immoral depravity and dissoluteness; as neglect of religious practice after such conviction: so active solicitude about it, and fair impartial consideration of its evidence before such conviction, is as really an exercise of a morally right temper; as is religious practice after. Thus, that religion is not intuitively true, but a matter of deduction and inference; that a conviction of its truth is not forced upon every one, but left to be, by some, collected with heedful attention to premises; this as much constitutes religious probation, as much

§ 12. (a) *In this subject, that matter 'may be true' obliges, as well as if it 'is true.'*

Secondly, It appears to be a thing as evident, though it is not so much attended to, that if, upon consideration of religion, the evidence of it should seem to any persons doubtful, in the highest supposable degree; even this doubtful evidence will, however, put them into a *general state of probation* in the moral and religious sense. For, suppose a man to be really in doubt, whether such a person had not done him the greatest favour; or, whether his whole temporal interest did not depend upon that person: no one, who had any sense of gratitude and of prudence, could possibly consider himself in the same situation, with regard to such person, as if he had no such doubt. In truth, it is as just to say, that certainty and doubt are the same; as to say, the situations now mentioned would leave a man as entirely at liberty in point of gratitude or prudence, as he would be, were he certain he had received no favour from such person, or that he no way depended upon him. And thus, though the evidence of religion which is afforded to some men should be little more than that they are given to see, the system of Christianity, or religion in general, to be supposable and credible; this ought in all reason to beget a serious practical apprehension, that it may be true.[1] And even this will afford matter of exercise for religious suspense and deliberation, for moral resolution and self-government; because the apprehension

[1] This obligation in cases of partial proof seems to extend to all matters (*a*) bearing upon moral conduct, (*b*) of grave interest; but to abstract and speculative matter only if, and when, we have special occasion to deal with it.

that religion may be true does as really lay men under obligations, as a full conviction that it is true. It gives occasion and motives to consider further the important subject; to preserve attentively upon their minds a general implicit sense that they may be under divine moral government, an awful solicitude about religion, whether natural or revealed. Such apprehension ought to turn men's eyes to every degree of new light which may be had, from whatever side it comes; and induce them to refrain, in the mean time, from all immoralities, and live in the conscientious practice of every common virtue.[1] Especially are they bound to keep at the greatest distance from all dissolute profaneness; for this the very nature of the case forbids; and to treat with highest reverence a matter, upon which their own whole interest and being, and the fate of nature, depends.

§ 13. (b) *Doubters in religion are bound to conform to its moral laws.*

This behaviour, and an active endeavour to maintain within themselves this temper, is the business, the duty, and the wisdom of those persons, who complain of the doubtfulness of religion: is what they are under the most proper obligations to. And such behaviour is an exertion of, and has a tendency to improve in them, that character, which the practice of all the several duties of religion, from a full conviction of its truth, is an exertion of, and has a tendency to improve in others: others, I say, to whom God has afforded such conviction. Nay, considering the infinite importance of religion, revealed as well as natural, I think it may be said in general, that whoever will weigh the matter thoroughly may see, there is not near so much difference, as is commonly imagined, between what ought in reason to be the rule of life, to those persons

[1] The idea of the author seems to be that conveyed in the Psalms: 'I will wash my hands in innocency, O Lord; and so will I go to thine altar' (xxvi. 6).

who are fully convinced of its truth, and to those who have only a serious doubting apprehension, that it may be true. Their hopes, and fears, and obligations, will be in various degrees: but, as the subject-matter of their hopes and fears is the same; so the subject-matter of their obligations, what they are bound to do and to refrain from, is not so very unlike.

§ 14. (c) *The obligation is enhanced by the weight attaching to example.*

It is to be observed further, that, from a character of understanding, or a situation of influence in the world, some persons have it in their power to do infinitely more harm or good, by setting an example of profaneness and avowed disregard to all religion, or, on the contrary, of a serious, though perhaps doubting, apprehension of its truth, and of a reverend regard to it under this doubtfulness; than they can do, by acting well or ill in all the common intercourses amongst mankind. And consequently they are most highly accountable for a behaviour, which, they may easily foresee, is of such importance, and in which there is most plainly a right and a wrong; even admitting the evidence of religion to be as doubtful as is pretended.

§ 15. (d) *Doubt implies the existence of some degree of evidence for the thing doubted.*

The ground of these observations, and that which renders them just and true, is, that doubting necessarily implies some degree of evidence for that, of which we doubt. For no person would be in doubt concerning the truth of a number of facts so and so circumstanced, which should accidentally come into his thoughts, and of which he had no evidence at all. And though in the case of an even chance, and where consequently we were in doubt, we should in common language say, that we had no evidence at all for either side; yet that situation of things, which renders it an even chance and no more, that such an event will happen, renders this case equivalent to all others, where there is such evidence on both sides of a question,[b] as leaves the mind in doubt concerning the truth. Indeed in all these cases, there is no more evidence on one side than on the other; but there is (what is equivalent to) much more for either, than for the truth of a number of facts which come into one's thoughts at random. And thus, in all these cases, doubt as much presupposes evidence, lower degrees of evidence, as belief presupposes higher, and certainty higher still. Any one, who will a little attend to the nature of evidence, will easily carry this observation on, and see, that between no evidence at all, and that degree of it which affords ground of doubt, there are as many intermediate degrees, as there are, between that degree which is the ground of doubt, and demonstration. And though we have not faculties to distinguish these degrees of evidence with any sort of exactness; yet, in proportion as they are discerned, they ought to influence our practice. For it is as real an imperfection in the moral character, not to be influenced in practice by a lower degree of evidence when discerned, as it is in the understanding, not to discern it.

§ 16. (e) *Corruption of the heart operates forcibly where the evidence is short of overbearing.*

And as, in all subjects which men consider, they discern the lower as well as higher degrees of evidence, proportionably to their capacity of understanding: so, in practical subjects, they are influenced in practice, by the lower as well as higher degrees of it, proportionably to their fairness and honesty. And as, in proportion to defects in the understanding, men are unapt to see lower degrees of evidence, are in danger of overlooking evidence when it is not glaring, and are easily imposed upon in such cases: so, in proportion to the corruption of the heart, they seem capable of

[b] Introduction, §§ 5, 6.

satisfying themselves with having no regard in practice to evidence acknowledged real, if it be not overbearing. From these things it must follow, that doubting concerning religion implies such a degree of evidence for it, as, joined with the consideration of its importance, unquestionably lays men under the obligations before mentioned, to have a dutiful regard to it in all their behaviour.

§ 17. (a) *The duty of effort is enhanced, as by doubtfulness in religion, so by temptations in conduct.*

Thirdly, The difficulties in which the evidence of religion is involved, which some complain of, is no more a just ground of complaint, than the external circumstances of temptation, which others are placed in; or than difficulties in the practice of it, after a full conviction of its truth. Temptations render our state a more improving state of discipline,[c] than it would be otherwise: as they give occasion for a more attentive exercise of the virtuous principle, which confirms and strengthens it more, than an easier or less attentive exercise of it could. Now speculative difficulties are, in this respect, of the very same nature with these external temptations. For the evidence of religion not appearing obvious, is to some persons a temptation to reject it, without any consideration at all; and therefore requires such an attentive exercise of the virtuous principle, seriously to consider that evidence, as there would be no occasion for, but for such temptation. And the supposed doubtfulness of its evidence, after it has been in some sort considered, affords opportunity to an unfair mind of explaining away, and deceitfully hiding from itself, that evidence which it might see; and also for men's encouraging themselves in vice, from hopes of impunity, though they do clearly see thus much at least, that these hopes are uncertain: in like manner as the common temptation to many instances of folly, which end in temporal infamy and

[c] Part I. chap. v.

ruin, is the ground for hope of not being detected, and of escaping with impunity; i.e. the doubtfulness of the proof beforehand, that such foolish behaviour will thus end in infamy and ruin. On the contrary, supposed doubtfulness in the evidence of religion calls for a more careful and attentive exercise of the virtuous principle, in fairly yielding themselves up to the proper influence of any real evidence, though doubtful; and in practising conscientiously all virtue, though under some uncertainty, whether the government in the universe may not possibly be such, as that vice may escape with impunity. And in general, temptation, meaning by this word the lesser allurements to wrong and difficulties in the discharge of our duty, as well as the greater ones; temptation, I say, as such and of every kind and degree, as it calls forth some virtuous efforts, additional to what would otherwise have been wanting, cannot but be an additional discipline and improvement of virtue, as well as probation of it in the other senses of that word.[d] So that the very same account is to be given, why the evidence of religion should be left in such a manner, as to require, in some, an attentive, solicitous, perhaps painful exercise of their understanding about it; as why others should be placed in such circumstances, as that the practice of its common duties, after a full conviction of the truth of it, should require attention, solicitude, and pains: or, why appearing doubtfulness should be permitted to afford matter of temptation to some; as why external difficulties and allurements should be permitted to afford matter of temptation to others. The same account also is to be given, why some should be exercised with temptations of both these kinds; as why others should be exercised with the latter in such very high degrees, as some have been, particularly as the primitive Christians were.

[d] Part I. chap. iv. and I. v. 42.

§ 18. (b) *As in nature, so in religion, doubts may constitute for some the capital article of trial.*

Nor does there appear any absurdity in supposing, that the speculative difficulties in which the evidence of religion is involved, may make even the principal part of some persons' trial. For, as the chief temptations of the generality of the world are, the ordinary motives to injustice or unrestrained pleasure; or to live in the neglect of religion from that frame of mind, which renders many persons almost without feeling as to any thing distant, or which is not the object of their senses: so there are other persons without this shallowness of temper, persons of a deeper sense as to what is invisible and future; who not only see, but have a general practical feeling, that what is to come will be present, and that things are not less real for their not being the objects of sense; and who, from their natural constitution of body and of temper, and from their external condition, may have small temptations to behave ill, small difficulty in behaving well, in the common course of life. Now when these latter persons have a distinct full conviction of the truth of religion, without any possible doubts or difficulties, the practice of it is to them unavoidable, unless they will do a constant violence to their own minds; and religion is scarce any more a discipline to them, than it is to creatures in a state of perfection. Yet these persons may possibly stand in need of moral discipline and exercise in a higher degree, than they would have by such an easy practice of religion. Or it may be requisite, for reasons unknown to us, that they should give some further manifestation [e] what is their moral character, to the creation of God, than such a practice of it would be. Thus in the great variety of religious situations in which men are placed, what constitutes, what chiefly and peculiarly constitutes, the probation, in all senses, of some persons, may be the difficulties in which the evidence of religion is involved: and

[e] *Sup.* I. v. 42.

their principal and distinguished trial may be, how they will behave under and with respect to these difficulties. Circumstances in men's situation in their temporal capacity, analogous in good measure to this respecting religion, are to be observed. We find some persons are placed in such a situation in the world, as that their chief difficulty with regard to conduct, is not the doing what is prudent when it is known; for this, in numberless cases, is as easy as the contrary: but to some the principal exercise is, recollection and being upon their guard against deceits, the deceits suppose of those about them; against false appearances of reason and prudence. To persons in some situations, the principal exercise with respect to conduct is, attention in order to inform themselves what is proper, what is really the reasonable and prudent part to act.

§ 19. *Also the doubts may be due to faults in the examinant.*

But as I have hitherto gone upon supposition, that men's dissatisfaction with the evidence of religion is not owing to their neglects or prejudices; it must be added, on the other hand, in all common reason, and as what the truth of the case plainly requires should be added, that such dissatisfaction possibly may be owing to those, possibly may be men's own fault. For,

If there are any persons, who never set themselves heartily and in earnest to be informed in religion: if there are any, who secretly wish it may not prove true; and are less attentive to evidence than to difficulties, and more to objections than to what is said in answer to them: these persons will scarce be thought in a likely way of seeing the evidence of religion, though it were most certainly true, and capable of being ever so fully proved. If any accustom themselves to consider this subject usually in the way of mirth and sport: if they attend to forms and representations, and inadequate manners of expression, instead of the real things intended by them: (for signs often can be no more than inadequately expressive of the things signified:) or if they substitute human errors in the room of divine truth: why may not all, or any of these things, hinder some men from seeing that evidence, which really is seen by others; as a like turn of mind, with respect to matters of common speculation and practice, does, we find by experience, hinder them from attaining that knowledge and right understanding, in matters of common speculation and practice, which more fair and attentive minds attain to? And the effect will be the same, whether their neglect of seriously considering the evidence of religion, and their indirect behaviour with regard to it, proceed from mere carelessness, or from the grosser vices; or whether it be owing to this, that forms and figurative manners of expression, as well as errors, administer occasions of ridicule, when the things intended, and the truth itself, would not. Men may indulge a ludicrous turn so far as to lose all sense of conduct and prudence in worldly affairs, and even, as it seems, to impair their faculty of reason. And in general, levity, carelessness, passion, and prejudice, *do* hinder us from being rightly informed, with respect to common things: and they *may*, in like manner, and perhaps in some further providential manner, with respect to moral and religious subjects: may hinder evidence from being laid before us, and from being seen when it is. The scripture [f] does declare, that every one *shall not*

---

[f] Dan. xii. 10. See also Is. xxix. 13, 14; Matth. vi. 23, and xi. 25, and xiii. 11, 12; John iii. 19 and v. 44; 1 Cor. ii. 14 and 2 Cor. iv. 4; 2 Tim. iii. 13; and that affectionate as well as authoritative admonition, so very many times inculcated, *He that hath ears to hear, let him hear.* Grotius saw so strongly the thing intended in these and other passages of scripture of the like sense, as to say, that the proof given us of Christianity was less than it might have been, for this very purpose: *Ut ita sermo Evangelii tanquam lapis esset Lydius ad quem ingenia sanabilia explorarentur.* De Ver. R. C. lib. ii. towards the end.

Texts; and Grotius on the purpose of restricted evidence.

understand. And it makes no difference, by what providential conduct this comes to pass: whether the evidence of Christianity was originally and with design, put and left so, as that those who are desirous of evading moral obligations should not see it; and that honest-minded persons should: or, whether it comes to pass by any other means.

§ 20. *The proof of religion, in both kinds, upon inquiry, lies level to common men.*

Further: The general proof of natural religion and of Christianity does, I think, lie level to common men; even those, the greatest part of whose time, from childhood to old age, is taken up with providing for themselves and their families the common conveniences, perhaps necessaries, of life: those, I mean, of this rank, who ever think at all of asking after proof, or attending to it. Common men, were they as much in earnest about religion, as about their temporal affairs, are capable of being convinced upon real evidence, that there is a God who governs the world: and they feel themselves to be of a moral nature, and accountable creatures. And as Christianity entirely falls in with this their natural sense of things, so they are capable, not only of being persuaded, but of being made to see, that there is evidence of miracles wrought in attestation of it, and many appearing completions of prophecy. But though this proof is real and conclusive, yet it is liable to objections, and may be run up into difficulties; which, however, persons who are capable, not only of talking of, but of really seeing, are capable also of seeing through: i.e. not of clearing up and answering them, so as to satisfy their curiosity, for of such knowledge we are not capable with respect to any one thing in nature; but capable of seeing that the proof is not lost in these difficulties, or destroyed by these objections. But then a thorough examination into religion, with regard to these objections, which cannot be the business of every man, is a matter of pretty large compass, and, from the nature of it, requires some knowledge, as well as time and attention; to see, how the evidence comes out, upon balancing one thing with another, and what, upon the whole, is the amount of it. Now if persons who have picked up these objections from others, and take for granted they are of weight, upon the word of those from whom they received them, or, by often retailing of them, come to see or fancy they see them to be of weight; will not prepare themselves for such an examination, with a competent degree of knowledge; or will not give that time and attention to the subject, which, from the nature of it, is necessary for attaining such information: in this case, they must remain in doubtfulness, ignorance, or error; in the same way as they must, with regard to common sciences, and matters of common life, if they neglect the necessary means of being informed in them.

§ 21. *Accrediting an ambassador is not a parallel case, as it aims only at a formal act.*

But still perhaps it will be objected, that if a prince or common master were to send directions to a servant, he would take care, that they should always bear the certain marks, who they came from, and that their sense should be always plain: so as that there should be no possible doubt, if he could help it, concerning the authority or meaning of them. Now the proper answer to all this kind of objections is, that, wherever the fallacy lies, it is even certain we cannot argue thus with respect to him, who is the Governor of the world: and particularly that he does not afford us such information, with respect to our temporal affairs and interests, as experience abundantly shows. However, there is a full answer to this objection, from the very nature of religion. For, the reason why a prince would give his directions in this plain manner is, that he absolutely desires such an external action should be done, without concerning himself with the motive or principle upon which it is done: i.e. he regards only the external event, or the thing's being done; and not at all, properly speaking, the doing of it, or the action. Whereas the whole of morality and religion consisting merely in action itself, there is no sort of parallel between the cases. But if the prince be supposed to regard only the action; i.e. only to desire to exercise, or in any sense prove, the understanding or loyalty of a servant; he would not always give his orders in such a plain manner.

§ 22. *Whether God's will be regarded, herein, as absolute, or as conditional, the argument remains.*

It may be proper to add, that the will of God, respecting morality and religion, may be considered either as absolute, or as only conditional. If it be absolute, it can only be thus, that we should act virtuously in such given circumstances; not that we should be brought to act so, by his changing of our circumstances. And if God's will be thus absolute, then it is in our power, in the highest and strictest sense, to do or to contradict his will; which is a most weighty consideration. Or his will may be considered only as conditional, that if we act so and so, we shall be rewarded; if otherwise, punished: of which conditional will of the Author of nature, the whole constitution of it affords most certain instances.

§ 23. *Sums up the foregoing Sections.*

Upon the whole: That we are in a state of religion necessarily implies, that we are in a state of probation: and the credibility of our being at all in such a state being admitted, there seems no peculiar difficulty in supposing our probation to be, just as it is, in those respects which are above objected against. There seems no pretence, from *the reason of the thing,* to say, that the trial cannot equitably be any thing, but whether persons will act suitably to certain information, or such as admits no room for doubt; so as that there can be no danger of miscarriage, but either from their not attending to what they certainly know, or from overbearing passion hurrying them on to act contrary to it. For, since ignorance and doubt afford scope for probation in all senses, as really as intuitive conviction or certainty; and since the two former are to be put to the same account as difficulties in practice; men's moral probation may also be, whether they will take due care to inform themselves by impartial consideration, and afterwards whether they will act as the case requires, upon the evidence which they have, however doubtful. And this, we find by *experience*, is frequently our probation,[g] in our temporal capacity. For, the information which we want with regard to our worldly interests is by no means always given us of course, without any care of our own. And we are greatly liable to self-deceits from inward secret prejudices, and also to the deceits of others. So that to be able to judge what is the prudent part, often requires much and difficult consideration. Then after we have judged the very best we can, the evidence upon which we must act, if we will live and act at all, is perpetually doubtful to a very high degree. And the constitution and course of the world in fact is such, as that want of impartial consideration what we have to do, and venturing upon extravagant courses because it is doubtful what will be the consequence, are often naturally, i.e. providentially, altogether as fatal, as misconduct occasioned by heedless inattention to what we certainly know, or disregarding it from overbearing passion.

§ 24. *Invites the objector to consider whether the obstacle lies within himself.*

Several of the observations here made may well seem strange, perhaps unintelligible, to many good men. But if the persons for whose sake they are made

[g] I. ii. 12, and *sup.* §§ 17–19.

think so; persons who object as above, and throw off all regard to religion under pretence of want of evidence; I desire them to consider again, whether their thinking so be owing to any thing unintelligible in these observations, or to their own not having such a sense of religion and serious solicitude about it, as even their state of scepticism does in all reason require? It ought to be forced upon the reflection of these persons, that our nature and condition necessarily require us, in the daily course of life, to act upon evidence much lower [1] than what is commonly called probable; to guard, not only against what we fully believe will, but also against what we think it supposable may, happen; and to engage in pursuits when the probability is greatly against success, if it be credible, that possibly we may succeed in them.

CHAPTER VII

OF THE PARTICULAR EVIDENCE FOR CHRISTIANITY

§ 1. *Will now try the evidences for Christianity by our rules of temporal action.*

THE presumptions against revelation, and objections against the general scheme of Christianity, and particular things relating to it, being removed; there remains to be considered, what positive evidence we have for the truth of it: chiefly in order to see, what the analogy of nature suggests with regard to that evidence, and the objections against it: or to see what is, and is allowed to be, the plain natural rule of judgment and of action, in our temporal concerns, in cases where we have the same kind of evidence, and the same kind of objections against it, that we have in the case before us.

[1] Comp. Introd. §§ 3, 6.

§ 2. *These evidences are* (a) *direct and particular*, (b) *general and resulting*.

Now in the evidence of Christianity there seem to be several things of great weight, not reducible to the head, either of miracles, or the completion of prophecy, in the common acceptation of the words.[1] But these

---

[1] After the discussions of the last century and a half, Butler would perhaps have somewhat altered what he has written respecting the twin office of miracle and prophecy as evidences of revealed religion.

As regards miracle, we may do well to remember—

1. The apostles were not converted by miracles as commonly understood.

2. The miracles of our Lord were of wide local notoriety, but we have no evidence of their having led to extended conversions. They may have had more powerful and extended operation through the preaching of the apostles.

3. The great miracle of Lazarus is noted for the specialty of its effect (John xi. 45).

4. There were three miracles which may be denominated as of the first order :—

(a) The Incarnation itself; which, as Butler observes, is not available as proof, but requires to be proved.

(b) The miracle of the Resurrection; which, after it had happened, became powerfully available, and may be taken as sustaining very broadly this declaration of Butler's.

(c) The miracle of our Lord's own person and character; which was too spiritual for the mass, but operated marvellously on a few.

It is well to observe that the apostles largely converted without miracle : and, in his address to the Athenians (Acts xvii. 31), St. Paul appeals to no miracle except the Resurrection. This appeal brought about an interruption, and he desisted from further speech.

With regard to prophecy—

1. It seems to imply the action of divine power operating with large combinations, such as belong to the government of the ages as a whole.

2. There are miracles ascribed to preternatural agencies of evil, as well as of good. But we have no similar recog-

two are its direct and fundamental proofs: and those other things, however considerable they are, yet ought never to be urged apart from its direct proofs, but always to be joined with them. Thus the evidence of Christianity will be a long series of things, reaching, as it seems, from the beginning of the world to the present time, of great variety and compass, taking in both the direct, and also the collateral, proofs; and making up, all of them together, one argument: the conviction arising from which kind of proof may be compared to what they call *the effect* in architecture or other works of art; a result from a great number of things so and so disposed, and taken into one view. I shall therefore, first, make some observations relating to miracles, and the appearing completions of prophecy; and consider what analogy suggests, in answer to the objections brought against this evidence. And, secondly, I shall endeavour to give some account of the general argument now mentioned, consisting both of the direct and collateral evidence, considered as making up one argument: this being the kind of proof, upon which we determine most questions of difficulty, concerning common facts, alleged to have happened, or seeming likely to happen; especially questions relating to conduct.

nition in Holy Writ of prophecy as being placed at the command of any evil agent.

It is obvious that the evidential force of the existence of the Church, and its operation on the world and on society, has grown progressively with the lapse of time, and the development of the varying conditions of life. In Great Britain, especially, it was to be expected that this idea should become more prominent and vivid with the great extension and increased efficiency of Christian missions during the nineteenth century. Also Christianity and the Church are far larger and weightier facts than heretofore in comparison with the rest of the world: nor is the great increase in the numerical proportion of Christians wholly without bearing on the case.

§ 3. *On the direct.* (A) *The miracles are told in narratives plain and unadorned;*

First, I shall make some observations upon the direct proof of Christianity from miracles and prophecy, and upon the objections alleged against it.

[I.] Now the following observations relating to the historical evidence of miracles wrought in attestation of Christianity, appear to be of great weight.

[1.] The Old Testament affords us the same historical evidence of the miracles of Moses and of the prophets, as of the common civil history of Moses and the kings of Israel; or, as of the affairs of the Jewish nation. And the *Gospels* and the *Acts* afford us the same historical evidence of the miracles of Christ and the apostles, as of the common matters related in them.[1] This indeed could not have been affirmed by any reasonable man, if the authors of these books, like many other historians, had appeared to make an entertaining manner of writing their aim; though they had interspersed miracles in their works, at proper distances and upon proper occasions. These might have animated a dull relation, amused the reader, and engaged his attention. And the same account would naturally have been given of them, as of the speeches and descriptions of such authors: the same account, in a manner, as is to be given, why the poets make use of wonders and prodigies. But the facts, both miraculous and natural, in scripture, are related in plain unadorned narratives: and both of them appear, in all respects, to stand upon the same foot of historical evidence.

---

[1] Fitzgerald cites Bolingbroke, *Posthumous Works*, iii. 279: 'The miracles in the Bible are not like those in Livy, detached pieces that do not disturb the civil history, which goes on very well without them. But the miracles of the Jewish historian are intimately connected with all the civil affairs, and make a necessary and inseparable part. The whole history is founded in them: it consists of little else; and, if it were not a history of them, it would be a history of nothing.'

§ 4. *Sustained by, and accounting for, great known consequent events;*

Further: Some parts of scripture, containing an account of miracles fully sufficient to prove the truth of Christianity, are quoted as genuine, from the age in which they are said to be written, down to the present: and no other parts of them, material in the present question, are omitted to be quoted in such manner, as to afford any sort of proof of their not being genuine. And, as common history, when called in question in any instance, may often be greatly confirmed by contemporary or subsequent events more known and acknowledged; and as the common scripture-history, like many others, is thus confirmed: so likewise is the miraculous history of it, not only in particular instances, but in general. For, the establishment of the Jewish and Christian religions, which were events contemporary with the miracles related to be wrought in attestation of both, or subsequent to them, these events are just what we should have expected, upon supposition such miracles were really wrought to attest the truth of those religions. These miracles are a satisfactory account of those events: of which no other satisfactory account can be given; nor any account at all, but what is imaginary merely and invented.

§ 5. *Hard to account for, except by supposing them true.*

It is to be added, that the most obvious, the most easy and direct account of this history, how it came to be written and to be received in the world, as a true history, is, that it really is so: nor can any other account of it be easy and direct. Now, though an account, not at all obvious, but very far-fetched and indirect, may indeed be, and often is, the true account of a matter; yet it cannot be admitted on the authority of its being asserted. Mere guess, supposition, and possibility, when opposed to historical evidence, prove nothing, but that historical evidence is not demonstrative.

§ 6. *Not mere objection, but disproof is here required.*

Now the just consequence from all this, I think, is, that the scripture-history in general is to be admitted as an authentic genuine history, till somewhat positive be alleged sufficient to invalidate it. But no man will deny the consequence to be, that it cannot be rejected, or thrown by as of no authority, till it can be proved to be of none; even though the evidence now mentioned for its authority were doubtful. This evidence may be confronted by historical evidence on the other side, if there be any: or general incredibility in the things related, or inconsistence in the general turn of the history, would prove it to be of no authority. But since, upon the face of the matter, upon a first and general view, the appearance is, that it is an authentic history; it cannot be determined to be fictitious without some proof that it is so. And the following observations in support of these and coincident with them, will greatly confirm the historical evidence for the truth of Christianity.

§ 7. *The Epistles of St. Paul possess distinct verifying evidences.*

[2.] The Epistles of St. Paul, from the nature of epistolary writing, and moreover from several of them being written, not to particular persons, but to churches, carry in them evidences of their being genuine, beyond what can be in a mere historical narrative, left to the world at large. This evidence, joined with that which they have in common with the rest of the New Testament, seems not to leave so much as any particular pretence for denying their genuineness considered, as an ordinary matter of fact, or of criticism: I say *particular* pretence, for *denying* it; because any single fact, of such a kind and such antiquity, may have *general doubts* raised concerning it, from the very nature of human affairs and human testimony. There is also to be mentioned a distinct and particular evidence of the genuineness of the Epistle chiefly referred to here, the First to the Corinthians; from the manner in which it is quoted by Clemens Romanus, in an epistle of his own to that church.[a] Now these epistles afford a proof of Christianity, detached from all others, which is, I think, a thing of weight; and also a proof of a nature and kind peculiar to itself. For,

In them the author declares, that he received the gospel in general, and the institution of the communion in particular, not from the rest of the apostles, or jointly together with them, but alone, from Christ himself; whom he declares likewise, conformably to the history in the Acts, that he saw after his ascension.[b] So that the testimony of St. Paul is to be considered, as detached from that of the rest of the apostles.

And he declares further, that he was endued with a power of working miracles, as what was publicly known to those very people, speaks of frequent and great variety of miraculous gifts as then subsisting in those very churches, to which he was writing; which he was reproving for several irregularities; and where he had personal opposers: he mentions these gifts incidentally, in the most easy manner and without effort; by way of reproof to those who had them, for their indecent use of them; and by way of depreciating them, in comparison of moral virtues; in short he speaks to these churches, of these miraculous powers, in the manner any one would speak to another of a thing, which was as familiar and as much known in common to them both, as any thing in the world.[c] And this, as hath been observed by several persons, is surely a very considerable thing.

[a] Clem. Rom. Ep. I. c. 47.
[b] Gal. i; 1 Cor. xi. 23, &c., xv. 8.
[c] Rom. xv. 19; 1 Cor. xii. 8, 9, 10–28, &c. and xiii. 1, 2, 8, and the whole fourteenth chapter; 2 Cor. xii. 12, 13; Gal. iii. 2, 5

§ 8. *Christianity and Judaism alone allege miracles publicly wrought.*

[3.] It is an acknowledged historical fact, that Christianity offered itself to the world, and demanded to be received, upon the allegation, i.e. as unbelievers would speak, upon the pretence, of miracles, publicly wrought to attest the truth of it, in such an age; and that it was actually received by great numbers in that very age, and upon the professed belief of the reality of these miracles. And Christianity, including the dispensation of the Old Testament, seems distinguished by this from all other religions. I mean, that this does not appear to be the case with regard to any other: for surely it will not be supposed to lie upon any person, to prove by positive historical evidence, that it was not. It does in no sort appear that Mahometanism was first received in the world upon the foot of supposed miracles,[d][1] i.e. public ones: for, as revelation is itself miraculous, all pretence to it must necessarily imply some pretence of miracles. And it is a known fact, that it was immediately, at the very first, propagated by other means. And as particular institutions, whether in paganism or popery, said to be confirmed by miracles after those institutions had obtained, are not to the purpose: so, were there what might be called historical proof, that any of them were introduced by a supposed divine command, believed to be attested by miracles; these would not be in any wise parallel. For single things of this sort are easy to be accounted for, after parties are formed, and have power in their hands; and the leaders of them are in veneration with the multitude; and political interests are blended with religious claims, and religious distinctions. But before any thing of

[d] See the Koran, chap. xiii and chap. xvii.

[1] See the argument hereupon in *The Beacon of Truth*, translated from the Arabic by Sir W. Muir, chap. i. (1895).

this kind, for a few persons, and those of the lowest rank, all at once, to bring over such great numbers to a new religion, and get it to be received upon the particular evidence of miracles; this is quite another thing. And I think it will be allowed by any fair adversary, that the fact now mentioned, taking in all the circumstances of it, is peculiar to the Christian religion. However, the fact itself is allowed, that Christianity obtained, i.e. was professed to be received in the world, upon the belief of miracles, immediately in the age in which it is said those miracles were wrought: or that this is what its first converts would have alleged, as the reason for their embracing it.

§ 9. *The converts, who sacrificed interest and pleasure, must be believed sincere.*

Now certainly it is not to be supposed, that such numbers of men, in the most distant parts of the world, should forsake the religion of their country, in which they had been educated; separate themselves from their friends, particularly in their festival shows and solemnities, to which the common people are so greatly addicted, and which were of a nature to engage them much more, than any thing of that sort amongst us; and embrace a religion, which could not but expose them to many inconveniences, and indeed must have been a giving up the world in a great degree, even from the very first, and before the empire engaged in form against them: it cannot be supposed, that such numbers should make so great, and, to say the least, so inconvenient a change in their whole institution of life, unless they were really convinced of the truth of those miracles, upon the knowledge or belief of which they professed to make it. And it will, I suppose, readily be acknowledged, that the generality of the first converts to Christianity must have believed them: that as by becoming Christians they declared to the world, they were satisfied of the truth of those miracles; so this declaration was to be credited. And this their testimony is the same kind of evidence for those miracles, as if they had put it in writing, and these writings had come down to us. And it is real evidence, because it is of facts, which they had capacity and full opportunity to inform themselves of. It is also distinct from the direct or express historical evidence, though it is of the same kind: and it would be allowed to be distinct in all cases. For were a fact expressly related by one or more ancient historians, and disputed in after ages; that this fact is acknowledged to have been believed by great numbers of the age in which the historian says it was done, would be allowed an additional proof of such fact, quite distinct from the express testimony of the historian. The credulity of mankind is acknowledged: and the suspicions of mankind ought to be acknowledged too; and their backwardness even to believe, and greater still to practise, what makes against their interest. And it must particularly be remembered, that education, and prejudice, and authority, were against Christianity, in the age I am speaking of. So that the immediate conversion of such numbers is a real presumption of somewhat more than human in this matter: I say presumption, for it is not alleged as a proof alone and by itself. Nor need any one of the things mentioned in this chapter be considered as a proof by itself: and yet all of them together may be one of the strongest.[e]

§ 10. *The* onus probandi *lies upon the objector.*

Upon the whole: As there is large historical evidence, both direct and circumstantial, of miracles wrought in attestation of Christianity, collected by those who have writ upon the subject; it lies upon unbelievers to show, why this evidence is not to be credited. This way of speaking is, I think, just; and what persons who write in defence of religion naturally fall into. Yet, in a matter of such unspeakable impor-

[e] *Inf.* § 60.

tance, the proper question is, not whom it lies upon, according to the rules of argument, to maintain or confute objections: but whether there really are any, against this evidence, sufficient, in reason, to destroy the credit of it. However, unbelievers seem to take upon them the part of showing that there are.

§ 11. *He says (a) other enthusiasts have borne erroneous witness. Yes: but to opinions, not facts.*

They allege, that numberless enthusiastic people, in different ages and countries, expose themselves to the same difficulties which the primitive Christians did; and are ready to give up their lives for the most idle follies imaginable. But it is not very clear, to what purpose this objection is brought. For every one, surely, in every case, must distinguish between opinions and facts. And though testimony is no proof of enthusiastic opinions, or of any opinions at all; yet it is allowed, in all other cases, to be a proof of facts. And a person's laying down his life in attestation of facts or of opinions, is the strongest proof of his believing them. And if the apostles and their contemporaries did believe the facts, in attestation of which they exposed themselves to sufferings and death; this their belief, or rather knowledge, must be a proof of those facts: for they were such as came under the observation of their senses.

§ 12. *Martyrs of the sub-apostolic age.*

And though it is not of equal weight, yet it is of weight, that the martyrs of the next age, notwithstanding they were not eye-witnesses of those facts, as were the apostles and their contemporaries, had, however, full opportunity to inform themselves, whether they were true or not, and gave equal proof of their believing them to be true.

§ 13. (β) *Enthusiasm weakens even testimony to facts. But were these witnesses enthusiasts?*

But enthusiasm, it is said, greatly weakens the evidence of testimony even for facts, in matters relating to religion: some seem to think it totally and absolutely destroys the evidence of testimony upon this subject. And indeed the powers of enthusiasm, and of diseases too, which operate in a like manner, are very wonderful, in particular instances. But if great numbers of men, not appearing in any peculiar degree weak, nor under any peculiar suspicion of negligence, affirm that they saw and heard such things plainly with their eyes and their ears, and are admitted to be in earnest; such testimony is evidence of the strongest kind we can have, for any matter of fact. Yet possibly it may be overcome, strong as it is, by incredibility in the things thus attested, or by contrary testimony. And in an instance where one thought it was so overcome, it might be just to consider, how far such evidence could be accounted for, by enthusiasm: for it seems as if no other imaginable account were to be given of it. But till such incredibility be shown, or contrary testimony produced, it cannot surely be expected, that so far-fetched, so indirect and wonderful an account of such testimony, as that of enthusiasm must be; an account so strange, that the generality of mankind can scarce be made to understand what is meant by it: it cannot, I say, be expected, that such account will be admitted of such evidence; when there is this direct, easy, and obvious account of it, that people really saw and heard a thing not incredible, which they affirm sincerely and with full assurance, they did see and hear.

§ 14. *The things not being incredible, the charge of enthusiasm is not to be entertained.*

Granting then that enthusiasm is not (strictly speaking) an absurd, but a possible account of such testimony: it is manifest, that the very mention of it goes upon the previous supposition that the things so attested are incredible; and therefore need not be considered, till they are shown to be so. Much less need it be considered, after the contrary has been proved. And I think it has been proved, to full satisfaction, that there is no incredibility in a revelation, in general; or in such an one as the Christian, in particular.

§ 15. *Many prejudices operate like enthusiasm; yet testimony prevails.*

However; as religion is supposed peculiarly liable to enthusiasm, it may just be observed, that prejudices [1] almost without number and without name, romance, affectation, humour, a desire to engage attention or to surprise, the party-spirit, custom, little competitions, unaccountable likings and dislikings, these influence men strongly in common matters. And as these prejudices are often scarce known or reflected upon by the persons themselves who are influenced by them, they are to be considered as influences of a like kind to enthusiasm. Yet human testimony in common matters is naturally and justly believed notwithstanding.

§ 16. *So it will, even if we assume partial untruth, exaggeration, or reticence.* [2]

It is intimated further, in a more refined way of observation, that though it should be proved, that the apostles and first Christians could not, in some respects,

[1] On the connection between virtue and sound judgment, see Aristotle, *Eth. Nic.* I. iv. 6; III. iv. 4; X. ix. 6.

[2] In estimating what Butler here says of the effect of partial untruth, we must bear in mind that we are dealing with the case of statements supposed to be made in the general interests, where the subject to be elucidated is truth at large; and not with evidence hostile to the life and property of an individual, where detection of untruth in a part is held to render the whole unavailable for carrying penal consequences home.

be deceived themselves, and, in other respects, cannot be thought to have intended to impose upon the world ; yet it will not follow, that their general testimony is to be believed, though truly handed down to us : because they might still in part, i.e. in other respects, be deceived themselves, and in part also designedly impose upon others ; which, it is added, is a thing very credible, from that mixture of real enthusiasm, and real knavery, to be met with in the same characters. And, I must confess, I think the matter of fact contained in this observation upon mankind is not to be denied ; and that somewhat very much akin to it is often supposed in scripture as a very common case, and most severely reproved.[1] But it were to have been expected, that persons capable of applying this observation as applied in the objection, might also frequently have met with the like mixed character, in instances where religion was quite out of the case. The thing plainly is, that mankind are naturally endued with reason, or a capacity of distinguishing between truth and falsehood ; and as naturally they are endued with veracity, or a regard to truth in what they say : but from many occasions they are liable to be prejudiced and biassed and deceived themselves, and capable of intending to deceive others, in every different degree : insomuch that, as we are all liable to be deceived by prejudice, so likewise it seems to be not an uncommon thing, for persons, who, from their regard to truth, would not invent a lie entirely without any foundation at all, to propagate it with heightening circumstances,[2] after it is once invented and set a-going. And others, though they would not *propagate* a lie, yet, which is a lower degree of false-

---

[1] As in the case of Balaam. See Serm. vii, on Balaam, and Serm. x, on Self-Deceit.

[2] Evidently we must understand this to refer to incidental exaggeration : not to what is systematic, which would go far to falsify. And, again, the reticence glanced at can only apply to secondary matters, or it might totally falsify.

hood, will let it pass without contradiction. But, notwithstanding all this, human testimony remains still a natural ground of assent; and this assent a natural principle of action.

§ 17. *No proof that danger here is more than ordinary.*

It is objected further, that however it has happened, the *fact* is, that mankind have, in different ages, been strangely deluded with pretences to miracles and wonders. But it is by no means to be admitted, that they have been oftener, or are at all more liable to be deceived by these pretences, than by others.

§ 18. *Nor does failure of like evidence in other cases prove this evidence fabulous.*

It is added, that there is a very considerable degree of historical evidence for miracles, which are, on all hands, acknowledged to be fabulous. But suppose there were even *the like* historical evidence for these, to what there is for those alleged in proof of Christianity, which yet is in no wise allowed, but suppose this; the consequence would not be, that the evidence of the latter is not to be admitted. Nor is there a man in the world, who, in common cases, would conclude thus. For what would such a conclusion really amount to but this, that evidence, confuted by contrary evidence, or any way overbalanced, destroys the credibility of other evidence, neither confuted, nor overbalanced? To argue, that because there is, if there were, like evidence from testimony, for miracles acknowledged false, as for those in attestation of Christianity, therefore the evidence in the latter case is not to be credited; this is the same as to argue, that if two men of equally good reputation had given evidence in different cases no way connected, and one of them had been convicted of perjury, this confuted the testimony of the other.

§ 19. *Testimony always liable to be weakened without being destroyed.*

Upon the whole then, the general observation that human creatures are so liable to be deceived, from enthusiasm in religion, and principles equivalent to enthusiasm in common matters, and in both from negligence; and that they are so capable of dishonestly endeavouring to deceive others; this does indeed weaken the evidence of testimony in all cases, but does not destroy it in any. And these things will appear, to different men, to weaken the evidence of testimony, in different degrees: in degrees proportionable to the observations they have made, or the notions they have any way taken up, concerning the weakness and negligence and dishonesty of mankind; or concerning the powers of enthusiasm, and prejudices equivalent to it. But it seems to me, that people do not know what they say, who affirm these things to destroy the evidence from testimony, which we have of the truth of Christianity. Nothing can destroy the evidence of testimony in any case, but a proof or probability, that persons are not competent judges of the facts to which they give testimony; or that they are actually under some indirect influence in giving it, in such particular case. Till this be made out, the *natural* laws of human actions require, that testimony be admitted. It can never be sufficient to overthrow direct historical evidence, indolently to say, that there are so many principles, from whence men are liable to be deceived themselves and disposed to deceive others, especially in matters of religion, that one knows not what to believe. And it is surprising persons can help reflecting, that this very manner of speaking supposes they are not satisfied that there is nothing in the evidence, of which they speak thus; or that they can avoid observing, if they do make this reflection, that it is, on such a subject, a very material one.[f]

[f] See the foregoing chapter.

§ 20. *Liability to error, how reduced in the Christian witnesses.*

And over against all these objections is to be set the importance of Christianity, as what must have engaged the attention of its first converts, so as to have rendered them liable to be deceived from carelessness, than they would in common matters; and likewise the strong obligations to veracity, which their religion laid them under: so that the first and most obvious presumption is, that they could not be deceived themselves, nor would deceive others. And this presumption, in this degree, is peculiar to the testimony we have been considering.

§ 21. *The objector is bound* in limine *to abate his objections.*

In argument, assertions are nothing in themselves, and have an air of positiveness, which sometimes is not very easy: yet they are necessary, and necessary to be repeated; in order to connect a discourse, and distinctly to lay before the view of the reader, what is proposed to be proved, and what is left as proved. Now the conclusion from the foregoing observations is, I think, beyond all doubt, this: that unbelievers must be forced to admit the external evidence for Christianity, i.e. the proof of miracles wrought to attest it, to be of real weight and very considerable; though they cannot allow it to be sufficient, to convince them of the reality of those miracles. And as they must, in all reason, admit this; so it seems to me, that upon consideration they would, in fact, admit it; those of them I mean, who know any thing at all of the matter: in like manner as persons, in many cases, own they see strong evidence from testimony, for the truth of things, which yet they cannot be convinced are true: cases, suppose, where there is contrary testimony: or things which they think, whether with or without reason, to be incredible. But there is no testimony contrary to that which we have been considering: and it has been fully proved, that there is no incredibility in Christianity in general, or in any part of it.

§ 22. (B) *In prophecy, the parts understood are not impaired by those not understood.*

[II.] As to the evidence for Christianity from prophecy, I shall only make some few general observations, which are suggested by the analogy of nature; i.e. by the acknowledged natural rules of judging in common matters, concerning evidence of a like kind to this from prophecy.

[1.] The obscurity or unintelligibleness of one part of a prophecy does not, in any degree, invalidate the proof of foresight, arising from the appearing completion of those other parts which are understood. For the case is evidently the same, as if those parts, which are not understood, were lost, or not written at all, or written in an unknown tongue. Whether this observation be commonly attended to or not, it is so evident, that one can scarce bring oneself to set down an instance in common matters, to exemplify it. However, suppose a writing, partly in cypher, and partly in plain words at length; and that in the part one understood, there appeared mention of several known facts: it would never come into any man's thoughts to imagine, that if he understood the whole, perhaps he might find, that those facts were not in reality known by the writer. Indeed, both in this example and the thing intended to be exemplified by it, our not understanding the whole (the whole, suppose, of a sentence or a paragraph) might sometimes occasion a doubt, whether one understood the literal meaning of such a part: but this comes under another consideration.

§ 23. *Why general fulfilment, short of absolute, may suffice.*

For the same reason, though a man should be incapable, for want of learning, or opportunities of inquiry, or from not having turned his studies this way, even so much as to judge, whether particular prophecies have been throughout completely fulfilled; yet he may see, in general, that they have been fulfilled to such a degree, as, upon very good ground, to be convinced of foresight more than human in such prophecies, and of such events being intended by them. For the same reason also, though, by means of the deficiencies in civil history, and the different accounts of historians, the most learned should not be able to make out to satisfaction, that such parts of the prophetic history have been minutely and throughout fulfilled; yet a very strong proof of foresight may arise, from that general completion of them, which is made out: as much proof of foresight, perhaps, as the giver of prophecy intended should ever be afforded by such parts of prophecy.

§ 24. *Applicability is to be presumed intentional.*

[2.] A long series of prophecy being applicable to such and such events, is itself a proof that it was intended of them: as the rules, by which we naturally judge and determine, in common cases parallel to this, will show. This observation I make in answer to the common objection against the application of the prophecies, that, considering each of them distinctly by itself, it does not at all appear, that they were intended of those particular events to which they are applied by Christians; and therefore it is to be supposed, that, if they meant any thing, they were intended of other events unknown to us, and not of these at all.

§ 25. *Is taken as proving intention in writings,*
(a) *mythological,* (b) *satirical.*

Now there are two kinds of writing, which bear a great resemblance to prophecy, with respect to the matter before us: the mythological,[1] and the satirical,

[1] The word is used by Butler as relating not to mythology, but to fable.

where the satire is, to a certain degree, concealed. And a man might be assured, that he understood what an author intended by a fable or parable, related without any application or moral, merely from seeing it to be easily capable of such application, and that such a moral might naturally be deduced from it. And he might be fully assured, that such persons and events were intended in a satirical writing, merely from its being applicable to them. And, agreeably to the last observation, he might be in a good measure satisfied of it, though he were not enough informed in affairs, or in the story of such persons, to understand half the satire. For, his satisfaction, that he understood the meaning, the intended meaning, of these writings, would be greater or less in proportion as he saw the general turn of them to be capable of such application: and in proportion to the number of particular things capable of it. And thus, if a long series of prophecy is applicable to the present state of the church, and to the political situations of the kingdoms of the world, some thousand years after these prophecies were delivered, and a long series of prophecy delivered before the coming of Christ is applicable to him; these things are in themselves a proof, that the prophetic history was intended of him, and of those events: in proportion as the general turn of it is capable of such application, and to the number and variety of particular prophecies capable of it. And though, in all just way of consideration, the appearing completion of prophecies is to be allowed to be thus explanatory of, and to determine their meaning; yet it is to be remembered further, that the ancient Jews applied the prophecies to a Messiah before his coming, in much the same manner as Christians do now: and that the primitive Christians interpreted the prophecies respecting the state of the church and of the world in the last ages, in the sense which the event seems to confirm and verify. And from these things it may be made appear:

§ 26. *Intentional, but not necessarily with the utterer,*

[3.] That the showing even to a high probability, if that could be, that the prophets thought of some other events, in such and such predictions, and not those at all which Christians allege to be completions of those predictions; or that such and such prophecies are capable of being applied to other events than those, to which Christians apply them—that this would not confute or destroy the force of the argument from prophecy, even with regard to those very instances. For, observe how this matter really is. If one knew such a person to be the sole author of such a book, and was certainly assured, or satisfied to any degree, that one knew the whole of what he intended in it; one should be assured or satisfied to such degree, that one knew the whole meaning of that book: for the meaning of a book is nothing but the meaning of the author. But if one knew a person to have compiled a book out of memoirs, which he received from another, of vastly superior knowledge in the subject of it, especially if it were a book full of great intricacies and difficulties; it would in no wise follow, that one knew the whole meaning of the book, from knowing the whole meaning of the compiler: for the original memoirs, i.e. the author of them, might have, and there would be no degree of presumption, in many cases, against supposing him to have, some further meaning than the compiler saw.

§ 27. *But with the Inspirer.*

To say then, that the scriptures and the things contained in them can have no other or further meaning than those persons thought or had, who first recited or wrote them; is evidently saying, that those persons were the original, proper, and sole authors of those books, i.e. that they are not inspired: which is absurd, whilst the authority of these books is under examination; i.e. till you have determined they are of no divine authority at all. Till this be determined, it must in all reason be supposed, not indeed that they have, for this is taking for granted that they are inspired, but that they may have, some further meaning than what the compilers saw or understood. And upon this supposition, it is supposable also, that this further meaning may be fulfilled. Now events corresponding to prophecies, interpreted in a different meaning from that, in which the prophets are supposed to have understood them; this affords, in a manner, the same proof, that this different sense was originally intended, as it would have afforded, if the prophets had not understood their predictions in the sense it is supposed they did : because there is no presumption of their sense of them being the whole sense of them. And it has been already shown, that the apparent completions of prophecy must be allowed to be explanatory of its meaning. So that the question is, whether a series of prophecy has been fulfilled, in a natural or proper, i.e. in any real, sense of the words of it. For such completion is equally a proof of foresight more than human, whether the prophets are, or are not, supposed to have understood it in a different sense. I say, supposed : for, though I think it clear, that the prophets did not understand the full meaning of their predictions ; it is another question, how far they thought they did, and in what sense they understood them.

§ 28. *Merely proving capability of some other interpretation is wasted labour.*

Hence may be seen, to how little purpose those persons busy themselves, who endeavour to prove, that the prophetic history is applicable to events of the age in which it was written, or of ages before it. Indeed to have proved this before there was any appearance of a further completion of it, might have answered some purpose ; for it might have prevented the expectation of any such further completion. Thus could Porphyry have shown, that some principal parts of the Book of Daniel, for instance, the seventh verse of the seventh chapter, which the Christians interpreted of the latter ages, was applicable to events which happened before or about the age of Antiochus Epiphanes; this might have prevented them from expecting any further completion of it. And, unless there was then, as I think there must have been, external evidence concerning that book, more than is come down to us; such a discovery might have been a stumbling-block in the way of Christianity itself: considering the authority which our Saviour has given to the Book of Daniel,[1] and how much the general scheme of Christianity presupposes the truth of it. But even this discovery, had there been any such,[g] would be of very little weight, with reasonable men now; if this passage, thus applicable to events before the age of Porphyry, appears to be applicable also to events, which succeeded the dissolution of the Roman empire. I mention this, not at all as intending to insinuate, that the division of this empire into ten parts, for it plainly was divided into about that number, were, alone and by itself, of any moment in verifying the prophetic history: but only as an example of the thing I am speaking of. And thus upon the whole, the

[g] It appears, that Porphyry did nothing worth mentioning in this way. For Jerome on the place says, *Duas posteriores bestias —— in uno Macedonum regno ponit.* And as to the ten kings; *Decem reges enumerat, qui fuerunt saevissimi: ipsosque reges non unius ponit regni, verbi gratia, Macedoniae, Syriae, Asiae, et Aegypti; sed de diversis regnis unum efficit regum ordinem.* And in this way of interpretation, any thing may be made of any thing.

[1] St. Matt. xxiv. 15; St. Mark xiii. 14. Two reports of the same incident: 'the abomination of desolation, spoken of by Daniel the prophet, standing in the holy place.' Our Lord's reference is marked with a rather peculiar solemnity, as in each case we find appended to it the words, 'whoso readeth, let him understand' (Matt.); 'let him that readeth understand' (Mark).

matter of inquiry evidently must be, as above put, Whether the prophecies are applicable to Christ, and to the present state of the world and of the church; applicable in such a degree, as to imply foresight: not whether they are capable of any other application; though I know no pretence for saying the general turn of them is capable of any other.

§ 29. *Men shrink from laborious inquiries with indeterminate result; prefer summary rejection.*

These observations are, I think, just; and the evidence referred to in them real: though there may be people who will not accept of such imperfect information from scripture. Some too have not integrity and regard enough to truth, to attend to evidence, which keeps the mind in doubt, perhaps perplexity, and which is much of a different sort from what they expected. And it plainly requires a degree of modesty and fairness, beyond what every one has, for a man to say, not to the world, but to himself, that there is a real appearance of somewhat of great weight in this matter, though he is not able thoroughly to satisfy himself about it; but it shall have its influence upon him, in proportion to its appearing reality and weight. It is much more easy, and more falls in with the negligence, presumption, and wilfulness of the generality, to determine at once, with a decisive air, There is nothing in it. The prejudices arising from that absolute contempt and scorn, with which this evidence is treated in the world, I do not mention. For what indeed can be said to persons, who are weak enough in their understandings to think this any presumption against it; or, if they do not, are yet weak enough in their temper to be influenced by such prejudices, upon such a subject?

§ 30. *The evidence, (a) direct, and (b) circumstantial, to be weighed as a whole.*

I shall now, secondly, endeavour to give some account of the general argument for the truth of Christianity, consisting both of the direct and circumstantial evidence, considered as making up one argument. Indeed to state and examine this argument fully, would be a work much beyond the compass of this whole Treatise: nor is so much as a proper abridgment of it to be expected here. Yet the present subject requires to have some brief account of it given. For it is the kind of evidence, upon which most questions of difficulty, in common practice, are determined: evidence arising from various coincidences, which support and confirm each other, and in this manner prove, with more or less certainty, the point under consideration. And I choose to do it also: first, because it seems to be of the greatest importance, and not duly attended to by every one, that the proof of revelation is, not some direct and express things only, but a great variety of circumstantial things also; and that though each of these direct and circumstantial things is indeed to be considered separately, yet they are afterwards to be joined together; for that the proper force of the evidence consists in the result of those several things, considered in their respects to each other, and united into one view: and in the next place, because it seems to me, that the matters of fact here set down, which are acknowledged by unbelievers, must be acknowledged by them also to contain together a degree of evidence of great weight, if they could be brought to lay these several things before themselves distinctly, and then with attention consider them together; instead of that cursory thought of them, to which we are familiarized. For being familiarized to the cursory thought of things really hinders the weight of them from being seen, as from having its due influence upon practice.

§ 31. *Over and above our reason and affections, God has given us* (a) *natural religion; and, further,*

The thing asserted, and the truth of which is to be inquired into, is this: That over and above our reason and affections, which God has given us for the information of our judgment and the conduct of our lives, he has also, by external revelation, given us an account of himself and his moral government over the world, implying a future state of rewards and punishments; i.e. hath revealed the system of natural religion: for natural religion may be externally [h] revealed by God, as the ignorant may be taught it by mankind their fellow-creatures:

§ 32. (b) *A revealed dispensation for the recovery of mankind.*

That God, I say, has given us the evidence of revelation, as well as the evidence of reason, to ascertain this moral system; together with an account of a particular dispensation of Providence, which reason could no way have discovered, and a particular institution of religion founded on it, for the recovery of mankind out of their present wretched condition, and raising them to the perfection and final happiness of their nature.

§ 33. *This revelation alone stands upon matters of fact,* (a) *past, or* (b) *alleged in the future.*

This revelation, whether real or supposed, may be considered as wholly historical.[1] For prophecy is nothing but the history of events before they come to

[h] *Sup.* II. i. 5, 6; also ii. 10.

---

[1] The connection of Christianity with fact is one of its most distinctive characteristics. In one sense 'doctrines are matters of fact'; but the great bulk of essential Christian doctrine, as set forth in the Apostles' Creed, rests on matters of fact already past, and subjected to the testing power of the common experience of mankind.

pass: doctrines also are matters of fact: and precepts come under the same notion. And the general design of scripture, which contains in it this revelation, thus considered as historical, may be said to be, to give us an account of the world, in this one single view, as God's world: by which it appears essentially distinguished from all other books, so far as I have found, except such as are copied from it. It begins with an account of God's creation of the world, in order to ascertain, and distinguish from all others, who is the object of our worship, by what he has done: in order to ascertain, who he is, concerning whose providence, commands, promises, and threatenings, this sacred book, all along, treats; the Maker and Proprietor of the world, he whose creatures we are, the God of nature: in order likewise to distinguish him from the idols of the nations, which are either imaginary beings, i. e. no beings at all; or else part of that creation, the historical relation of which is here given.[1] And St. John, not improbably, with an eye to this Mosaic account of the creation, begins his gospel with an account of our Saviour's pre-existence, and that *all things were made by him; and without him was not any thing made that was made:*[j] agreeably to the doctrine of St. Paul, that *God created all things by Jesus Christ.*[k] This being premised, the scripture, taken together, seems to profess to contain a kind of an abridgment of the history of the world, in the view just now mentioned: that is,

[j] John i. 3.   [k] Eph. iii. 9.

Thus the recorded facts become a guarantee for those not yet recorded. It is in quite another sense that, e. g., the freedom of the will, or the Calvinian doctrine of reprobation, may be handled as matters of fact.

[1] There seems now to be little room for doubt that the greater gods of the ancient religions are to a large extent deteriorated and corrupted reproductions of the original divine idea, as to both Creator and Redeemer: to which we may add (*a*) impersonations of the abstract or of external nature, (*b*) deifications of the deceased, (*c*) personified conceptions of the evil agent or agents

a general account of the condition of religion and its professors, during the continuance of that apostasy from God, and state of wickedness, which it every where supposes the world to lie in. And this account of the state of religion carries with it some brief account of the political state of things, as religion is affected by it. Revelation indeed considers the common affairs of this world, and what is going on in it, as a mere scene of distraction; and cannot be supposed to concern itself with foretelling at what time Rome, or Babylon, or Greece, or any particular place, should be the most conspicuous seat of that tyranny and dissoluteness, which all places equally aspire to be; cannot, I say, be supposed to give any account of this wild scene for its own sake. But it seems to contain some very general account of the chief governments of the world, as the general state of religion has been, is, or shall be, affected by them, from the first transgression, and during the whole interval of the world's continuing in its present state, to a certain future period, spoken of both in the Old and New Testament, very distinctly, and in great variety of expression: *The times of the restitution of all things:*[1] when *the mystery of God shall be finished, as he hath declared to his servants the prophets:* [m] when *the God of heaven shall set up a kingdom, which shall never be destroyed: and the kingdom shall not be left to other people,*[n] as it is represented to be during this apostasy, but *judgment shall be given to the saints,*[o] and *they shall reign:* [p] *and the kingdom and dominion, and the greatness of the kingdom under the whole heaven, shall be given to the people of the saints of the Most High.*[q]

§ 34. *That in so long a time it* has *not been confuted, gives a presumption that it* cannot *be.*

Upon this general view of the scripture, I would remark, how great a length of time the whole relation

[1] Acts iii. 21.   [m] Rev. x. 7.   [n] Dan. ii. 44.
[o] Dan. vii. 22.   [p] Rev. xxii. 5.   [q] Dan. vii. 27.

takes up, near six thousand years [1] of which are past: and how great a variety of things it treats of; the natural and moral system or history of the world, including the time when it was formed, all contained in the very first book, and evidently written in a rude and unlearned age; and in subsequent books, the various common and prophetic history, and the particular dispensation of Christianity. Now all this together gives the largest scope for criticism; and for confutation of what is capable of being confuted, either from reason, or from common history, or from any inconsistence in its several parts. And it is a thing which deserves, I think, to be mentioned, that whereas some imagine the supposed doubtfulness of the evidence for revelation implies a positive argument that it is not true; it appears, on the contrary, to imply a positive argument that it is true. For, could any common relation, of such antiquity, extent, and variety, (for in these things the stress of what I am now observing lies,) be proposed to the examination of the world: that it could not, in an age of knowledge and

---

[1] Obviously to be taken as an *obiter dictum*, which assumes the popular and most accepted chronology, that of the Hebrew text, but is not to be construed as an authoritative judgment upon the age of the world in its present condition. There seems, however, to be no tendency in scientific opinion to any wholesale or vast extension of the term. Butler's argument in no way demands an exact specification.

From another point of view, this passage is open to the remark that the favourable presumption applies to other religions also, which are as old as, or older than, Christianity. We are dealing here with presumption only. But even as to presumption the case is by no means parallel. For (1) Christianity has stimulated the forces and faculties of human nature into an effective vitality and activity quite unknown under other now current religions. (2) It has been the only religion which has constantly practised aggression, and this as a rule by legitimate, that is to say by non-coercive, means: and has thus delivered a perpetual challenge to all other creeds.

liberty, be confuted, or shown to have nothing in it, to the satisfaction of reasonable men; this would be thought a strong presumptive proof of its truth. And indeed it must be a proof of it, just in proportion to the probability, that if it were false, it might be shown to be so: and this, I think, is scarce pretended to be shown, but upon principles and in ways of arguing, which have been clearly obviated.[r] Nor does it at all appear, that any set of men who believe natural religion, are of the opinion, that Christianity has been thus confuted. But to proceed:

§ 35. *The Old Testament gives a detailed history of God's covenant with the Jews;*

Together with the moral system of the world, the Old Testament contains a chronological account of the beginning of it, and from thence, an unbroken genealogy of mankind for many ages before common history begins; and carried on as much further as to make up a continued thread of history of the length of between three and four thousand years. It contains an account of God's making a covenant with a particular nation, that they should be his people, and he would be their God, in a peculiar sense; of his often interposing miraculously in their affairs; giving them the promise, and, long after, the possession, of a particular country; assuring them of the greatest national prosperity in it, if they would worship him, in opposition to the idols which the rest of the world worshipped, and obey his commands; and threatening them with unexampled punishments, if they disobeyed him, and fell into the general idolatry; insomuch that this one nation should continue to be the observation and the wonder of all the world.

§ 36. *Threat of dispersion, and promise of restoration;*

It declares particularly, that *God would scatter them among all people, from one end of the earth unto the*

[r] Chap. ii, iii, &c.

other : but that when they should return unto the Lord their God, he would have compassion upon them, and gather them from all the nations, whither he had scattered them : that Israel should be saved in the Lord, with an everlasting salvation ; and not be ashamed or confounded world without end. And as some of these promises are conditional, others are as absolute, as any thing can be expressed : that the time should come, when *the people should be all righteous, and inherit the land for ever :* that *though God would make a full end of all nations whither he had scattered them, yet would he not make a full end of them :* that *he would bring again the captivity of his people Israel, and plant them upon their land, and they should be no more pulled up out of their land :* that *the seed of Israel should not cease from being a nation for ever.*[s]

§ 37. *It predicts a Messiah ;*

It foretells, that God would raise them up a particular person, in whom all his promises should finally be fulfilled ; the Messiah, who should be, in an high and eminent sense, their anointed Prince and Saviour. This was foretold in such a manner, as raised a general expectation of such a person in the nation, as appears from the New Testament, and is an acknowledged fact ; an expectation of his coming at such a particular time before any one appeared claiming to be that person, and when there was no ground for such an expectation but from the prophecies: which expectation, therefore, must in all reason be presumed to be explanatory of those prophecies, if there were any doubt about their meaning. It seems moreover to foretell, that this person should be rejected by that nation, to whom he had been so long promised, and though he was so much desired by them.[t]

[s] Deut. xxviii. 64, xxx. 2, 3 ; Isa. xlv. 17, lx. 21 ; Jer. xxx. 11, xlvi. 28 ; Amos ix. 14, 15 ; Jer. xxxi. 36.
[t] Isa. viii. 14, 15, xlix. 5, ch. liii ; Mal. i. 10, 11, and ch. iii.

§ 38. *And a redemption reaching far beyond the Jewish race.*

And it expressly foretells, that he should be the Saviour of the Gentiles; and even that the completion of the scheme, contained in this book, and then begun, and in its progress, should be somewhat so great, that, in comparison with it, the restoration of the Jews alone would be but of small account. *It is a light thing that thou shouldest be my servant to raise up the tribes of Jacob, and to restore the preserved of Israel: I will also give thee for a light to the Gentiles, that thou mayest be for salvation unto the end of the earth.* And, *In the last days, the mountain of the Lord's house shall be established in the top of the mountains, and shall be exalted above the hills; and all nations shall flow into it——for out of Zion shall go forth the law, and the word of the Lord from Jerusalem. And he shall judge among the nations——and the Lord alone shall be exalted in that day, and the idols he shall utterly abolish.*[u]

§ 39. *Messiah was expected; came; and fulfilled his mission.*

The scripture further contains an account, that at the time the Messiah was expected, a person rose up, in this nation, claiming to be that Messiah, to be the person, whom all the prophecies referred to, and in whom they should centre: that he spent some years in a continued course of miraculous works; and endued his immediate disciples and followers with a power of doing the same, as a proof of the truth of that religion, which he commissioned them to publish: that, invested with this authority and power, they made numerous converts in the remotest countries, and

---

[u] Isa. xlix. 6, ch. ii, ch. xi, ch. lvi. 7; Mal. i. 11. To which must be added, the other prophecies of the like kind, several in the New Testament, and very many in the Old; which describe what shall be the completion of the revealed plan of Providence.

Add other prophecies from both Testaments.

settled and established his religion in the world; to the end of which, the scripture professes to give a prophetic account of the state of this religion amongst mankind.

§ 40. *Suppose an inquirer, at first view:*

Let us now suppose a person utterly ignorant of history, to have all this related to him out of the scripture. Or suppose such an one, having the scripture put into his hands, to remark these things in it, not knowing but that the whole, even its civil history, as well as the other parts of it, might be, from beginning to end, an entire invention; and to ask, What truth was in it, and whether the revelation here related was real, or a fiction? And, instead of a direct answer, suppose him, all at once, to be told the following confessed facts; and then to unite them into one view.

§ 41. *Finds* (a) *how much of the force of natural religion is due to scripture:*

Let him first be told, in how great a degree the profession and establishment of natural religion, the belief that there is one God to be worshipped, that virtue is his law, and that mankind shall be rewarded and punished hereafter, as they obey and disobey it here; in how very great a degree, I say, the profession and establishment of this moral system in the world is owing to the revelation, whether real or supposed, contained in this book: the establishment of this moral system, even in those countries which do not acknowledge the proper authority of the scripture.[x]

§ 42. (b) *That the establishment of Christianity is the greatest event in history.*

Let him be told also, what number of nations do acknowledge its proper authority. Let him then take

---

[x] *Sup.* II. vi. 5.

in the consideration, of what importance religion is to mankind. And upon these things he might, I think, truly observe, that this supposed revelation's obtaining and being received in the world, with all the circumstances and effects of it, considered together as one event, is the most conspicuous and important event in the story of mankind: that a book of this nature, and thus promulged and recommended to our consideration, demands, as if by a voice from heaven, to have its claims most seriously examined into: and that, before such examination, to treat it with any kind of scoffing and ridicule, is an offence against natural piety.

§ 43. (*But revelation imports no disparagement to any proof from reason.*)

But it is to be remembered, that how much soever the establishment of natural religion in the world is owing to the scripture-revelation, this does not destroy the proof of religion from reason; any more than the proof of Euclid's Elements is destroyed, by a man's knowing or thinking, that he should never have seen the truth of the several propositions contained in it, nor had those propositions come into his thoughts, but for that mathematician.

§ 44. (c) *The antiquity of scripture;* (d) *its corroborations;*

Let such a person as we are speaking of, be, in the next place, informed of the acknowledged antiquity of the first parts of this book: and that its chronology, its account of the time when the earth, and the several parts of it, were first peopled with human creatures, is no way contradicted, but is really confirmed, by the natural and civil history of the world, collected from common historians, from the state of the earth, and from the late invention of arts and sciences.[1] And

---

[1] This confirmation has been immensely enlarged since

as the scripture contains an unbroken thread of common and civil history, from the creation to the captivity, for between three and four thousand years: let the person we are speaking of be told, in the next place, that this general history, as it is not contradicted, but is confirmed by profane history as much as there would be reason to expect, upon supposition of its truth; so there is nothing in the whole history *itself*, to give any reasonable ground of suspicion of its not being, in the general, a faithful and literally true genealogy of men, and series of things.

§ 45. (e) *Its self-congruity.*

I speak here only of the common scripture-history, or of the course of ordinary events related in it; as distinguished from miracles, and from the prophetic history. In all the scripture-narrations of this kind, following events arise out of foregoing ones, as in all other histories. There appears nothing related as done in any age, not conformable to the manners of that age: nothing in the account of a succeeding age, which, one would say, could not be true, or was

Butler wrote, for monuments and scientific results are histories. However, while in itself a most solid and weighty fact, it is not exact and particular on behalf of the Hebrew chronology, or of any of the three competing chronologies of the Old Testament: but it confirms the Old Testament history in its basis, from which we learn that the history of the Adamic race is confined to a very few *millennia* before the Advent. This proposition is in no way interfered with by the discovery of the geologic man; for there seems to be no reason for associating him with the Adamic race, and much reason, perhaps some of it possibly derived from scripture, to assume the existence of other races of men, some of them perhaps less perfect or less capable of perfection.

It is needless to dwell upon the marked concurrence between the belief now generally received as to the origin of our solar system, and the general framework of the first chapter of Genesis.

improbable, from the account of things in the preceding one. There is nothing in the characters, which would raise a thought of their being feigned; but all the internal marks imaginable of their being real.

§ 46. (f) *Its neutrality as to ornament: its frank encountering of facts.*

It is to be added also, that mere genealogies, bare narratives of the number of years, which persons called by such and such names lived, do not carry the face of fiction; perhaps do carry some presumption of veracity: and all unadorned narratives, which have nothing to surprise, may be thought to carry somewhat of the like presumption too. And the domestic and the political history is plainly credible.

§ 47. (*It has strange incidents; as have most lives, or many; but nothing to destroy credit.*)

There may be incidents in scripture, which, taken alone in the naked way they are told, may appear strange; especially to persons of other manners, temper, education: but there are also incidents of undoubted truth, in many or most persons' lives, which, in the same circumstances, would appear to the full as strange. There may be mistakes of transcribers, there may be other real or seeming mistakes, not easy to be particularly accounted for: but there are certainly no more things of this kind in the scripture, than what were to have been expected in books of such antiquity; and nothing, in any wise, sufficient to discredit the general narrative.

§ 48. (g) *Divers points: and how, in scripture, proof of the common goes to support the miraculous.*

Now, that a history, claiming to commence from the creation, and extending in one continued series, through so great a length of time, and variety of events, those parts of it which require to be believed upon the mere authority of its Author; that this religion, I say, gradually spread and supported itself, for some hundred years, not only without any assistance from temporal power, but under constant discouragements, and often the bitterest persecutions from it; and then became the religion of the world.

§ 51. (k) *With the dispersion and standing isolation of the Jews;*

That in the mean time, the Jewish nation and government were destroyed, in a very remarkable manner, and the people carried away captive and dispersed through the most distant countries; in which state of dispersion they have remained fifteen hundred years: and that they remain a numerous people, united amongst themselves, and distinguished from the rest of the world, as they were in the days of Moses, by the profession of his law; and every where looked upon in a manner, which one scarce knows how distinctly to express, but in the words of the prophetic account of it, given so many ages before it came to pass; *Thou shalt become an astonishment, a proverb, and a byword, among all nations whither the Lord shall lead thee.*[a]

§ 52. *Insufficiently accounted for as a mere fact, by secondary provisions.*

The appearance of a standing miracle, in the Jews remaining a distinct people in their dispersion, and the confirmation which this event appears to give to the truth of revelation, may be thought to be answered, by their religion's forbidding them intermarriages with those of any other, and prescribing them a great many peculiarities in their food, by which they are debarred from the means of incorporating with the people in whose countries they live.[1] This is not, I think, a

[a] Deut. xxviii. 37.

---

[1] Now let us suppose that these prohibitions were

satisfactory account of that which it pretends to account for. But what does it pretend to account for? The correspondence between this event and the prophecies; or the coincidence of both, with a long dispensation of Providence, of a peculiar nature, towards that people formerly? No. It is only the event itself, which is offered to be thus accounted for; which single event, taken alone, abstracted from all such correspondence and coincidence, perhaps would not have appeared miraculous: but that correspondence and coincidence may be so, though the event itself be supposed not. Thus the concurrence of our Saviour's being born at Bethlehem, with a long foregoing series of prophecy and other coincidences, is doubtless miraculous; the series of prophecy, and other coincidences, and the event, being admitted: though the event itself, his birth at that place, appears to have been brought about in a natural way; of which, however, no one can be certain.[1]

§ 53. *The part-fulfilment of historical prophecy seems to foreshadow the entire,*

And as several of these events seem, in some degree expressly, to have verified the prophetic history already; so likewise they may be considered further, as having a peculiar aspect towards the full completion of it; as affording some presumption that the whole of it shall, one time or other, be fulfilled. Thus, that the Jews have been so wonderfully preserved in their sufficient to account for the isolation. The argument perhaps would not be weakened; because they spring from the original divine appointment, so that the entire chain of phenomena would hang, unbroken, upon that appointment.

[1] In this section, the word miraculous appears to imply marked adjustments in the order of nature, but not any variance from it; differing from other places where miracle does imply such a variance, either self-attested, by the evidence of the human senses; or (as in the Incarnation) without that kind of attestation.

long and wide dispersion; which is indeed the direct fulfilling of some prophecies, but is now mentioned only as looking forward to somewhat yet to come: that natural religion came forth from Judæa, and spread, in the degree it has done over the world, before lost in idolatry; which, together with some other things, have distinguished that very place, in like manner as the people of it are distinguished: that this great change of religion over the earth was brought about under the profession and acknowledgment, that Jesus was the promised Messiah: things of this kind naturally turn the thoughts of serious men towards the full completion of the prophetic history, concerning the final restoration of that people; concerning the establishment of the everlasting kingdom among them, the kingdom of the Messiah; and the future state of the world, under this sacred government. Such circumstances and events, compared with these prophecies, though no completions of them, yet would not, I think, be spoken of as nothing in the argument, by a person upon his first being informed of them. They fall in with the prophetic history of things still future, give it some additional credibility, have the appearance of being somewhat in order to the full completion of it.

§ 54. *For those capable of handling the question.*

Indeed it requires a good degree of knowledge, and great calmness and consideration, to be able to judge, thoroughly, of the evidence for the truth of Christianity, from that part of the prophetic history, which relates to the situation of the kingdoms of the world, and to the state of the Church, from the establishment of Christianity to the present time. But it appears, from a general view of it, to be very material. And those persons who have thoroughly examined it, and some of them were men of the coolest tempers, greatest capacities, and least liable to imputations of prejudice, insist upon it as determinately conclusive.[1]

---

[1] 'He had probably in his mind Sir Isaac Newton and Dr. Clarke.'—Fitzgerald.

§ 55. *But also the many, large, and plain coincidences will weigh much with any impartial mind:*

Suppose now a person quite ignorant of history, first to recollect the passages above mentioned out of scripture, without knowing but that the whole was a late fiction, then to be informed of the correspondent facts now mentioned, and to unite them all into one view: that the profession and establishment of natural religion in the world is greatly owing, in different ways, to this book, and the supposed revelation which it contains; that it is acknowledged to be of the earliest antiquity; that its chronology and common history are entirely credible; that this ancient nation, the Jews, of whom it chiefly treats, appear to have been, in fact, the people of God, in a distinguished sense; that, as there was a national expectation amongst them, raised from the prophecies, of a Messiah to appear at such a time, so one at this time appeared claiming to be that Messiah; that he was rejected by this nation, but received by the Gentiles, not upon the evidence of prophecy, but of miracles; that the religion he taught supported itself under the greatest difficulties, gained ground, and at length became the religion of the world; that in the mean time the Jewish polity was utterly destroyed, and the nation dispersed over the face of the earth; that notwithstanding this, they have remained a distinct numerous people for so many centuries, even to this day; which not only appears to be the express completion of several prophecies concerning them, but also renders it, as one may speak, a visible and easy possibility, that the promises made to them as a nation, may yet be fulfilled.

§ 56. *Extending to facts beyond Jewish and Christian history.*

And to these acknowledged truths, let the person we have been supposing add, as I think he ought, whether every one will allow it or no, the obvious appearances which there are, of the state of the world, in other respects besides what relates to the Jews, and of the Christian Church, having so long answered, and still answering to the prophetic history. Suppose, I say, these facts set over against the things before mentioned out of the scripture, and seriously compared with them; the joint view of both together must, I think, appear of very great weight to a considerate reasonable person: of much greater indeed, upon having them first laid before him, than is easy for us, who are so familiarized to them, to conceive, without some particular attention for that purpose.

§ 57. *Even this rude sketch shows something more than human;*

All these things, and the several particulars contained under them, require to be distinctly and most thoroughly examined into; that the weight of each may be judged of, upon such examination, and such conclusion drawn as results from their united force. But this has not been attempted here. I have gone no further than to show, that the general imperfect view of them now given, the confessed historical evidence for miracles, and the many obvious appearing completions of prophecy, together with the collateral things [b] here mentioned, and there are several others of the like sort; that all this together, which, being fact, must be acknowledged by unbelievers, amounts to real evidence of somewhat more than human in this matter: evidence much more important, than careless men, who have been accustomed only to transient and partial views of it, can imagine; and indeed abundantly sufficient to act upon. And these things, I apprehend, must be acknowledged by unbelievers.

[b] All the particular things mentioned in this chapter, not reducible to the head of certain miracles, or determinate completions of prophecy. See *sup.* §§ 2 *sqq.*

§ 58. *And with claims upon unbelievers.*

For though they may say, that the historical evidence of miracles wrought in attestation of Christianity, is not sufficient to convince them that such miracles were really wrought; they cannot deny, that there is such historical evidence, it being a known matter of fact that there is. They may say, the conformity between the prophecies and events is by accident: but there are many instances in which such conformity itself cannot be denied. They may say, with regard to such kind of collateral things as those above mentioned, that any odd accidental events, without meaning, will have a meaning found in them by fanciful people: and that such as are fanciful in any one certain way, will make out a thousand coincidences, which seem to favour their peculiar follies.

§ 59. *To competent judges, circumstantial evidence often as strong as direct.*

Men, I say, may talk thus: but no one who is serious, can possibly think these things to be nothing, if he considers the importance of collateral things, and even of lesser circumstances, in the evidence of probability, as distinguished, in nature, from the evidence of demonstration. In many cases indeed it seems to require the truest judgment, to determine with exactness the weight of circumstantial evidence:[1] but it is very often altogether as convincing, as that which is the most express and direct.

§ 60. *Serious men, taking aggregate account, will find a high probable proof.*

This general view of the evidence for Christianity, considered as making one argument, may also serve

[1] Meaning in this place not evidence from fact as opposed to evidence from testimony: but evidence from matter circumjacent, according to the etymology of the word; or collateral evidence, which evidently gives scope for largeness of view in the inquirer.

to recommend to serious persons, to set down every thing which they think may be of any real weight at all in proof of it, and particularly the many seeming completions of prophecy: and they will find, that, judging by the natural rules, by which we judge of probable evidence in common matters, they amount to a much higher degree of proof, upon such a joint review, than could be supposed upon considering them separately, at different times; how strong soever the proof might before appear to them, upon such separate views of it. For probable proofs, by being added, not only increase the evidence, but multiply it.

§ 61. *And should examine which is the safest side.*

Nor should I dissuade any one from setting down, what he thought made for the contrary side. But then it is to be remembered, not in order to influence his judgment, but his practice, that a mistake on one side may be, in its consequences, much more dangerous, than a mistake on the other. And what course is most safe, and what most dangerous, is a consideration thought very material, when we deliberate, not concerning events, but concerning conduct in our temporal affairs. To be influenced by this consideration in our judgment, to believe or disbelieve upon it, is indeed as much prejudice, as any thing whatever. And, like other prejudices, it operates contrary ways, in different men; for some are inclined to believe what they hope, and others what they fear. And it is manifest unreasonableness to apply to men's passions in order to gain their assent. But in deliberations concerning conduct, there is nothing which reason more requires to be taken into the account, than the importance of it. For, suppose it doubtful, what would be the consequence of acting in this, or in a contrary manner: still, that taking one side could be attended with little or no bad consequence, and taking the other might be attended with the greatest, must appear, to unprejudiced reason, of the highest moment towards determining, how we are to act.

§ 62. *The stress of our argument lies here: this cannot as a whole* (a) *be accident, or* (b) *be otherwise set aside.*

But the truth of our religion, like the truth of common matters, is to be judged of by all the evidence taken together. And unless the whole series of things which may be alleged in this argument, and every particular thing in it, can reasonably be supposed to have been by accident; (for here the stress of the argument for Christianity lies;) then is the truth of it proved: in like manner, as if in any common case, numerous events acknowledged, were to be alleged in proof of any other event disputed; the truth of the disputed event would be proved, not only if any one of the acknowledged ones did of itself clearly imply it, but, though no one of them singly did so, if the whole of the acknowledged events taken together could not in reason be supposed to have happened, unless the disputed one were true.

§ 63. *Advantages given by attack in detail.*

It is obvious, how much advantage the nature of this evidence gives to those persons who attack Christianity, especially in conversation. For it is easy to show, in a short and lively manner, that such and such things are liable to objection, that this and another thing is of little weight in itself; but impossible to show, in like manner, the united force of the whole argument in one view.

§ 64. *Summary in three propositions.*

However, lastly, as it has been made appear,[1] that there is no presumption against a revelation as miraculous; that the general scheme of Christianity, and the principal parts of it, are conformable to the experienced constitution of things, and the whole

[1] Especially in chapters ii, iv, v, vii.

perfectly credible: so the account now given of the positive evidence for it, shows, that this evidence is such, as, from the nature of it, cannot be destroyed, though it should be lessened.

CHAPTER VIII

OF THE OBJECTIONS WHICH MAY BE MADE AGAINST ARGUING FROM THE ANALOGY OF NATURE, TO RELIGION

§ 1. *Chief objections of thinking and unthinking men;*

IF every one would consider, with such attention as they are bound, even in point of morality, to consider, what they judge and give characters of; the occasion of this chapter would be, in some good measure at least, superseded. But since this is not to be expected; for some we find do not concern themselves to understand even what they write against: since this Treatise, in common with most others, lies open to objections, which may appear very material to thoughtful men at first sight; and, besides that, seems peculiarly liable to the objections of such as can judge without thinking, and of such as can censure without judging; it may not be amiss to set down the chief of these objections which occur to me, and consider them to their hands. And they are such as these:

§ 2. (a) *To the plan of meeting difficulties by showing the like elsewhere.*

' That it is a poor thing to solve difficulties in revelation, by saying, that there are the same in natural religion; when what is wanting is to clear both of them of these their common, as well as other their respective, difficulties; but that it is a strange way indeed of convincing men of the obligations of religion, to show them, that they have as little reason for their worldly pursuits : and a strange way of vindicating the justice and goodness of the Author of nature, and of removing the objections against both, to which the system of religion lies open, to show, that the like objections lie against natural providence ; a way of answering objections against religion, without so much as pretending to make out, that the system of it, or the particular things in it objected against, are reasonable——especially, perhaps some may be inattentive enough to add, must this be thought strange, when it is confessed that analogy is no answer to such objections : that when this sort of reasoning is carried to the utmost length it can be imagined capable of, it will yet leave the mind in a very unsatisfied state : and that it must be unaccountable ignorance of mankind, to imagine they will be prevailed with to forego their present interests and pleasures, from regard to religion, upon doubtful evidence.'[1]

§ 3. *Such pleas may partially affect considerate men.*

Now, as plausible as this way of talking may appear, that appearance will be found in a great measure owing to half-views, which show but part of an object, yet show that indistinctly, and to undeterminate language. By these means weak men are often deceived by others, and ludicrous men, by themselves. And even those, who are serious and considerate, cannot always readily disentangle, and at once clearly see through the perplexities, in which subjects themselves are involved ; and which are heightened by the

---

[1] No adversary or critic within my knowledge has ever stated the objections against Butler's argument with as much force as Butler himself has given them in this section. Also, he exerts himself to bring that argument to a head :

1. I show you, on the basis of experience, what is true (§ 6) ;
2. And, in the way of inducement, what is useful (§ 7).

deficiencies and the abuse of words. To this latter sort of persons, the following reply to each part of this objection severally, may be of some assistance; as it may also tend a little to stop and silence others.

§ 4. *Removal of all difficulties would mean comprehension of God's entire plan.*

First, The thing wanted, i.e. what men require, is to have all difficulties cleared. And this is, or, at least for any thing we know to the contrary, it may be, the same, as requiring to comprehend the divine nature, and the whole plan of Providence from everlasting to everlasting.

§ 5. *The method is one of regular use in common life.*

But it hath always been allowed to argue, from what is acknowledged, to what is disputed. And it is in no other sense a poor thing, to argue from natural religion to revealed, in the manner found fault with, than it is to argue in numberless other ways of probable deduction and inference, in matters of conduct, which we are continually reduced to the necessity of doing. Indeed the epithet *poor* may be applied, I fear, as properly to great part or the whole of human life, as it is to the things mentioned in the objection. Is it not a poor thing, for a physician to have so little knowledge in the cure of diseases, as even the most eminent have? to act upon conjecture and guess, where the life of man is concerned? Undoubtedly it is: but not in comparison of having no skill at all in that useful art, and being obliged to act wholly in the dark.

§ 6. *His principal recourse is to the course of providence experimentally ascertained.*

Further: since it is as unreasonable, as it is common, to urge objections against revelation, which are of equal weight against natural religion; and those who do this, if they are not confused themselves, deal unfairly with others, in making it seem, that they are arguing only against revelation, or particular doctrines of it, when in reality they are arguing against moral providence; it is a thing of consequence to show, that such objections are as much levelled against natural religion as against revealed. And objections, which are equally applicable to both, are properly speaking answered, by its being shown that they are so, provided the former be admitted to be true. And, without taking in the consideration how distinctly this is admitted, it is plainly very material to observe, that as the things objected against in natural religion are of the same kind with what is certain matter of experience in the course of providence, and in the information which God affords us concerning our temporal interest under his government; so the objections against the system of Christianity, and the evidence of it, are of the very same kind with those which are made against the system and evidence of natural religion. However, the reader upon review may see, that most of the analogies insisted upon, even in the latter part of this Treatise, do not necessarily require to have more taken for granted than is in the former; that there is an Author of nature, or natural Governor of the world: and Christianity is vindicated, not from its analogy to natural religion, but chiefly from its analogy to the experienced constitution of nature.

§ 7. *Shows also that our interest is profoundly involved.*

Secondly, Religion is a practical thing, and consists in such a determinate course of life; as being what, there is reason to think, is commanded by the Author of nature, and will, upon the whole, be our happiness under his government. Now if men can be convinced, that they have the like reason to believe this, as to believe, that taking care of their temporal affairs will be to their advantage; such conviction cannot but be an argument to them for the practice of religion. And if there be really any reason for believing one of these, and endeavouring to preserve life, and secure ourselves the necessaries and conveniences of it: then there is reason also for believing the other, and endeavouring to secure the interest it proposes to us. And if the interest, which religion proposes to us, be infinitely greater than our whole temporal interest; then there must be proportionably greater reason for endeavouring to secure one, than the other: since, by the supposition, the probability of our securing one is equal to the probability of our securing the other. This seems plainly unanswerable; and has a tendency to influence fair minds, who consider what our condition really is, or upon what evidence we are naturally appointed to act; and who are disposed to acquiesce in the terms upon which we live, and attend to and follow that practical instruction, whatever it be, which is afforded us.

§ 8. *The main objection is: 'the evidence is doubtful, therefore the claim is unfounded.'*

But the chief and proper force of the argument referred to in the objection, lies in another place. For, it is said that the proof of religion is involved in such inextricable difficulties, as to render it doubtful; and that it cannot be supposed, that, if it were true, it would be left upon doubtful evidence. Here then, over and above the force of each particular difficulty or objection, these difficulties and objections taken together are turned into a positive argument against the truth of religion; which argument would stand thus. If religion were true, it would not be left doubtful, and open to objections to the degree in which it is: therefore that it is thus left, not only renders the evidence of it weak, and lessens its force, in proportion to the weight of such objections; but also shows it to be false, or is a general presumption of its being so.

§ 9. *Like doubt is frequent in matters of high temporal interest.*

Now the observation, that, from the natural constitution and course of things, we must in our temporal concerns, almost continually, and in matters of great consequence, act upon evidence of a like kind and degree to the evidence of religion, is an answer to this argument: because it shows, that it is according to the conduct and character of the Author of nature to appoint we should act upon evidence like to that, which this argument presumes he cannot be supposed to appoint we should act upon: it is an instance, a general one made up of numerous particular ones, of somewhat in his dealing with us, similar to what is said to be incredible. And as the force of this answer lies merely in the parallel, which there is between the evidence for religion and for our temporal conduct; the answer is equally just and conclusive, whether the parallel be made out, by showing the evidence of the former to be higher, or the evidence of the latter to be lower.

§ 10. *His aim is, not to vindicate God, but to point out our duty as men.*

Thirdly, The design of this Treatise is not to vindicate the character of God, but to show the obligations of men: it is not to justify his providence, but to show what belongs to us to do. These are two subjects, and ought not to be confounded. And though they may at length run up into each other, yet observations may immediately tend to make out the latter, which do not appear, by any immediate connection, to the purpose of the former; which is less our concern than many seem to think. For, first, it is not necessary we should justify the dispensations of Providence against objections, any further than to show, that the things objected against may, for ought we know, be consistent with justice and goodness.

§ 11. *Things, unjust if taken alone, may be vindicable by things circumjacent.*

Suppose then, that there are things in the system of this world, and plan of Providence relating to it, which taken alone would be unjust: yet it has been shown unanswerably, that if we could take in the reference, which these things may have, to other things present, past, and to come; to the whole scheme, which the things objected against are parts of; these very things might, for ought we know, be found to be, not only consistent with justice, but instances of it. Indeed it has been shown, by the analogy of what we see, not only possible that this may be the case, but credible that it is. And thus objections, drawn from such things, are answered, and Providence is vindicated, as far as religion makes its vindication necessary.

§ 12. *He leaves none but inconclusive objections to lie against nature.*

Hence it appears, secondly, that objections against the divine justice and goodness are not endeavoured to be removed, by showing that the like objections, allowed to be really conclusive, lie against natural Providence: but those objections being supposed and shown not to be conclusive, the things objected against, considered as matters of fact, are further shown to be credible, from their conformity to the constitution of nature; for instance, that God will reward and punish men for their actions hereafter, from the observation, that he does reward and punish them for their actions here. And this, I apprehend, is of weight.

§ 13. *If the objections remain unanswered, so does religion, with its proofs.*

And I add, thirdly, it would be of weight, even though those objections were not answered. For, there being the proof of religion above set down; and religion implying several facts; for instance again, the fact last mentioned, that God will reward and punish men for their actions hereafter; the observation, that his present method of government is by rewards and punishments, shows that future fact not to be incredible: whatever objections men may think they have against it, as unjust or unmerciful, according to their notions of justice and mercy; or as improbable from their belief of necessity. I say, *as improbable:* for it is evident no objection against it, *as unjust,* can be urged from necessity; since this notion as much destroys injustice, as it does justice.

§ 14. *The credibility of a religion based on fact may be proved apart from its reasonableness.*

Then, fourthly, Though objections against the reasonableness of the system of religion cannot indeed be answered without entering into consideration of its reasonableness; yet objections against the credibility or truth of it may. Because the system of it is reducible into what is properly matter of fact: and the truth, the probable truth, of facts, may be shown without consideration of their reasonableness. Nor is it necessary, though, in some cases and respects, it is highly useful and proper, yet it is not necessary, to give a proof of the reasonableness of every precept enjoined us, and of every particular dispensation of Providence, which comes into the system of religion.

§ 15. *Unless religion has been disproved, the practice of it is reasonable.*

Indeed the more throughly a person of a right disposition is convinced of the perfection of the divine nature and conduct, the further he will advance towards that perfection of religion, which St. John speaks of.[a] But the general obligations of religion are fully made out, by proving the reasonableness of the practice of

[a] 1 John iv. 18.

it. And that the practice of religion *is* reasonable, may be shown, though no more could be proved, than that the system of it *may be* so, for ought we know to the contrary: and even without entering into the distinct consideration of this.

§ 16. *Repeats* § 14.

And from hence, fifthly, it is easy to see, that though the analogy of nature is not an immediate answer to objections against the wisdom, the justice, or goodness, of any doctrine or precept of religion: yet it may be, as it is, an immediate and direct answer to what is really intended by such objections; which is, to show that the things objected against are incredible.

§ 17. *Proof in religion does not reach to satisfaction; nor in temporal affairs; e. g. as to health.*[1]

Fourthly, It is most readily acknowledged, that the foregoing Treatise is by no means satisfactory; very far indeed from it: but so would any natural institution of life appear, if reduced into a system, together with its evidence. Leaving religion out of the case, men are divided in their opinions, whether our pleasures overbalance our pains: and whether it be, or be not, eligible to live in this world. And were all such controversies settled, which perhaps, in speculation, would

---

[1] Butler seems to use the word *satisfaction*, or its adjective *satisfactory*, in the following senses:—

(*a*) In a popular manner, as the equivalent of comfort or enjoyment.

(*b*) With regard to our Saviour's sacrifice, as the equivalent of atonement. See *sup.* II. vi. 17, 18, 22.

(*c*) In a more scientific way, with regard to sufficiency of evidence.

He supplies in the next section a subjective definition of the words 'satisfactory evidence,' viz. *what we wish it*. In itself it seems to be the equivalent of the Greek αὐτάρκης, that is to say, self-sufficing or ideally complete, not requiring aid or supplement from without.

be found involved in great difficulties; and were it determined upon the evidence of reason, as nature has determined it to our hands, that life is to be preserved: yet still, the rules which God has been pleased to afford us, for escaping the miseries of it, and obtaining its satisfactions, the rules, for instance, of preserving health, and recovering it when lost, are not only fallible and precarious, but very far from being exact. Nor are we informed by nature, in future contingencies and accidents, so as to render it at all certain, what is the best method of managing our affairs. What will be the success of our temporal pursuits, in the common sense of the word success, is highly doubtful. And what will be the success of them, in the proper sense of the word; i. e. what happiness or enjoyment we shall obtain by them, is doubtful in a much higher degree. Indeed the unsatisfactory nature of the evidence, with which we are obliged to take up, in the daily course of life, is scarce to be expressed. Yet men do not throw away life, or disregard the interests of it, upon account of this doubtfulness.

§ 18. *The demand is to change 'the very condition of our being,'*

The evidence of religion then being admitted real, those who object against it, as not satisfactory, i. e. as not being what they wish it, plainly forget the very condition of our being: for satisfaction, in this sense, does not belong to such a creature as man. And, which is more material, they forget also the very nature of religion.

§ 19. *And the probative power of religious evidences.*

For, religion presupposes, in all those who will embrace it, a certain degree of integrity and honesty; which it was intended to try whether men have or not, and to exercise in such as have it, in order to its improvement. Religion presupposes this as much, and in the same sense, as speaking to a man presupposes he understands the language in which you speak; or as warning a man of any danger presupposes that he hath such a regard to himself, as that he will endeavour to avoid it. And therefore the question is not at all, Whether the evidence of religion be satisfactory: but Whether it be, in reason, sufficient to prove and discipline that virtue, which it presupposes. Now the evidence of it is fully sufficient for all those purposes of probation; how far soever it is from being satisfactory, as to the purposes of curiosity, or any other: and indeed it answers the purposes of the former in several respects, which it would not do, if it were as overbearing as is required.

§ 20. *Ask, not, does it satisfy? but, does it bind to action?*

One might add farther; that whether the motives or the evidence for any course of action be satisfactory, meaning here, by that word, what satisfies a man, that such a course of action will in event be for his good; this need never be, and I think, strictly speaking, never is, the practical question in common matters. But the practical question in all cases is, Whether the evidence for a course of action be such, as, taking in all circumstances, makes the faculty within us, which is the guide and judge of conduct,[b] determine that course of action to be prudent. Indeed, satisfaction that it will be for our interest or happiness, abundantly determines an action to be prudent: but evidence almost infinitely lower than this, determines actions to be so too; even in the conduct of every day.

§ 21. *His object is to show how men ought in reason to behave;*

Fifthly, As to the objection concerning the influence which this argument, or any part of it, may, or may not,

[b] See Dissert. II. § 8.

be expected to have upon men; I observe, as above, that religion being intended for a trial and exercise of the morality of every person's character, who is a subject of it; and there being, as I have shown, such evidence for it, as is sufficient, in reason, to influence men to embrace it: to object, that it is not to be imagined mankind will be influenced by such evidence, is nothing to the purpose of the foregoing Treatise. For the purpose of it is not to inquire, what sort of creatures mankind are; but what the light and knowledge, which is afforded them, requires they should be: to show how, in reason, they ought to behave; not how, in fact, they will behave. This depends upon themselves, and is their own concern; the personal concern of each man in particular.

§ 22. *And so to put them into probation; with some he may succeed.*

And how little regard the generality have to it, experience indeed does too fully show. But religion, considered as a probation, has had its end upon all persons, to whom it has been proposed with evidence sufficient in reason to influence their practice: for by this means they have been put into a state of probation; let them behave as they will in it. And thus, not only revelation, but reason also, teaches us, that by the evidence of religion being laid before men, the designs of Providence are carrying on, not only with regard to those who will, but likewise with regard to those who will not, be influenced by it. However, lastly, the objection here referred to, allows the things insisted upon in this Treatise to be of some weight: and if so, it may be hoped it will have some influence. And if there be a probability that it will have any at all, there is the same reason in kind, though not in degree, to lay it before men, as there would be, if it were likely to have a greater influence.

§ 23. *Has all along worked from points of departure not chosen by him.*

And further, I desire it may be considered, with respect to the whole of the foregoing objections, that in this Treatise I have argued upon the principles of others,[c] not my own: and have omitted what I think true, and of the utmost importance, because by others thought unintelligible, or not true. Thus I have argued upon the principles of the Fatalists, which I do not believe:

§ 24. *Has waived the two great principles,* (a) *of moral fitness,* (b) *of liberty;*

And have omitted a thing of the utmost importance which I do believe, the moral fitness and unfitness of actions, prior to all will whatever; which I apprehend as certainly to determine the divine conduct, as speculative truth and falsehood necessarily determine the divine judgment. Indeed the principle of liberty, and that of moral fitness, so force themselves upon the mind, that moralists, the ancients as well as moderns, have formed their language upon it. And probably it may appear in mine: though I have endeavoured to avoid it; and, in order to avoid it, have sometimes been obliged to express myself in a manner, which will appear strange to such as do not observe the reason for it: but the general argument here pursued does not at all suppose or proceed upon these principles.

§ 25. *And has treated religion only as matter of fact.*

Now, these two abstract principles of liberty and moral fitness being omitted, religion can be considered in no other view, than merely as a question of fact: and in this view it is here considered. It is obvious,

[c] By *arguing upon the principles of others,* the reader will observe is meant; not proving any thing *from* those principles, but *notwithstanding* them. Thus religion is proved, not *from* the opinion of necessity; which is absurd: but, *notwithstanding* or *even though* that opinion were admitted to be true.

that Christianity, and the proof of it, are both historical. And even natural religion is, properly, a matter of fact. For, that there is a righteous Governor of the world, is so: and this proposition contains the general system of natural religion. But then, several abstract truths, and in particular those two principles, are usually taken into consideration in the proof of it: whereas it is here treated of only as a matter of fact. To explain this: that the three angles of a triangle are equal to two right ones, is an abstract truth: but that they appear so to our mind, is only a matter of fact. And this last must have been admitted, if any thing was, by those ancient sceptics, who would not have admitted the former; but pretended to doubt, Whether there were any such thing as truth, or Whether we could certainly depend upon our faculties of understanding for the knowledge of it in any case. So likewise, that there is, in the nature of things, an original standard of right and wrong in actions, independent upon all will, but which unalterably determines the will of God, to exercise that moral government over the world, which religion teaches, i. e. finally and upon the whole to reward and punish men respectively as they act right or wrong;[1] this assertion contains an abstract truth, as well as matter of fact. But suppose, in the present state, every man, without exception, was rewarded and punished, in exact proportion as he followed or transgressed that sense of right and wrong, which God has implanted in the nature of every man: this would not be at all an abstract truth, but only a matter of fact. And though this fact were acknowledged by every one; yet the very same difficulties might be raised, as are now, concerning the abstract questions of liberty and moral fitness: and we should have a proof, even the certain one of experience, that the government of the world was perfectly moral, without taking in the consideration of those questions: and this proof would remain, in what way soever they were determined.

[1] Comp. *sup.* I. vi. 16 *n.*

§ 26. *Has thus lost much in the proof of final reward and punishment.*

And thus, God having given mankind a moral faculty, the object of which is actions, and which naturally approves some actions as right, and of good desert, and condemns others as wrong, and of ill desert; that he will, finally and upon the whole, reward the former and punish the latter, is not an assertion of an abstract truth, but of what is as mere a fact, as his doing so at present would be. This future fact I have not indeed proved with the force with which it might be proved, from the principles of liberty and moral fitness; but without them have given a really conclusive practical proof of it, which is greatly strengthened by the general analogy of nature : a proof easily cavilled at, easily shown not to be demonstrative, for it is not offered as such; but impossible, I think, to be evaded, or answered. And thus the obligations of religion are made out, exclusively of the questions concerning liberty and moral fitness; which have been perplexed with difficulties and abstruse reasonings, as every thing may.

§ 27. *Has shown it absurd to denounce Christianity as false : also that it is credible : and more.*

Hence therefore may be observed distinctly, what is the force of this Treatise. It will be, to such as are convinced of religion upon the proof arising out of the two last-mentioned principles, an additional proof and a confirmation of it: to such as do not admit those principles, an original proof of it,[d] and a confirmation of that proof. Those who believe, will here find the scheme of Christianity cleared of objections, and the evidence of it in a peculiar manner strengthened: those who do not believe, will at least be shown the absurdity of all attempts to prove Christianity false, the plain undoubted credibility of it; and, I hope, a good deal more.

[1] *Sup.* I. vi. 12-14.

§ 28. *Analogy has a firm basis, and special claims on those who prefer facts to abstractions.*

And thus, though some perhaps may seriously think, that analogy, as here urged, has too great stress laid upon it; and ridicule, unanswerable ridicule, may be applied, to show the argument from it in a disadvantageous light: yet there can be no question, but that it is a real one. For religion, both natural and revealed, implying in it numerous facts; analogy, being a confirmation of all facts to which it can be applied, as it is the only proof of most, cannot but be admitted by every one to be a material thing, and truly of weight on the side of religion, both natural and revealed: and it ought to be particularly regarded by such as profess to follow nature, and to be less satisfied with abstract reasonings.

CHAPTER IX

CONCLUSION

§ 1. *Upon the known facts, disregard of religion would be incredible but for experience.*

WHATEVER account may be given of the strange inattention and disregard, in some ages and countries, to a matter of such importance as religion; it would, before experience, be incredible, that there should be the like disregard in those, who have had the moral system of the world laid before them, as it is by Christianity, and often inculcated upon them: because this moral system carries in it a good degree of evidence for its truth, upon its being barely proposed to our thoughts.

§ 2. *A simple matter is obscured by intricacies of speculation.*

There is no need of abstruse reasonings and distinctions, to convince an unprejudiced understanding, that there is a God who made and governs the world, and will judge it in righteousness; though they may be necessary to answer abstruse difficulties, when once such are raised: when the very meaning of those words, which express most intelligibly the general doctrine of religion, is pretended to be uncertain; and the clear truth of the thing itself is obscured by the intricacies of speculation. But to an unprejudiced mind, ten thousand thousand instances of design cannot but prove a designer. And it is intuitively manifest, that creatures ought to live under a dutiful sense of their Maker; and that justice and charity must be his laws, to creatures whom he has made social, and placed in society.

§ 3. *Revelation requires proofs; offers them: to refuse inquiry is immoral;*

Indeed the truth of revealed religion, peculiarly so called, is not self-evident, but requires external proof, in order to its being received. Yet inattention, among us, to revealed religion, will be found to imply the same dissolute immoral temper of mind, as inattention to natural religion: because, when both are laid before us, in the manner they are in Christian countries of liberty, our obligations to inquire into both, and to embrace both upon supposition of their truth, are obligations of the same nature. For, revelation claims to be the voice of God: and our obligation to attend to his voice is surely moral in all cases. And as it is insisted, that its evidence is conclusive, upon thorough consideration of it; so it offers itself to us with manifest obvious appearances of having something more than human in it, and therefore in all reason requires to have its claims most seriously examined into.

§ 4. *Especially in view of its claim as miraculous.*

It is to be added, that though light and knowledge, in what manner soever afforded us, is equally from God; yet a miraculous revelation has a peculiar tendency, from the first principles of our nature, to awaken mankind, and inspire them with reverence and awe: and this is a peculiar obligation, to attend to what claims to be so with such appearances of truth. It is therefore most certain, that our obligations to inquire seriously into the evidence of Christianity, and, upon supposition of its truth, to embrace it, are of the utmost importance, and moral in the highest and most proper sense.

§ 5. *Negation is apt to pass into virulent hostility.*

Let us then suppose, that the evidence of religion in general, and of Christianity, has been seriously inquired into, by all reasonable men among us. Yet we find many professedly to reject both, upon speculative principles of infidelity. And all of them do not content themselves with a bare neglect of religion, and enjoying their imaginary freedom from its restraints. Some go much beyond this. They deride God's moral government over the world. They renounce his protection, and defy his justice. They ridicule and vilify Christianity, and blaspheme the Author of it; and take all occasions to manifest a scorn and contempt of revelation. This amounts to an active setting themselves against religion; to what may be considered as a positive principle of irreligion: which they cultivate within themselves, and, whether they intend this effect or not, render habitual, as a good man does the contrary principle. And others, who are not chargeable with all this profligateness, yet are in avowed opposition to religion, as if discovered to be groundless.

§ 6. *His opponents proceed on* (a) *prejudice against revelation;* (b) *strange things in Scripture;* (c) *pleas as* sup. ch. vi. ; (d) *that doubt warrants denial.*

Now admitting, which is the supposition we go upon, that these persons act upon what they think principles of reason, and otherwise they are not to be argued with ; it is really inconceivable, that they should imagine they clearly see the whole evidence of it, considered in itself, to be nothing at all : nor do they pretend this. They are far indeed from having a just notion of its evidence : but they would not say its evidence was nothing, if they thought the system of it, with all its circumstances, were credible, like other matters of science or history. So that their manner of treating it must proceed, either from such kind of objections against all religion, as have been answered or obviated in the former part of this Treatise ; or else from objections, and difficulties, supposed more peculiar to Christianity. Thus, they entertain prejudices against the whole notion of a revelation, and miraculous interpositions. They find things in scripture, whether in incidental passages, or in the general scheme of it, which appear to them unreasonable. They take for granted, that if Christianity were true, the light of it must have been more general, and the evidence of it more satisfactory, or rather overbearing : that it must and would have been, in some way, otherwise put and left, than it is. Now this is not imagining they see the evidence itself to be nothing, or inconsiderable ; but quite another thing. It is being fortified against the evidence, in some degree acknowledged, by thinking they see the system of Christianity, or somewhat which appears to them necessarily connected with it, to be incredible or false : fortified against that evidence, which might, otherwise, make great impression upon them. Or, lastly, if any of these persons are, upon the whole, in doubt concerning the truth of Christianity ; their behaviour seems owing to their taking for granted, through strange inattention, that such doubting is, in a manner, the same thing, as being certain against it.

§ 7. *This treatise meets them by* (a) *establishing a moral government ;* (b) *removing presumptions against Christianity as* fact ;

To these persons, and to this state of opinion concerning religion, the foregoing Treatise is adapted. For, all the general objections against the moral system of nature having been obviated, it is shown, that there is not any peculiar presumption at all against Christianity, either considered as not discoverable by reason, or as unlike to what is so discovered ; nor any worth mentioning against it as miraculous, if any at all ; none, certainly, which can render it in the least incredible. It is shown, that, upon supposition of a divine revelation, the analogy of nature renders it beforehand highly credible, I think probable, that many things in it must appear liable to great objections ; and that we must be incompetent judges of it, to a great degree. This observation is, I think, unquestionably true, and of the very utmost importance : but it is urged, as I hope it will be understood, with great caution of not vilifying the faculty of reason,[1] which is *the candle of the Lord within us* ;[a] though it can afford no light, where it does not shine ; nor judge, where it has no principles to judge upon.

§ 8. (c) *As against its goodness, by showing their failure as against nature.*

The objections here spoken of, being first answered in the view of objections against Christianity as a matter of fact, are in the next place considered as urged more immediately against the wisdom, justice,

[a] Prov. xx. 27.

[1] *Sup.* II. iii. 3.

and goodness of the Christian dispensation. And it is fully made out, that they admit of exactly the like answer, in every respect, to what the like objections against the constitution of nature admit of: that, as partial views give the appearance of wrong to things, which, upon further consideration and knowledge of their relations to other things, are found just and good; so it is perfectly credible, that the things objected against the wisdom and goodness of the Christian dispensation, may be rendered instances of wisdom and goodness, by their reference to other things beyond our view: because Christianity is a scheme as much above our comprehension, as that of nature; and like that, a scheme in which means are made use of to accomplish ends, and which, as is most credible, may be carried on by general laws. And it ought to be attended to, that this is not an answer taken merely or chiefly from our ignorance; but from somewhat positive, which our observation shows us. For, to like objections, the like answer is experienced to be just, in numberless parallel cases.

§ 9. *Particular objections are next met: e.g. that the remedy was not summary.*

The objections against the Christian dispensation, and the method by which it is carried on, having been thus obviated, in general and together; the chief of them are considered distinctly, and the particular things objected to are shown credible, by their perfect analogy, each apart, to the constitution of nature. Thus, if man be fallen from his primitive state, and to be restored, and infinite wisdom and power engages in accomplishing our recovery: it were to have been expected, it is said, that this should have been effected at once; and not by such a long series of means, and such a various economy of persons and things; one dispensation preparatory to another, this to a further one, and so on through an indefinite number of ages, before the end of the scheme proposed can be completely accomplished: a scheme conducted by infinite wisdom, and executed by almighty power. But now, on the contrary, our finding that every thing in the constitution and course of nature is thus carried on, shows such expectations concerning revelation to be highly unreasonable; and is a satisfactory answer to them, when urged as objections against the credibility, that the great scheme of Providence in the redemption of the world may be of this kind, and to be accomplished in this manner.

§ 10. *As to operating through a mediator.*

As to the particular method of our redemption, the appointment of a mediator between God and man: this has been shown to be most obviously analogous to the general conduct of nature, i. e. the God of nature, in appointing others to be the instruments of his mercy, as we experience in the daily course of Providence.

§ 11. *Heathen recognition of our fallen state.*

The condition of this world, which the doctrine of our redemption by Christ presupposes, so much falls in with natural appearances, that heathen moralists inferred it from those appearances: inferred, that human nature was fallen from its original rectitude, and, in consequence of this, degraded from its primitive happiness. Or, however this opinion came into the world, these appearances must have kept up the tradition, and confirmed the belief of it.

§ 12. *As to the insufficiency of repentance;*

And as it was the general opinion under the light of nature, that repentance and reformation, alone and by itself, was not sufficient to do away sin, and procure a full remission of the penalties annexed to it; and as the reason of the thing does not at all lead to any such conclusion: so every day's experience shows us, that reformation is not, in any sort, sufficient to prevent the present disadvantages and miseries, which, in the natural course of things, God has annexed to folly and extravagance.

§ 13. *And the further provision made;*

Yet there may be ground to think, that the punishments, which, by the general laws of divine government, are annexed to vice, may be prevented: that provision may have been, even originally, made, that they should be prevented by some means or other, though they could not by reformation alone. For we have daily instances of *such mercy*, in the general conduct of nature: compassion provided for misery,[b] medicines for diseases, friends against enemies. There is provision made, in the original constitution of the world, that much of the natural bad consequences of our follies, which persons themselves alone cannot prevent, may be prevented by the assistance of others; assistance, which nature enables, and disposes, and appoints them to afford. By a method of goodness analogous to this, when the world lay in wickedness, and consequently in ruin, *God so loved the world, that he gave his only begotten Son* to save it: and *he being made perfect by suffering, became the Author of eternal salvation to all them that obey him.*[c]

§ 14. *Beyond comprehension in its mode, but efficacious, agreeably to experience.*

Indeed neither reason nor analogy would lead us to think, in particular, that the interposition of Christ, in the manner in which he did interpose, would be of that efficacy for recovery of the world, which the scripture teaches us it was: but neither would reason

---

[b] Sermons V, VI, at the Rolls.
[c] John iii. 16; Heb. v. 9.

nor analogy lead us to think, that other particular means would be of the efficacy, which experience shows they are, in numberless instances. And therefore, as the case before us does not admit of experience; so, that neither reason nor analogy can show how, or in what particular way, the interposition of Christ, as revealed in scripture, is of that efficacy, which it is there represented to be; this is no kind nor degree of presumption against its being really of that efficacy.

§ 15. *As to partial propagation, and imperfect evidence.*

Further: the objections against Christianity, from the light of it not being universal, nor its evidence so strong as might possibly be given us, have been answered by the general analogy of nature. That God has made such variety of creatures, is indeed an answer to the former: but that he dispenses his gifts in such variety, both of degrees and kinds, amongst creatures of the same species, and even to the same individuals at different times; is a more obvious and full answer to it. And it is so far from being the method of Providence in other cases, to afford us such overbearing evidence, as some require in proof of Christianity; that, on the contrary, the evidence upon which we are naturally appointed to act in common matters, throughout a very great part of life, is doubtful in a high degree. And admitting the fact, that God has afforded to some no more than doubtful evidence of religion: the same account may be given of it, as of difficulties and temptations with regard to practice.

§ 16. *The doubtfulness may be due to ourselves;*

But as it is not impossible,[d] surely, that this alleged doubtfulness may be men's own fault; it deserves their most serious consideration, whether it be not so.

---

[d] *Sup.* II. vi. 19.

§ 17. *And doubtful evidence binds.*

However, it is certain, that doubting implies a degree of evidence for that of which we doubt: and that this degree of evidence, as really lays us under obligations, as demonstrative evidence.

§ 18. *Religion varies from nature not more than nature from herself.*

The whole then of religion is throughout credible: nor is there, I think, any thing relating to the revealed dispensation of things, more different from the experienced constitution and course of nature, than some parts of the constitution of nature are from other parts of it.

§ 19. *Reason almost intuitively approves of natural religion, taken up by the gospel: so the guilt of immorality is aggravated.*

And if so, the only question which remains is, What positive evidence can be alleged for the truth of Christianity? This too in general has been considered, and the objections against it estimated. Deduct, therefore, what is to be deducted from that evidence, upon account of any weight which may be thought to remain in these objections, after what the analogy of nature has suggested in answer to them: and then consider, what are the practical consequences from all this, upon the most sceptical principles one can argue upon: (for I am writing to persons who entertain these principles:) and upon such consideration it will be obvious, that immorality, as little excuse as it admits of in itself, is greatly aggravated, in persons who have been made acquainted with Christianity, whether they believe it or not: because the moral system of nature, or natural religion, which Christianity lays before us, approves itself, almost intuitively, to a reasonable mind, upon seeing it proposed.

§ 20. *The sceptic must own that Christianity may be true; by this he is bound.*

In the next place, with regard to Christianity, it will be observed; that there is a middle between a full satisfaction of the truth of it, and a satisfaction of the contrary. The middle state of mind between these two consists in a serious apprehension, that it may be true; joined with doubt whether it be so. And this, upon the best judgment I am able to make, is as far towards speculative infidelity, as any sceptic can at all be supposed to go, who has had true Christianity, with the proper evidence of it, laid before him, and has in any tolerable measure considered them. For I would not be mistaken to comprehend all who have ever heard of it: because it seems evident, that in many countries called Christian, neither Christianity, nor its evidence, are fairly laid before men. And in places where both are, there appear to be some, who have very little attended to either, and who reject Christianity with a scorn proportionate to their inattention; and yet are by no means without understanding in other matters. Now it has been shown, that a serious apprehension that Christianity may be true, lays persons under the strictest obligations of a serious regard to it, throughout the whole of their life: a regard not the same exactly, but in many respects nearly the same, with what a full conviction of its truth would lay them under.

§ 21. *Blasphemy is without excuse.*

Lastly, it will appear, that blasphemy and profaneness, I mean with regard to Christianity, are absolutely without excuse. For there is no temptation to it, but from the wantonness of vanity or mirth: and these, considering the infinite importance of the subject, are no such temptations as to afford any excuse for it.

§ 22. *For it, and for disregard, even demonstration might fail as remedy.*[1]

If this be a just account of things, and yet men can go on to vilify or disregard Christianity, which is to talk and act as if they had a demonstration of its falsehood; there is no reason to think they would alter their behaviour to any purpose, though there were a demonstration of its truth.

---

[1] If we project the following classification:

1. Things demonstrated;
2.   ,,   of moral certainty;
3.   ,,   likely;
4.   ,,   not unlikely;
5.   ,,   neutral;
6.   ,,   improbable;
7.   ,,   demonstrated false;

Butler's arguments for religion will range from (2) down to (4). (The distinction between (2), (3), (4), is taken by Maurice, *Mor. and Met. Phil.* ch. viii. § 31.) Butler's complaint is that men so irrational as to place it in (7) are such offenders against reason, that they would probably defy even a demonstration on behalf of religion.

THE END OF THE SECOND PART

TWO BRIEF DISSERTATIONS

I
OF PERSONAL IDENTITY

II
OF THE NATURE OF VIRTUE

ADVERTISEMENT

IN the first copy of these Papers, I had inserted the two following Dissertations into the chapters, *Of a Future Life*, and, *Of the Moral Government of God*; with which they are closely connected. But as they do not directly fall under the *title* of the foregoing Treatise, and would have kept the subject of it too long out of sight; it seemed more proper to place them by themselves.

DISSERTATION I

OF PERSONAL IDENTITY

§ 1. *There are misleading subtleties on personal identity;*

WHETHER we are to live in a future state, as it is the most important question which can possibly be asked, so it is the most intelligible one which can be expressed in language. Yet strange perplexities have been raised about the meaning of that identity or sameness of person, which is implied in the notion of our living now and hereafter, or in any two successive moments. And the solution of these difficulties hath been stranger than the difficulties themselves. For, personal identity has been explained so by some, as to render the inquiry concerning a future life of no consequence at all to us the persons who are making it. And though few men can be misled by such subtleties; yet it may be proper a little to consider them.

§ 2. *An idea, which definition can only perplex:*

Now when it is asked, wherein personal identity consists, the answer should be the same, as if it were asked, wherein consists similitude, or equality; that all attempts to define would but perplex it. Yet there is no difficulty at all in ascertaining the idea. For as, upon two triangles being compared or viewed together, there arises to the mind the idea of similitude; or upon twice two and four, the idea of equality: so likewise, upon comparing the consciousnesses of one's self, or one's own existence, in any two moments, there as immediately arises to the mind the idea of personal identity. And as the two former comparisons not only give us the ideas of similitude and equality; but also show us, that two triangles are alike, and twice two and four are equal: so the latter comparison not only gives us the idea of personal identity, but also shows us the identity of ourselves in those two moments; the present, suppose, and that immediately past; or the present, and that a month, a year, or twenty years past. Or in other words, by reflecting upon that, which is my self now, and that, which was my self twenty years ago, I discern they are not two, but one and the same self.[1]

§ 3. *Not constituted by, but presupposed in, recollection (or consciousness of the past).*

But though consciousness of what is past does thus ascertain our personal identity to ourselves, yet to say, that it makes personal identity, or is necessary to our being the same persons, is to say, that a person has not existed a single moment, nor done one action, but what he can remember; indeed none but what he reflects upon. And one should really think it self-evident, that consciousness of personal identity presupposes, and therefore cannot constitute, personal identity; any more than knowledge, in any other case, can constitute truth, which it presupposes.

This wonderful mistake may possibly have arisen from hence; that to be endued with consciousness is inseparable from the idea of a person, or intelligent being. For, this might be expressed inaccurately thus, that consciousness makes personality: and from hence it might be concluded to make personal identity.[2]

---

[1] Reflection on the past, or recollection, is for us, consciousness of the past. But brutes have memory, perhaps not recollection, without consciousness proper.

[2] This is a bold description of personality. But can a better be supplied? As to dictionaries, Johnson gives, 'The existence or individuality of any one.' Latham and Webster withdraw the first phrase. Locke says, 'Person

§§ 3, 4] OF PERSONAL IDENTITY 347

<u>But though present consciousness of what we at present do and feel is necessary to our being the persons we now are; yet present consciousness of past actions or feelings is not necessary to our being the same persons who performed those actions, or had those feelings.</u>

§ 4. *Differs from sameness in vegetables ; where all the parts may be different :*

The inquiry, what makes vegetables the same in the common acceptation of the word, does not appear to have any relation to this of personal identity: because, the word *same*, when applied to them and to person, is not only applied to different subjects, but it is also used in different senses. For when a man swears to the same tree, as having stood fifty years in the same place, he means only the same as to all the purposes of property and uses of common life, and not that the tree has been all that time the same in the strict philosophical sense of the word. For he does not know, whether any one particle of the present tree be the same with any one particle of the tree which stood in the same place fifty years ago.[1] And

belongs only to intelligent agents, capable of a law, and happiness and misery.' This definition, or account, seems to go beyond the personality of God. For a law is something extrinsic ; and capability of misery is surely here a thing utterly beyond our power to predicate. What is consciousness ? It is a developed intelligence, in act or habit; it is a doubled mental function : it presents to us an active and a passive function, or perhaps a reciprocation of activities implying dualism. Not two intelligences, but one, gifted with the power of turning back upon itself. The personality of brutes is defective ; is not this because their consciousness is defective ? Do we gain anything by adding to Butler's succinct phrase ? Consciousness is, at the least, personality in action, and is the basis and distinctive mark of all that belongs to personality.

[1] May there not, however, remain behind, and un-

if they have not one common particle of matter, they cannot be the same tree in the proper philosophic sense of the word *same:* it being evidently a contradiction in terms, to say they are, when no part of their substance, and no one of their properties is the same: no part of their substance, by the supposition: no one of their properties, because it is allowed, that the same property cannot be transferred from one substance to another. And therefore, when we say the identity or sameness of a plant consists in a continuation of the same life, communicated under the same organization, to a number of particles of matter, whether the same or not: the word *same,* when applied to life and to organization, cannot possibly be understood to signify, what it signifies in this very sentence, when applied to matter. In a loose and popular sense then, the life and the organization and the plant are justly said to be the same, notwithstanding the perpetual change of the parts. But in a strict and philosophical manner of speech, no man, no being, no mode of being, no anything, can be the same with that, with which it hath indeed nothing the same. Now sameness is used in this latter sense, when applied to persons. The identity of these, therefore, cannot subsist with diversity of substance.

§ 5. *And consciousness, if at different times, is different.*

The thing here considered, and demonstratively, as I think, determined, is proposed by Mr. Locke in these

touched by this argument, the question, What is it that constitutes life in a vegetable, and wherein and whereby is it transmitted? If we look to parts alone, how does a vegetable differ from any mineral, subject only to mechanical or chemical action? But the total absence of consciousness seems of itself to supply the immeasurable separation, which Butler's argument requires. He uses below the phrase 'same life': but this life cannot be regarded as exchangeable.

§ 5] OF PERSONAL IDENTITY 349

words, *Whether it*, i. e. the same self or person, *be the same identical substance?* And he has suggested what is a much better answer to the question, than that which he gives it in form. For he defines Person, *a thinking intelligent being*, &c., and personal identity, *the sameness of a rational being.*[a] The question then is, whether the same rational being is the same substance: which needs no answer, because Being and Substance, in this place, stand for the same idea. The ground of the doubt, whether the same person be the same substance, is said to be this; that the consciousness of our own existence, in youth and in old age, or in any two joint successive moments, is not [1] the *same individual action*,[b] i. e. not the same consciousness, but different successive consciousnesses.[2] Now it is strange that this should have occasioned such perplexities. For it is surely conceivable, that a person may have a capacity of knowing some object or other to be the same now, which it was when he contemplated it formerly: yet in this case, where, by the supposition, the object is perceived to be the same, the perception of it in any two moments cannot be one and the same perception. And thus though the successive consciousnesses, which we have of our own existence, are not the same, yet are they consciousnesses of one and the same thing or object; of the same person, self, or living agent. The person, of whose existence the consciousness is felt now, and was felt an hour or a year ago, is discerned to be, not two persons, but one and the same person; and therefore is one and the same.

[a] Locke's *Works*, vol. i. p. 146.
[b] Locke, pp. 146, 147.

---

[1] See *Anal.* I. i. 1.
[2] The argument ascribed to Locke is frivolous: as if, because I saw and loved A last year and B this year, it should be argued that the faculty or affection of love is in me not the same.

§ 6. *Locke's hasty ideas pushed by others to confusion.*

Mr. Locke's observations upon this subject appear hasty: and he seems to profess himself dissatisfied with suppositions, which he has made relating to it.[c] But some of those hasty observations have been carried to a strange length by others, whose notion, when traced and examined to the bottom, amounts, I think, to this:[d] 'That personality is not a permanent, but a transient thing: that it lives and dies, begins and ends continually: that no one can any more remain one and the same person two moments together, than two successive moments can be one and the same moment: that our substance is indeed continually changing; but whether this be so or not, is, it seems, nothing to the purpose; since it is not substance, but consciousness alone, which constitutes personality; which consciousness, being successive, cannot be the same in any two moments, nor consequently the personality constituted by it.' And from hence it must follow, that it is a fallacy upon ourselves, to charge our present selves with any thing we did, or to imagine our present selves interested in any thing which befell us yesterday; or that our present self will be interested in what will befall us to-morrow: since our present self is not, in reality, the same with the self of yesterday, but another like self or person coming in its room, and mistaken for it; to which another self will succeed to-morrow. This, I say, must follow: for if the self or person of to-day, and that of to-morrow, are not the same, but only like persons; the person of to-day is really no more interested in what will befall the person of to-morrow, than in what will befall any other person. It may be thought, perhaps, that this is not a just representation of the opinion we are speaking of: because those who maintain it allow, that a person is the same as far back

[c] Locke, p. 152.
[d] See an *Answer to Dr. Clarke's Third Defence of his Letter to Mr. Dodwell*, 2nd edit. pp. 44, 56, &c.

as his remembrance reaches. And indeed they do use the *words, identity* and *same* person. Nor will language permit these words to be laid aside; since if they were, there must be I know not what ridiculous periphrasis substituted in the room of them. But they cannot, consistently with themselves, mean, that the person is really the same. For it is self-evident, that the personality cannot be really the same, if, as they expressly assert, that in which it consists is not the same. And as, consistently with themselves, they cannot, so, I think it appears, they do not, mean, that the person is *really* the same, but only that he is so in a fictitious sense: in such a sense only as they assert, for this they do assert, that any number of persons whatever may be the same person. The bare unfolding this notion, and laying it thus naked and open, seems the best confutation of it. However, since great stress is said to be put upon it, I add the following things.

§ 7. *It is imagination against conviction;*

First, This notion is absolutely contradictory to that certain conviction, which necessarily and every moment rises within us, when we turn our thoughts upon ourselves, when we reflect upon what is past, and look forward upon what is to come. All imagination of a daily change of that living agent which each man calls himself, for another, or of any such change throughout our whole present life, is entirely borne down by our natural sense of things. Nor is it possible for a person in his wits to alter his conduct, with regard to his health or affairs, from a suspicion, that, though he should live to-morrow, he should not, however, be the same person he is to-day. And yet, if it be reasonable to act, with respect to a future life, upon this notion, that personality is transient; it is reasonable to act upon it, with respect to the present.

§ 8. *As all perceive in temporal concerns.*

Here then is a notion equally applicable to religion and to our temporal concerns; and every one sees and feels the inexpressible absurdity of it in the latter case. If, therefore, any can take up with it in the former, this cannot proceed from the reason of the thing, but must be owing to an inward unfairness, and secret corruption of heart.

§ 9. *The experiences of a being supply a bond independent of memory.*

Secondly, It is not an idea, or abstract notion, or quality, but a being only, which is capable of life and action, of happiness and misery. Now all beings confessedly continue the same, during the whole time of their existence. Consider then a living being now existing, and which has existed for any time alive: this living being must have done and suffered and enjoyed, what it has done and suffered and enjoyed formerly, (this living being, I say, and not another,) as really as it does and suffers and enjoys, what it does and suffers and enjoys this instant. All these successive actions, enjoyments, and sufferings, are actions, enjoyments, and sufferings, of the same living being. And they are so, prior to all consideration of its remembering or forgetting: since remembering or forgetting can make no alteration in the truth of past matter of fact. And suppose this being endued with limited powers of knowledge and memory, there is no more difficulty in conceiving it to have a power of knowing itself to be the same living being which it was some time ago, of remembering some of its actions, sufferings, and enjoyments, and forgetting others, than in conceiving it to know or remember or forget any thing else.

§ 10. *Whether the self be property or substance, consciousness declares its identity;*

Thirdly, Every person is conscious, that he is now the same person or self he was as far back as his remembrance reaches: since when any one reflects upon a past action of his own, he is just as certain of the person who did that action, namely, himself, the person who now reflects upon it, as he is certain that the action was at all done. Nay, very often a person's assurance of an action having been done, of which he is absolutely assured, arises wholly from the consciousness that he himself did it. And this he, person, or self, must either be a substance, or the property of some substance. If he, if person, be a substance; then consciousness that he is the same person is consciousness that he is the same substance. If the person, or he, be the property of a substance, still consciousness that he is the same property is as certain a proof that his substance remains the same, as consciousness that he remains the same substance would be: since the same property cannot be transferred from one substance to another.

§ 11. *And is deceivable in all, if in this.*

But though we are thus certain, that we are the same agents, living beings, or substances, now, which we were as far back as our remembrance reaches; yet it is asked, whether we may not possibly be deceived in it? And this question may be asked at the end of any demonstration whatever: because it is a question concerning the truth of perception by memory. And he who can doubt, whether perception by memory can in this case be depended upon, may doubt also, whether perception by deduction and reasoning, which also include memory, or indeed whether intuitive perception can. Here then we can go no further. For it is ridiculous to attempt to prove the truth of those perceptions, whose truth we can no otherwise prove, than by other perceptions of exactly the same kind with them, and which there is just the same ground to suspect; or to attempt to prove the truth of our faculties, which can no otherwise be proved, than by the use or means of those very suspected faculties themselves.

DISSERTATION II

OF THE NATURE OF VIRTUE

§ 1. *We have powers of reflection and approval, and by this become capable of moral government.*[1]

THAT which renders beings capable of moral government, is their having a moral nature, and moral faculties of perception and of action. Brute creatures are impressed and actuated by various instincts and propensions; so also are we. But additional to this,

[1] I extract from Dr. Angus (*in loc.*) portions of his concise account of the tacit references of Butler in this Dissertation to the doctrines of immediately preceding writers:

'Within a hundred years, Hobbes had published his *Theory of Human Nature*, in which he taught that personal gratification was the sole end of every act, that every exercise of passion or faculty was equally authoritative, and that man has no moral faculties of perception or action. . . . The first and last part of Hobbes's theory Butler here refutes; the second he notices in his Sermons. . . .

'By denying that prudence is the whole of virtue, he meets the abuse which Hobbes committed, and which some modern writers have revived. Benevolence he reckons a most important virtue, and yet denies, against Leibnitz, that all virtue is resolvable into it. In his doctrine of a moral sense, he agrees substantially with Hutcheson, his contemporary, and in the importance he attaches to the distinction between mere acts and the dispositions or principles from which they spring, he condemns Hobbes and sanctions Malebranche.'

we have a capacity of reflecting upon actions and
characters, and making them an object to our thought:
and on doing this, we naturally and unavoidably
approve some actions, under the peculiar view of
their being virtuous and of good desert; and disapprove others, as vicious and of ill desert. <u>That we
have this moral approving and disapproving [a] faculty,
is certain from our experiencing it in ourselves, and
recognizing it in each other.</u>

§ 2. *Shown by our common language, judgments, behaviour; and by moral systems.*

It appears from our exercising it unavoidably, in
the approbation and disapprobation even of feigned
characters: from the words, *right* and *wrong, odious*
and *amiable, base* and *worthy,* with many others of like
signification in all languages, applied to actions and
characters:[1] from the many written systems of morals
which suppose it; since it cannot be imagined, that
all these authors, throughout all these treatises, had
absolutely no meaning at all to their words, or a meaning merely chimerical: from our natural sense of

---

[a] This way of speaking is taken from Epictetus,* and is made
use of as seeming the most full, and least
Phrase of Epictetus, liable to cavil. And the moral faculty may
why employed. be understood to have these two epithets,
δοκιμαστική and ἀποδοκιμαστική, upon a double account:
because, upon a survey of actions, whether before or after they
are done, it determines them to be good or evil; and also because
it determines itself to be the guide of action and of life, in con-
tradistinction from all other faculties, or natural principles of
action: in the very same manner as speculative reason *directly*
and naturally judges of speculative truth and falsehood; and
at the same time is attended with a consciousness upon *reflection,*
that the natural right to judge of them belongs to it.

* Arr. Epict. lib. i. cap. 1.

---

[1] We may add the ἔπαινος and ψόγος of Aristotle;
but it is characteristic of Butler not to rest upon a basis
merely subjective, and to look rather for tests founded
in the nature of the thing itself.

§§ 2, 3]   OF THE NATURE OF VIRTUE   357

gratitude, which implies a distinction between merely being the instrument of good, and intending it: from the like distinction, every one makes, between injury and mere harm, which, Hobbes says, is peculiar to mankind;[1] and between injury and just punishment, a distinction plainly natural, prior to the consideration of human laws.[2] It is manifest great part of common language, and of common behaviour over the world, is formed upon supposition of such a moral faculty;[3] whether called conscience, moral reason, moral sense, or divine reason; whether considered as a sentiment of the understanding, or as a perception of the heart;[4] or, which seems the truth, as including both.

§ 3. *It has an acknowledged standard; and conclusive tests.*

Nor is it at all doubtful in the general, what course of action this faculty, or practical discerning power within us, approves, and what it disapproves. For, as much as it has been disputed wherein virtue consists, or whatever ground for doubt there may be about particulars; yet, in general, there is in reality an universally acknowledged standard of it. It is that, which all ages and all countries have made profession of in public: it is that, which every man

---

[1] Evidently Butler's intention is rather to record as against Hobbes generally this valuable admission, than to imply that the opposite opinion was one anywhere held.

[2] On the distinction see Serm. viii. 6, 8.

[3] Comp. Serm. xii. 6.

[4] Is this not an exercise of the faculty by which, as in a court of first instance, we discern good and evil. When the perception thus acquired has passed under the view, and received the judicial sanction, of the conscience, it has passed under the view of the court of appeal.

This sentence is one in which Butler allows himself more elasticity in the use of terms than is quite usual with him.

358 OF THE NATURE OF VIRTUE [Diss. II.

you meet puts on the show of : it is that, which the primary and fundamental laws of all civil constitutions over the face of the earth make it their business and endeavour to enforce the practice of upon mankind : namely, justice, veracity, and regard to common good. It being manifest then, in general, that we have such a faculty or discernment as this, it may be of use to remark some things more distinctly concerning it.

§ 4. *Has action for its object, apart from* (a) *mere truth,* (b) *consequences.*

First, It ought to be observed, that the object of this faculty is actions,[b] comprehending under that name active or practical principles: those principles from which men would act, if occasions and circumstances gave them power; and which, when fixed and habitual in any person, we call his character. It does not appear, that brutes have the least reflex sense of actions, as distinguished from events: or that will and design, which constitute the very nature of actions as such, are at all an object to their perception. But to ours they are: and they are the object, and the only one, of the approving and disapproving faculty. Acting, conduct, behaviour, abstracted from all regard to what is, in fact and event, the consequence of it, is itself the natural object of the moral discernment; as speculative truth and falsehood is of speculative reason. Intention of such and such consequences, indeed, is always included; for it is part of the action itself: but though the intended good or bad consequences do not follow, we have exactly the same sense of the action as if they did. In like manner we think well or ill of characters, abstracted from all consideration of the good or the evil, which persons of such characters have it actually in their power to do. We never, in the moral way, applaud or blame either

---

[b] Οὐδὲ ἡ ἀρετὴ καὶ κακία.... ἐν πείσει, ἀλλὰ ἐνεργείᾳ. M. Anton. lib. ix. 16. Virtutis laus omnis in actione consistit. Cic. *Off.* lib. i. cap. 6.

ourselves or others, for what we enjoy or what we suffer, or for having impressions made upon us which we consider as altogether out of our power: but only for what we do, or would have done had it been in our power; or for what we leave undone which we might have done, or would have left undone though we could have done it.

§ 5. *By nature, we link vice with misery for ill desert.*

Secondly, Our sense or discernment of actions as morally good or evil, implies in it a sense or discernment of them as of good or ill desert. It may be difficult to explain this perception, so as to answer all the questions which may be asked concerning it: but every one speaks of such and such actions as deserving punishment; and it is not, I suppose, pretended that they have absolutely no meaning at all to the expression. Now the meaning plainly is not, that we conceive it for the good of society, that the doer of such actions should be made to suffer. For if unhappily it were resolved, that a man, who, by some innocent action, was infected with the plague, should be left to perish, lest, by other people's coming near him, the infection should spread; no one would say he deserved this treatment. Innocence and ill desert are inconsistent ideas. Ill desert always supposes guilt: and if one be no part of the other, yet they are evidently and naturally connected in our mind. The sight of a man in misery raises our compassion towards him; and, if this misery be inflicted on him by another, our indignation against the author of it. But when we are informed, that the sufferer is a villain, and is punished only for his treachery or cruelty; our compassion exceedingly lessens, and in many instances our indignation wholly subsides. Now what produces this effect is the conception of that in the sufferer, which we call ill-desert. Upon considering then, or viewing together, our notion of vice and that of misery, there results a third, that of ill-desert. And thus there is in human creatures an association of the two ideas, natural and moral evil, wickedness and punishment. If this association were merely artificial or accidental, it were nothing: but being most unquestionably natural, it greatly concerns us to attend to it, instead of endeavouring to explain it away.

§ 6. *Desert is higher or lower according to circumstances.*

It may be observed farther, concerning our perception of good and of ill desert, that the former is very weak with respect to common instances of virtue. One reason of which may be, that it does not appear to a spectator, how far such instances of virtue proceed from a virtuous principle, or in what degree this principle is prevalent: since a very weak regard to virtue may be sufficient to make men act well in many common instances. And on the other hand, our perception of ill desert in vicious actions lessens, in proportion to the temptations men are thought to have had to such vices. For, vice in human creatures consisting chiefly in the absence or want of the virtuous principle; though a man be overcome, suppose, by tortures, it does not from thence appear to what degree the virtuous principle was wanting. All that appears is, that he had it not in such a degree, as to prevail over the temptation: but possibly he had it in a degree, which would have rendered him proof against common temptations.

§ 7. *Judgment on acts must measure them by the agent.*[1]

Thirdly, Our perception of vice and ill desert arises from, and is the result of, a comparison of actions with the nature and capacities of the agent. For the mere neglect of doing what we ought to do would, in many

[1] Comp. Serm. ii. 15, iii. 13.

cases, be determined by all men to be in the highest degree vicious. And this determination must arise from such comparison, and be the result of it; because such neglect would not be vicious in creatures of other natures and capacities, as brutes. And it is the same also with respect to positive vices, or such as consist in doing what we ought not. For, every one has a different sense of harm done by an idiot, madman, or child, and by one of mature and common understanding; though the action of both, including the intention, which is part of the action, be the same: as it may be, since idiots and madmen, as well as children, are capable not only of doing mischief, but also of intending it. Now this difference must arise from somewhat discerned in the nature or capacities of one, which renders the action vicious; and the want of which, in the other, renders the same action innocent or less vicious: and this plainly supposes a comparison, whether reflected upon or not, between the action and capacities of the agent, previous to our determining an action to be vicious. And hence arises a proper application of the epithets, *incongruous, unsuitable, disproportionate, unfit,* to actions which our moral faculty determines to be vicious.

§ 8. *Prudence, or a due regard to our own welfare, is a part of virtue.*

Fourthly, It deserves to be considered, whether men are more at liberty, in point of morals, to make themselves miserable without reason, than to make other people so: or dissolutely to neglect their own greater good, for the sake of a present lesser gratification, than they are to neglect the good of others, whom nature has committed to their care. It should seem, that a due concern about our own interest or happiness, and a reasonable endeavour to secure and promote it, which is, I think, very much the meaning of the word *prudence,* in our language; it should seem, that this is virtue, and the contrary behaviour faulty and blamable: since, in the calmest way of reflection, we approve of the first, and condemn the other conduct, both in ourselves and others.[1] This approbation and disapprobation are altogether different from mere desire of our own, or of their happiness, and from sorrow upon missing it. For the object or occasion of this last kind of perception is satisfaction or uneasiness: whereas the object of the first is active behaviour. In one case, what our thoughts fix upon is our condition: in the other, our conduct.

§ 9. *Why not fortified so strongly, as other parts, with disapproval of the contrary.*

It is true indeed, that nature has not given us so sensible a disapprobation of imprudence and folly, either in *ourselves* or *others*, as of falsehood, injustice, and cruelty: I suppose, because that constant habitual sense of private interest and good, which we always carry about with us, renders such sensible disapprobation less necessary, less wanting, to keep us from imprudently neglecting our own happiness, and

---

[1] I suppose it indisputable that the study and prosecution of good with a practical aim is virtuous. Let us suppose then that it is done for the benefit of x. If x mean another person than ourselves, this is benevolence, and benevolence is a virtue. But let x mean a man's own self. The act is still the same, done to one person instead of another; it continues to be the study and prosecution of good with a practical aim: how can the act have changed its own essential nature, because it is now for the benefit, not of B, but of A? So that Butler's contention appears perfectly just. It undergoes perhaps some disadvantage from the fact that prudence, as the wise choice of means for an end, extends to all common matters lying beyond the territory of vice and virtue.

This may well be considered the classical passage of Butler on prudence. Compare Aristotle (*Eth. Nic.* VI. v. 4) on φρόνησις:

Λείπεται ἄρα αὐτὴν εἶναι ἕξιν ἀληθῆ μετὰ λόγου πρακτικὴν περὶ τὰ ἀνθρώπῳ ἀγαθὰ καὶ κακά.

foolishly injuring ourselves, than it is necessary and wanting to keep us from injuring others, to whose good we cannot have so strong and constant a regard: and also because imprudence and folly, appearing to bring its own punishment more immediately and constantly than injurious behaviour, it less needs the additional punishment, which would be inflicted upon it by others, had they the same sensible indignation against it, as against injustice, and fraud, and cruelty. Besides, unhappiness being in itself the natural object of compassion; the unhappiness which people bring upon themselves, though it be wilfully, excites in us some pity for them: and this of course lessens our displeasure against them.

§ 10. *Still disapproval is strong in grave cases.*

But still it is matter of experience, that we are formed so as to reflect very severely upon the greater instances of imprudent neglects and foolish rashness, both in ourselves and others. In instances of this kind, men often say of themselves with remorse, and of others with some indignation, that they deserved to suffer such calamities, because they brought them upon themselves, and would not take warning. Particularly when persons come to poverty and distress by a long course of extravagance, and after frequent admonitions, though without falsehood or injustice; we plainly do not regard such people as alike objects of compassion with those, who are brought into the same condition by unavoidable accidents. From these things it appears, that prudence is a species of virtue, and folly of vice: meaning by *folly*, somewhat quite different from mere incapacity; a thoughtless want of that regard and attention to our own happiness, which we had capacity for. And this the word properly includes; and, as it seems, in its usual acceptation; for we scarce apply it to brute creatures.

§ 11. *We may dispense with vice and virtue as predicates.*

However, if any person be disposed to dispute the matter, I shall very willingly give him up the words virtue and vice, as not applicable to prudence and folly; but must beg leave to insist, that the faculty within us, which is the judge of actions, approves of prudent actions, and disapproves imprudent ones; I say prudent and imprudent *actions* as such, and considered distinctly from the happiness or misery which they occasion. And, by the way, this observation may help to determine what justness there is in that objection against religion, that it teaches us to be interested and selfish.

§ 12. *Benevolence, and its opposite, are only parts of virtue and vice;*

Fifthly, Without inquiring how far, and in what sense, virtue is resolvable into benevolence, and vice into the want of it; it may be proper to observe, that benevolence, and the want of it, singly considered, are in no sort the whole of virtue and vice.[1] For if this were the case, in the review of one's own character, or that of others, our moral understanding and moral sense would be indifferent to everything, but the degrees in which benevolence prevailed, and the degrees in which it was wanting. That is, we should neither approve of benevolence to some persons rather than to others, nor disapprove injustice and falsehood upon any other account, than merely as an overbalance of happiness was foreseen likely to be produced by the first, and of misery by the second. But now, on the contrary, suppose two men competitors for any thing whatever, which would be of equal advantage to each of them: though nothing indeed would be more im-

---

[1] On benevolence see *Anal.* I. iii. 3. Also compare the statement from a different point of view, Serm. xii. 18, 19, 22.

pertinent, than for a stranger to busy himself to get one of them preferred to the other; yet such endeavour would be virtue, in behalf of a friend or benefactor, abstracted from all consideration of distant consequences: as that examples of gratitude, and the cultivation of friendship, would be of general good to the world. Again, suppose one man should, by fraud or violence, take from another the fruit of his labour, with intent to give it to a third, who he thought would have as much pleasure from it as would balance the pleasure which the first possessor would have had in the enjoyment, and his vexation in the loss of it; suppose also that no bad consequences would follow: yet such an action would surely be vicious. Nay farther, were treachery, violence and injustice, no otherwise vicious, than as foreseen likely to produce an overbalance of misery to society; then, if in any case a man could procure to himself as great advantage by an act of injustice, as the whole foreseen inconvenience, likely to be brought upon others by it, would amount to; such a piece of injustice would not be faulty or vicious at all: because it would be no more than, in any other case, for a man to prefer his own satisfaction to another's in equal degrees.

§ 13. *Which include matter other than the overbalance of enjoyment or suffering.*

The fact then appears to be, that we are constituted so as to condemn falsehood, unprovoked violence, injustice, and to approve of benevolence to some preferably to others, abstracted from all consideration, which conduct is likeliest to produce an overbalance of happiness or misery. And therefore, were the Author of nature to propose nothing to himself as an end but the production of happiness, were his moral character merely that of benevolence; yet ours is not so. Upon that supposition indeed the only reason of his giving us the above-mentioned approbation of benevolence to some persons rather than others, and disapprobation of falsehood, unprovoked violence, and injustice, must be, that he foresaw this constitution of our nature would produce more happiness, than forming us with a temper of mere general benevolence. But still, since this is our constitution; falsehood, violence, injustice, must be vice in us, and benevolence to some, preferably to others, virtue; abstracted from all consideration of the overbalance of evil or good, which they may appear likely to produce.

§ 14. *Moral government makes awards by a moral rule.*

Now if human creatures are endued with such a moral nature as we have been explaining, or with a moral faculty, the natural object of which is actions; moral government must consist in rendering them happy and unhappy, in rewarding and punishing them, as they follow, neglect, or depart from, the moral rule of action interwoven in their nature, or suggested and enforced by this moral faculty; [c] in rewarding and punishing them upon account of their so doing.

§ 15. *Some authors are open to misapprehension on benevolence.*

I am not sensible that I have, in this fifth observation, contradicted what any author designed to assert. But some of great and distinguished merit have, I think, expressed themselves in a manner, which may occasion some danger, to careless readers, of imagining the whole of virtue to consist in singly aiming, according to the best of their judgment, at promoting the happiness of mankind in the present state; [1] and the whole of vice, in doing what they foresee, or might foresee, is likely to produce an overbalance of unhappiness in it: than which mistakes, none can be conceived

[c] Page 121. [So stands the reference in the edition of 1844. The reference seems really to be to I. iii. 2, 3.—ED.]

---

[1] Is the allusion to Shaftesbury and Hutcheson? See Leslie Stephen, *English Thought*, ix. 60.

more terrible. For it is certain, that some of the most shocking instances of injustice, adultery, murder, perjury, and even of persecution, may, in many supposable cases, not have the appearance of being likely to produce an overbalance of misery in the present state: perhaps sometimes may have the contrary appearance. For this reflection might easily be carried on, but I forbear.

§ 16. *We are to promote happiness, not* simpliciter, *but within bounds, and according to likelihoods.*

The happiness of the world is the concern of him, who is the Lord and the Proprietor of it: nor do we know what we are about, when we endeavour to promote the good of mankind in any ways, but those which he has directed; that is indeed in all ways not contrary to veracity and justice. I speak thus upon supposition of persons really endeavouring, in some sort, to do good without regard to these. But the truth seems to be, that such supposed endeavours proceed, almost always, from ambition, the spirit of party, or some indirect principle, concealed perhaps in great measure from persons themselves. And though it is our business and our duty to endeavour, within the bounds of veracity and justice, to contribute to the ease, convenience, and even cheerfulness and diversion of our fellow-creatures: yet, from our short views, it is greatly uncertain, whether this endeavour will, in particular instances, produce an overbalance of happiness upon the whole; since so many and distant things must come into the account. And that which makes it our duty is, that there is some appearance that it will, and no positive appearance sufficient to balance this, on the contrary side; and also, that such benevolent endeavour is a cultivation of that most excellent of all virtuous principles, the active principle of benevolence.

§ 17. *Veracity is part of the rule of life, but not easy in application.*

However, though veracity, as well as justice, is to be our rule of life; it must be added, otherwise a snare will be laid in the way of some plain men, that the use of common forms of speech, generally understood, cannot be falsehood; and, in general, that there can be no designed falsehood without designing to deceive. It must likewise be observed, that in numberless cases, a man may be under the strictest obligations to what he foresees will deceive, without his intending it. For it is impossible not to foresee, that the words and actions of men, in different ranks and employments, and of different educations, will perpetually be mistaken by each other: and it cannot but be so, whilst they will judge with the utmost carelessness, as they daily do, of what they are not, perhaps, enough informed to be competent judges of, even though they considered it with great attention.

CORRESPONDENCE

BETWEEN

DR. BUTLER AND DR. CLARKE

[The Letters are numbered consecutively, and the references in the Index are to Corr. I., Corr. II., and so forth.]

I

THE FIRST LETTER

(A)

Butler, apparently admitting place to be a condition or incident of divine existence, conceives that Clarke has offered, as proving the divine omnipresence, this: that if absent somewhere, He might be absent everywhere; which contradicts His self-existence being non-existence. No, says Butler: partial absence might be possible, yet universal impossible.

Further, to prove the unity of the self-existent, Clarke says, were there two, each might be supposed existing alone, so that the other might be conceived not to exist. Butler denies this consequence: whether we take alone as independent, or as solitary.

REVEREND SIR,

I SUPPOSE you will wonder at the present trouble from one who is a perfect stranger to you, though you are not so to him; but I hope the occasion will excuse my boldness. I have made it, sir, my business, ever since I thought myself capable of such sort of reasoning, to prove to myself the being and attributes of God. And being sensible that it is a matter of the last consequence, I endeavoured after a demonstrative proof; not only more fully to satisfy my own mind, but also in order to defend the great truths of natural religion, and those of the Christian revelation which follow from them, against all opposers; but must own with concern, that hitherto I have been unsuccessful; and though I have got very probable arguments, yet I can go but a very little way with demonstration in the proof of those things. When first your book on those subjects (which by all, whom I have discoursed with, is so justly esteemed) was recommended to me, I was in great hopes of having all my inquiries answered. But since in some places, either through my not understanding your meaning, or what else I know not, even that has failed me, I almost despair of ever arriving to such a satisfaction as I aim at, unless by the method I now use. You cannot but know, sir, that of two different expressions of the same thing, though equally clear to some persons, yet to others one of them is sometimes very obscure, though the other be perfectly intelligible. Perhaps this may be my case here; and could I see those of your arguments, of which I doubt, differently proposed, possibly I might yield a ready assent to them. This, sir, I cannot but think a sufficient excuse for the present trouble; it being such an one as I hope may prevail for an answer, with one who seems to aim at nothing more than that good work of instructing others.

In your Demonstration of the Being and Attributes of God, Prop. VI.[a] [edit. 2nd, pp. 69, 70] you propose to prove the infinity of omnipresence of the self-existent Being. The former part of the proof seems highly probable; but the latter part, which seems to aim at demonstration, is not to me convincing. The latter part of the paragraph is, if I mistake not, an entire argument of itself, which runs thus: 'To suppose a finite being to be self-existent, is to say that it is a contradiction for that being not to exist, the absence of which may yet be conceived without a contradiction; which is the greatest absurdity in the world.' The sense of these words [' the absence of which '] seems plainly to be determined by the following sentence, to mean its absence from any

[a] P. 45, edit. 4; p. 41, edit. 6; p. 43, edit. 7; p. 44, edit. 8.

particular place. Which sentence is to prove it to be an absurdity; and is this: 'For if a being can, without a contradiction, be absent from one place, it may, without a contradiction, be absent from another place, and from all places.' Now supposing this to be a consequence, all that it proves is, that if a being can, without a contradiction, be absent from one place at one time, it may, without a contradiction, be absent from another place, and so from all places, at different times; (for I cannot see, that if a being can be absent from one place at one time, therefore it may, without a contradiction, be absent from all places at the same time, i.e. may cease to exist.) Now, if it proves no more than this, I cannot see that it reduces the supposition to any absurdity. Suppose I could demonstrate, that any particular man should live a thousand years; this man might, without a contradiction, be absent from one and from all places at different times; but it would not from thence follow, that he might be absent from all places at the same time, i.e. that he might cease to exist. No; this would be a contradiction, because I am supposed to have demonstrated that he should live a thousand years. It would be exactly the same, if, instead of a thousand years, I should say, for ever; and the proof seems the same, whether it be applied to a self-existent or a dependent being.

What else I have to offer is in relation to your proof, that the self-existent being must of necessity be but one. Which proof is as follows, in Prop. VII.[b] [edit. 2nd, p. 74]. 'To suppose two or more different natures existing of themselves, necessarily, and independent from each other, implies this plain contradiction; that, each of them being independent from the other, they may either of them be supposed to exist alone; so that it will be no contradiction to imagine the other not to exist, and consequently neither of them will be necessarily existing.' The supposition indeed implies, that since each of these beings is independent from the other, they may either of them exist alone, i.e. without any relation to, or dependence on, the other: but where is the third idea, to connect this proposition and the following one, viz. 'so that it will be no contradiction to imagine the other not to exist'? Were this a consequence of the former pro-

[b] P. 48, edit. 4; p. 44, edit. 6; p. 46, edit. 7; p. 47, edit. 8.

position, I allow it would be demonstration, by the first corollary of Prop. III.[c] [2nd edit. p. 26]; but since these two propositions, ['they may either of them be supposed to exist alóne,'] and, ['so that it will be no contradiction to imagine the other not to exist,'] are very widely different; since likewise it is no immediate consequence, that because either may be supposed to exist independent from the other, therefore the other may be supposed not to exist at all; how is what was proposed, proved? That the propositions are different, I think is plain; and whether there be an immediate connection, every body that reads your book must judge for themselves. I must say, for my own part, the absurdity does not appear at first sight, any more than the absurdity of saying that the angles below the base in an isosceles triangle are unequal; which though it is absolutely false, yet I suppose no one will lay down the contrary for an axiom; because, though it is true, yet there is need of a proof to make it appear so.

Perhaps it may be answered, that I have not rightly explained the words, 'to exist alone;' and that they do not mean only, to exist independent from the other; but that 'existing alone' means that nothing exists with it. Whether this or the other was meant I cannot determine: but, whichever it was, what I have said will hold. For if this last be the sense of those words, ['they either of them may be supposed to exist alone;'] it indeed implies that it will be no contradiction to suppose the other not to exist: but then I ask, how come these two propositions to be connected; that to suppose two different natures existing, of themselves, necessarily and independent from each other, implies that each of them may be supposed to exist alone in this sense? Which is exactly the same as I said before, only applied to different sentences. So that if 'existing alone' be understood as I first took it, I allow it is implied in the supposition; but cannot see that the consequence is, that it will be no contradiction to suppose the other not to exist. But if the words, 'existing alone,' are meant in the latter sense, I grant, that if either of them may be supposed thus to exist alone, it will be no contradiction to suppose the other not to exist: but then I cannot see

[c] Pp. 16, 17, edit. 4, 6, 7, and 8.

that to suppose two different natures existing, of themselves, necessarily and independent from each other, implies that either of them may be supposed to exist alone in this sense of the words; but only, that either of them may be supposed to exist without having any relation to the other, and that there will be no need of the existence of the one in order to the existence of the other. But though upon this account, were there no other principle of its existence, it might cease to exist; yet on the account of the necessity of its own nature, which is quite distinct from the other, it is an absolute absurdity to suppose it not to exist.

Thus, sir, I have proposed my doubts, with the reasons of them. In which if I have wrested your words to another sense than you designed them, or in any respect argued unfairly, I assure you it was without design. So I hope you will impute it to mistake. And, if it will not be too great a trouble, let me once more beg the favour of a line from you, by which you will lay me under a particular obligation to be, what, with the rest of the world, I now am,

Reverend Sir,

Your most obliged servant, &c.

Nov. 4, 1713.

II

THE ANSWER

(B)

1. *Clarke contends in reply that if necessary self-existing presence can be dispensed with anywhere, it can be dispensed with everywhere. If so, his argument holds.*
2. *Also independent self-existence may imply solitary self-existence: and here, too, he holds his ground.*

Sir,

Did men who publish controversial papers accustom themselves to write with that candour and ingenuity, with which you propose your difficulties, I am persuaded almost all disputes might be very amicably terminated, either by men's coming at last to agree in opinion, or at least finding reason to suffer each other friendly to differ.

Your two objections are very ingenious, and urged with great strength and acuteness. Yet I am not without hopes of being able to give you satisfaction in both of them. To your first, therefore, I answer: Whatever may, without a contradiction, be absent from any one place, at any one time, may also, without a contradiction, be absent from all places at all times. For, whatever is absolutely necessary at all, is absolutely necessary in every part of space, and in every point of duration. Whatever can at any time be conceived possible to be absent from any one part of space, may for the same reason [viz. the implying no contradiction in the nature of things] be conceived possible to be absent from every other part of space at the same time; either by ceasing to be, or by supposing it never to have begun to be. Your instance about demonstrating a man to live a thousand years, is what, I think, led you into the mistake; and is a good instance to lead you out of it again. You may suppose a man shall live a thousand years, or God may reveal and promise he shall live a thousand years; and upon that supposition, it shall not be possible for the man to be absent from all places in any part of that time. Very true: but why shall it not be possible? only because it is contrary to the supposition, or to the promise of God; but not contrary to the absolute nature of things; which would be the case, if the man existed necessarily, as every part of space does. In supposing you could demonstrate, a man should live a thousand years, or one year; you make an impossible and contradictory supposition. For though you may know certainly (by revelation suppose) that he will live so long; yet this is only the certainty of a thing true in fact, not in itself necessary: and demonstration is applicable to nothing but what is necessary in itself, necessary in all places and at all times equally.

To your second difficulty, I answer: What exists necessarily, not only must so exist alone, as to be independent of any thing else; but (being self-sufficient) may also so exist alone, as that every thing else may possibly (or without any contradiction in the nature of things) be supposed not to exist at all: and consequently, (since that which may possibly be supposed not to exist at all, is not necessarily existent,) no other thing can be necessarily existent. Whatever is necessarily existing, there is need of its existence in order to the supposal of the existence of any other thing; so that nothing can possibly be supposed to exist, without presupposing and including antecedently the existence of that which is necessary. For instance; the supposal of the existence of any thing whatever includes necessarily a presupposition of the existence of space and time; and if any thing could exist without space or time, it would follow that space and time were not necessarily existing. Therefore, the supposing any thing possibly to exist alone, so as not necessarily to include the presupposal of some other thing, proves demonstrably that that other thing is not necessarily existing; because, whatever has necessity of existence cannot possibly, in any conception whatsoever, be supposed away. There cannot possibly be any notion of the existence of any thing, there cannot possibly be any notion of existence at all, but what shall necessarily preinclude the notion of that which has necessary existence. And consequently the two propositions, which you judged independent, are really necessarily connected. These sorts of things are indeed very difficult to express, and not easy to be conceived but by very attentive minds: but to such as can and will attend, nothing, I think, is more demonstrably convictive.

If any thing still sticks with you in this or any other part of my books, I shall be very willing to be informed of it; who am,

Sir,
Your assured friend and servant,
S. C.

Nov. 10, 1713.

PS. Many readers, I observe, have misunderstood my second general proposition; as if the words ['some one unchangeable and independent being,'] meant [one only—being;] whereas the true meaning, and all that the argument there requires, is, [some one at least.] That there can be but one, is the thing proved afterwards in the seventh proposition.

III

THE SECOND LETTER

(C)

Butler argues in reply that ubiquity and self-existence are separable; and the necessity of ubiquity has to be proved.

On the second head, demands the title for asserting that the necessary being is required in order to the existence of any other being.

REVEREND SIR,

I HAVE often thought that the chief occasions of men's differing so much in their opinions, were, either their not understanding each other; or else that, instead of ingenuously searching after truth, they have made it their business to find out arguments for the proof of what they have once asserted. However, it is certain there may be other reasons for persons not agreeing in their opinions: and where it is so, I cannot but think with you, that they will find reason to suffer each other to differ friendly; every man having a way of thinking, in some respects, peculiarly his own.

I am sorry I must tell you, your answers to my objections are not satisfactory. The reasons why I think them not so are as follow:

You say, 'Whatever is absolutely necessary at all is absolutely necessary in every part of space, and in every point of duration.' Were this evident, it would certainly prove what you bring it for; viz. that 'Whatever may, without a contradiction, be absent from one place at one time, may also be absent from all places at all times.' But I do not conceive, that the idea of ubiquity is contained in the idea of self-existence, or directly follows from it; any otherwise than as, whatever exists must exist somewhere. You add, 'Whatever can at any time be conceived possible to be absent from any one part of space, may for the same reason [viz. the implying no contradiction in the nature of things] be conceived possible to be absent from every other part of space, at the same time.' Now I cannot see, that I can make

these two suppositions for the same reason, or upon the
same account. The reason why I conceive this being
may be absent from one place, is because it doth not
contradict the former proof, [drawn from the nature of
things,] in which I proved only that it must necessarily
exist. But the other supposition, viz. that I can conceive
it possible to be absent from every part of space at one
and at the same time, directly contradicts the proof that
it must exist somewhere; and so is an express contradiction. Unless it be said, that as, when we have proved
the three angles of a triangle equal to two right ones,
that relation of the equality of its angles to two right
ones will be wherever a triangle exists; so, when we
have proved the necessary existence of a being, this
being must exist everywhere. But there is a great difference between these two things: the one being the proof
of a certain relation, upon supposition of such a being's
existence with such particular properties; and consequently, wherever this being and these properties exist,
this relation must exist too: but from the proof of the
necessary existence of a being, it is no evident consequence
that it exists everywhere. My using the word *demonstration*, instead of *proof which leaves no room for doubt*,
was through negligence, for I never heard of strict demonstration of matter of fact.

In your answer to my second difficulty, you say, 'Whatsoever is necessarily existing, there is need of its existence,
in order to the supposal of the existence of any other
thing.' All the consequences you draw from this proposition, I see proved demonstrably; and consequently
that the two propositions I thought independent are
closely connected. But how, or upon what account, is
there need of the existence of whatever is necessarily
existing, in order to the existence of any other thing?
Is it as there is need of space and duration, in order to
the existence of any thing; or is it needful only as the
cause of the existence of all other things? If the former
be said, as your instance seems to intimate: I answer;
space and duration are very abstruse in their natures,
and, I think, cannot properly be called things, but are
considered rather as affections which belong, and in the
order of our thoughts are antecedently necessary, to the
existence of all things. And I can no more conceive

how a necessarily existent being can, on the same account, or in the same manner as space and duration are, be needful in order to the existence of any other being, than I can conceive extension attributed to a thought; that idea no more belonging to a thing existing, than extension belongs to thought. But if the latter be said, that there is need of the existence of whatever is a necessary being, in order to the existence of any other thing; only as this necessary being must be the cause of the existence of all other things: I think this is plainly begging the question; for it supposes that there is no other being exists, but what is casual, and so not necessary. And on what other account, or in what other manner than one of these two, there can be need of the existence of a necessary being in order to the existence of any thing else, I cannot conceive.

Thus, sir, you see I entirely agree with you in all the consequences you have drawn from your suppositions, but cannot see the truth of the suppositions themselves.

I have aimed at nothing in my style, but only to be intelligible; being sensible that it is very difficult (as you observe) to express one's self on these sorts of subjects, especially for one who is altogether unaccustomed to write upon them.

I have nothing at present more to add, but my sincerest thanks for your trouble in answering my letter, and for your professed readiness to be acquainted with any other difficulty that I may meet with in any of your writings. I am willing to interpret this, as somewhat like a promise of an answer to what I have now written, if there be any thing in it which deserves one.

I am,

Reverend Sir,

Your most obliged humble servant.

Nov. 23, 1713.

IV

THE ANSWER

(D)

Clarke holds in reply that necessity of existence is original, absolute, and antecedent to all besides ; so that the necessary, if anywhere, must for the same reason be everywhere.

Declares Butler assumes a finite necessary being.

On No. 2: a necessary being is a sine qua non to the existence of any (= every) other being.

SIR,

IT seems to me, that the reason why you do not apprehend ubiquity to be necessarily connected with self-existence, is because, in the order of your ideas, you first conceive a being, (a finite being, suppose,) and then conceive self-existence to be a property of that being; as the angles are properties of a triangle, when a triangle exists: whereas, on the contrary, necessity of existence, not being a property consequent upon the supposition of the things existing, but antecedently the cause or ground of that existence; it is evident this necessity, being not limited to any antecedent subject, as angles are to a triangle; but being itself original, absolute, and (in order of nature) antecedent to all existence; cannot but be everywhere, for the same reason that it is anywhere. By applying this reasoning to the instance of space, you will find, that by consequence it belongs truly to that substance, whereof space is a property,[d] as duration also is. What you say about a necessary being existing somewhere, supposes it to be finite; and being finite, supposes some cause which determined that such a certain quantity of that being should exist, neither more nor less: and that cause must either be a voluntary cause; or else such a necessary cause, the quantity of whose power must be determined and limited by some other cause. But in original absolute necessity, antecedent (in order of nature) to the existence of any thing, nothing of all this can have place; but the necessity is necessarily everywhere alike.

[d] Or, mode of existence.

Concerning the second difficulty, I answer: That which exists necessarily, is needful to the existence of any other thing; not considered now as a cause, (for that indeed is begging the question,) but as a *sine qua non;* in the sense as space is necessary to every thing, and nothing can possibly be conceived to exist, without thereby presupposing space: which therefore I apprehend to be a property or mode of the self-existent substance; and that, by being evidently necessary itself, it proves that the substance, of which it is a property, must also be necessary; necessary both in itself, and needful to the existence of any thing else whatsoever. Extension indeed does not belong to thought, because thought is not a being; but there is need of extension to the existence of every being, to a being which has or has not thought, or any other quality whatsoever.

I am, Sir,
Your real friend and servant.

London, *Nov.* 28, 1713.

V

THE THIRD LETTER

(E)

Disclaims the finite being: holds by one eternal and necessary. Admits great force of Clarke's argument on head No. 1; continues to contest No. 2.

Reverend Sir,

I do not very well understand your meaning, when you say that you think, 'in the order of my ideas I first conceive a being (finite suppose) to exist, and then conceive self-existence to be a property of that being.' If you mean that I first suppose a finite being to exist I know not why; affirming necessity of existence to be only a consequent of its existence; and that, when I have supposed it finite, I very safely conclude it is not infinite; I am utterly at a loss, upon what expressions in my letter this conjecture can be founded. But if you mean, that I first of all prove a being to exist from eternity, and then, from the reasons of things, prove that such a being must be eternally necessary; I freely own it. Neither do I conceive it to be irregular or absurd; for there is a great difference between the order in which things exist, and the order in which I prove to myself that they exist. Neither do I think my saying a necessary being exists somewhere, supposes it to be finite; it only supposes that this being exists in space, without determining whether here, or there, or everywhere.

To my second objection, you say, 'That which exists necessarily, is needful to the existence of any other thing, as a *sine qua non;* in the sense space is necessary to every thing: which is proved (you say) by this consideration, that space is a property of the self-existent substance; and, being both necessary in itself, and needful to the existence of every thing else; consequently the substance, of which it is a property, must be so too.' Space, I own, is in one sense a property of the self-existent substance; but, in the same sense, it is also a property of all other substances. The only difference is in respect to the quantity. And since every part of space, as well as the whole, is necessary; every substance consequently must be self-existent, because it hath this self-existent property. Which since you will not admit for true; if it directly follows from your arguments, they cannot be conclusive.

What you say under the first head proves, I think, to a very great probability, though not to me with the evidence of demonstration: but your arguments under the second I am not able to see the force of.

I am so far from being pleased that I can form objections to your arguments, that, besides the satisfaction it would have given me in my own mind, I should have thought it an honour to have entered into your reasonings, and seen the force of them. I cannot desire to trespass any more upon your better employed time; so shall only add my hearty thanks for your trouble on my account, and that I am, with the greatest respect,

Reverend Sir,

Your most obliged humble servant.

Dec. 5, 1713.

VI

THE ANSWER

(F)

Nothing finite can be (antecedently) necessary: nothing (thus) necessary finite. Matter. Motion.

Space a property or mode of the self-existent: of it only. It alone does not exist in space. Space and duration necessary.

SIR,

THOUGH, when I turn my thoughts every way, I fully persuade myself there is no defect in the argument itself; yet in my manner of expression I am satisfied there must be some want of clearness, when there remains any difficulty to a person of your abilities and sagacity. I did not mean that your saying a necessary being exists somewhere, does necessarily suppose it to be finite; but that the manner of expression is apt to excite in the mind an idea of a finite being, at the same time that you are thinking of a necessary being, without accurately attending to the nature of that necessity by which it exists. Necessity absolute, and antecedent (in order of nature) to the existence of any subject, has nothing to limit it; but, if it operates at all, (as it must needs do,) it must operate (if I may so speak) everywhere and at all times alike. Determination of a particular quantity, or particular time or place of existence of any thing, cannot arise but from somewhat external to the thing itself. For example: why there should exist just such a small determinate quantity of matter, neither more nor less, interspersed in the immense vacuities of space, no reason can be given. Nor can there be any thing in nature, which could have determined a thing so indifferent in itself, as is the measure of that quantity; but only the will of an intelligent and free agent. To suppose matter, or any other substance, necessarily existing in a finite determinate quantity; in an inch-cube, for instance; or in any certain number of cube-inches, and no more; is exactly the same absurdity, as supposing it to exist necessarily, and yet for a finite duration only:

which every one sees to be a plain contradiction. The
argument is likewise the same, in the question about
the original of motion. Motion cannot be necessarily
existing; because, it being evident that all determinations of motion are equally possible in themselves, the
original determination of the motion of any particular
body this way rather than the contrary way, could not
be necessarily in itself, but was either caused by the
will of an intelligent and free agent, or else was an effect
produced and determined without any cause at all;
which is an express contradiction: as I have shown in
my *Demonstration of the Being and Attributes of God.*
[Page 14, edit. 4th and 5th; page 12, edit. 6th and 7th.]

To the second head of argument, I answer: Space
is a property [or mode] of the self-existent substance;
but not of any other substances. All other substances
are in space, and are penetrated by it; but the self-
existent substance is not in space, nor penetrated by it,
but is itself (if I may so speak) the substratum of space,
the ground of the existence of space and duration itself.
Which [space and duration] being evidently necessary,
and yet themselves not substances, but properties or
modes, show evidently that the substance, without which
these properties could not subsist, is itself much more
(if that were possible) necessary.[1] And as space and
duration are needful (i.e. *sine qua non*) to the existence

---

[1] We may suppose, say, that love, justice, power, the
faculty of knowing, exist in God: and so are above
and outside the idea of creation. But who can suppose
that space or time, such as we conceive them, are in God?

The assumption of necessary existence, which I cannot
but question as to both, seems to be especially questionable as to time, because the idea of time, if it have an
ending, involves that of a *beginning*.

Out of this difficulty we slide, in the text, by treating
time as synonymous with duration. But is not this to
pass from one *impasse* into another? Who will upon
reflection venture to *define* eternity? and to define it,
moreover, as 'time without a beginning and interminably
prolonged'? I cannot help surmising that within the
veil there may lie explanations of these, as well as of
many other secrets.

of every thing else; so consequently is the substance, to which these properties belong in that peculiar manner which I before mentioned.

I am, Sir,
Your affectionate friend and servant.

Dec. 10, 1713.

VII

THE FOURTH LETTER

(G)

Now admits the first of the arguments impugned in A. Both spirit and body exist in space. He cannot tell the mode. Does not accept 'substratum.' Thinks space antecedently necessary, and necessary even to the self-existent substance. Search for truth is the business of his life.

REVEREND SIR,

WHATEVER is the occasion of my not seeing the force of your reasonings, I cannot impute it to [what you do] the want of clearness in your expression. I am too well acquainted with myself, to think my not understanding an argument, a sufficient reason to conclude that it is either improperly expressed, or not conclusive; unless I can clearly show the defect of it. It is with the greatest satisfaction I must tell you, that the more I reflect on your first argument, the more I am convinced of the truth of it; and it now seems to me altogether unreasonable to suppose absolute necessity can have any relation to one part of space more than to another; and if so, an absolutely necessary being must exist everywhere.

I wish I was as well satisfied in respect to the other. You say, 'All substances, except the self-existent one, are in space, and are penetrated by it.' All substances doubtless, whether body or spirit, exist in space: but when I say that a spirit exists in space, were I put upon telling my meaning, I know not how I could do it any other way than by saying, such a particular quantity of space terminates the capacity of acting in finite spirits at one and the same time; so that they cannot act beyond that determined quantity. Not but that I think there is somewhat in the manner of the existence of spirits in respect of space, that more directly answers to the manner of the existence of body; but what that is, or of the manner of their existence, I cannot possibly form an idea. And it seems (if possible) much more difficult to determine what relation the self-existent Being hath to space. To say he exists in space, after the same manner that other substances do, (somewhat like which I too rashly asserted in my last,) perhaps would be placing the Creator too much on a level with the creature; or however, it is not plainly and evidently true: and to say the self-existent substance is the substratum of space, in the common sense of the word, is scarce intelligible, or at least is not evident. Now though there may be an hundred relations distinct from either of these; yet how we should come by ideas of them, I cannot conceive. We may indeed have ideas to the words, and not altogether depart from the common sense of them, when we say the self-existent substance is the substratum of space, or the ground of its existence: but I see no reason to think it true, because space seems to me to be as absolutely self-existent, as it is possible any thing can be: so that, make what other supposition you please, yet we cannot help supposing immense space; because there must be either an infinity of being, or (if you will allow the expression) an infinite vacuity of being. Perhaps it may be objected to this, that though space is really necessary, yet the reason of its being necessary is its being a property of the self-existent substance; and that, it being so evidently necessary, and its dependence on the self-existent substance not so evident, we are ready to conclude it absolutely self-existent, as well as necessary; and that this is the reason why the idea of space forces itself on our minds, antecedent to, and exclusive of (as to the ground of its existence) all other things. Now this, though it is really an objection, yet is no direct answer to what I have said; because it supposes the only thing to be proved, viz. that the reason why space is necessary is its being a property of a self-existent substance. And supposing it not to be evident, that space is absolutely self-existent; yet, while it is doubtful, we cannot argue as though the contrary were certain, and we were sure that space was only a property of the self-existent substance. But now, if space be not absolutely independent, I do not see what we can conclude is so: for it is manifestly necessary itself, as well as antecedently needful to the existence of all other things, not excepting (as I think) even the self-existent substance.

All your consequences, I see, follow demonstrably from your supposition; and, were that evident, I believe it would serve to prove several other things as well as what you bring it for. Upon which account, I should be extremely pleased to see it proved by any one. For, as I design the search after truth as the business of my life, I shall not be ashamed to learn from any person; though, at the same time, I cannot but be sensible, that instruction from some men is like the gift of a prince, it reflects an honour on the person on whom it lays an obligation.

I am, Reverend Sir,
Your obliged servant.

Dec. 16, 1713.

VIII

THE ANSWER

(H)

Clarke replies that space and time are not substances, but qualities or relations necessarily existing which infer a substance. Illustrated by the ideas formable of body by men without touch or sight respectively.

SIR,

My being out of town most part of the month of January, and some other accidental avocations, hindered me from answering your letter sooner. The sum of the difficulties it contains is, I think, this: that 'it is difficult to determine what relation the self-existent substance has to space:' that 'to say it is the substratum of space, in the common sense of the word, is scarce intelligible, or, at least, is not evident:' that 'space seems to be as absolutely self-existent, as it is possible any thing can be:' and that 'its being a property of the self-existent substance is supposing the thing that was to be proved.' This is entering indeed into the very bottom of the matter; and I will endeavour to give you as brief and clear an answer as I can.

That the self-existent substance is the substratum of space, or space a property of the self-existent substance, are not perhaps very proper expressions; nor is it easy to find such. But what I mean is this: The idea of space (as also of time or duration) is an abstract or partial idea; an idea of a certain quality or relation, which we evidently see to be necessarily existing; and yet which (not being itself a substance) at the same time necessarily presupposes a substance, without which it could not exist; which substance consequently must be itself (much more, if possible) necessarily existing. I know not how to explain this so well as by the following similitude. A blind man, when he tries to frame to himself the idea of body, his idea is nothing but that of hardness. A man that had eyes, but no power of motion, or sense of feeling at all; when he tried to frame to himself the idea of body, his idea would be nothing but that of colour. Now as, in these cases, hardness is not body, and colour is not body; but yet, to the understanding of these persons, those properties necessarily infer the being of a substance, of which substance itself the persons have no idea: so space to us is not itself substance, but it necessarily infers the being of a substance, which affects none of our present senses; and, being itself necessary, it follows, that the substance, which it infers, is (much more) necessary.

I am, Sir,

Your affectionate friend and servant.

Jan. 29, 1713.

IX

THE FIFTH LETTER

(1)

Cannot disprove, but pauses before admitting that space and duration are properties of a substance. Is at a loss about their nature. If the thesis could be demonstrated, Atheism would be confuted.

Apologizes for his observations on omnipresence.

REVEREND SIR,

You have very comprehensively expressed, in six or seven lines, all the difficulties of my letter; which I should have endeavoured to have made shorter, had I not been afraid an improper expression might possibly occasion a mistake of my meaning. I am very glad the debate is come into so narrow a compass; for I think now it entirely turns upon this, whether our ideas of space and duration are partial, so as to presuppose the existence of some other thing. Your similitude of the blind man is very apt, to explain your meaning, (which I think I fully understand,) but does not seem to come entirely up to the matter. For what is the reason that the blind man concludes there must be somewhat external, to give him that idea of hardness? It is because he supposes it impossible for him to be thus affected, unless there were some cause of it; which cause, should it be removed, the effect would immediately cease too; and he would no more have the idea of hardness, but by remembrance. Now to apply this to the instance of space and duration: Since a man, from his having these ideas, very justly concludes that there must be somewhat external, which is the cause of them; consequently, should this cause (whatever it is) be taken away, his ideas would be so too: therefore, if what is supposed to be the cause be removed, and yet the idea remains, that supposed cause cannot be the real one. Now, granting the self-existent substance to be the substratum of these ideas, could we make the supposition of its ceasing to be, yet space and duration would still remain unaltered: which seems to show, that the self-existent substance is not the substratum of space and duration. Nor would it be an answer to the difficulty, to say that every property of the self-existent substance is as necessary as the substance itself; since that will only hold, while the substance itself exists; for there is implied, in the idea of a property, an impossibility of subsisting without its substratum. I grant, the supposition is absurd: but how otherwise can we know whether any thing be a property of such a substance, but by examining whether it would cease to be, if its supposed substance should do so? Notwithstanding what I have now said, I cannot say that I believe your argument not conclusive; for I must own my ignorance, that I am really at a loss about the nature of space and duration. But did it plainly appear that they were properties of a substance, we should have an easy way with the atheists: for it would at once prove demonstrably an eternal, necessary, self-existent Being; that there is but one such; and that he is needful in order to the existence of all other things. Which makes me think, that though it may be true, yet it is not obvious to every capacity: otherwise it would have been generally used, as a fundamental argument to prove the being of God.

I must add one thing more; that your argument for the omnipresence of God seemed always to me very probable. But being very desirous to have it appear demonstrably conclusive, I was sometimes forced to say what was not altogether my opinion: not that I did this for the sake of disputing, (for, besides the particular disagreeableness of this to my own temper, I should surely have chosen another person to have trifled with;) but I did it to set off the objection to advantage, that it might be more fully answered. I heartily wish you as fair treatment from your opponents in print, as I have had from you; though, I must own, I cannot see, in those that I have read, that unprejudiced search after truth, which I would have hoped for.

I am,
Reverend Sir,
Your most humble servant.

Feb. 3, 1713.

X

THE ANSWER

(J)

Clarke thinks that Butler, in allowing that the removal of the self-existent substance is an absurd idea, has conceded his argument.

Animadverts on the mischief done by Descartes in referring origins to mechanical laws, as drawing us away from God. Other animadversions.

SIR,

IN a multitude of business, I mislaid your last letter; and could not answer it, till it came again to my hands by chance. We seem to have pushed the matter in question between us as far as it will go; and, upon the whole, I cannot but take notice, I have very seldom met with persons so reasonable and unprejudiced as yourself, in such debates as these.

I think all I need say, in answer to the reasoning in your letter, is, that your granting the absurdity of the supposition you were endeavouring to make, is consequently granting the necessary truth of my argument.[1] If [d] space and duration necessarily remain, even after they are supposed to be taken away; and be not (as it is plain they are not) themselves substances; then the [e] sub-

[d] Ut partium temporis ordo est immutabilis, sic etiam ordo partium spatii. Moveantur hae de locis suis, et movebuntur (ut ita dicam) de seipsis, Newton, *Princip. Mathemat. Schol. ad definit.* 8.

[e] Deus non est aeternitas vel infinitas, sed aeternus et infinitus; non est duratio vel spatium, sed durat et adest. Durat semper, et adest ubique; et existendo semper et ubique, durationem et spatium, aeternitatem et infinitatem, constituit. Cum unaquae-

---

[1] This seems to be a fallacy. The concession, that a certain supposition was absurd, was grounded on considerations drawn *aliunde;* and did not deprive Butler of his right to point out that space and time do not logically depend upon our recognition.

stance, on whose existence they depend, will necessarily remain likewise, even after it is supposed to be taken away : which shows that supposition to be impossible and contradictory.[1]

As to your observation at the end of your letter ; that the argument I have insisted on, if it were obvious to every capacity, should have more frequently been used as a fundamental argument for a proof of the being of God : the true cause why it has been seldom urged, is, I think, this ; that the universal prevalency of Cartes's absurd notions (teaching that [f] matter is necessarily infinite and necessarily eternal, and ascribing all things to mere mechanic laws of motion, exclusive of final causes, and of all will and intelligence and Divine Providence from the government of the world) hath incredibly blinded the eyes of common reason, and prevented men from discerning *him in whom they live, and move, and have their being*. The like has happened in some other instances. How universally have men for many ages believed, that eternity is no duration at all, and infinity no amplitude !

que spatii particula sit semper ; et unumquodque durationis indivisibile momentum ubique ; certe rerum omnium Fabricator ac Dominus non erit nunquam nusquam. Omnipraesens est, non per virtutem solam, sed etiam per substantiam : nam virtus sine substantia subsistere non potest. In ipso continentur et moventur universa, &c. Newton, *Princip. Mathemat. Schol. general. sub finem.*

[f] Puto implicare contradictionem, ut mundus [meaning the material world] sit finitus. Cartes. *Epist.* 69 *Partis primae.*

---

[1] We have here (1) space, (2) time, set down as—

(*a*) Being each of them a quality or relation. (Why a quality or relation only ? Why more than sound or light ?)

(*b*) 'Evidently seen to be necessarily existing.'

This evidence, this necessity, I have never been able to see. No one has taught us so well as Butler the limitedness of our faculties. When we say that this or that necessarily exists, do we not run a risk of travelling too fast and far ? For we place that particular thing outside the creative power, and in independence of it. What title have we to lay down such a proposition as to either space or time ?

Something of the like kind has happened in the matter of transubstantiation, and, I think, in the scholastic notion of the Trinity, &c.

I am, Sir,
Your affectionate friend and servant.

April 8, 1713 [? 1714].

INDEX

[References to the *body* of the *Analogy* are indicated by figures only: thus I. ii. 3 means the First Part, Second Chapter, Section 3. Those to the Introduction by Intr. To the Advertisement by Adv. To the Dissertations by Diss. I., Diss. II. Those to the Butler and Clarke Correspondence by Corr.]

ACTION, is the main instrument appointed for the formation of character, I. v. 40.
includes consequences intended to follow it, Diss. II. 4.
judgment on acts should measure them by the agent, Diss. II. 7.

AFFECTION. See LIVING POWERS; also PROPENSIONS.

AGENT, nature of, to be regarded in estimating virtuous action, Diss. II. 7.

ANALOGY, false, drawn by prince whom Locke names, Intr. 3.
true counter-analogy, *ibid.*
omits to discuss its general nature, Intr. 7.
between scripture and nature, Intr. 8.
as dealt with by author, between nature and religion natural and revealed, supplies answers to almost all objections, Intr. 15.
with varying force in different parts of the argument, *ibid.*
its force as regards ridicule, *ibid.*
applies to religion natural and revealed alike, Intr. 17.
furnishes argument generally unanswerable; undoubtedly of weight, in whatever degree, *ibid.*
what materials it furnishes for estimating probable effects of death on us, I. i. 1.
affords no presumption of the loss of living powers at death or otherwise, I. i. 7.
between relation of early to later life, and of this life to survival, I. v. 3, 18.
might hold even were the mode of our discipline inscrutable, I. v. 19.
of nature, does not disprove waste of souls, I. v. 35.
between acquisition of right qualities, and supply of wants, I. v. 41.

ANALOGY (*continued*).
    begins with proving the fact rather than the right of divine government, I. vii. 1.
    leads us to expect a scheme, and one imperfectly comprehended, I. vii. 2.
    many analogies show we are bad judges of schemes not fully known, I. vii. 22.
    none from nature against the gospel idea, II. ii. 3–6.
    between nature and revelation, brings the like objectors against both, II. iii. 5.
    between nature and revelation, as to advance into the ulterior stages of knowledge, II. iii. 20, 21.
    between unlikeness of creatures and unlikeness of environment for like creatures, II. vi. 8.
    between scanty evidence in religion, and temptation in environment, II. vi. 17.

ANALOGIES, PRINCIPAL, BETWEEN NATURE AND THE GOSPEL, OR CHRISTIANITY.
    the provisions made in each are open to abuse, II. i. 14, iii. 18, 19.
    between our obligations under natural and under divine relations, II. i. 22, 23.
    in the injunction to use means for the attainment of benefits, II. i. 24.
    the gospel undiscoverable; so is much in nature, II. ii. 4.
    the want of uniform agreement with nature, and the inconformity of nature to herself, II. ii. 5.
    adverse presumptions in each are to be set aside by proofs, II. ii. 13, iii. 13.
    our incompetence to anticipate in nature, what it should be, and in revelation, II. iii. 5 *seqq*.
    and like incompetency to judge, II. iii. 9.
    in the modes, inscrutable to us, by which the different parts of knowledge are opened to us, II. iii. 15.
    as to progress through the stages of knowledge, II. iii. 20, 21.
    modes of giving it, in each, not such as we should choose, II. iii. 22.
    the supply of light in each is only partial, II. iii. 23, ix. 15.
    in both schemes remedies are incomplete, II. iii. 24.
    in both, the scheme imperfectly comprehended, II. iv. 1.
    in both, apparent want of aptitude in means, II. iv. 3.
    in nature, method of operation is by general laws; may be so in the gospel, II. iv. 4–6.
    would not of itself lead us to anticipate the efficacy of Christ's mediation, II. ix. 14.
    the cumbrousness of the methods used, II. iv. 7, 8.
    mediation, proposed in the gospel, is interwoven with all nature, II. v. 1.

INDEX

ANALOGIES (*continued*).
  in the arrival of punishment as natural consequence, II. v. 2.
  reliefs from full consequences of misconduct, II. v. 4, 5.
  in nature reformation does not cancel the past : so it may be in the gospel, II. v. 7, 8.
  between mediation in the world, and in the Christian system, II. v. 1, 22.
  as to great diversities in the evidence, referably to times, persons, and otherwise, II. vi. 4–6.
  is real, though some may think it here overstrained, II. viii. 28.
  that the Christian remedy is not summary, II. ix. 9.
  principal analogy, to vindicate the gospel, not with natural religion, but with nature, II. viii. 6.
ANCIENTS were alive to the power dwelling in liberty and moral fitness, II. viii. 24.
ANTICIPATION, formed by us, no safe guide to the provisions made by God, II. iii. 25.
ARGUMENT, that as 'we see not the *why*, *ergo* it cannot be,' illegitimate, almost infatuated, II. v. 24.
ARGUMENTS, in a Treatise like this, are important unless futile, Adv. 1.
ASTRONOMY compared with medicine, as to amount and nature of progress made, and in reference to our probable anticipations respecting them, II. iii. 15.
ATHEISM does not disprove a future state, I. i. 32.
  objections taken to Christianity from its perversions, lead to, II. i. 13.
  would be confuted, could we prove that space and time were properties of a substance, Corr. ix.
ATONEMENT of Christ. See SATISFACTION.
AUTHOR. See NATURE.

BAPTISM, why triune, II. i. 18.
BEHAVIOUR, enjoyment (all) and suffering (much) dependent on, I. ii. 1.
  possible reasons hereof : forewarning is one of them, II. ii. 2.
BENEVOLENCE, not the whole of virtue, I. iii. 3.
  examined at large, Diss. II. 12–16.
BIRTH, its possible analogy with death, I. i. 27.
  second, figuratively but expressly declared by John iii. 5, II. i. 24.
BLASPHEMY, how the spirit of negation may carry men to it, II. ix. 5.
  wholly without excuse in the face of the Christian argument, II. ix. 21.
  demonstration might fail to arrest it, II. ix. 22.
BODY, is no more part of ourselves than any other matter, I. i. 11.
  we may exist out of the body, or in a new body, *ibid.*

INDEX

BODY (*continued*).
    its destruction, no more tends to destroy the *ego* than that of any other foreign matter, I. i. 11.
    large and important parts of it can be dispensed with, I. i. 12, 15.
    probably even of the small body of childhood, I. i. 12.
    its particles in continual flux, change their owners, I. i. 13.
    unless the living being exceed an atom in bulk, which we do not know, how can death dissolve it? I. i. 14.
    if body be not the *ego*, no other matter can be supposed it, I. i. 15.
    original solids of, may not be dissolved or removed at death, I. i. 16.
    only reciprocal action of, and living agent, provable, *ibid.*
    true in degree of foreign matter generally, *ibid.*
    i. e. sense, conveys but does not perceive, I. i. 17.
    on parting with it: we act, in dreams, without it, I. i. 18, 25.
    limbs, are instruments not agents, I. i. 19.
    if dissolution of such matter (I. i. 17–19) do not destroy, why of any matter? I. i. 20.
BRUTES, can they attain immortality? I. i. 21.
    with or without, their rational and moral rank, *ibid.*
    may, but need not, *ibid.*
    puzzles about them are founded only in our ignorance, I. i. 22.
    certain, stronger than man, yet reason tends to obtain superiority, I. iii. 22.
    their faculties work with greater security, II. iii. 16.
BURDEN of proof; there is evidence for the gospel sufficient to throw *onus probandi* on the opponent, II. vii. 10.

CAESAR, presumptions against the story of, II. ii. 11.
CHANCES, adverse, even when enormous may be countervailed by slight proof, II. ii. 11, 12.
    there can be no such thing as chance, II. iv. 4.
CHILD trained as a necessitarian, his case supposed, I. vi. 7.
CHRISTIANITY. See GOSPEL.
    now extensively assumed to be false, Adv. 2.
    assumption wholly unproven, *ibid.*
    Judaism is just what we should expect it to be supposing the miracles true, II. vii. 4.
    and Judaism are alone in claiming assent on the ground of miracles publicly wrought, II. vii. 8.
CHURCH, visible, included in the gospel plan; its object, II. i. 10, 11.
CIVIL punishments are natural, and often temporally final, I. ii. 16.
    government, an aid to virtue, I. iii. 16.
CLEMENS ROMANUS, quoted, II. vii. 7.

INDEX

COMMANDS, distinguished as (a) positive, and (b) moral, II. i. 26; they both agree and differ, *ibid. n.*
  (a) precepts founded on command, (b) anterior to it, II. i. 26.
  yet (a) have a moral force, and may rest on natural religion, or revealed (example), II. i. 27, 33.
  have moral force, especially in principle apart from form, II. i. 28.
  in case of conflict, the moral command prevails, II. i. 29.
  has a double title (a) from scripture, (b) from nature, II. i. 30.
  as between (a) and (b) our Lord has determined the case, II. i. 32; and this from the Old Testament, *ibid.* 33.
  makes moral some precepts that would be otherwise immoral, II. iii. 27.
  they must not be contrary to immutable morality, *ibid.*
CONDUCT, difficulty of, sometimes consists in discovering the right, more than in doing it, II. vi. 18.
CONSCIOUSNESS makes personality but not identity, Diss. I. 2, 3.
CONSENT as to religion in all ages and countries, I. vi. 16.
CONTINUANCE of existence is to be presumed in the absence of reasons to the contrary, I. i. 4, 8.
  this extends to all substances; and, except as to the self-existent, is the only reason for presuming a future, I. i. 4.
  presumption higher for our substances, than for our living powers, I. i. 4 *n.*
  mere contrary apprehension is of no weight, I. i. 5.
CONVERSIONS to the gospel, with the sacrifice of interest and pleasure, must be believed sincere, and perhaps something more, II. vii. 9.
CORRUPTION of heart begets intellectual error, Diss. I. 8.
CORRUPTIONS in religion, obscure the evidence, II. i. 13, vi. 5.
  have been great and shocking; form no argument against the gospel, I. iv. 9, II. i. 13.
COURSE of nature, as now known, has no application to the *Origines*, II. ii. 7, 8.
CREDENTIALS of an ambassador, contemplating only formal outward acts, not analogous to proofs in religion, II. vi. 21.
CYPHER, illustration from part use of, in a writing, to case of a prophecy dark in a part of it, II. vii. 22.

DANIEL, Book of, authority given it by our Lord, II. vii. 28.
  its truth presupposed in the general scheme of Christianity, *ibid.*
DEATH, change at, may be no greater than other changes known to allow survival, I. i. 3, 8.
  relation of, to the living powers, essentially unknown, I. i. 6.
  removes only the sensible proof of our having them, I. i. 7.
  not known in itself, but only in certain effects, I. i. 6.
  cannot be presumed to end our existence unless the soul be discerptible, I. i. 10.

DEATH (*continued*).

    the argument to show that it is indiscerptible, I. i. 10.

    yields no sign of destroying anything that belongs to our 'state of reflection,' I. i. 24.

    may not even suspend our reflective life, I. i. 26.

    may be analogous to birth, as continuance with alteration, I. i. 27.

    argument *a fortiori* against the idea that death destroys, I. i. 27 *n.*

    may be a birth into a higher state, I. i. 27.

    to presume extinction at death is 'palpably absurd,' I. viii. 4.

    scope given to hope and fear in the future bears upon conduct, I. viii. 5.

    See RUIN.

DEMONSTRATION of the Being of God, has not succeeded in finding, Corr. i.

DEPRAVITY, imported into our natures, enhances need for discipline, I. v. 30.

    neglect of evidence is a real depravity, II. vi. 11.

DESCARTES builds a world upon hypothesis, Intr. 9.

    censured by Clarke, as leading away from God, Corr. x.

DESERT, associated by us with the moral quality of actions, Diss. II. 5.

    higher or lower, according to the particulars of the case, Diss. II. 6.

DESIGN, is to be inferred (*a*) from creation, (*b*) from natural government, I. iii. 1.

    in no way disproved by necessity, I. vi. 5.

DIFFICULTY, in the evidence of religion may be indispensable as a means of training, II. vi. 10, 18.

    the difficulties of the moral scheme may be things good, the best possible, indispensable, I. vii. 13, 15, II. iv. 1.

    total removal of, demanded, II. viii. 4.

    which removal may mean demand to comprehend the divine nature and plan, *ibid.*

DISCERPTIBILITY. See DEATH.

DISCIPLINE, moral; describes our condition in this life, I. v. *passim.*

    the viciousness of the world makes the discipline of life specially effective, I. v. 34.

    wrought out principally through action, I. v. 40.

    of religion less stringent where conviction is absolute, II. vi. 18.

DISCOVERIES, greatness of recent, in the material world, I. iii. 28, II. iii. 21.

DISEASES, some though mortal leave the *ego* unaffected all through, I. i. 25.

DISOBEDIENCE, single, produces disorder; and repeated, habit, I. v. 28.

DISREGARD of the gospel argument betokens a temper which even demonstration might fail to rouse, II. ix. 22.

DOUBT: presupposes evidence for that of which we doubt, II. vi. 1, ix. 17.

promoted by corruption of the heart where the evidence is not overbearing, II. vi. 16.

commands increase of effort, as temptations do in conduct, II. vi. 17.

may even constitute the capital article of our trial, II. vi. 18.

may be due to our own fault; remissness of thought, levity, prejudice, II. vi. 19, ix. 16.

as to the evidence of the miracles, would not warrant their rejection, II. vii. 5.

the doubtfulness of the evidence for religion, bearing the test of long experience and examination, becomes an evidence in its favour, II. vii. 34.

the middle or doubtful state of mind is the most negative of what is found among persons of tolerable capacity and opportunity, II. ix. 19.

DREAMS show we have latent powers of perception, not dependent on sense, I. i. 18.

ENTHUSIASM, weakens testimony; but the Christian witnesses were not enthusiasts, II. vii. 13.

can only be imputed if the things be incredible, II. vii. 14.

EPICTETUS: why his phrase is employed, Diss. II. 1 *n*.

EVIDENCE, real but doubtful, imposes a moral obligation, Intr. 5, II. vi. 12.

implied alike by doubt, belief, certainty; but in different degrees, II. vi. 15; obligations entailed by the lower degrees, *ibid.*

for the gospel, to be viewed as a whole, and in the reciprocal relations of its parts, II. vii. 30, 59, 62.

series of generally uncontested propositions (II. vii. 41–56) which may be laid before an unprepossessed mind, and their proper effect in giving proof of something more than human, II. vii. 40, 57.

summary of propositions available for this purpose, II. vii. 41–56, viz.:

natural religion, how rooted in scripture, II. vii. 41.

the establishment of Christianity is the greatest fact in history, without any disparagement to reason, II. vii. 42, 43.

the antiquity of scripture, and the corroborations it has received, II. vii. 44.

the marks of reality in the simple self-congruous narratives, II. vii. 45.

frank dealing with facts, and disregard of ornament, II. vii. 46.

INDEX

EVIDENCE (*continued*).
    strange incidents in it, as in other narratives, but nothing to destroy credit, II. vii. 47.
    vast range joined with apparent truthfulness, and force of the common in supporting the miraculous, II. vii. 48.
    add the grand sign of the Jews, a nationality dependent on belief, II. vii. 49.
    with the Advent, and establishment of the gospel, II. vii. 50.
    and the dispersion and standing isolation of the Jews, ill accounted for by secondary causes, II. vii. 51, 52.
    and the presumption from part-fulfilment in favour of entire, II. vii. 53.
    fair capacity in the judge presupposed, II. vii. 54.
    all these particulars to be taken in consideration, II. vii. 55.
    their range going beyond that of Jewish and Christian history, II. vii. 56.
    something more than human is shown, with claims on unbelievers, II. vii. 57, 58.
    with competent judges, circumstantial evidence weighs largely, II. vii. 59.
    serious men, dealing with the aggregate, will admit high probable proof, II. vii. 60.
    stress of the argument; this cannot as a whole be accident, and cannot otherwise be set aside, II. vii. 62.
    advantages enjoyed by attack in detail, II. vii. 63.
    summed up in three propositions:
      (*a*) no adverse presumption on the ground of miracle, II. vii. 64.
      (*b*) general scheme agrees with the constitution of things, *ibid*.
      (*c*) direct evidence, even if lessened, cannot be destroyed, *ibid*.
    to ask for the removal of all difficulties is really asking for an entire comprehension of the divine nature, II. viii. 4.
    as presented in this Treatise, is far from satisfactory, II. viii. 17.
    commonly accepted to guide conduct, is most unsatisfactory, *ibid*.
    demand for full, changes the very condition of our being, II. viii. 18.
    its nature is appointed for our probation, II. viii. 19.
    true question, does it bind to action? not, does it satisfy? II. viii. 20.
EXAMPLE: there may be those who exist only to serve as examples, I. ii. 21.
    the weight of our responsibility enhanced by the power of our example, II. vi. 14.
EXPERIENCE of moral government, how an answer to fatalists, I. vi. 20–22.

INDEX

EXPERIENCE (*continued*).
teaches, that often means we deem unsuitable are available for their ends, I. vii. 14.
used in this Treatise exclusively as the plea for religion, II. viii. 25.
EXTENSION does not belong to thought, Corr. iii.
EXTERIOR of religion, provided by a visible church, II. i. 10.
an essential part of Christianity, II. i. 19.
its form fixed by command, II. i. 21.
EYES are vehicles which convey to the perceiving power, I. i. 17.

FABLE: applicability having been shown, intention is presumed, II. vii. 24, 25.
FACT, its peculiar relation to the gospel, as foundation, II. vii. 33.
a religion founded on, may be proved credible, apart from its reasonableness, II. viii. 14, 16.
plea for religion herein confined to the authority of fact and experience, II. viii. 25.
foregoing the aid of argument from freedom and moral fitness, author has provided an independent proof of future righteous judgment from this source, II. viii. 26.
in matter of, strict demonstration is unheard of, Corr. iii.
FATALISM. See NECESSITY.
FEAR, as also hope, a legitimate motive to obedience, I. v. 36.
FITNESS, moral, has waived reasoning from, though true and important, II. viii. 24.
FREEDOM, its contrast with necessity, I. vi. 5.
our entire state is what it would be if we were free, I. vi. 9.
our experience shows its truth, I. vi. 14.
FUTURE LIFE, the foundation of all our hopes and fears, Intr. 17.
in proof, relies mainly on presumption from the doctrine of continuance, and on the incapacity of death to destroy, I. i. 30.
has quashed the negative presumption, I. i. 32.
has shown a high probability of survival, *ibid.*
to predicate extinction at death is palpably absurd, I. viii. 4.
draws its importance from our capacity to enjoy and suffer, I. ii. 1.
analogy between relation of early to later life, and of this life to a future one, I. v. 3, 18.
probably active, and under the more sensible dominion of God, I. v. 21.
awakens hope and fear; these bear upon conduct, I. viii. 5.
enlarged action of moral elements probable in, I. viii. 7.
future righteous judgment, proved here from fact, may be separately proved from liberty and moral fitness, II. viii. 26.
proof of, would not *per se* prove religion, I. i. 32.
amendment in, of those capable of amendment, I. iii. 28.
has natural and moral proofs commonly insisted on, I. i. 5.

INDEX

GENERAL LAWS, attended with particular irregularities, I. iii. 20.
the method appointed for natural government, I. vii. 18.
allow of action with forethought, *ibid.*
as to corrective interposition, we are no judges, I. vii. 18, 19.

GOD: the manifold proofs of his existence (fivefold); not denied by opponents, Intr. 10.
uses pleasures and pains for government, I. ii. 8, vi. 23.
has a natural government over the world, I. iii. 1.
and a moral government, I. ii. 2–4, iii. 10, 35, 36, iv. 2, II. iv. 1, v. 2, 7, 20, viii. 2.
carried on by general laws, I. vii. 18, 19.
even now takes the side of the good, I. iii. 21, 34.
an infinite and immense eternal Being exists by necessity, I. vi. 4; but this is only a manner of speaking, *ibid.*
his character and will, untouched by fatalism, I. vi. 12.
his will determined by the right and reason of the case, I. vi. 16 *n.*
disobedience to him, its weighty and terrible character, II. i. 2, v. 6.
his plans liable to abuse, II. i. 14.
the form of his purposes only knowable to us by experience, II. iii. 7.
has appointed our existence to be in progressive stages, II. iv. 8.
argument from his government here to his government hereafter, II. v. 1, 2.
his goodness in remedies and mitigations of evil, II. v. 4.
we cannot expect instruction on the divine conduct as large as on our own duty, II. v. 25.
whether we regard his will as absolute or as conditional, the case is the same, II. vi. 22.
Treatise does not seek to vindicate, but to show our duty, II. viii. 10, 21; author has made it his business to seek proof of the being and attributes, Corr. 1; has only found probable arguments. Not convinced by Clarke's demonstration, *ibid.*
exists in space, Corr. v.

GOSPEL, the, republishes natural religion with new authority, II. i. 5, 6.
derives additional credibility from miracle, II. i. 7, 8.
illuminates doctrines of immortality and the efficacy of repentance, II. i. 9.
as a republication of natural religion has a title to be examined, II. i. 15.
is a dispensation for the recovery of a world in ruins, II. i. 16.
is especially a revelation of the Son and Spirit, hence triune baptism, II. i. 17, 18.
method of, has two essential parts, (*a*) inward, and (*b*) outward, II. i. 19.
no presumption against it as undiscoverable, II. ii. 4.

INDEX

GOSPEL (*continued*).
    nor as being unlike nature, which herself has inequalities, II. ii. 5.
    things objected to in, may be good or the very best, as is the case in nature, II. iv. 1.
    is a dispensation of righteousness, but like nature beyond our competency to judge, II. iv. 2.
    means for ends, though not seen by us to be good, may be the very best, I. vii. 13, 15, II. iv. 3.
    our ignorance bars our objections, II. iv. 2.
    method of general laws operates alike in nature and grace, II. iv. 4, 5.
    the parallel found in each as to gaps and anomalies, II. iv. 7.
    objection to the modes as circuitous and cumbrous; we are incompetent, *ibid.*
    objection to mediation: most common, most causeless, II. v. 1.
    partial reliefs and remedies are often mercifully provided for us, II. v. 11.
    total impunity blindly reckoned on, II. v. 5.
    evidence for, suffices to throw *onus probandi* on the objector, II. vii. 10.
    every Christian bound to share in its propagation, II. i. 15.

GOVERNMENT, God is a Governor, by rewarding and punishing, I. ii. 9.
    by punishments, not incidental, but systematic, I. ii. 17.
    its indications confirmed by religion as to the future, *ibid.*
    extreme gravity of the present scheme of punishments, its effect on teaching as to the future, I. ii. 18.
    scheme of natural punishments operates perceptibly but not uniformly, I. ii. 19.
    it ought to check the audacity of this age, I. ii. 20.
    as known by experience, like creation, implies design, I. iii. 1.
    God is a moral Governor, by rewarding and punishing righteously, I. iii. 2, 3, 8, Diss. II. 14.
    balance in favour of virtue; not invariable, nor always clear, I. iii. 5.
    especially in cases of reformed life, I. iii. 6.
    no presumption against perfectly righteous final award, I. iii. 8.
    good acts sometimes punished, but never as being good, I. iii. 12.
    regard is had to quality and intent of acts, not acts only, I. iii. 13.
    the sum of results is favourable (*a*) in what is, (*b*) in indicating what will be, I. iii. 17.
    this regard to the *quale* is due (*a*) to our moral nature, (*b*) to the effects upon related destinies, I. iii. 18.
    even now God takes the side of the *vir bonus*, I. iii. 21, 34.
    the tendencies of, run ahead of the present facts, I. iii. 22.

GOVERNMENT (*continued*).

> providential, must be vast in proportion to the material universe, I. iii. 28.
>
> objection taken, that this mixed state may continue: even so, vice would not triumph, I. iii. 32, 33.
>
> doctrine of a future rectification strongly sustained by the points here shown, I. iii. 33.
>
> its having veracity and justice for its rule, and its correspondence with nature, not impaired by necessity, I. vi. 13, 14.
>
> divine, corresponds with our nature, I. vi. 15.
>
> is a scheme, and a scheme imperfectly comprehended, in both points analogous to nature, I. vii. 3, 4.
>
> may have relations to all, or some, other parts of the universe, I. vii. 5.
>
> our ignorance of the whole precludes judgment upon the parts, I. vii. 9.
>
> and bars objections against Providence, I. vii. 10.
>
> which holds, apart from any question of scheme; but the objection is valueless, I. vii. 11, 12.
>
> solution may lie in some unknown relation, or possibility, I. vii. 13.
>
> may even be good, and indispensable, I. vii. 13, 15, II. iv. 1.
>
> experience proves means to be effective which we judge unfit, I. vii. 14.
>
> permission of evil may under conditions tend to good, like diseases which act as remedies, I. vii. 16, 17.
>
> makes our temporal, and probably our higher interest, depend upon behaviour, I. viii. 7.
>
> we can furnish the reason of it only in part, I. viii. 8.
>
> and can trace an intention of our improvement, I. viii. 9.
>
> its provisions are left open to abuse, II. i. 14.
>
> both governments are by general laws, II. iv. 4.
>
> a linked succession of stages in both, with complication, II. iv. 7, 8.
>
> the plan of divine, one of allowance and universal equity, II. vi. 7.
>
> alone in standing upon matters of fact (*a*) past, or (*b*) anticipated, II. vii. 33.
>
> has shown (*a*) it absurd to denounce this plan as fable, (*b*) it is credible, and (*c*) more, II. viii. 27.
>
> carrying so much moral evidence, makes the prevailing disregard of religion incredible but for experience, II. ix. 1.
>
> simplicity of the argument for, is darkened by intricacies of speculation, II. ix. 2.
>
> immoral to refuse examination of the proofs it freely offers, II. ix. 3.
>
> especially in view of the high claims of miracle, II. ix. 4.

INDEX

GOVERNMENT, MORAL, essence of, lies in righteous award, I. iii. 3, Diss. II. 14.
   subsists in the world not absolutely but in degree, I. iii. 4.
   further indicated by mental states attaching to virtue and vice, and by our power of forecast, I. iii. 10.
   and by civil punishments, and the fear of them, I. iii. 11.
   is implied in the natural, is a voice of God, and the seen tendencies are a promise of the future, I. iii. 38.
   enhances view of life as a preparatory stage, I. v. 20.
   as a fact, proves that Action is not Necessary, I. vi. 21, 22.
GOVERNMENT, NATURAL, implies a probation for this life, I. iv. 2.
   may be subservient to moral, and one part of moral to another, I. vii. 7, 8.
   is under general laws, I. vii. 18, 19. See GENERAL LAWS.
   has a moral element already in part operative, I. viii. 6; exemplifies moral do., *ibid.* 11.
   is everywhere pervaded by mediation, II. v. 1.
   is conditioned by faculty of moral approval and disapproval, Diss. II. 1.
GROTIUS, cited, II. vi. 19 *n*.

HABITS are of perception or of action, I. v. 6.
   of the body or of the mind, produced by use; both due to repeated acts, I. v. 6, 7.
   passive or active, I. v. 6.
   mental, formed by carrying principles into action or decision, I. v. 7.
   thoughts regardless of action, and passive impressions, lose force by repetition, I. v. 8.
   but active habits gain, *ibid.*
   this gain may be attended with loss of emotion, I. v. 9.
   passive, if bent towards action, may help to form active, I.v. 10.
   formation of, not easy to trace, I. v. 11.
   contribute to readiness, ease, and satisfaction in action, I. v. 12.
   the means whereby we attain maturity, I. v. 13.
   without it, duration would not give capacity, I. v. 14.
   nature casts us forth unfurnished, but capable of furnishing, I. v. 15, 16.
   by effort, and the education of life, I. v. 17.
   improve character, I. v. 20.
   the fitting antidote for our liability to lapse through particular propensions, I. v. 22.
   giving us a security *ab intra*, I. v. 24.
   may have place in a future state, is an advance in virtue, I. v. 25.
   evil, produced by repetition of disobedience, I. v. 28.
   enhancement of good, by continual battle and wariness against temptation, I. v. 32.

HABITS (*continued*).

    law of confirmation in good, may perhaps have limits, I. v. 33.

    immoral habit would grow out of multiplied acts, not out of few, in certain cases, II. iii. 27, 28.

HAPPINESS is to be pursued, not *simpliciter*, but within bounds, Diss. II. 16.

    if now perfect, would make strange the teaching of our uncertain future, I. iv. 11.

HEALTH, extreme deficiency of evidence on which we have to act, II. viii. 17.

HEATHEN: condition of the heathen world was such as to require revelation, II. i. 1.

    moralists were partially conscious of our fall from rectitude, II. ix. 11.

    and felt repentance to be insufficient, II. ix. 12.

HISTORY: tradition refers the origin of religion to primitive revelation, I. vi. 18, II. ii. 10.

HOBBES says that to distinguish between injury and harm is peculiar to mankind, Diss. II. 2.

HOLY GHOST: God the Son and God the Holy Ghost principally brought into our view by the gospel, II. i. 17, 18.

HOPE, like fear, a legitimate motive of obedience, I. v. 36.

IDENTITY, strange difficulties raised as to personal, I. i. 1, Diss. I. 1.

    in us and in animals, survives great changes, than which death may be no greater, I. i. 2, 3.

    so handled by some as to leave no interest in a future life, Diss. I. 1.

    hard, not to ascertain, but to define; so with equality, similitude, Diss. I. 2.

    not constituted by, but presupposed in, recollection, Diss. I. 3.

    differs from sameness in vegetables, Diss. I. 4.

    according to Locke, the sameness of a rational being, where being means substance, Diss. I. 5.

    shown also by continuity of act, enjoyment, suffering, Diss. I. 9.

    I did it, is as certain as *it was done*: and often serves as a basis, Diss. I. 10.

    we are no more deceivable in this than in our other surest perceptions, Diss. I. 11.

IGNORANCE: we cannot give the whole account of any one thing whatever, I. vii. 6.

    does not disable us from judging of the proofs of religion, I. vii. 20.

    we may be bad judges of schemes not fully known, yet good ones of proofs, I. vii. 23.

    absurd to suppose we know the whole case, II. v. 20, 21.

INDEX 407

IMAGINATION, a forward delusive faculty, apt to trespass beyond its sphere, but of some utility, I. i. 9.

IMMORTALITY, natural, of the soul, an hypothesis, I. i. 21, 31, iii. 26.
within possibility for brutes, I. i. 21.
eminently brought to light by the gospel, II. i. 9.

IMPUNITY, partial, familiar to us in provisions of nature, II. v. 4.

INSUFFICIENCY of the supply of light by revelation; so in nature, II. iii. 22, 23.

INTEREST, sense of. See SELF-LOVE.
an abstract idea, worthless, I. v. 24 n.; or may be a part of virtue, *ibid,*
our interest is profoundly involved in the religious argument, II. viii. 7.

JEWS. See JUDAISM.

JUDAISM: the prosperity promised to the Jews, I. iii. 30.
like Christianity, is such as we should expect it to be on the supposition that the miracles are true, II. vii. 4.
alone among religions, together with Christianity, in appealing to miracle, II. vii. 8.
God's dealings with the Jews, II. vii. 35–39.
the Jews as an historical phenomenon, II. vii. 49.
their dispersion and isolation, II. vii. 51–55; confirm Christianity, *ibid.* 52.

JUSTICE, distributive, or award according to right, the most natural rule, I. iii. 9.
things which taken singly seem unjust may be compatible with and even instances of justice, II. viii. 11.

KNOWLEDGE: great advances recently made in natural, I. iii. 28, II. iii. 21.
reasons for placing us in this state of hazard unknown, I. v. 1; to know, might not be for our advantage, *ibid.*
natural, sometimes of high consequence, II. iii. 22; is not given according to our notions of advantage, *ibid.*
not absolute and exhaustive, as to any one thing in nature, II. vi. 20.

LANGUAGE inadequate to its purpose, and liable to abuse, II. ii. 15.

LIBERTY, its relation to lapse from right, I. v. 26.
a consideration powerful in this argument, which has been waived, II. viii. 24.

LIFE. See PRESENT LIFE; FUTURE LIFE.

LIMBS. See BODY.

INDEX

LIVING POWERS, or LIVING BEING, or LIVING AGENT, or LIVING PERSON.
  powers, I. i. 4 *n.*, 5; agent, *ibid.* 6; being, *ibid.* 10; person, *ibid.* 19.
  of enjoyment, action, suffering, I. i. 4.
  as they exist, their continuance presumable, in the absence of reasons against it, *ibid.*
  capable of existence in a state of suspension, I. i. 6.
  may depend on something quite apart from death, *ibid.*
  unless the living being exceed an atom in bulk, how can death destroy it? I. i. 14.
  acts and is acted on by the body: no more provable, I. i. 16.
  which is true in a degree of other foreign matter, *ibid.*
  reason, memory, affection, do not depend on, like as sense does, or so as to raise any presumption of end at death, I. i. 23.
  our dual state of sensation and of reflection, I. i. 24.
  no sign that the latter is dissolved by death, *ibid.*
  some mortal diseases, leaving the *ego* unaffected to the last, raise a presumption that it will remain untouched in death, I. i. 25.
  suspensions in drowsiness and sleep would lead, but for experience, to false inferences, *ibid.*
  may not even be suspended by death, *ibid.*
  suspension of, distinguish from destruction, I. i. 28.
  has continuity of act, enjoyment, and suffering, Diss. I. 9.
LOCKE, his story of the Prince of Siam, Intr. 3.
  on personal identity, Diss. I. 5, 6.

MAHOMETANISM was not received on the evidence of miracle, II. vii. 8.
MAHOMETANS, modern, compared with ancient Persians, II. vi. 5.
MAN, the acknowledged governing animal upon earth, I. iii. 22.
MANIFESTATION of character may have unknown uses: is a great instrument in the actual course, I. v. 42, II. vi. 18.
MATURITY, is attained by habit, I. v. 13.
  if given at birth would not confer capacity, I. v. 14.
MEANING, of scripture, to be accepted, not imposed, II. i. 34, iii. 12.
  of revelation, to be judged of by reason, II. iii. 26.
MEANS (for ends), shown by experience to be good, though in our eyes unlikely, I. vii. 14; may even be indispensable, *ibid.* 2–15.
  their suitability often beyond our power to judge, as in nature, so in the gospel, II. iv. 3.
MEDIATION, for good and evil, is interwoven with the whole scheme of natural government, II. v. 1, 22, ix. 10.
  explained to mean the instrumentality of others, II. v. 1.
  was appropriate, necessary, and effectual, II. v. 11.
  is by means of a foreshadowed Priest-victim, II. v. 13.

INDEX

MEDIATION (*continued*).
has an efficacy beyond instruction, example, and government, II. v. 14.
was by a Prophet, II. v. 15.
who had a Church or Kingdom, II. v. 16.
and made an atonement or expiation, whereof the mode is not revealed to us, and has been unduly distended or reduced, II. v. 17–19, 21, ix. 14.
thus we are enabled to escape wrath and obtain life, II. v. 19.
how far these means might have been varied, we cannot judge, II. v. 20.
tends to vindicate the authority of the divine laws, II. v. 23.

MEDICINE, the rarity, lateness, and incompleteness of remedies for disease, II. iii. 24.

MEMORY. See LIVING POWERS.

METHOD, of this Treatise, to take known facts for a basis of reasoning about unknown, Intr. 10, 14.
of divine government, leaves its provisions open to abuse, II. i. 14.
of general laws, in government by nature, I. vii. 18.
and in government by revelation, II. iv. 4.

MIRACLE, *sing.* or *plur.*, adds to the credibility of a revealed moral system, II. i. 7, 8.
has advanced natural religion, II. i. 10.
presumption against the gospel as miraculous, is frivolous; why discussed, II. ii. 1, 2.
has been sufficiently defined, II. ii. 6.
the Incarnation, a miracle but not a proof, requires to be proved, *ibid.*
a thing relative to the course of nature, and departing from it, II. ii. 7.
origin of mankind, wholly outside the present course of nature, II. ii. 8.
our Lord's, not a question of degree, II. ii. 9.
the essential question is, are they credible ? II. ii. 12.
presumption against, less than against many common facts, II. ii. 13.
strong positive reasons for, II. ii. 14.
proper standard of comparison is with things extraordinary, II. ii. 15.
presumption on the whole favourable, II. ii. 16.
disorderly use of miraculous gifts no ground of objection, II. iii. 18.
other gifts open to like animadversions, II. iii. 19.
is, with prophecy, the direct and fundamental proof of Christianity, II. vii. 2.
of the gospel, have the same evidence as the non-miraculous contents, II. vii. 3.

410 INDEX

MIRACLE (*continued*).
   narratives of them plain and unadorned, II. vii. 3.
   some of Holy Scripture largely confirmed by history, II. vii. 4.
   of Holy Scripture hard to account for, except by their truth, II. vii. 5.
   can be set aside only by disproof, II. vii. 6.
   subsequent to the institution of a religion, are not available in the argument, II. vii. 8.
   miracles publicly wrought form a main ground of appeal by Christianity and Judaism alone among religions, *ibid*.
   pretences to, may and have deceived, but not more than other pretences, II. vii. 17.
   enhances force of the claim to examination, II. ix. 4.
MORALITY, the right and reason of the case determine the will of God, I. vi. 16 *n*.
   its obligation being based upon our nature, does not depend upon the consequences of acts, I. vii. 21.
   all moral duty is enjoined by scripture, II. ii. 30.
   of revelation, is within the cognisance of reason, II. iii. 26.
   moral fitness, a consideration of great power in this argument, which has been waived, II. viii. 24.

NATURAL: means stated, fixed, settled, similar, uniform, I. i. 31; conformable to God's other dealings, *ibid*.
   our present 'supernatural,' may to us hereafter, or now to beings of wider view, be natural, *ibid*.
   knowledge given us, in measures, not as we expect, II. iii. 22.
   as to immortality of the soul, I. i. 10, 21, 31.
   government of God, has a great deal moral in it, II. v. 8.
   And see RELIGION, NATURAL.
NATURE: an Author of nature is here presupposed, Intr. 8, 10, I. ii. 3.
   has been often proved from four sources, Intr. 10, I. viii. 2.
   denied by few among the non-acceptors of religion, Intr. 10.
   imaginary optimistic schemes of nature, wholly beyond the scope of our faculties to frame aright, Intr. 11, 12.
   especially as to the means for attaining ends, Intr. 12, 13.
   nature, in this case a true voice of God, prompts us to ascribe to God all perfection, Intr. 13.
   observed facts of, to be resolved into general laws, Intr. 14.
   objections taken against scheme of, in common with religion natural and revealed, are of little weight, Intr. 17, I. vii. 3, II. ix. 7.
   present dispensation of: puts enjoyment wholly, suffering largely, in our own power, I. ii. 2.
   due to nature, which means the Author of nature, I. ii. 3.
   has a scheme of government by punishments, I. ii. 10–18.
   not uniform, yet sufficient to warn, I. ii. 19.

INDEX

NATURE (*continued*).
   its voice not drowned by the undoubted intrusion of perverse rules, I. iii. 20.
   greatness of recent discoveries in the material world, I. iii. 28, II. iii. 21.
   leaves us unfurnished, but capable of furnishing, I. v. 15, 16.
   by effort, and the education of life, I. v. 17.
   exhibits waste, unaccountable, but vast, I. v. 35.
   Author of, his character and goodness gives us an interest in the scheme under which we live, I. viii. 3.
   supplies no presumption against the gospel-idea of rule by Christ, II. ii. 3–6.
   scheme of, is vast beyond imagination, II. ii. 4.
   as we object to nature, so we are likely to object to revelation, II. iii. 5.
   like revelation, partial in remedies, and incomplete, II. iii. 24.
   the things objected to in, may be good, nay, the very best, I. vii. 13, 15, II. iv. 1.
   subsequent good behaviour does not cancel an evil past, II. v. 7.
   the complexity of, suggests the likelihood of large varieties in the divine plans, II. vii. 9.
   all objections here admitted to lie against nature are inconclusive, II. viii. 12.
NECESSITY, or necessitarianism, its position *quoad* nature and *quoad* religion, the favourite basis of unbelief, I. vi. 14.
   exactly parallel, I. vi. 1, 24.
   the supposition of universal necessity absurd, I. vi. 1, 8.
   fate or no fate, agency by choice is matter of experience, I. vi. 2.
   only asserts an incident of being, in no way explains the *how*, I. vi. 3.
   God's existence by necessity, a manner of speech, I. vi. 4.
   requires and supposes a necessary agent, as freedom a free, I. vi. 5.
   proves nothing as against intelligent design, or religion, I. vi. 5, 6.
   case of a child trained as a necessitarian, I. vi. 7.
   our state is as if we were free, I. vi. 9.
   in the known sphere only misleads, may do the like in the unknown, I. vi. 10.
   being *as if* false, to entertain it is against reason, I. vi. 11.
   it comports with will and character in us, may do the same in God, I. vi. 12.
   on the general proof of religion, is mute, I. vi. 16.
   and on the evidence from duration and extension, I. vi. 17.
   admitting that necessary action is not punishable, the *fact* of

NECESSITY (*continued*).
    moral government shows that action is not necessary, I. vi. 20–22.
    thus proved false as an opinion referable to practice, I. vi. 23.
    estopped from objecting, I. viii. 10.
    author has argued on principles (of fatalism) though rejecting them, II. viii. 23.
NEGATION, passing into virulent defiance, II. ix. 5.
NEGLECT often operates as positive misbehaviour, I. ii. 15.
NICETY, which rejects all religion of hope or fear, is illegitimate, I. v. 36.

OBEDIENCE founded on hope and fear is materially virtuous, a natural principle of action, grows into morality, I. v. 36.
    passive = resignation, is also a requisite, as a training in patience, I. v. 37.
    as resignation, a barrier against bias of self-love, I. v. 38.
    receives a training from affliction, I. v. 39.
    and integrates active obedience, *ibid*.
OBJECTIONS to the gospel, except to its proofs, mostly frivolous, II. iv. 1, 2.
    to want of universality and to deficiency of proof, in no case justify rejection, II. vi. 1, ix. 15.
    how both run through the whole system of nature, II. vi. 2, 3.
    ground of, often lies in the objector, II. vi. 24.
    to the gospel, why to be at least abated *in limine*, II. vii. 21.
    that it is a poor thing to solve difficulties by showing the like elsewhere, II. viii. 1, 2.
    how such avails with certain minds, II. viii. 3.
    the method is one of constant use in common life, II. viii. 5.
    is legitimate, if the standard of appeal be acknowledged, II. viii. 6.
    the burden is shifted not on natural religion, but ultimately on the experienced constitution of nature, *ibid*.
    on the plea of doubtfulness, the objection treats the claim of religion as unfounded, II. viii. 8.
    like doubt in matters of temporal interest is not so treated, II. viii. 9.
    even if unanswered, leaves religion with its proofs unanswered also, II. viii. 13.
    until religion has been disproved, the practice of it is proper, II. viii. 15.
    largely taken from (*a*) prejudice *in limine*, (*b*) strange things in scripture, (*c*) points raised in II. vi, (*d*) it treats doubt as warranting denial, II. ix. 6.
    are met in this Treatise by—
        (*a*) establishing the fact of a moral government, II. ix. 7.
        (*b*) removing presumptions against Christianity as *fact*, *ibid*.

OBJECTIONS (*continued*).
    (*c*) and against its righteousness by showing that the like objections are invalid as against nature, II. ix. 8 ; lie against nature rather than against natural religion, II. viii. 6, 12.

    (*d*) and as taken against nature are insufficient, Intr. 17, I. vii. 3, II. ix. 6.

    things objected to in the moral scheme, may be good, even indispensable, I. vii. 13, 15, II. iv. 1.

OLD TESTAMENT history and prophecy, their vast range, and the manner in which they have stood the test of experience, II. vii. 35-39.

OMNIPRESENCE : author contests the doctrine of Clarke that if God could be absent somewhere he might be absent everywhere, Corr. i.

    ubiquity is separable from self-existence and has to be proved, *ibid.*

    accepts Clarke's argument, Corr. vii.

OPPORTUNITY, if lost, rarely returns, I. ii. 14.

ORIGEN supplies the germ of the entire argument, Intr. 8.

PAIN. See PLEASURE.

PAUL, ST., his epistles present distinct verifying evidence, II. vii. 7. 1 Corinthians, quoted by St. Clement, witness to the supernatural, *ibid.*

PERSIANS, of old, may be said to have had natural religion, but not revelation, II. vi. 5.

PERSONALITY, how said to constitute identity, Diss. I. 3.

    wrongly said to reach back only as far as remembrance, Diss. I. 6.

    also that the same personality can exist in many individuals, *ibid.*

    imagination is here set up against our natural sense of things, Diss. I. 7.

    to apply this idea to temporal affairs would be ridiculous, Diss. I. 8.

    whether viewed as substance or as property, identity remains, Diss. I. 10.

PLEASURE AND PAIN, given us as general guides to action, I. ii. 4.

    doubtful which preponderates in life, II. viii. 17.

PORPHYRY and the Book of Daniel, II. vii. 28 and *n.*

POSITIVE. See COMMANDS.

POWER ; reason tends to acquire as against force, I. iii. 23.

    and virtue, as against vice, I. iii. 24.

    virtue, with less of, avails against vice with more of, I. iii. 25.

PRECEPTS, things otherwise immoral, in some cases made moral by command, II. iii. 27.

    acts under them, if multiplied, would create an immoral habit, II. iii. 27, 28.

INDEX

PREJUDICE operates to warp the judgment: testimony prevails notwithstanding, II. vii. 15.

PRESENT LIFE, is under government, I. ch. ii.; moral government, I. ch. iii.; probation, I. ch. iv.; probation for improvement = moral discipline, I. ch. v.

a preparation for future life, as youth is for age, I. v. 3, 18.

well suited for discipline by the variety of its lessons, I. v. 31, 34.

seems to be for the generality a discipline of vice, I. v. 34.

and to be (*a*) related to something beyond it, (*b*) progressive, (*c*) not fully comprehensible, I. viii. 1.

no escape herefrom by denying an Author of nature, I. viii. 2.

survey of, entails obligation to self-government and piety, I. viii. 12.

is it worth living? II. viii. 17.

PRESUMPTION in favour of the gospel, from its having lain so long open to confutation and not been confuted, II. vii. 34.

even if strong, readily overcome by 'anything of proof,' II. ii. 11.

PROBABILITY, or probable evidence, unlike demonstrative, admits of degree, Intr. 1, 2.

founded in likeness to known truths and observed facts, Intr. 3.

is limited, and is concerned with limited beings, Intr. 4.

is for us the very guide of life, *ibid.*

when low may still bind to action, Intr. 5.

PROBATION, implies trial, difficulty, danger, and future account, I. iv. 1.

we are also in a probation for this life under natural government, I. iv. 2; of our prudence, *ibid.* 5.

comes (*a*) by temptation of circumstance *ab extra*, I. iv. 3; (*b*) by habits and passions *ab intra*; each aiding the other, *ibid.* 4.

in the sphere of religion, is of our virtue, I. iv. 6.

some deceived into wrong, others rush at it, I. iv. 7.

analogy between the two probationary states, I. iv. 8.

aggravation of danger. See DANGER.

our state has ill symptoms, but is not intolerable in either sphere (of nature and of religion), I. iv. 10.

doctrine of religious probation accredited by the facts of temporal, I. iv. 11.

the *why* of our hazardous condition is beyond us, I. iv. 12, v. 1.

in both spheres, we have to acquire, not merely accept, I. iv. 13.

our probation is meant for our benefit, I. v. 2.

relations of youth to age, and this life to future life, analogous, I. v. 3, 18; pointing to acquisition of quality, *ibid.* 3.

our powers of storage, self-adaptation, fitness, and facility through use, I. v. 5.

INDEX

PROBATION (*continued*).

may minister to the highest condition of perfection, I. v. 31.

a part of moral, may be furnished by doubtfulness in the evidence, II. vi. 10.

presentation of evidence imposes it upon us, II. vi. 11.

state of, is thoroughly in accord with limitations of evidence, II. vi. 23.

constituted by presentation of evidence; as some recognise, II. viii. 22.

PROOF, insufficiency of, charge lies against religion, both natural and revealed, I. iii. 3 *n*.

of revelation, to be judged of by reason, II. iii. 26.

objections to the proofs: here lies the stress of the argument, II. iii. 29.

of religion, in both kinds, lies level to common sense, II. vi. 20.

with varieties of demand and opportunity, *ibid*.

PROOFS, even when slight, may countervail vast adverse chances, II. ii. 11, 12.

PROPENSIONS, particular, entail danger of lapse, I. v. 23.

often the road to lapse, I. v. 27.

are the counterpart to our capacity of betterment and eventual safety, I. v. 29.

PROPHECY and miracle are the two direct and fundamental proofs of Christianity, II. vii. 2; any others are subsidiary, *ibid*.

if part be unknown, it cannot invalidate the part known, II. vii. 22.

fulfilment short of absolute may give proof of foresight (*a*) sufficient, (*b*) as much as intended, II. vii. 23.

applicability to the facts is to be presumed intentional, II. vii. 24.

as in the cases of (*a*) fable, (*b*) satire, II. vii. 25.

intention need not be that of the utterer, but of the Inspirer, II. vii. 26, 27.

it is futile simply to show susceptibility of another interpretation, II. vii. 28.

of the Old Testament, partly fulfilled; argument hence arising, II. vii. 53.

PROVIDENCE. See GOVERNMENT.

its plans must be proportioned to the vastness of the universe, I. iii. 28.

provision made for us: (*a*) reason and affections, (*b*) natural religion, (*c*) revealed religion, II. vii. 31, 32.

PRUDENCE obliges us to act upon low probability, Intr. 5.

with some, it is harder to discover the prudent course than to act on it, II. vi. 18.

the main question of conduct: is such and such an act prudent? II. viii. 19.

PRUDENCE (*continued*).

includes a due regard to our own happiness; and defined to be as such a part of virtue, Diss. II. 8.

why not fortified as strongly as other virtues with disapproval of its opposite? Diss. II. 9.

disapproval is, however, strong in grave cases, Diss. II. 10.

holding by the disapproval, we may dispense with virtue and vice as predicates, Diss. II. 11.

PUNISHMENT. See REWARD.

why to be the more particularly considered, I. ii. 10.

miseries due to our own conduct are natural punishments, I. ii. 11.

often (*a*) following after pleasure reaped, (*b*) exceeding it, (*c*) long delayed, (*d*) hard to foresee, I. ii. 12.

often due to habits formed in youth, I. ii. 13.

civil, being natural, often temporally final, I. ii. 16.

future, viewed by Gentiles (heathens) as by scripture, I. ii. 16 *n*.

religion is distinctive in annexing them to our next state, *ibid*.

may follow vice in the manner of natural consequence, II. v. 2.

partial impunity is familiar to us in nature, II. v. 4.

and total impunity blindly reckoned on, II. v. 5.

REASON. See LIVING POWERS.

tends to superiority over brute force: may use union, require time, and not be uniform, I. iii. 23.

the lessons derivable from the defects of our faculties, I. vi. 19.

our only instrument for judging even of revelation, II. iii. 3.

action of revealed proofs in no way disparages proof from reason, II. vii. 43.

RECOLLECTION is our consciousness of the past: does not constitute identity, Diss. I. 2, 3.

REDEMPTION: nothing said to confine it to those who know of it here, II. v. 11 *n*.

REFLECTION, state of, distinguished from our state of sensation, I. i. 24.

may not even be suspended by death, I. i. 26.

REGENERATION, necessity of renewal by the Holy Ghost shown by the declaration, John iii. 5, II. i. 24.

RELIGION will be argued for, upon the postulate of a deity, Intr. 10.

summed up: (*a*) Natural, in four heads; (*b*) Revealed, in six, Intr. 16.

both natural and revealed religion rest on the same basis of analogy to nature, Intr. 17.

as principle of conduct, is not illegitimate when proceeding from hope or fear, I. v. 36.

in no way disproved by necessity, I. vi. 6.

proofs of, are motives to, I. viii. 14.

RELIGION (*continued*).
   does not vary from nature more than nature from herself, II. ix. 18.
   duty of an 'awful solicitude' about, and of avoiding all immorality and profaneness, II. vi. 12.
   doubts upon, do not absolve from moral obedience, II. vi. 13.
   proof of, in both kinds, lies level to common sense, II. vi. 20.

RELIGION, EXTERNAL: provided for in the gospel scheme of a visible church, II. i. 10.
   an essential part of Christianity, II. i. 19.
   form of its manifestation is fixed by command, II. i. 21.

RELIGION, NATURAL: its four heads, Intr. 16.
   its origin, probably by revelation, I. vi. 18, II. ii. 10.
   doubtful whether it could have been reasoned out, or would, II. i. 1.
   republished by Christianity, II. i. 4, 5.
   miracle added to its credibility, II. i. 7.
   obtained supernatural aid, II. i. 12.
   specially contemplates God the Father, II. i. 19.
   effect of, in aggravating the guilt of immorality, as it has the almost intuitive approval of reason, II. ix. 19.
   scripture can never contradict it, II. i. 35.

RELIGION, REVEALED, OR REVELATION.
   summed up in six heads, Intr. 16.
   is distinctive in annexing punishments to a future state, I. ii. 16 *n*.
   early consent in certain beliefs due to a primitive revelation, I. vi. 18.
   came to be (*a*) requisite, (*b*) serviceable, II. i. 1.
   if of divine authority, its importance undeniable, II. i. 3.
   Christianity republishes natural religion, and adds another dispensation, II. i. 4, 5; with fresh authority, *ibid*. 6.
   specially contemplates God the Son and the Holy Ghost, II. i. 19, 20, 21.
   our relation to Christ is strictly moral, under moral sanctions, II. i. 22.
   disregard whereof, punishable in a natural way, I. i. 31, II. i. 23.
   our need of divine grace, and duty as to appointed means, II. i. 24.
   levity in treating it is the extreme of rashness, II. i. 25.
   was there a primitive, a question of fact, not presumption, II. ii. 7.
   there is no presumption against, at the beginning, II. ii. 9.
   primitive; the evidence is in favour of, II. ii. 10.
   later; how presumptions lie against many known facts, II. ii. 11.

RELIGION, REVEALED, OR REVELATION (*continued*).
    objections taken to the substance, mostly frivolous, except those against the proofs, II. iii. 1, 2.
    subject to the judgment of reason, *quoad* (*a*) immoralities, (*b*) contradictions, II. iii. 3.
    dislike of consequences, an invalid plea, II. iii. 4.
    as a bad judge of ordinary government will be the same of extraordinary, so here in the field of religion, II. iii. 6.
    we are bad judges what revelation or inspiration should be, II. iii. 7, 9.
    bad judges as between written and unwritten form, II. iii. 7, 8.
    our deficiency of power, either to anticipate or to judge, II. iii. 9.
    attack is feasible only as to proofs, (*a*) of miracle, (*b*) of prophecy, II. iii. 10.
    even partial proof of them will bind, II. iii. 11.
    the common tests of judgment are not uniformly applicable to scripture, II. iii. 12.
    we cannot judge with what conditions miraculous gifts should be conferred, II. iii. 18.
    urgency of our need does not prove that light given will be more than partial, II. iii. 23.
    supplies only partial light: nature partial too, II. iii. 24.
    reason is to judge, (*a*) the meaning, (*b*) the proof, (*c*) the morality, II. iii. 25.
    whether it tends to virtue, and is not fanatical or political, we are competent judges, II. iii. 30.
    if founded on fact, may be proved credible, apart from its reasonableness, II. viii. 14, 16.
    proved credibility of a, makes its practice reasonable, II. viii. 15.
    proof in, does not reach to satisfaction; nor in temporal things, e. g. health, II. viii. 17.

REMEDIES, incomplete both in nature and revelation, II. iii. 24.
    demand for complete, would warrant a demand to banish disease, II. iii. 25.

REPENTANCE: ill behaviour is not in nature cancelled by good, following it, II. v. 7, 8.
    felt to be insufficient while standing alone, II. ix. 12.
    divine provisions, and that by the gospel, II. ix. 13.

REPUBLICATION of natural religion by the gospel, II. i. 4–7.
    gives the gospel a title to be examined, II. i. 15.

RESIGNATION. See OBEDIENCE.

REWARD and punishment, for conduct, are already in operation, I. ii. 6.
    whether by propelled or self-acting laws, I. ii. 7.
    and by small pains as well as great, I. ii. 8.

INDEX

RIGHTEOUSNESS, as the rule of reward and punishment, makes government moral, I. iii. 2.
requires more than simple benevolence, I. iii. 3.

RUIN: this world in a state of apostasy, wickedness, and ruin, Intr. 16, II. i. 16, iii. 23, v. 11, 12.
the depravity imported into our nature enhances need for discipline, I. v. 30.
life a discipline of vice for the generality, I. v. 34.
bad example almost universal, II. i. 8.
mankind are corrupted and depraved; need regeneration, II. i. 24.
the present state one of vice, misery, and darkness, II. v. 5.
what confusion and misery we have brought into the kingdom of God, II. v. 6.
manifold miseries, extreme wickedness of the world, and advancing deterioration of the generality with their age, II. v. 12.
perceived in part by heathen moralists, II. ix. 11.

SACRIFICE: its prevalence proves a sense of the insufficiency of repentance, II. v. 9.
of Christ, its efficacy, II. vi. 17.

SATIRE: where applicability has been proved, intention is presumed, II. vii. 25.

SATISFACTION, (a) of Christ, II. vi. 17, 18, 22; (b) in evidence, that which supplies all we desire, II. viii. 18.

SCEPTIC, immorality of, much aggravated in view of the case of natural religion, II. ix. 19.
if owning that the gospel may be true, thereby becomes bound, II. ix. 20.
how far in negation any tolerably informed sceptic is found to go, *ibid.*

SCRIPTURE, required as part of our training, I. v. 17.
prefers moral precepts to positive, II. i. 28.
enjoins every moral virtue, II. i. 30.
we are to accept its sense, not impose it, II. i. 34, iii. 12.
cannot contradict natural religion, II. i. 36.
informs us of a scheme of revealed Providence additional to nature, II. iii. 5.
not to be judged wholly as other books are, e. g. as to prophecy, II. iii. 12; and improbabilities, *ibid.* 13.
preconceived expectations no guide in interpreting, II. iii. 14.
nor are they as to comparative access to different kinds of knowledge, or inventions, or the efficiency of language, II. iii. 15.
same arguments applicable to any prospective revelation, II. iii. 17.
the whole scheme of, is not yet understood, II. iii. 21.

INDEX

SCRIPTURE (*continued*).
    how variously made known to times, places, persons, II. vi. 4, 5.
    gives imperfect information: trouble saved by summary rejection, II. vii. 29.

SELF-DENIAL, necessary for our present not less than our future interest, I. iv. 4, 11.
    not of the essence of virtue and piety, I. v. 32.
    tends to moderate both particular affections and self-love, I. v. 38.

SELF-EXISTENT, the, its relation to space, very hard to determine; is not the 'substratum' of space, Corr. vii.

SELF-INTEREST. See SELF-LOVE.

SELF-LOVE: there is a reasonable self-love, I. iv. 4.
    as a sense of self-interest, wants education and improvement, I. v. 24 n.
    enters into the idea of virtue, *ibid.*
    is at variance with the passions, I. iv. 4.
    apt to diverge from the will of God, and to distort and rend the mind; stands in need of discipline; may require habits of resignation; denials of self-love tend to moderate it, I. v. 38.
    a reasonable self-love with worldly interest for its end, I. iv. 4.
    not coincident with the passions, *ibid.*

SENSE. See BODY.

SIN. See RUIN.

SLEEP (compare *swoon*) shows that living powers exist without being exercised at will, I. i. 8.

SON: God the Son, with the Holy Ghost, principally brought into view by the gospel, II. i. 17.

SOUL. See BODY; LIVING POWERS.

SPACE and time are necessarily presupposed in the existence of anything whatever, Corr. ii., iii.
    are rather mental affections than things objective, Cor. iii.
    absolutely self-existent, Corr. vii.; presupposed even in the self-existent, *ibid.*
    with time, exists necessarily, but dependently (Clarke), Corr. viii., x.
    does not admit that space and duration presuppose anything else, but cannot fathom their nature, Corr. ix.

STATE. See CIVIL.
    ideal state, deriving power from virtue, I. iii. 29.
    would obtain a great pre-eminence, I. iii. 30.

SUPERNATURAL. See NATURAL.

SUSPENSION of living powers, to be distinguished from destruction, I. i. 28.

SWOON. See SLEEP.

TESTIMONY prevails on the whole, despite the known force of prejudices, II. vii. 15.

INDEX

TESTIMONY (*continued*).
   also despite partial untruth, reticence, or exaggeration in the witnesses, II. vii. 16.
   the failure even of *like* testimony in some other case would be no proof of its falsity here, II. vii. 18.
   all human, liable to be weakened without being destroyed, II. vii. 19.
   is destroyed, only where the witnesses are (*a*) incompetent, (*b*) under falsifying influence, *ibid*.
   liability to error was at a minimum in the Christian witnesses, II. vii. 20.
   for gospel facts, is (*a*) real, (*b*) considerable, (*c*) not incredible, (*d*) not overthrown by contrary evidence, II. vii. 21.

THOUGHT, cursory, danger of, if habitual, II. vii. 30.
   has no extension, Corr. iii. ; because not a being, *ibid*. iv.

TIME and space are necessarily presupposed in the existence of anything whatever, Corr. ii., iii.
   are rather incidents of the order of our ideas, than things objective, Corr. iii.
   And see SPACE.

TRADITION, historical, in favour of a primitive revelation, has weight due to it, I. vii. 18.

TREATISE (this), its force to be measured by the aggregate effect of its arguments, Adv. 1, II. vii. 30, 40, 57, 62, 63.
   its design is not to vindicate God, but to establish the duty of man, II. viii. 10.
   object of, is to show how man ought in reason to behave, II. viii. 21.
   has all along worked from points of departure chosen by opponents, II. viii. 23.
   has waived the use of powerful weapons, liberty and moral fitness, II. viii. 24.
   has dealt with religion only as fact, II. viii. 25.
   meets objectors by showing (*a*) the existence of a moral government, and that there is no presumption against Christianity, (*b*) as fact, (*c*) as righteous, II. ix. 7, 8.
   general upshot of, II. viii. 27.
   is very far from satisfactory, II. viii. 17.

UBIQUITY. See OMNIPRESENCE.

UNDERSTANDING : not all are to understand, II. vi. 19.

UNIFORMITY OF NATURE : the gospel does not more vary from, than nature from herself, II. ix. 18.

UNIVERSE : dispensations of earth may operate beyond its limits, I. iii. 26, 28.
   material, its immensity, and presumption thence arising, I. iii. 28.
   creatures in very high states of perfection may perhaps owe it to probation, I. v. 31.

UNIVERSE (*continued*).
   manifestation of human character to other portions of creation, its possible intent and uses, I. v. 42.
   the scheme of government under which we live may have relations extending throughout the universe, I. vii. 5.
UNKNOWN : we may reason about, on the basis of the known, Intr. 9.

VEGETABLES, not having perception or action, supply no analogy, I. i. 29.
VERACITY is, with justice, our rule of life; but is not easy of application, Diss. II. 17.
VICARIOUS punishment may be fit and necessary, II. v. 22; a providential appointment of every day's experience, *ibid.*
VICE. See Virtue.
   becomes possible through liberty, I. v. 26.
   and through the nature of particular propensions, I. v. 27.
   this world a discipline of vice for most men, I. v. 34.
   absurd to feel secure in a life of : its pleasures trivial, I. vii. 12.
   punishment may follow it in the way of natural consequence, which is the act of God, II. v. 2, 3.
   its terrible aggravations, must have consequences in proportion, II. v. 6.
   linked with misery in our faculty of approval and disapproval, Diss. II. 5.
   vicious acts are also unfit, incongruous, and so forth, Diss. II. 7.
   not required as a predicate for the opposite of prudence, Diss. II. 11.
   produces an overbalance of misery, but this is not all, Diss. II. 13.
VIRTUE : has the balance cast in its favour, but not invariable, nor always clear, I. iii. 5.
   especially in cases of lives once bad but reformed, I. iii. 6.
   balance clear as a whole, but initial, I. iii. 7.
   has support in the mental states annexed to it, and the forecast, I. iii. 10.
   also in civil punishments and in the fear of them, I. iii. 11.
   never punished *as such*, nor vice as such rewarded, I. iii. 12, 13.
   fears and hopes of a future life count on the same side as facts, I. iii. 14.
   also the favour and disfavour of the good, I. iii. 15.
   and the moral qualities in (*a*) civil government, (*b*) treatment of children, (*c*) regard to virtue as such, (*d*) pardons given in absence of guilt, I. iii. 16.
   a reversal of the relative estimates of virtue and vice, imaginary or unnatural, I. iii. 19.
   already God takes the side of, as against vice, I. iii. 21, 34.
   tendencies are, on its behalf, in excess of the facts, I. iii. 22, 24.

INDEX 423

VIRTUE (*continued*).

this tendency, as against vice, compared with the tendency of reason to overcome force, I. iii. 23.

can, with much less of power, hold its ground against vice, and is likely to prevail with a fair field, I. iii. 25.

the hindrances to it may disappear hereafter, I. iii. 26.

is, *per se*, a bond of union, I. iii. 27.

may supposably attract hereafter spirits inaccessible to it here, I. iii. 28.

if these advantages seem trifling matters, what should we say were they on the side of vice? I. iii. 31.

the change we anticipate is of degree, not kind, I. iii. 35.

the lower degree warrants hope of the higher, I. iii. 36.

the tendency is essential, the hindrances accidental, I. iii. 37.

how men corruptly strive to substitute rites for virtuous action, II. i. 31.

we have a faculty of moral approval and disapproval, Diss. II. 1.

this is shown by evidence from many sources, Diss. II. 2.

it has (*a*) a standard, (*b*) tests, Diss. II. 3.

has action for its object, not consequences, nor abstract truth, Diss. II. 4.

includes the notion of desert, and links misery with vice, Diss. II. 5.

desert higher or lower according to the particulars of the case, Diss. II. 6.

acts to be measured with reference to the agent, Diss. II. 7.

includes a due regard to the happiness of ourselves, as of others, Diss. II. 8.

virtue and vice not required as predicates in the discussion on prudence, Diss. II. 11.

benevolence is a part only of virtue, its opposite of vice, I. iii. 3, Diss. II. 12 *seqq*.

includes other matter besides the balance of enjoyment and suffering, Diss. II. 13.

some authors open to misapprehension on the point, Diss. II. 15.

basis for the pursuit of happiness, Diss. II. 16.

WASTE IN NATURE, enormous, but unaccountable: does not disprove design, I. v. 35.

WATERLAND, DR., cited, II. i. 18 *n*.

WHOLE: evidences of religion are to be viewed as a whole and in the reciprocal relations of their parts, II. vii. 30.

WILL, of God, follows moral fitness, or the right and reason of the case, I. vi. 16 *n*., II. viii. 25.

moral fitness anterior to will, II. viii. 24.

WITNESSES, to the gospel: how their sacrifices, and all their

WITNESSES (*continued*).
    circumstances, show their sincerity and otherwise give weight to their evidence, II. vii. 9.

    of the sub-apostolic age have also a great weight, II. vii. 12.

    their testimony may be weakened by enthusiasm; but are they enthusiasts? II. vii. 13.

    the Christian: liability to error, how reduced in them to a minimum, II. vii. 20.

WORLDS, evidences of design in, I. iii. 1.

WORSHIP, a duty to be inferred from the harmony of God's government with our nature, I. vi. 15.

WRITING: whether revelation should be transmitted by, we are incompetent to judge, II. iii. 7, 8.

YOUTH, related to maturity, as present life to future, I. v. 3, 18.

THE WORLD'S CLASSICS
(SIZE 6 x 4 INCHES)

ORDINARY EDITION
Published in SEVEN different Styles

Cloth, boards	1/- net
Sultan-red Leather, limp, gilt top	1/9 net
Lambskin, limp, gilt top	2/6 net
Quarter Vellum, hand-tooled, paneiled lettering-piece, gilt top. Superior library style	4/6 net
Half Calf, marbled edges	4/6 net
Whole Calf, marbled edges	6/6 net
Tree Calf, marbled edges	6/6 net

POCKET EDITION

of THE WORLD'S CLASSICS (each with a portrait) is printed on THIN OPAQUE PAPER, by means of which the bulk of the stouter volumes is reduced by one-half. Some of the works printed in two volumes can be had bound in one volume, in sultan-red leather, limp, gilt top, at 3/- net.

Cloth, limp, gilt back, gilt top	1/3 net
Sultan-red Leather, limp, gilt top	1/9 net
Italian, thin boards, gilt design, gilt top	2/6 net
Quarter Vellum, hand-tooled, panelled lettering-piece, gilt top	4/6 net

OF ALL BOOKSELLERS

HUMPHREY MILFORD
OXFORD UNIVERSITY PRESS
LONDON, EDINBURGH, GLASGOW
NEW YORK, TORONTO, MELBOURNE, BOMBAY
CAPE TOWN, & SHANGHAI

The World's Classics

THE best recommendation of **The World's Classics** is the books themselves, which have earned unstinted praise from critics and all classes of the public. Some two million copies have been sold, and of the volumes already published nearly one-half have gone into a second, third, fourth, fifth, sixth, seventh, eighth, ninth, or tenth impression. It is only possible to give so much for the money when large sales are certain. The clearness of the type, the quality of the paper, the size of the page, the printing, and the binding—from the cheapest to the best—cannot fail to commend themselves to all who love good literature presented in worthy form. That a high standard is insisted upon is proved by the list of books already published and of those on the eve of publication. A great feature is the brief critical introductions written by leading authorities of the day. The volumes of The World's Classics are obtainable, bound in cloth and leather, at the prices given on page 1; and special attention is directed to the sultan-red limp leather style, which is unsurpassable in leather bindings at the price of 1/9 net.

The **Pocket Edition** is printed on **thin opaque paper,** by means of which the bulk is greatly reduced.

February, 1916.

THE WORLD'S CLASSICS

LIST OF THE SERIES

The figures in parentheses denote the number of the book in the series

Aeschylus. The Seven Plays. Translated by LEWIS CAMPBELL. (117)
Ainsworth (W. Harrison). The Tower of London. (162)
A Kempis (Thomas). Of the Imitation of Christ. (49)
Aristophanes. Frere's translation of the Acharnians, Knights, Birds, and Frogs. Introduction by W. W. MERRY. (134)
Arnold (Matthew). Poems. Intro. by Sir A. T. QUILLER-COUCH. (85)
Aurelius (Marcus). The Thoughts. A new translation by JOHN JACKSON. (60)
Austen (Jane). Emma. Introduction by E. V. LUCAS. (129)
Bacon. The Advancement of Learning, and the New Atlantis. Introduction by Professor CASE. (93)
    Essays. (24)
Barham. The Ingoldsby Legends. (9)
Barrow (Sir John). The Mutiny of the Bounty. Introduction by Admiral Sir CYPRIAN BRIDGE. (195)
Betham-Edwards (M.) The Lord of the Harvest. Introduction by FREDERIC HARRISON. (194)
Blackmore (R. D.). Lorna Doone. Intro. by T. H. WARREN. (171)
Borrow. The Bible in Spain. (75)
    Lavengro. (66)
    The Romany Rye. (73)
Brontë Sisters.
    Charlotte Brontë. Jane Eyre. (1)
    Shirley. (14)
    Villette. (47)
    The Professor, and the Poems of Charlotte, Emily, and Anne Brontë. Introduction by THEODORE WATTS-DUNTON. (78)
    Emily Brontë. Wuthering Heights. (10)
    Anne Brontë. Agnes Grey. (141)
    The Tenant of Wildfell Hall. (67)
Brown (Dr. John). Horae Subsecivae. Intro. by AUSTIN DOBSON. (118)
Browning (Elizabeth Barrett). Poems: A Selection. (176)
Browning (Robert). Poems and Plays, 1833-1842. (58)
    Poems, 1842-1864. (137)
Buckle. The History of Civilization in England. 3 vols. (41, 48, 53)
Bunyan. The Pilgrim's Progress. (12)
Burke. Works. 6 vols.
    Vol. I. General Introduction by Judge WILLIS and Preface by F. W. RAFFETY. (71)
    Vols. II, IV, V, VI. Prefaces by F. W. RAFFETY. (81, 112-114)
    Vol. III. Preface by F. H. WILLIS. (111)

List of the Series—*continued*

Burns. Poems. (34)
Butler. The Analogy of Religion. Edited, with Notes, by W. E. GLADSTONE. (136)
Byron. Poems: A Selection. (180)
Carlyle. On Heroes and Hero-Worship. (62)
    Past and Present. Introduction by G. K. CHESTERTON. (153)
    Sartor Resartus. (19)
    The French Revolution. Introduction by C. R. L. FLETCHER. 2 vols. (125, 126)
    The Life of John Sterling. Introduction by W. HALE WHITE. (144)
Cervantes. Don Quixote. Translated by C. JERVAS. Intro. and Notes by J. FITZMAURICE-KELLY. 2 vols. With a frontispiece. (130, 131)
Chaucer. The Canterbury Tales. (76)
Chaucer. The Works of. From the text of Professor SKEAT. 3 vols. Vol. I (42); Vol. II (56); Vol. III, containing the whole of the Canterbury Tales (76)
Cobbold. Margaret Catchpole. Intro. by CLEMENT SHORTER. (119)
Coleridge. Poems. Introduction by Sir A. T. QUILLER-COUCH. (99)
Cooper (T. Fenimore). The Last of the Mohicans. (163)
Cowper. Letters. Selected, with Introduction, by E. V. LUCAS. (138)
Darwin. The Origin of Species. With a Note by GRANT ALLEN. (11)
Defoe. Captain Singleton. Intro. by THEODORE WATTS-DUNTON. (82)
    Robinson Crusoe. (17)
De Quincey. Confessions of an English Opium-Eater. (23)
Dickens. Great Expectations. With 6 Illustrations by WARWICK GOBLE. (128)
    Oliver Twist. (8)
    Pickwick Papers. With 43 Illustrations by SEYMOUR and 'PHIZ.' 2 vols. (120, 121)
    Tale of Two Cities. (38)
Dufferin (Lord). Letters from High Latitudes. Illustrated. With Introduction by R. W. MACAN. (158)
Eliot (George). Adam Bede. (63)
    Felix Holt. Introduction by VIOLA MEYNELL. (179)
    Romola. Introduction by VIOLA MEYNELL. (178)
    Scenes of Clerical Life. Introduction by ANNIE MATHESON. (155)
    Silas Marner, The Lifted Veil, and Brother Jacob. Introduction by THEODORE WATTS-DUNTON. (80)
    The Mill on the Floss. (31)
Emerson. English Traits, and Representative Men. (30)
    Essays. First and Second Series. (6)
English Critical Essays (Nineteenth Century). Selected and Edited by EDMUND D. JONES. (206)

List of the Series—*continued*

English Essays. Chosen and arranged by W. PEACOCK. (32)

English Essays, 1600-1900 (Book of). Chosen by S. V. MAKOWER and B. H. BLACKWELL. (172)

English Letters. (Fifteenth to Nineteenth Centuries.) Selected and edited by M. DUCKITT and H. WRAGG. (192)

English Prose from Mandeville to Ruskin. Chosen and arranged by W. PEACOCK. (45)

English Prose: Narrative, Descriptive, and Dramatic. Selected by H. A. TREBLE. (204)

English Short Stories. (Nineteenth Century.) Introduction by Prof. HUGH WALKER. (193)

English Songs and Ballads. Compiled by T. W. H. CROSLAND. (13)

English Speeches, from Burke to Gladstone. Selected by EDGAR R. JONES, M.P. (191)

Fielding. Journal of a Voyage to Lisbon, etc. Introduction and Notes by AUSTIN DOBSON. 2 Illustrations. (142)

Galt (John). The Entail. Introduction by JOHN AYSCOUGH. (177)

Gaskell (Mrs.). Introductions by CLEMENT SHORTER.
  Cousin Phillis, and other Tales, etc. (168)
  Cranford, The Cage at Cranford, and The Moorland Cottage. (110)
  The 'Cage' has not hitherto been reprinted.
  Lizzie Leigh, The Grey Woman, and other Tales, etc. (175)
  Mary Barton. (86)
  North and South. (154)
  Right at Last, and other Tales, etc. (205)
  Round the Sofa. (190)
  Ruth. (88)
  Sylvia's Lovers. (156)
  Wives and Daughters. (157)

Gibbon. Decline and Fall of the Roman Empire. With Maps. 7 vols. (35, 44, 51, 55, 64, 69, 74)
  Autobiography. Introduction by J. B. BURY. (139)

Goethe. Faust, Part I (with Marlowe's Dr. Faustus). Translated by JOHN ANSTER. Introduction by Sir A. W. WARD. (135)

Goldsmith. Poems. Introduction and Notes by AUSTIN DOBSON. (123)
  The Vicar of Wakefield. (4)

Grant (James). The Captain of the Guard. (159)

Hawthorne. The Scarlet Letter. (26)

Hazlitt. Characters of Shakespeare's Plays. Introduction by Sir A. QUILLER-COUCH. (205)
  Lectures on the English Comic Writers. Introduction by R. BRIMLEY JOHNSON. (124)
  Sketches and Essays. (15)
  Spirit of the Age. (57)
  Table-Talk. (5)
  Winterslow. (25)

Herbert (George). Poems. Introduction by ARTHUR WAUGH. (109)

Herrick. Poems. (16)

List of the Series—*continued*

Holmes (Oliver Wendell). The Autocrat of the Breakfast-Table. (61)
The Poet at the Breakfast-Table. Introduction by Sir W. ROBERTSON NICOLL. (95)
The Professor at the Breakfast-Table. Introduction by Sir W. ROBERTSON NICOLL. (89)

Homer. Iliad. Translated by Pope. (18)
Odyssey. Translated by Pope. (36)

Hood. Poems. Introduction by WALTER JERROLD. (87)

Horne (R. Hengist). A New Spirit of the Age. Introduction by WALTER JERROLD. (127)

Hume. Essays. (33)

Hunt (Leigh). Essays and Sketches. Introduction by R. BRIMLEY JOHNSON. (115)
The Town. Introduction and Notes by AUSTIN DOBSON, and a Frontispiece. (132)

Irving (Washington). The Conquest of Granada. (150)
The Sketch-Book of Geoffrey Crayon, Gent. Introduction by T. BALSTON. (173)

Jerrold (Douglas). Mrs. Caudle's Curtain Lectures, Mr. Caudle's Breakfast Talk, and other Stories and Essays. Introduction by WALTER JERROLD, and 90 Illustrations by KEENE, LEECH, and DOYLE. (122)

Johnson. Lives of the English Poets. Introduction by ARTHUR WAUGH. 2 vols. (83, 84)

Keats. Poems. (7)

Keble. The Christian Year. (181)

Lamb. Essays of Elia, and The Last Essays of Elia. (2)

Landor. Imaginary Conversations. Selected with Introduction by Prof. E. DE SÉLINCOURT. (196)

Lesage. Gil Blas. Translated by T. SMOLLETT, with Introduction and Notes by J. FITZMAURICE-KELLY. 2 vols. (151, 152)

Letters written in War Time. Selected and edited by H. WRAGG. (202)

Longfellow. Evangeline, The Golden Legend, etc. (39)
Hiawatha, Miles Standish, Tales of a Wayside Inn, etc. (174)

Lytton. Harold. With 6 Illustrations by CHARLES BURTON. (165)

Macaulay. Lays of Ancient Rome; Ivry; The Armada. (27)

Machiavelli. The Prince. Translated by LUIGI RICCI. (43)

Marcus Aurelius. See Aurelius.

Marlowe. Dr. Faustus (with Goethe's Faust, Part I). Introduction by Sir A. W. WARD. (135)

Marryat. Mr. Midshipman Easy. (160)
The King's Own. With 6 Illustrations by WARWICK GOBLE. (164)

Mill (John Stuart). On Liberty, Representative Government, and the Subjection of Women. With an Introduction by Mrs. FAWCETT. (170)

Milton. The English Poems. (182)

Montaigne. Essays. Translated by J. FLORIO. 3 vols. (65, 70, 77)

Morris (W.). The Defence of Guinevere, The Life and Death of Jason, and other Poems. (183)

List of the Series—*continued*

Motley. Rise of the Dutch Republic. Introduction by CLEMENT SHORTER. 3 vols. (96, 97, 98)

Palgrave. The Golden Treasury. With additional Poems, including FITZGERALD'S translation of Omar Khayyám. (133)

Peacock (W.). English Prose from Mandeville to Ruskin. (45)
Selected English Essays. (32)

Poe (Edgar Allan). Tales of Mystery and Imagination. (21)

Porter (Jane). The Scottish Chiefs. (161)

Prescott (W. H.). History of the Conquest of Mexico. Introduction by Mrs. ALEC-TWEEDIE. 2 vols. (197, 198)

Reid (Mayne). The Rifle Rangers. With 6 Illustrations by J. E. SUTCLIFFE. (166)
The Scalp Hunters. With 6 Illustrations by A. H. COLLINS. (167)

Reynolds (Sir Joshua). The Discourses, and the Letters to 'The Idler.' Introduction by AUSTIN DOBSON. (149)

Rossetti (Christina). Goblin Market, The Prince's Progress, and other Poems. (184)

Rossetti (D. G.). Poems and Translations, 1850-1870. (185)

Ruskin. (*Ruskin House Editions, by arrangement with Messrs. Allen, and Unwin, Ltd.*)
'A Joy for Ever,' and The Two Paths. Illustrated. (147)
Sesame and Lilies, and The Ethics of the Dust. (145)
Time and Tide, and The Crown of Wild Olive. (146)
Unto this Last, and Munera Pulveris. (148)

Scott. Ivanhoe. (29)
Lives of the Novelists. Introduction by AUSTIN DOBSON. (94)
Poems. A Selection. (186)

Selected Speeches on British Foreign Policy (1738-1914). Edited by EDGAR R. JONES, M.P. (201)

Shakespeare. Plays and Poems. With a Preface by A. C. SWINBURNE and general Introductions to the several plays and poems by EDWARD DOWDEN, and a Note by T. WATTS-DUNTON on the special typographical features of this Edition. 9 vols.
Comedies. 3 vols. (100, 101, 102)
Histories and Poems. 3 vols. (103, 104, 105)
Tragedies. 3 vols. (106, 107, 108)

Shakespeare's Contemporaries. Six Plays by BEAUMONT and FLETCHER, DEKKER, WEBSTER, and MASSINGER. Edited by C. B. WHEELER. (199)

Shelley. Poems. A Selection. (187)

Sheridan. Plays. Introduction by JOSEPH KNIGHT. (79)

Smith (Adam). The Wealth of Nations. 2 vols. (54, 59)

Smith (Alexander). Dreamthorp, with Selections from Last Leaves. Introduction by Prof. HUGH WALKER. (200)

Smollett. Travels through France and Italy. Introduction by THOMAS SECCOMBE. (90)

Sophocles. The Seven Plays. Translated by the late LEWIS CAMPBELL. (116)

List of the Series—*continued*

Southey (Robert). Letters. Selected, with an Introduction and Notes, by MAURICE H. FITZGERALD. (169)
Sterne. Tristram Shandy. (40)
Swift. Gulliver's Travels. (20)
Taylor (Meadows). Confessions of a Thug. (207)
Tennyson (Lord). Poems. (3)
Thackeray. Book of Snobs, Sketches and Travels in London, &c. (50)
   Henry Esmond. (28)
   Pendennis. Introduction by EDMUND GOSSE. 2 vols. (91, 92)
Thoreau. Walden. Introduction by THEODORE WATTS-DUNTON. (68)
Tolstoy. Essays and Letters. Translated by AYLMER MAUDE. (46)
   Twenty-three Tales. Translated by L. and A. MAUDE. (72)
   The Cossacks.
   Resurrection.   } *In Preparation.*
   Anna Karenina.
Trollope. The Three Clerks. Intro. by W. TEIGNMOUTH SHORE. (140)
Virgil. Translated by DRYDEN. (37)
Watts-Dunton (Theodore). Aylwin. (52)
Wells (Charles). Joseph and his Brethren. With an Introduction by ALGERNON CHARLES SWINBURNE, and a Note on Rossetti and Charles Wells by THEODORE WATTS-DUNTON. (143)
White (Gilbert). The Natural History of Selborne. (22)
Whittier. Poems. A Selection. (188)
Wordsworth. Poems: A Selection. (189)

Other Volumes in Preparation.

Bookcases for the World's Classics

To hold 50 Volumes ordinary paper, or 100 Volumes thin paper:

In Fumed Oak, with two fixed shelves. (22 x 21½ x 4¾ inches) 0 6 0

To hold 100 Volumes ordinary paper, or 200 Volumes thin paper:

In Mahogany, French Stained and Ebonized, with fancy ornamental top, and three adjustable shelves, best cabinet make. (44 x 36 x 6 inches)   1 15 0

OF ALL BOOKSELLERS

HUMPHREY MILFORD
OXFORD UNIVERSITY PRESS
LONDON, EDINBURGH, GLASGOW
NEW YORK, TORONTO, MELBOURNE, BOMBAY
CAPE TOWN, & SHANGHAI

THE WORLD

HUMPHREY·MILFORD·OXFORD·UNIVERSITY·PRESS